Guide to International Human Rights Practice

Fourth Edition

Guide to International Human Rights Practice

Fourth Edition

edited by

Hurst Hannum

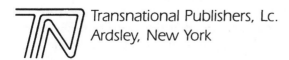 Transnational Publishers, Lc.
Ardsley, New York

Published and distributed by Transnational Publishers, Inc.
Ardsley Park Science and Technology Center
410 Saw Mill River Road
Ardsley, NY 10502

———————————————

Phone: 914-693-5100
Fax: 914-693-4430
E-mail: info@transnationalpubs.com
Web: www.transnationalpubs.com

Library of Congress Cataloging-in-Publication Data

Guide to international human rights practice / edited by Hurst
    Hannum.—4th ed.
    p.   cm.
    At bottom of title: Procedural Aspects of International Law Institute.
    Includes index.
    ISBN 1-57105-320-4
    1. Human rights.   I. Hannum, Hurst.   II. Procedural Aspects
of International Law Institute.
K3240.4.G94 2004
341.4'8—dc22

                                                    2004053656

Manufactured in the United States of America

To the memory and legacy of

Richard B. Lillich (1933–1996)
Diana Vincent-Daviss (1943–1993)
Joan M. Fitzpatrick (1950–2003)

Someone must have traduced Joseph K., for without having done anything wrong he was arrested one fine morning. . . .

Who could these men be? What were they talking about? What authority could they represent? K. lived in a country with a legal constitution, there was universal peace, all the laws were in force; who dared seize him in his own dwelling?

. . . "What are your papers to us?" cried the tall warder. . . . "We are humble subordinates who can scarcely find our way through a legal document and have nothing to do with your case except to stand guard over you for ten hours a day and draw our pay for it. That's all we are, but we're quite capable of grasping the fact that the high authorities we serve, before they would order such an arrest as this, must be quite well informed about the reasons for the arrest and the person of the prisoner. There can be no mistake about that. Our officials, so far as I know them, and I know only the lowest grades among them, never go hunting for crime in the populace, but, as the Law decrees, are drawn toward the guilty and must then send out us warders. This is the Law. How could there be a mistake in that?"

Franz Kafka, The Trial

It is essential, if man is not to be compelled to have recourse, as a last resort, to rebellion against tyranny and oppression, that human rights should be protected by the rule of law. . . .

Universal Declaration of Human Rights

Contents

Part III   Regional Systems for the Protection of Human Rights

Part IV   Other Techniques and Forums for Protecting Rights

Appendixes

Acknowledgments

The genesis of the *Guide to International Human Rights Practice* lies in the vision of the late Richard B. Lillich, founding President of The Procedural Aspects of International Law Institute; Sidney Liskofsky, then Director of the Jacob Blaustein Institute for the Advancement of Human Rights (which provided financial support for the first two editions of the *Guide*); and Amy Young, Executive Director of the International Human Rights Law Group (now Global Rights) from its creation until 1991. In the early days of human rights activism, they saw the need for a practice-oriented guide to international human rights law which could provide concrete advice to individuals and NGOs around the world. The explosion of human rights norms and procedures since the first edition of the *Guide* was written in the early 1980s makes that need even greater today.

Of course, the greatest debt of gratitude is owed to the contributors to the present volume, who were frequently called upon to sacrifice more than one well-turned phrase (and numerous endnotes) in the interest of greater consistency for the work as a whole. The gathering of expertise represented in this work is perhaps unparalleled, and each author has advanced the cause of human rights in many ways well beyond writing the chapter that he or she has so generously contributed.

Hurst Hannum
*The Fletcher School of Law
and Diplomacy
Tufts University
April 2004*

Part I
Preliminary
Considerations

Chapter 1
An Overview of International Human Rights Law

Richard B. Bilder

The international human rights movement is based on the concept that every nation has an obligation to respect the human rights of its citizens and that other nations and the international community have a right, and responsibility, to protest if states do not adhere to this obligation. International human rights law consists of the body of international rules, procedures, and institutions developed to implement this concept and to promote respect for human rights in all countries.

While international human rights law focuses on international rules, procedures, and institutions, it typically also requires at least some knowledge of and sensitivity to the relevant domestic law of countries with which the practitioner is concerned. In particular, one must be aware of national laws regarding the implementation of treaties and other international obligations, the conduct of foreign relations, and domestic protection of human rights. Indeed, since international law is generally applicable only to states and may not normally create rights directly enforceable by individuals in national courts, international human rights law can be made most effective only if each state makes these rules part of its domestic legal system. Many human rights initiatives are directed at encouraging countries to incorporate international human rights standards into their own internal legal order in this way. Thus, the work of international human rights lawyers and national human rights (or "civil rights") lawyers is closely related.

In practice, the differences between international human rights and national civil rights often lie more in emphasis than substance. Concern for human rights rarely begins or ends at any single nation's boundaries, and effective action to protect and promote human rights, whether at home or abroad, can be furthered by the imaginative use of both national and international techniques.

3

It is not necessary to be an expert in international human rights law to be able to make a significant contribution to the promotion of human rights. However, a knowledge of this body of law may suggest ways in which such efforts can be pursued more effectively. This introductory chapter presents a broad overview of the field.

A Brief Historical Note

Although the idea that human beings are inherently entitled to certain fundamental rights and freedoms has roots early in human thinking, the concept that human rights are an appropriate subject for international regulation is very new. Throughout most of human history, the way a government treated its own citizens was considered solely its own business and not a proper concern of any other state. From an international legal standpoint, human rights questions were regarded as matters entirely within each state's own domestic jurisdiction and wholly inappropriate for regulation by international law. The United States, for example, could properly complain to France if France mistreated *American* citizens living in France; international law had early established rules as to how each nation had to behave regarding nationals of another state ("aliens") present within its territory, and a state could protest or extend its diplomatic protection to its own nationals if their rights were violated. But, under traditional international law, the United States could *not* legitimately complain solely because France mistreated its own *French* citizens; if the United States tried to interfere in such matters, France could claim that the United States was violating French sovereignty by illegally intervening in its domestic affairs.

While this attitude—that human rights questions were generally outside the purview of international concern or regulation—was broadly accepted until World War II, several developments before then suggested at least limited exceptions to the rule that human rights questions were wholly internal. These included the antislavery movement of the nineteenth and early twentieth centuries, which culminated in adoption of the Slavery Convention of 1926; early international expressions of concern over the treatment of Jews in Russia and Armenians in the Ottoman empire; the inclusion in certain post-World War I treaties establishing new states in Eastern Europe of provisions and procedures to protect minorities within those countries; certain aspects of the League of Nations mandates system; and the establishment in 1919 of the International Labor Organization (ILO) and the subsequent activities of that organization.

However, most of what we now regard as "international human rights law" has emerged only since 1945, when, with the implications of the holocaust and other Nazi denials of human rights very much in mind, the nations of the world decided that the promotion of human rights and fundamental freedoms should be one of the principal purposes of the new United Nations organization. To implement this purpose, the UN Charter established general obligations requiring member states to respect human rights and provided for the creation of a Human Rights Commission to protect and advance those rights.

UN concern with human rights has expanded dramatically since 1945. Numerous international instruments have been adopted, among the most notable of which are the Universal Declaration of Human Rights and the Genocide Convention (1948); the Convention on the Political Rights of Women (1952); the Standard Minimum Rules for the Treatment of Prisoners (1957); the Convention on the Elimination of All Forms of Racial Discrimination (1965); the International Covenant on Civil and Political Rights and International Covenant on Economic, Social and Cultural Rights (1966); the Protocol relating to the Status of Refugees (1967); the Convention on the Elimination of All Forms of Discrimination against Woman (1979); the Convention against Torture and other Cruel, Inhuman or Degrading Treatment or Punishment (1984); the Convention on the Rights of the Child (1989); and the Convention on Migrant Workers (1990). In 1993, the Second World UN Conference on Human Rights, held in Vienna, focussed renewed attention on human rights issues; other recent international conferences have focussed attention on the environment (1991, Rio de Janeiro), population and development (1994, Cairo), social development (1995), and women (Beijing, 1995). In 1998, agreement was reached on creation of an international criminal court, and the Rome Statute of the International Criminal Court entered into force on 1 July 2002.

Increased UN involvement in human rights matters has been mirrored by growing adoption of regional human rights instruments, as illustrated by the entry into force in 1953 and subsequent evolution of the European Convention on Human Rights (which now covers forty-five countries and over 800 million people), the establishment of the Inter-American Commission on Human Rights in 1960, the entry into force of the American Convention on Human Rights in 1978, and the entry into force of the African Charter on Human and Peoples' Rights in 1986.

By the late 1960s, human rights had become relatively well established on the international agenda. Before 1960, human rights questions were regularly debated in the United Nations, but few states paid such discussions much attention. The rapid growth of UN membership in the early 1960s to include a significant number of African and other developing nations deeply concerned with problems of self-determination and racial discrimination, particularly in southern Africa, and the growing emphasis by Arab countries on human rights aspects of the Palestine question after 1967, resulted in these specific human rights issues being given a prominent role in UN politics. Increasing interest in human rights on the part of the U.S. Congress beginning in the early 1970s and President Jimmy Carter's decision that international human rights should play a leading role in U.S. foreign policy raised interest in human rights in the United States and around the world. Both the European Union and the Organization for Security and Cooperation in Europe now give considerable attention to human rights, and creation in 1994 of the post of UN High Commissioner for Human Rights has cemented the central place that human rights issues have assumed in international relations.

The international human rights movement received further world attention when the Nobel Prize for Peace was awarded in 1977 to Amnesty International for its human rights work for "prisoners of conscience," and, in 1980, to the Argentine human rights activist Adolfo Perez Esquivel. Since that time, other Peace Prize recipients whose work primarily concerned human rights or political freedoms include Lech Walesa (1983), Bishop Desmond Tutu (1984), the Dalai Lama (1989), Aung San Kuu Kyi (1991), Rigoberta Menchu Tum (1992), Bishop Carlos Bello and Jose Ramos-Horta (1996), Médecins Sans Frontières (1999), and Shirin Ebadi (2003).

Considering the relatively recent emergence of much international human rights law (compared to established international legal concepts such as sovereignty), it is not surprising that the field is one in which rules are still imprecise, fragmentary, and sometimes overlapping, and in which institutions and procedures continue to evolve. Today, however, the basic concept of international human rights is firmly established in international law and practice.

What Is the Content of International Human Rights Law?

International human rights law is derived from a variety of sources and involves many kinds of instruments, both international and national. The details of international procedures to protect human rights are examined in the remainder of this book. However, a few examples may illustrate the many different types of materials with which lawyers and others concerned with international human rights should be familiar.

First, there are now dozens of important multilateral treaties in force in the field of human rights, which create legally binding obligations for the states that are parties to them.[1] The most important of these is the United Nations Charter itself. The Charter is binding on almost every country in the world and establishes general obligations to respect and promote human rights. More specific international obligations are established in a series of UN-sponsored international human rights agreements of global scope and the three regional human rights conventions now in force. Many other relevant and important treaties have been concluded under the auspices of the ILO, UNESCO, and other UN specialized agencies, as well as various regional organizations.

Second, there are a great number of international declarations, resolutions, and recommendations relevant to international human rights that have been adopted by the United Nations, other international organizations or conferences, or nongovernmental and professional organizations concerned with human rights. While these instruments are not directly binding in a legal sense, they establish broadly recognized standards and are frequently invoked in connection with human rights issues.[2] The most important of these is the Universal Declaration of Human Rights, adopted without a dissenting vote by the UN General Assembly in 1948, which has provided a framework for much subsequent work. Another important instrument is the 1975 Helsinki Final Act and subsequent documents adopted by of the Conference on Security and Cooperation in Europe, which in 1994 became the Organization for Security and Cooperation in Europe. Other examples of such "soft law" include the 1957 Standard Minimum Rules for the Treatment of Prisoners, the 1981 General Assembly Declaration on Religious Intolerance, and the 1992 General Assembly Declaration on the Rights of Persons belonging to National or Ethnic, Religious or Linguistic Minorities.

Third, a variety of actions by UN organs and other international bodies have supported specific efforts to protect human rights. Examples include the International Court of Justice's 1971 Advisory Opinion on the Continued Presence of South Africa in Namibia (South West Africa); Security Council resolutions imposing sanctions on or authorizing intervention in Rhodesia (1968), South Africa (1977), former Yugoslavia (1991), Somalia (1992), Haiti (1994), and (eventually) Rwanda (1994); Security Council resolutions creating criminal tribunals to deal with mass killings in former Yugoslavia (1993), Rwanda (1994), Sierra Leone (2002), and Cambodia (2004); General Assembly resolutions dealing with human rights issues in Southern Africa, Chile, and the Middle East; resolutions and other actions by the UN Commission on Human Rights and its Sub-Commission on the Promotion and Protection of Human Rights;[3] the activities of the various treaty-based supervisory bodies;[4] and a growing body of decisions by regional commissions and courts in Europe and the Americas.[5]

Fourth, there are a great many national laws, regulations, court and administrative decisions, and policy pronouncements relevant to implementing international human rights objectives, both within each country and with respect to its relations with other countries. In the United States, for example, these domestic tools include provisions of the U.S. Constitution and Bill of Rights; legislation prohibiting discrimination and slavery and ensuring the political rights of women; legislation and regulations implementing the Genocide and Torture Conventions; legislation denying security assistance to any country whose government engages in a consistent pattern of gross violations of internationally recognized human rights; the Alien Tort Claims and Torture Victims Protection Acts, which allow federal civil suits against individuals who violate certain internationally protected human rights; judicial decisions dealing with aspects of international human rights law; and federal, state, and municipal judicial and administrative decisions dealing with aspects of American corporate operations in foreign countries that engage in gross violations of human rights.[6] Many other countries also have extensive bodies of domestic law or policy relevant to international human rights.

Finally, many international and national institutions contribute to the protection of human rights, even if their primary concern may be with other issues. For example, the relationship among human rights, humanitarian assistance, and development is of growing interest to many international governmental and nongovernmental organizations (NGOs). At the domestic level, legislative bodies; ministries dealing with foreign relations, trade, and defense; and courts at all levels may on occasion become involved in human rights questions or serve as arenas for promoting human rights objectives.

Obtaining documents and other information relevant to international human rights law is not always easy, although the World Wide Web and Internet are increasingly useful sources for up-to-date information. The most important materials, in both printed and electronic form, are identified in the Bibliographical Essay contained in Appendix A.

Who Is Bound by International Human Rights Law?

Unlike individual sovereign states, the community of nations has no international legislature empowered to enact laws that are directly binding on all countries. (Resolutions adopted by the UN General Assembly are only recommendations and do not legally bind its members. Of course, decisions of the UN Security Council adopted under Chapter VII of the Charter are legally binding on all UN members, and a number of such decisions in the past decade have been directly relevant to human rights concerns.) Instead, states establish legally binding obligations among themselves in other ways, principally by expressly consenting to an obligation by ratifying a treaty or other international agreement or through wide acceptance of a rule as binding customary international law.

International law, including human rights law, is primarily applicable to states rather than to individuals. Consequently, these international rules generally can become a source of domestic legal obligation for a state's officials and of domestic rights for that nation's citizens only through their incorporation in some manner into the state's own internal law.

In practice, the most important source of international human rights law is likely to be international treaties, which directly create international obligations for the parties. But treaties are binding only when they are in force and only with respect to the nations that have expressly agreed to become parties to them. Thus, in determining whether a treaty is legally relevant to the human rights situation in a particular country, it is important to ascertain: (1) whether the treaty contains express language requiring the parties to respect the particular human rights at issue; (2) whether the treaty is in force, since multilateral treaties typically do not take effect until a certain number of nations have deposited their ratifications (formal instruments indicating their intent to be bound); (3) whether the nation involved has in fact ratified the treaty, since signature alone may not legally bind a nation to the obligations of a multilateral treaty; and (4) whether the nation in question has filed any reservations that expressly modify its treaty obligations.

As indicated above, the human rights treaties establish a widespread network of human rights obligations. Almost all nations in the world are now parties to the UN Charter. While the human rights provisions of the Charter are broadly stated, it is now generally accepted that at least gross and systematic government-imposed or endorsed denials of human rights, such as the imposition of apartheid or government-sanctioned genocide, may directly violate Charter obligations. Most human rights conventions have now been widely ratified, and there are now approximately 150 state parties to the two Covenants; 170 parties to the Convention on the Elimination of All Forms of Racial Discrimination and Convention on the Elimination of All Forms of Discrimination against Women; and over 190 parties to the Convention on the Rights of the Child and the Fourth Geneva Convention on the Protection of Civilian Persons in Times of War.

A second source of international human rights law is international custom. In order to establish the existence of a rule of customary international law, it is necessary to demonstrate a widespread practice by states conforming to the alleged rule, together with evidence that they follow this practice because they believe that they are under a normative obligation to comply with the rule. It may be particularly useful if a specific human rights rule has become part of customary international law, since customary international law is generally binding upon *all* states, without regard to whether they have expressly consented. However, the concept of customary law is somewhat technical, and proving the existence of a customary rule can be difficult.

The authoritative 1987 *Restatement (Third) of The Foreign Relations Law of The United States* takes the position that at least certain basic human rights are now protected by customary international law. Section 702 of the *Restatement* provides, "A state violates international law if, as a matter of state policy, it practices, encourages, or condones (a) genocide, (b) slavery or slave trade, (c) the murder of causing the disappearance of individuals, (d) torture or other cruel, inhuman or degrading treatment or punishment, (e) prolonged arbitrary detention, (f) systematic racial discrimination, or (g) a consistent pattern of gross violations of internationally recognized human rights." Other commentators have identified different lists, but there seems to be widespread agreement that a number of rights are now included within customary international law.[7]

Even if particular international human rights instruments such as treaties or declarations are not *legally* binding on a particular state (either because it has not ratified the treaty or because the particular rule is not recognized as customary law), such instruments may possess a moral or political force that may be useful in persuading government officials to observe human rights standards. Moreover, national courts may be responsive to arguments that domestic law should be interpreted consistently with international human rights standards, particularly in cases where an inconsistent interpretation, even if not technically a breach of international law, might nevertheless be politically embarrassing.

While international law has traditionally been concerned primarily with relations among states, it is becoming widely recognized that individuals are the real subjects and beneficiaries of international human rights law. Individuals may have access to assert the rights granted to them under international law in various ways.

First and most importantly, states may incorporate international obligations expressed in human rights treaties into their domestic law; the rights can then be invoked directly by individuals as part of that state's internal law. Whether and how such incorporation takes place depends on each state's domestic law, and states differ in this respect. Under the basic law of some countries, a ratified treaty automatically becomes part of domestic law; in others, specific implementing legislation is required to create any domestic effect or individual right.

Second, some human rights treaties establish standing for individuals and/or NGOs to bring complaints directly before international bodies. This is the case, for example, if a state has acceded to the European Convention on Human Rights, the American Convention on Human Rights, or the Optional Protocol to the International Covenant on Civil and Political Rights.

In certain circumstances, individuals also may be held personally accountable under international law for genocide, crimes against humanity, and grave breaches of the laws of war. Several treaties (including the conventions on genocide, apartheid, and torture) impose individual criminal responsibility on government officials and, in some cases, others who violate the human rights protected by these conventions. As noted above, the UN Security Council has created international criminal tribunals to try individuals accused of serious violations of international humanitarian law in the former Yugoslavia and genocide in Rwanda, and the International Criminal Court has jurisdiction over genocide, crimes against humanity, and serious war crimes. In addition, hybrid courts, enforcing a combination of domestic and international criminal law and comprising both local and international judges and staff have been established in Kosovo, East Timor, Sierra Leone, and Cambodia. Finally, individual states may exercise universal jurisdiction over some international crimes, as Belgium now does in a somewhat limited form, and as Spain and other states attempted to assert in 1998 with respect to former Chilean ruler Augosto Pinochet.

How Can International Human Rights Obligations Be Enforced?

Implementation is key to making the system of international protection of human rights effective, but it has proved a difficult and troublesome problem. The jurisdiction of international courts depends upon the consent of the states involved, and relatively few states have given such consent with respect to disputes involving human rights. (The notable exceptions are the forty-five parties to the European Convention on Human Rights, which now mandates acceptance of the jurisdiction of the European Court of Human Rights, and the more than twenty states that have accepted the optional jurisdiction of the Inter-American Court of Human Rights.) Moreover, international courts are generally open only to states and not to individuals, although the European and inter-American systems are, again, exceptions. Finally, even when international courts are able to render judgments against nations that violate human rights obligations, there is no international police force to enforce such orders. Consequently, international human rights law, like all international law, must rely heavily on voluntary compliance by states, buttressed by such moral and other influence as other countries are prepared to exert.

One way of examining enforcement or implementation options is in terms of the level at which they occur. Thus, international human rights obligations can be implemented through action within the domestic system of the state concerned, by other states in the course of international relations, or by international bodies.

The easiest and most effective way to implement human rights is through action within each country's own legal system. If domestic law provides an effective system of remedies for violations of international human rights obligations (or their domestic equivalents), the authority of a nation's own legal system can be mobilized to support compliance with international norms. Most human rights treaties require that parties incorporate relevant obligations into their domestic law and that they provide appropriate local remedies. This, in turn, provides the rationale for the common requirement that domestic remedies be exhausted before an international body will investigate a complaint of human rights violations. Human rights treaties also frequently require that nations make periodic reports on their compliance with their treaty obligations, including reference to how these obligations are incorporated into domestic law, to international institutions overseeing the treaties.

Enforcement also can occur at the interstate level. Thus, one state may complain directly to another state concerning the latter's alleged breach of human rights obligations and can bring diplomatic pressure to bear in an attempt to influence the other country to cease such violations. Such pressure might include traditional "quiet diplomacy," public criticism, denial of military and economic assistance, or, at the extreme, through the use of force for "humanitarian" intervention.

Enforcement by international organizations occurs through a variety of international forums in which complaints of human rights violations can be raised by states or individuals, most of which are discussed in greater detail in this book. These include regional and global procedures which offer avenues for inter-state and/or individual complaints to be filed. Some international institutions, e.g., UN bodies such as the General Assembly, Security Council, and Commission on Human Rights, and regional bodies, such as the Inter-American Commission on Human Rights and the Organization for Security and Cooperation in Europe, may consider human rights matters on their own initiative, without any formal complaint mechanism; this is also true of the international criminal tribunals established by the Security Council and the new International Criminal Court.

Another way of looking at enforcement and implementation options is in terms of the party which can institute a complaint. Depending on the procedure invoked, this may be a private individual or group, a state, or an international organization.

An effective system of international human rights law rests primarily on the concept of enforcement by states. In theory, when a state violates its international human rights obligations, it will be called to account by other states. In practice, however, this rarely occurs. States are often reluctant to antagonize friendly nations by criticizing their human rights behavior; they have typically been willing to raise human rights issues only with respect to either their enemies or politically unpopular states. While exceptions may be found—such as interstate complaints filed within the European system by Ireland against the United Kingdom and by several states against Turkey—even gross violations of human rights have often been ignored. Many have argued that, in view of the political factors which affect the willingness of states to criticize each other's human rights conduct, any system that is overly reliant on state-to-state complaints as the means of enforcement is almost certain to be illusory and ineffective.

One alternative is to rely on an international organization or institution, such as the UN High Commissioner for Human Rights or the Organization for Security and Cooperation in Europe, to raise human rights issues. Of course, the issue must somehow be brought to the attention of the international organization, and this almost invariably requires that the matter be raised by a state or group of states. Once it has jurisdiction over the matter, the body may be empowered to initiate a public or private investigation or take other action to encourage respect for human rights. However, since international organizations are composed of states, political considerations will remain foremost, and an influential country or regional group often can block any effective action.

Another alternative is to permit human rights issues to be raised by private individuals or nongovernmental organizations. Where human rights obligations are incorporated in domestic law, or where domestic law links foreign policy to human rights performance, individuals or groups may raise relevant human rights issues in national courts or agencies. They also may attempt to influence national legislatures, foreign relations ministries, or other agencies that either implement human rights obligations domestically or are supposed to encourage compliance by other countries. Institutions within the government apparatus with special concerns and responsibilities regarding human rights can be helpful in providing a focus and accessible forum for such efforts. Finally, as discussed in the following chapters, some treaties establish procedures under which individuals or groups may file complaints directly with international bodies.

A third way of looking at enforcement options is in terms of the types of enforcement techniques that can be employed in an attempt to secure compliance with human rights obligations. For example, a private individual or group may seek a decision from a national court or administrative agency or an international tribunal or other body. A state may employ techniques ranging from "quiet diplomacy" to public condemnation, trade embargoes, cessation of diplomatic relations, or perhaps even the use of force through so-called "humanitarian intervention." International organizations may similarly employ a wide range of enforcement devices, including the use of "good offices;" diplomatic persuasion; public exposure and criticism; expulsion of the offending state from the international organization; imposition of trade and diplomatic sanctions; indictment or trial of accused individuals, where possible; or, under some circumstances, the collective use of armed force.

As the twenty-first century opens, questions have arisen as to the advantages and disadvantages of various of these potential enforcement techniques. Debate continues regarding both the legality and efficacy of forcible humanitarian intervention as a means of seeking to protect human rights, particularly when employed by only one or a few states without express United Nations authorization, as was the case with NATO's 1999 bombing of Yugoslavia and expulsion of Serb forces from Kosovo. Controversy also continues over the legality and appropriateness both of individual states (such as Spain and Belgium) that claim universal jurisdiction to prosecute non-nationals for alleged international crimes, and over the increasing number of international criminal tribunals. Indeed, as of early 2004, the United States has not only actively opposed the International Criminal Court but made clear that it will vigorously resist any attempt to subject U.S. nationals to that Court's jurisdiction.

Problems and Prospects

Despite the rapid growth of international human rights law during the last half-century, massive and shocking violations of fundamental human rights continue to occur in many countries, and progress in achieving greater respect for these rights has been sporadic and slow. Some commentators are skeptical as to the potential effectiveness of international law and institutions in promoting human rights objectives, and a number of basic questions remain unanswered.[8]

First, what is meant by human rights? Can over 190 different countries with different cultures, political systems, and ideologies, and at different stages of economic development, really hope to agree on the rights that ought to be protected through international rules and institutions, or on the priorities among them when these rights conflict with one another? Differences in perspective have emerged in the past, for example, between Western developed nations, which have generally emphasized the importance of civil and political rights, and the developing and socialist nations, which have emphasized economic and social rights. Some nations have pressed for greater recognition for "collective" human rights, such as the right to development or peace; others believe that collective rights are ill-defined and inconsistent with individual human rights.

Today, however, there is growing agreement that human rights must be considered in their entirety. Questions about "cultural relativism" were answered in part by the 1993 Vienna Declaration, adopted by the Second World UN Conference on Human Rights, which concluded by consensus:

> All human rights are universal, indivisible and interdependent and interrelated. The international community must treat human rights globally in a fair and equal manner, on the same footing, and with the same emphasis. While the significance of national and regional particularities and various historical, cultural and religious back-grounds must be borne in mind, it is the duty of States, regardless of their political, economic and cultural systems, to promote and protect all human rights and fundamental freedoms.[9]

There has been some concern that international organizations and some NGOs label too many aspirations as "human rights" and that this proliferation may diminish the concept of human rights as a claim of individual freedom and dignity that the state must respect. At the same time, most people have welcomed the expansion of human rights efforts over the past decade to address more seriously issues of women, children, and minorities, as well as individual criminal responsibility for human rights violations.

Second, can one expect government officials to support human rights objectives and efforts impartially, even when this poses foreign policy risks, or will they only give such support selectively, when it serves what is perceived as their country's more immediate foreign policy interests? It is apparent that many nations apply a "double standard" in their attitudes toward human rights, harshly condemning violations by political enemies but ignoring equally serious violations on the part of nations with which they wish to maintain good relations. For example, critics attacked the Reagan administration's attempt to distinguish between so-called "authoritarian" and "totalitarian" regimes as, in effect, the use of such a "double standard." Other countries and regional blocs have equally problematic records of consistency on human rights; similarly, the United Nations focused its early human rights efforts principally on problems involving South Africa and the Israeli-occupied territories, while paying little or no attention to equally or more serious violations in other countries. If governments do not accept the basic moral premises of international human rights but only pay them lip service, how can international human rights law ever work?

Third, can one hope through international law and institutions to affect the ways governments behave toward their own citizens, or do the roots of repression, discrimination, and other denials of human rights lie in deeper and more complex political, social, and economic problems? And if, as some believe, humanity faces an increasingly uphill struggle against the relentless pressures of increasing population, resource depletion, environmental degradation, and economic scarcity, can one ever hope to reach conditions of economic well-being in which social competition will become less intense and human rights can flourish?

These problems must be taken seriously. It is neither realistic nor useful to pretend that international human rights law can produce an immediate change in the way human beings and their governments have behaved for millennia or to promise any quick and dramatic improvement in the human condition.

But there is some basis for optimism. Today, human rights are a part of every government's foreign policy, even if only rhetorically. Almost all former colonies have achieved independence, and apartheid in South Africa was abolished in 1994. Even when governments employ international human rights concepts hypocritically and for selfish political purposes, their actions serve to reinforce human rights principles and establish important precedents. International human rights institutions have acquired their own momentum, expanding their human rights activities in ways that governments have found difficult to curb.

At the very least, international human rights law has probably exerted some check on government actions and kept matters from getting worse—although the carnage in Cambodia, former Yugoslavia, Sudan, Rwanda, Liberia, Sierra Leone, Sri Lanka, and elsewhere demonstrates only too clearly how human rights are often forgotten when widespread violence breaks out. But if international efforts and activities can succeed in ratcheting respect for and observance of human rights gradually upwards, even if only slowly and incrementally, the game will be worth the candle.

Finally, the growing number of local and national human rights NGOs, especially in countries of the developing world and countries in transition in Eastern Europe, has significantly expanded the impact of NGO work; such groups have become increasingly active at the international level. Such activism has been facilitated by a 1996 revision to the resolution that governs the formal relationship between NGOs and the United Nations; regional and national NGOs, as well as international ones, may now apply for "consultative status" with ECOSOC and thus participate more fully in UN meetings.[10]

Certainly, the international human rights movement will continue to encounter reverses as well as advances, and dedication, persistence, and much more work is needed to achieve the goal of bringing human rights to all peoples everywhere. Among the directions such work might take are the following:

- increasing efforts to embed international human rights norms more firmly within national legal systems and to sensitize lawyers, judges, and other officials to the relevance and usefulness of international human rights law as a tool to advance human rights within national societies;
- strengthening and providing adequate resources for existing international institutions, such as the various human rights commissions and courts and the Office of the UN High Commissioner for Human Rights;
- expanding cooperation and coordination among the various human rights institutions to avoid inconsistency and unnecessary duplication of effort;
- developing regional human rights institutions in the Arab World and Asia;
- enhancing the role and influence of NGOs involved in the promotion of human rights and increasing their access to national and international human rights institutions and processes, while increasing their accountability and transparency;
- giving increased attention to massive and urgent human rights issues, such as pervasive hunger and disease (particularly among children), widespread and deeply entrenched discrimination against women, recurrent violations of human rights and humanitarian law in international and civil conflict, and the continuing problem of refugees and internally displaced persons;
- focussing greater attention on economic, social, and cultural rights and the relationship between human rights and economic development;
- exploring the relationship between human rights and other agreed-upon international objectives, such as protection of the environment, promotion of trade, and suppression of transnational crime;
- ensuring the accountability of nonstate actors, such as transnational corporations or private armies, for complicity in human rights violations;
- devising criteria to guide forceful intervention intended to prevent or stop massive violations of human rights;
- achieving wider dissemination of human rights ideas and documentation among people throughout the world and ensuring access by individuals to national and international institutions for redress for violations;
- learning more about the root causes of discrimination and intolerance, in order to devise better ways of trying to eliminate them;

- developing better indicators for measuring and monitoring the observance of human rights and better fact-finding mechanisms and techniques;
- depoliticizing human rights questions, so as to increase the willingness of governments to address such issues fairly and on their own merits in international forums;
- ensuring that the post-2001 "war against terrorism" does not lead to unjustifiable restrictions on human rights and, in particular, the activities of human rights defenders and critics of the government; and
- persuading government officials that human rights *are* an appropriate and legitimate concern of national foreign policy, not only because support for human freedom and dignity is "decent" and "right," but also because it is in each nation's pragmatic long-term national interest to acquire the respect and friendship of other nations and to achieve a world in which people can live securely and in peace.

In many cases, the day-to-day problems involved in work in the field of international human rights law will be undramatic, and broader goals and issues may not be apparent. But practitioners are nonetheless sharing in an important and exciting enterprise, albeit one whose ultimate success remains still distant and elusive.

Notes

1. A list of ratifications of some of the major human rights treaties is contained in Appendix E.
2. See chap 11.
3. See chap 4.
4. See chaps 3, 10.
5. See chaps 7, 8.
6. See chap 13.
7. See generally Hurst Hannum, The Status of the Universal Declaration of Human Rights in National and International Law, 25 *Ga J. Int'l & Comp. L.* 287 (1995/96).
8. These questions are discussed further in Richard Bilder, Rethinking International Human Rights: Some Basic Questions, 1969 *Wis L. Rev.* 171, reprinted in 2 *Hum. Rts. J.* 557 (1969).
9. Vienna Declaration and Programme of Action, UN Doc. A/CONF.157/23 (1993), para. I.5.
10. ECOSOC Res. 1996/31 (1996), amending ECOSOC Res. 1296.

Chapter 2
Implementing Human Rights: An Overview of NGO Strategies and Available Procedures

Hurst Hannum

As the preceding chapter indicates, international human rights norms are drawn from a wide range of sources. Whether "hard" or "soft" law, binding or nonbinding, each set of norms and principles contributes to the evolving definition of international human rights.

The chapters which follow describe in detail the many mechanisms available to promote, monitor, and enforce human rights law, ranging from the national to the global. Some of these mechanisms are concerned with specific categories of rights; others are limited geographically. The present chapter addresses some of the considerations that should go into selecting which procedure or procedures to use under various circumstances. It also discusses some political or tactical concerns of which human rights advocates should be aware.

NGO Mandates and Strategies

Nongovernmental organizations (NGOs) may be found in all regions of the world. They range from truly mass-based international organizations, such as Amnesty International, which has 1.5 million members, donors, and supporters in over 150 countries, to one-person offices created to monitor the human rights situation in a single country. While many human rights lawyers and other activists provide services to victims on an individual basis, most tend to work in cooperation with one or more NGOs.

The goals or mandates of NGOs range across the entire spectrum of internationally recognized human rights. An NGO's definition of its primary aims will have a profound impact in determining which procedures it may be in the NGO's interest to invoke.

The first significant distinction among NGOs is their substantive focus: is an NGO's mandate general and universal, or is it limited either geographically or substantively? Many well-known NGOs have found it more efficient to focus on only a narrow range of human rights, in order to develop greater expertise or to address more effectively those rights which it may deem to be the most important. For example, Amnesty International began as an organization concerned with rights of personal integrity, including protection against physical ill-treatment, arbitrary detention, and unfair trials; the mandate of Defense for Children International is clearly expressed in its name; the London-based group, Article 19, takes its name from Article 19 of the Universal Declaration of Human Rights and is concerned with freedom of expression. Other NGOs—such as Human Rights Watch, International Commission of Jurists, Global Human Rights (formerly the International Human Rights Law Group), Human Rights First (formerly the Lawyers Committee for Human Rights), the Fédération Internationale des Droits de l'Homme, and today's Amnesty International—choose not to limit their substantive concerns and take up issues spanning all of the rights in the Universal Declaration and other international instruments.

Many NGOs were created to respond to a specific concern or to the situation in a particular country. Others have adopted a regional focus, seeking to maximize available expertise (including linguistic ability) or utilize existing regional mechanisms for the protection of human rights. Such NGOs obviously do not need to concern themselves with regional institutions outside the area of their concern, although UN or other global mechanisms may still be useful.

Perhaps every human rights NGO in the world, even the largest, is understaffed and underfunded, and each must make almost daily decisions as to which violations it can address and which it must ignore because of limited time and resources. Such decisions are often strategic rather than ideological, and one of the most difficult tasks faced by the governing boards and staffs of NGOs is to develop criteria which can help determine which issues they can and should address. Should individual cases be given priority over more general human rights concerns? Should a kind of "triage" be exercised, pursuant to which only those cases in which there is the greatest chance that NGO action will have real impact are accepted? Should more "serious" cases be dealt with before less vital ones? Can choices be based on distinctions among categories of rights, such as civil and political rights, on the one hand, and economic, social, and cultural rights, on the other? Should larger societal issues which may encourage human rights violations be addressed, such as the unequal distribution of wealth, or should an NGO restrict itself to the violations which result from such situations?

It is almost impossible to adopt a clear policy which responds to these questions in every instance, and most NGOs find themselves addressing many different kinds of violations, each requiring different tactics, at the same time. Individual cases are often urgent, and they serve as powerful illustrations of the existence of larger human rights problems. One cannot easily judge the chances for success in every instance, and it is often those cases which seem most hopeless that are the most compelling. In many instances, the limited amount of information available, linguistic competence, and financial resources may prevent an NGO from taking up even a deserving case in a thorough manner, although *some* response to urgent appeals will almost always be forthcoming.

As noted later in this chapter, it is essential for a human rights NGO both to be and to appear to be nonpartisan and nonideological. When an NGO deals with situations in a wide number of countries, decisions regarding future initiatives should include consideration of the geopolitical or cultural balance reflected in the NGO's work as a whole. For example, an NGO which purports to monitor compliance with the minority rights norms adopted by the Organization for Security and Cooperation in Europe should not focus only on Eastern Europe; an organization concerned with religious intolerance might wish to examine the situations in China and Israel, for example, as well as that in Saudi Arabia. An NGO might decide to investigate North Korea or Tajikistan precisely because information about such countries is difficult to obtain, and, as a result, the country may have received disproportionately less attention from human rights bodies than is warranted.

Such considerations might seem overly Machiavellian, but they are part of the real world of daily NGO activities. Most NGOs do not have the leisure to examine such questions in the abstract—appeals for help arrive daily, and decisions as to the kind and degree of activity that can be undertaken must be made relatively quickly—but they should not allow their actions to be determined simply by what appeal arrives first.

International human rights *law* is directed to states and governments; they have the responsibility to ensure that rights are protected from violation either by government officials or by private individuals acting with the acquiescence or complicity of governments. However, the activities of armed opposition groups in a number of countries have given rise to accusations of "human rights violations" being directed against these nongovernmental actors, as well as against governments.

Without entering fully into the debate, it should be noted that many advocates believe that their concern is only with the action (or inaction) of governments; killings and other assaults by nongovernmental forces are crimes under domestic law and should be treated as such. Other groups, particularly when dealing with situations in which violent conflicts are long-standing (e.g., Sudan, Sri Lanka, Colombia) choose to address "human rights violations" by guerrillas in at least a summary fashion. In such situations, the humanitarian law of armed conflict is obviously relevant, although the precise scope of its application often may be confusing.

An NGO generally should not ignore the existence of a conflict entirely, if only because some conflicts may justify derogations from or limitations on rights that would otherwise be impermissible. At the same time, however, human rights law is distinct from the law relating to armed conflict, and one must be careful to utilize the legal arguments which are most protective of individual rights in the particular circumstances. Similar considerations apply to the often complex situations of refugees or displaced persons, although one must remember that they, too, have the right to be protected from human rights violations.

As international criminal law takes firmer hold, many NGOs have begun to advocate criminal liability for "human rights crimes," particularly in transitional situations where repressive or despotic regimes have been replaced by arguably more rights-respecting governments. International or mixed tribunals have been established to address international crimes in the former Yugoslavia, Rwanda, Cambodia, Sierra Leone, East Timor, and Liberia, and a new International Criminal Court was created in 2002. Again, however, one should distinguish between a human rights violation and an international crime—each is defined in different instruments, and most human rights violations do not constitute crimes.

Finally, some NGOs have become increasingly active in promoting human rights through assistance and educational programs, rather than just responding to violations. Such activities are often particularly important in "transitional" states, where respecting human rights and establishing a meaningful rule of law are essential to long-term stability and democratization.

Questions of mandate and long-term strategy arise most frequently in the early stages of an NGO's existence, although they may usefully be reviewed every few years. Even the most well-established NGOs need to reassess fact-finding and other tactics on the basis of experience, and mandates may be expanded or restricted depending on the changing nature of human rights violations in the world. Some of these issues are addressed in greater detail in the works on NGOs listed in the Bibliographic Essay in Appendix A.

Domestic Activities

Redressing Human Rights Violations in One's Own Country

If there has not been a wholesale breakdown in the rule of law in a country, there are a number of domestic initiatives that an NGO can undertake to promote human rights generally or to change national policies which appear to conflict with international norms.

The *invocation of formal legal procedures*, such as *habeas corpus* or *amparo* proceedings or civil suits to challenge government acts, is an obvious first step which should not be ignored (at least where there is a regularly functioning judicial system). As discussed in chapter 13, there also may be ways to implement international human rights norms directly through the domestic/national legal system, although this possibility depends on the domestic law of each country.

Nonjudicial *administrative appeals* also should be attempted, if necessary by challenging the exercise of executive discretion in particular cases. Constitutional and administrative courts often have the authority to redress governmental abuses of power, and they should not be ignored. It may be easier to persuade a government to change its rules and policies where they are perceived to be inconsistent with international human rights norms, before trying to force it to change through litigation.

An often overlooked, but vitally important, avenue of legal and political redress is the *legislative branch of government*, particularly where the system of government gives the legislature a power base separate from the executive. In the United States, for example, most human rights initiatives originated in the U.S. Congress, and many significant pieces of legislation were adopted over the opposition of the executive branch. Legislation also may be required to reform judicial procedures or comply with a country's obligations to promote economic and social rights.

Legislative hearings and fact-finding investigations provide forums in which human rights violations can be publicized and pressure brought to bear on governments to halt them. The parliamentary immunity enjoyed by legislators in many countries may enable them to speak out more forthrightly, and NGOs often have much closer ties to the legislative than to the executive branch of government. Human rights ombudsman or similar institutions also are frequently responsible to the legislative rather than the executive branch of government.

Urging the government to *ratify international treaties* concerning human rights can be an effective tool to educate the public about human rights and increase the substantive protections available to a country's citizens. The international oversight that accompanies most human rights treaties also can provide a useful (if limited) potential check on government actions, as discussed in chapters 3 and 10. While mere ratification is no guarantee that a government will take its obligations seriously, international treaty commitments are often important to prevent a government from back-sliding on its human rights promises.

The importance of the *mass media* cannot be overemphasized. While one most often thinks of exposing human rights violations in the press, the media also can be extremely helpful in educating the public (and politicians) about human rights issues. When human rights norms are invoked by a government to justify its criticism of foreign regimes, the media can legitimately ask why the same norms are not also adhered to at home.

Abstract human rights appeals are less likely to receive serious attention than more specific appeals regarding an issue that is already newsworthy. NGOs should find a "hook" to which their human rights concerns can be attached, such as the visit of a foreign dignitary or an increased flow of refugees from a country in which human rights are being violated. Where an immigrant or other group in one country is ethnically or culturally linked to a group which is being victimized in another country, "foreign" human rights concerns may suddenly acquire much greater importance in domestic politics.

Countries which systematically violate human rights also persecute human rights activists and rigidly control access to their territory by the media. Thus, exile or other groups in foreign countries are often the best source of information on human rights abuses, and domestic NGOs can assist these groups in contacting local (and international) media.

Successful human rights NGOs develop good personal contacts with journalists, who may provide information to NGOs and also serve as a means of making NGO information public. In addition, NGOs and individuals should attempt to gain direct access to the media where that is possible, through letters to the editor, short "op-ed" pieces, soliciting radio and television interviews, and similar techniques.

Domestic Activities Aimed at Promoting Human Rights in Other Countries

Today, both governments and the public view human rights as a legitimate issue of foreign policy, and seeking to influence the foreign policy of one's own country can be one of the most effective means of promoting human rights in another country. Many foreign ministries now have specific bureaus or divisions dedicated to monitoring human rights, and foreign policy pronouncements from governments around the world frequently cite human rights concerns as influencing political decisions.

Few countries have gone as far as the United States, where the administration is required by law to prepare a public annual report on the state of human rights in all countries. However, it should be possible in many countries to provide information informally to a foreign ministry regarding the human rights situation in another country with which there are close economic or political relations. In addition, NGOs should demand that every government pay greater attention to human rights considerations in formulating its foreign policy.

Of course, there is a danger that human rights may become overly politicized if they are too closely entwined with foreign policy. The United States favored friendly "authoritarian" regimes over Communist "totalitarian" regimes during the Reagan administration; the Soviet Union hypocritically promoted economic and social rights while violating political rights; and many Asian and African governments have excused gross human rights violations by their neighbors by invoking specious arguments of interference with "sovereignty" or "cultural relativism."

Nevertheless, the mobilization of world public opinion against human rights violators almost necessarily includes influencing the political decisions of governments. So-called "quiet diplomacy," in which a government may privately raise individual cases or larger human rights issues in a bilateral diplomatic setting, can be an important tool. Public expressions of concern over alleged human rights violations may lay the groundwork for a government later to support multilateral initiatives in the United Nations or elsewhere. However, while human rights NGOs should take "political" considerations into account when they make tactical decisions as to which situations are most likely to receive attention at a given time, they must always be conscious of the need to deal with human rights in the most objective, nonpartisan manner possible.

International Initiatives

International treaties and human rights bodies have proliferated in the past three decades, and anyone seeking to invoke international human rights procedures is presented with a bewildering array of choices. This section summarizes some of the most significant differences among the various international mechanisms available; the reader should then turn to succeeding chapters for more detailed information on the substantive and procedural requirements of each option.[1]

Individual Cases

Perhaps the most crucial distinction to be kept in mind when surveying available procedures is that between protecting the rights of a particular individual and promoting broader human rights concerns within a particular country. While there is obviously a close relationship between the two in most instances, the international community has developed quite different mechanisms to address each.

Where the concern is, for example, to release an individual from prison, to protect her from torture, to allow a banned newspaper to resume publication, or to secure a family's right to emigrate, the primary motivation must be to secure the rights of the individual victim. In such a context, a human rights advocate or NGO should not worry about setting precedents, proving the "guilt" of a government, or gaining publicity, unless any of these steps might help the individual concerned.

The danger in focusing exclusively on an individual case is that a government may attempt to "buy off" an NGO by acceding to its demands, at least in part. The bargain may take the form of an early release from detention or permission to leave a country, so long as the NGO ceases its public condemnation or agrees to discuss the problem confidentially. Such a "bargain" may be more insidious, if governments threaten to persecute victims to an even greater extent if international publicity continues.

Under such circumstances, the primary loyalty of an NGO must be to the individual victim. Of course, the victim may reject a proposed bargain, for example, by refusing to recant an unpopular political belief or even refusing release while others remain imprisoned. On the other hand, a victim may understandably choose to accept a government's offer of release, exile, or compensation, even if such a "settlement" may unwillingly undermine broader efforts to redress human rights violations in a particular country. However, this must be the victim's decision, and an NGO should honor whatever that decision may be.

At the same time, however, an NGO should not hesitate to apprise its individual client of the implications of a particular settlement or offer, particularly if the situation is not life-threatening or where formal legal proceedings have been invoked. The European and inter-American human rights systems require approval of any "friendly settlement" by the appropriate international body, to ensure that it is on the basis of respect for human rights; an NGO can play a similar role in ensuring that a victim is not tricked or coerced by a government.

Exhausting domestic remedies

The requirement that a complainant exhaust all domestic remedies before invoking international procedures is common to nearly every international mechanism discussed in this book. This is not surprising, for a state should be given the first opportunity to redress at least those occasional human rights violations that occur in every country.

This requirement need be fulfilled only where the domestic remedies are real, not illusory. Where theoretical remedies are ineffective or inadequate for any reason—such as inordinate delay in judicial proceedings, lack of an independent judiciary, clear judicial precedent which upholds the challenged action, or limits on the judiciary's jurisdiction which prevents the courts from interfering with actions taken by the executive branch—a petitioner need not go through the motions of pursuing useless domestic proceedings.

Not only is exhaustion of domestic remedies normally required before international procedures can be invoked, but, where they do exist, domestic remedies are likely to be faster and more effective than mere political or moral exhortations emanating from an international body. Indeed, when it is possible to separate an individual case from broader complaints about human rights abuses, NGOs should always consider whether a "nonpolitical" domestic approach might be more persuasive in a particular case.

Humanitarian appeals

A purely humanitarian approach may be faster and more effective at the international level than an initiative that is accusatory or emphasizes the broader political context in which an individual violation occurs. A humanitarian approach involves direct contact with international bodies, without attempting to fulfill the requirements for a formal petition or communication. The goal is to protect the victim from immediate danger (e.g., torture or execution), without regard to the underlying causes or formal governmental responsibility for a violation of human rights.

The mere fact that an inquiry is instituted by an intergovernmental body may deter a government from physically assaulting, executing, or deporting someone in custody. However, there is no guarantee that this will occur, particularly if the government concerned is a gross violator of human rights. If the appeal is successful in preventing immediate harm, the case can then be continued by initiating a formal application.

There are several mechanisms which can respond to humanitarian appeals:

- The UN High Commissioner for Human Rights has created a "hot line" for reporting urgent human rights violations, which can be used by victims, their relatives, or NGOs.[2] This number also may be used to contact the so-called "thematic" rapporteurs and working groups established by the UN Commission on Human Rights, which are specifically authorized to take "effective action" in response to individual complaints; they should be among the first international entities contacted in urgent cases.[3] These mechanisms cannot investigate or pronounce on violations, but their humanitarian functions have become increasingly accepted; all can be contacted through the Office of the UN High Commissioner for Human Rights in Geneva.
- The secretariats of the Inter-American Commission on Human Rights and the European Court of Human Rights have the authority to request (although not to order) that a government take action to

safeguard the human rights of an individual on whose behalf they have been approached.[4]

- Staff members who serve international bodies, such as the Human Rights Committee, UNESCO, and others, may be willing to contact a government informally about urgent situations. Here, much depends on the goodwill and initiative of the individual staff member, as well as the general practice in the office.

- Country-specific rapporteurs appointed by the Commission on Human Rights also can be contacted privately, although many governments have refused to cooperate with such rapporteurs, and they tend to have less immediate influence than the thematic rapporteurs. If a rapporteur is about to conduct an on-site investigation in a country or issue a report, however, the government concerned may be much more receptive to appeals from the rapporteur on behalf of a particular individual.

- The International Committee of the Red Cross is perhaps the best-known humanitarian organization in the world, but its mandate is quite limited. In situations of armed conflict, however, Red Cross representatives may make confidential approaches to governments to search for missing persons, visit prisons and detention camps, and otherwise seek to alleviate individual suffering and provide information to the families of victims. There also are a number of NGOs whose interests are purely or primarily humanitarian, such as Médecins sans Frontières and Oxfam.

Humanitarian appeals also can be made by one government to another, in the context of bilateral diplomacy. Particularly when the inquiring government is perceived as having friendly relations with the target government, it may be easier for the latter to take positive action with respect to an individual case than to anger its ally by refusing to cooperate. Even if two countries are not allies, the likelihood of a successful humanitarian appeal may increase if an important state visit is to occur or if a positive response to human rights issues is viewed as contributing to achieving economic or political goals.

Invoking formal international procedures

Just as the domestic lawyer's ultimate threat is that "I'll see you in court," the international human rights activist is most likely to invoke formal international procedures as a last resort. While many procedures can and should be invoked at the same time that other avenues of redress are being explored, they should rarely be the first option considered.

In addition to the specific procedural hurdles that must be overcome with respect to each mechanism, all the international procedures share a serious problem of delay. It is not uncommon for it to take three or four years for a case to be finally decided, although initial hearings and/or decisions on admissibility may be made within a few months to a year or two. While many international bodies have the authority to request a government to take "interim" or "precautionary" measures to prevent irreparable harm from occurring while a complaint is being considered, there is no guarantee that a government will honor such a request.

At the same time, it should be recognized that submission of a formal communication and, in particular, its transmittal to the government concerned may be an effective tool in itself in encouraging a government to take action. Full consideration of a case may lead to a great deal of publicity and pressure on a government to change its practices, especially when the complaint raises an issue of concern to more people than just the individual petitioner.

Another problem with international procedures is that their decisions are not legally binding on governments, with the exception of judgments rendered by the inter-American and European courts of human rights. Only such judicial forums have the power to order that compensation be paid to victims of human rights violations. The distinction between legally binding judgments and nonbinding recommendations does not always have great practical significance, however, and many governments have taken an action recommended by an international body even when the recommendation was not formally binding.

Of course, much depends on whether there is a good supervisory mechanism to follow-up on even non-binding recommendations or effective publicity designed to pressure a government to abide by an international decision. The systematic supervision by the International Labor Organization, for example, is more likely to encourage compliance than is the mere issuance of "views" by the Human Rights Committee.[5]

The right of an individual to invoke formal international complaint procedures must be specifically accepted by individual states, and the geographical scope of many treaties remains unfortunately limited. All members of the Organization of American States fall within the jurisdiction of the Inter-American Commission on Human Rights, and all parties to the European Convention on Human Rights accept the right of individual petition. As of early 2004, 104 of the 151 parties to the Covenant on Civil and Political Rights had accepted the right of individual petition under the Optional Protocol, but fewer than half of the state parties to the Convention on the Elimination of All Forms of Racial Discrimination, Convention on the Elimination of All Forms of Discrimination against Women, Convention against Torture and other Forms of Cruel, Inhuman or Degrading Treatment, or American Convention on Human Rights, had accepted the right of individual petition.

Procedures which have been adopted under the inherent constitutional authority of international organizations—such as the UNESCO procedure,[6] the procedures to protect freedom of association developed by the ILO,[7] and the United Nations "1503 procedure"[8]—are universal, but they do not lead to legally binding judgments and are restricted to cases falling within the subject-matter jurisdiction of the organization.

Many mechanisms that address individual communications are confidential, but judicious use of the media and mobilization of international public opinion is nevertheless possible. It is essential to seek advice from the secretariats of the relevant bodies and from knowledgeable NGOs or lawyers, in order to determine whether publicity is appropriate in a particular case. The decision to seek or avoid publicity is a tactical one and may depend on the circumstances of the particular victim, but the mere fact that a case has been filed should certainly be considered to be public information.

Large-Scale Human Rights Violations in a Particular Country

An individual petition should be drawn narrowly and need not necessarily impugn widespread government policies. A government which does not feel that its very existence is being challenged may be more willing to respond favorably to a humanitarian appeal or comply with the opinion of an international human rights body, and depoliticizing a complaint is often a worthwhile tactic in individual cases.

This is not true for actions which seek to redress widespread human rights abuses or a consistent practice of violations within a country. Such allegations are inevitably viewed by governments as potentially dangerous, as they call into question the willingness or ability of a government to live up to internationally recognized norms and may even challenge the government's political legitimacy. Under such circumstances, it is rarely fruitful to depoliticize issues, although NGOs must still guard against appearing to be ideologically motivated.

Of course, where the goal is to overturn a law in a more-or-less democratic country, a finding by an international body that the law does, in fact, violate international norms may provide sufficient impetus for the government concerned to amend or repeal the offending legislation. If a state is subject to the binding jurisdiction of the European or inter-American courts of human rights, such a direct international legal challenge may be the most effective way of ensuring compliance with international standards.

But when the goal is to challenge the overall human rights situation in a country or a widespread practice of violations, formal international procedures may be less relevant than they are in an individual case. It may be more effective to increase awareness of the violations and thereby mobilize public pressure to end them, through tactics such as publishing reports, sending fact-finding missions, and publicizing eyewitness accounts; invoking formal international mechanisms may supplement such direct methods.

One of the goals of mobilizing public opinion is to influence the policies of both foreign governments and international organizations, and international mechanisms offer the possibility of increased visibility and greater credibility for NGO efforts. The fact that a country's human rights situation is even discussed at the international diplomatic level is in itself a form of pressure, and promoting that discussion is a primary goal of much NGO activity.

The most visible action that an international body can take is to initiate an investigation of the human rights situation in a country. This may be followed or accompanied by a formal resolution, whose diplomatic phraseology may range from the relatively benign ("noting" or "expressing concern") to outright condemnation. A country which is the subject of such attention is likely to resist with all the political and diplomatic weapons available to it.

The UN Commission on Human Rights is the most important forum with global jurisdiction that can initiate a country-specific investigation.[9] Lobbying for appointment of a special rapporteur on a country, who will undertake an investigation of the human rights situation and report back to the commission the following year, requires a substantial commitment of time and resources, including physical presence in Geneva during at least part of the Commission's annual session. Many NGOs arrive in Geneva having woefully underestimated the political and practical difficulties which they face in mounting such an initiative, and the coordinated effort of several NGOs is often required for success. In addition, it is helpful if the human rights situation is sufficiently serious to have already acquired a certain notoriety among government representatives on the Commission.

Having the Commission on Human Rights or its Sub-Commission on the Promotion and Protection of Human Rights simply adopt a resolution concerning a specific country may be marginally easier, but geopolitical considerations will play a major role in determining how a country votes. For example, a resolution on human rights in Iraq was adopted by the Commission only *after* the outbreak of the first Gulf War in 1990–91; the Chinese government successfully opposed adoption of any resolution by the Commission referring to the 1989 massacres in Tian An Mien Square; and the success or failure of U.S. attempts to secure passage of various resolutions on Cuba in the 1990s probably depends more on the general political climate than on careful evaluation of the human rights situation in Cuba. Another alternative is adoption of a "Chairman's statement" on an issue by consensus, which is seen as less intrusive and therefore somewhat more politically feasible than adoption of a formal resolution. Of course, serious public discussion of human rights in a particular country at the Commission or Sub-Commission may itself create useful political pressure, even if no resolution is adopted.

A somewhat less onerous challenge is to try to convince the Commission and Sub-Commission to launch a confidential investigation of "situations which appear to reveal a consistent pattern of gross violations of human rights." This procedure, known as the "1503 procedure" for the resolution which created it in 1970, is described more fully in chapter 4; while its use requires a substantial effort to gather and present the relevant facts, this should not be beyond the capability of an NGO which seeks to address massive human rights violations. The entire procedure is confidential and suffers from other weaknesses, although the annual public identification by the chairman of the Commission of those countries under consideration does provide a form of public opprobrium. In rare instances, the confidentiality of the 1503 procedure may even be an advantage in dealing with a relatively receptive government which may be more susceptible to private than to public pressure, since yielding to confidential diplomatic inquiries is less embarrassing than yielding to public pressure or condemnation.

The Committee against Torture and the Committee on the Elimination of All Forms of Discrimination against Women enjoy a somewhat similar authority to investigate situations which appear to reveal the existence of a systematic practice of torture or discrimination against women, respectively.[10] Although their proceedings are confidential, they may receive information from NGOs or any other reliable source.

At the regional level, the Inter-American Commission on Human Rights has the most extensive jurisdiction of any international body to investigate the general human rights situation in a country; on its own initiative, it may investigate and issue a public report on human rights violations in any OAS member state.[11] While NGOs have no formal role in such an investigation, they can play a crucial role both in urging that an investigation be undertaken and in providing information. The Commission's public reports on the human rights situation in specific countries have had significant political impact, and any NGO concerned with human rights in the Western Hemisphere should certainly consider the possibility of encouraging an IACHR investigation.

Although its consideration of individual cases has only begun recently, the African Commission on Human and People's Rights has the theoretical authority to draw the attention of the Organization of African Unity's Assembly of Heads of State and Government to allegations of "serious and massive violations," which the Assembly may then request the Commission to investigate.[12] Unfortunately, it is not clear whether this procedure has yet been utilized.

While the Inter-American Commission on Human Rights and the UN Commission on Human Rights have issued reports on a large number of countries, such international investigations remain relatively rare. As noted above, perhaps the next most ambitious goal with respect to human rights violations in a country is the adoption of a resolution by a UN body. No matter how mild the language, any specific reference to a country by name should be counted a success. Country-specific resolutions also facilitate continuing consideration of the situation in subsequent sessions and in other UN bodies.

Chapter 4 discusses NGO interventions at the United Nations, most of which are relevant to attempts to increase awareness of widespread violations of human rights in a country. While less dramatic, consideration also should be given to critiquing or challenging a government's view of its own human rights record, when that record is reviewed by an international monitoring body to which a government must submit regular reports.[13] Publicizing those government reports, along with NGO commentaries and criticisms, can make a valuable contribution to the domestic discussion of human rights, utilizing international norms as the reference point.

Finally, it should be remembered that there are a few political bodies dedicated to monitoring human rights in specific countries or circumstances, although their number has decreased since the achievement of majority rule in South Africa in the mid-1990s. Access to these bodies is relatively easy, so long as the NGO or individual has information which is directly relevant. At present, they include the General Assembly's Special Committee to Investigate Israeli Practices Affecting the Human Rights of the Population of the Occupied Territories and the "Committee of 24" on the Granting of Independence to Colonial Countries.[14]

Concerns Over Specific Rights

Some NGOs are created to promote specific human rights, and others may begin to focus their substantive concerns as their expertise develops in a particular area. The methods appropriate to such promotional work may be different from those that seek primarily to halt violations, as the concern is not only with implementing existing norms but also with creating new standards.

NGOs often need to adopt a longer-term strategy in order to convince the international community that a particular issue deserves special attention. While it is not the only scenario, this process is exemplified by the approach of Amnesty International (AI) to the issue of torture in the 1970s and 1980s.

As it became more expert in the situation of "prisoners of conscience," AI realized that the torture and other ill-treatment of detainees was a serious and apparently increasing problem. In 1972, AI launched a world-wide "Campaign against Torture" that sought to educate diplomats, politicians, and the general public about the prevalence of torture in the world and to reinforce the absolute rejection of the use of torture under any circumstances. In 1975, prodded and lobbied by AI (with the support of sympathetic states), the UN Congress on the Prevention of Crime and Treatment of Offenders and subsequently the UN General Assembly adopted declarations condemning torture and other cruel, inhuman, and degrading treatment or punishment. Intensive work on drafting and lobbying led to the adoption of a Convention against Torture in 1984, monitored by an expert Committee against Torture. To ensure that no country could escape scrutiny merely by failing to ratify the Torture Convention, AI and others also successfully lobbied for the appointment of a Special Rapporteur on Torture by the UN Commission on Human Rights in 1985.

AI's concern with torture led to related initiatives concerning, inter alia, detention without trial; the protection of human rights during states of emergency; procedures for the investigation of summary or arbitrary executions; and guidelines for the actions of law enforcement officials, doctors, lawyers, and judges.[15]

While focusing on the development of new standards, AI was able to draw attention to violations of existing standards by way of illustration. Thus, what might wrongly be seen as merely theoretical legal debates or drafting exercises in fact reinforced AI's work in combating specific violations.

Similar successful initiatives have been undertaken by other NGOs. The International Commission of Jurists began in the 1980s to devote particular attention to interference with the independence of judges and lawyers. The General Assembly endorsed a set of Basic Principles on the Independence of the Judiciary in 1985, and a Commission Rapporteur on the subject was appointed in 1994. A number of NGOs played an influential role in the drafting and adoption of the Convention on the Rights of the Child in 1989; it now is the most widely ratified international human rights treaty. An informal coalition of NGOs pressed the Commission on Human Rights for years to adopt a declaration on the protection of human rights defenders, which the Commission finally did in 1998. An effort by a similar coalition of NGOs to gain approval for a treaty on the rights of people with disabilities appears to be close to success.

The 1995 Beijing Conference on Women was both a capstone to efforts by NGOs to draw greater attention to women's human rights issues and an impetus for greater international cooperation and coordination on women's issues. A Commission Rapporteur on violence against women was appointed in 1994, and NGOs that focus on women's rights have become more active at meetings of the Commission on the Status of Women and the Committee on the Elimination of All Forms of Discrimination against Women.[16]

Finally, mention should be made of two highly political, global efforts to adopt new international norms in the 1990s in which both traditional "human rights" NGOs and a large number of single-issue organizations participated. Primarily through pressuring their own governments in a coordinated manner, as well as raising global awareness, ad hoc NGO coalitions succeeded in pressuring governments to adopt a treaty banning land mines in 1997[17] and, in 1998, the statute that led to creation of the International Criminal Court in 2002. NGO representatives participated actively in the intergovernmental conferences that adopted the treaties; during the latter meeting, NGOs provided formal advisers to some government delegations.

A key element in ensuring that new standards are not merely empty documents is the creation of some form of monitoring mechanism, even if its powers are only advisory. While their specific powers vary considerably, international forums do now exist for discussion of the human rights of racial and ethnic groups; women; children; migrant workers; indigenous peoples; minorities; and the victims of torture, arbitrary killings, disappearances, slavery-like practices, and religious intolerance. Many of these bodies can be of help in drawing attention to specific violations of human rights or issue-oriented campaigns, even if they are not technically competent to consider complaints formally.

The Human Rights Campaign: Using Procedures Simultaneously

Rarely does an NGO adopt only a single course of action when combatting a particular human rights violation, unless an effective procedure is available to deal with an isolated individual case. In most instances, the goal is to resolve a problem, and that goal may be promoted through a variety of means.

Bearing in mind that limited resources will generally not permit all options to be undertaken in every case, an NGO might consider adopting a number of the following actions to address a serious human rights concern:

- send letters to the country in which the violations are taking place, to the appropriate foreign ministry department in one's own country, and to other countries that enjoy friendly relations with the target country, requesting the resolution of specific aspects of the situation and a commitment to undertake at least private diplomatic initiatives;
- ensure that any available domestic remedies are engaged;
- contact the media with information regarding the human rights violations that have occurred or are threatened;
- contact any rapporteur or body that might be able to take "urgent action" to resolve the situation on a humanitarian basis;
- file a formal individual complaint under the relevant treaty;
- issue a report on the human rights situation in question, based on an on-site investigation or, where that is not feasible, on other means of fact-finding;
- file a communication alleging the existence of a "consistent pattern" of violations under the 1503 procedure;
- promote public discussion of the violations in UN forums, including, if feasible, calls for a country-specific rapporteur or adoption of an appropriate resolution;
- publicize all (or most) of the above, bearing in mind rules of confidentiality where relevant.

In general, one can safely utilize most international procedures simultaneously, although care should be given to the particular requirements of each. For example, an individual complaint may be filed under the Optional Protocol to the Covenant on Civil and Political Rights and used at the same time to illustrate a "consistent pattern" under the 1503 procedure, as the latter procedure cannot determine the rights of any specific victim. On the other hand, the Human Rights Committee may not consider a complaint if it is being simultaneously considered under another international procedure, for example, by the European Court of Human Rights.

Tactical considerations also may dictate that not every conceivable forum be engaged at once or in every possible manner. International bodies do have a sense of proportion, and they are unlikely to respond positively if they are bombarded with information about a situation that clearly is less compelling than others of which they are aware.

One should remember that significant differences exist between domestic human rights forums and international forums. In many respects, international implementation and supervision are still rudimentary, even if substantive norms are fairly well developed; at the national level, on the other hand, well-developed, independent judicial systems and rules may exist. At the national level, legal factors may prevail, whereas political factors often dominate in international intergovernmental forums.

As a result of these and other differences, certain methods and techniques that may be relevant to a domestic judicial or administrative process are less likely to be as useful within the UN system. One example is the role of precedent, which is very important in the Anglo-American and many other domestic judicial systems. Within the United Nations, however, it should not be automatically assumed that procedures adopted to investigate the human rights situation in Chile, for example, will necessarily serve as a model or precedent for other countries where a military coup occurs and gross violations of human rights ensue. On the other hand, precedent is more likely to play a role in the deliberations of, for example, the Human Rights Committee and the European Court of Human Rights, with respect to legal issues which arise in individual cases.

The fact that intergovernmental institutions are ultimately political may render less meaningful other elements common to the domestic legal process, such as the force of logical argument or the conclusive character of evidence determined by a fact-finding body. But even if sound legal argument or well-proved facts may yield to political considerations, the value of well-prepared, nonideological submissions by NGOs should not be underestimated.

Competence and Professionalism

The primary influence of NGOs and human rights activists comes through the mobilization of public and governmental opinion, except in those relatively rare instances when a formal international legal mechanism may be invoked. The success of this mobilization, in turn, depends on the credibility of the group providing the information. To be credible does not require infallibility, and information should not be withheld in urgent situations simply because it cannot be verified. However, maintaining the credibility of an individual NGO and the human rights movement in general does require competence and professionalism.

Objective and thorough fact-finding lies at the heart of human rights work, and it is important for individuals and NGOs to distinguish between facts relevant to human rights and broader political concerns. This does not mean that NGOs should be oblivious to the political context in which they work; it is certainly legitimate, for example, to time the release of a report on human rights in a country or the initiation of legal proceedings to coincide with a legislative debate on economic assistance or the visit of a head of state to the NGO's home country.

However, political issues should be dealt with politically. Allegations of human rights violations must be legitimate in and of themselves and should not be used merely as a means to achieve larger political objectives. Unfortunately, human rights issues are regularly manipulated by all sides to a conflict, as demonstrated by the use and abuse of human rights rhetoric in Central America throughout the 1980s, the former Yugoslavia in the 1990s, and Iraq in 2003. It is legitimate for an NGO to call for the release of detainees, an end to torture, or free and fair elections; it is not legitimate for a *human rights* NGO to favor one side over another in an election or prefer one economic system to another, unless those preferences are firmly grounded in internationally accepted human rights norms relating to, e.g., political participation or economic rights.

Finally, one must recognize the limits of human rights advocacy—although those limits are increasingly being brought into question by the proponents of so-called "humanitarian intervention." The protection of internationally recognized human rights cannot by itself reform society, redistribute wealth, protect the environment, achieve peace, and ensure tolerance—although achieving a democratic, participatory society in which human rights and the rule of law are respected is likely to make these goals more realizable. Law is not a substitute for politics, and there are many choices that societies face that need not and should not be determined by reference to a universal legal standard. Respect for international human rights does not require the obliteration of cultural, economic, and political differences among peoples, although it does mandate the rejection of dictatorship and exploitation.

At the same time, appeals to "cultural relativism" by rights-violating governments should be rejected as the hypocritical sophistry they so often are. We should remember the 1993 Vienna Declaration of the UN World Conference on Human Rights, which concluded that "[w]hile the significance of national and regional particularities and various historical, cultural and religious backgrounds must be borne in mind, it is the duty of States, regardless of their political, economic and cultural systems, to promote and protect all human rights and fundamental freedoms."

In the past decade, international organizations or self-proclaimed "coalitions of the willing" have intervened in states in various stages of disintegration or conflict. In most of these situations, the protection of human rights has been proclaimed as one of the primary goals of the intervention. While there should be little hesitation in using force to protect large numbers of people from imminent death, such a demanding standard is a far cry from the loose invocation of "human rights." Human rights advocates must guard against calling too loosely for "action" to be taken against even a gross violator of human rights, lest their advocacy be misused by those with less noble purposes. At the very least, we need to recognize that armed intervention and subsequent reconstruction are much more difficult than generally imagined, as evidenced by the continuing debacles in Bosnia and Herzegovina, Kosovo, Haiti, Afghanistan, and Iraq.

Everyone has the right to an adequate standard of living, to be free from arbitrary treatment by government, to participate in society on a basis of equality. But, in many respects, international human rights law is concerned primarily with ensuring fairness, with ensuring that the rules of the game are observed rather than with determining the winner. International human rights law seeks to hold governments accountable to the norms they themselves have proclaimed as universal values. Other political and social decisions must be left to the rights-protective societies which one hopes will result from the universal guarantee of human rights.

Notes

1. Also see Appendixes B and C, which set forth a series of questions designed to elicit the information most relevant to choosing the right forum(s).

2. Contact information for such appeals is contained in Appendix D.

3. See chap. 4.

4. See chaps. 7 and 8, respectively.

5. On the ILO, see chap. 6. The Human Rights Committee now also attempts to monitor compliance with its opinions, although its success is not overly impressive; see chap. 3.

6. See chap. 6.

7. See chap. 5.

8. See chap. 4.

9. See chap. 4.

10. See chap. 3.

11. See chap. 7.

12. See chap. 9.

13. See chap. 10.

14. As of early 2004, the latter Committee's jurisdiction extended to Western Sahara, New Caledonia, Gibraltar, and several small islands or island groups belonging to the United States or the United Kingdom.

15. Many of these initiatives are discussed in chap. 11.

16. See chap. 10.

17. The treaty entered into force in 1998. An international coalition of NGOs known as the International Campaign to Ban Landmines was awarded the 1997 Nobel Peace Prize for its work in promoting the treaty's adoption.

Part II
International Procedures
for Making Human Rights
Complaints within the
UN System

Chapter 3
Treaty-Based Procedures for Making Human Rights Complaints Within the UN System

Siân Lewis-Anthony and Martin Scheinin[1]

Within the United Nations human rights treaty system, there are now four bodies competent to receive and consider, in a quasi-judicial manner, communications[2] from individuals who claim to be victims of human rights violations. They are the Human Rights Committee (HRC), the Committee against Torture (CAT), the Committee on the Elimination of Racial Discrimination (CERD), and the Committee for the Elimination of Discrimination against Women (CEDAW).[3] Each was established by treaty in order to monitor state parties' compliance with their treaty obligations. The system of individual petition is optional; ratification of the treaties alone does not empower the four bodies to scrutinize petitions alleging violations by a state. States must specifically declare that they recognize the competence of the relevant committee to receive and consider applications from individuals within their jurisdiction.

All four committees operate along similar lines in the consideration of individual communications, and all proceedings are held in private. Since the Human Rights Committee has had the most experience in considering individual communications, its practice will be examined in greatest detail. The practice of CERD and CAT will be explored more briefly, highlighting the main differences in the procedures. The Optional Protocol to the Convention for the Elimination of Discrimination against Women entered into force only in 2000, and there had been no decided cases at the time this chapter was written.

The Optional Protocol to the International Covenant on Civil and Political Rights

The Optional Protocol to the Covenant on Civil and Political Rights allows individuals to petition the Human Rights Committee alleging violations of the Covenant. As of March 2004, 104 of the 151 parties to the

Covenant had ratified the Optional Protocol; as of February 2004, the committee had registered 1,245 cases and concluded 963 cases concerning seventy-five different countries. Worthy of note is the unfortunate precedent set by Jamaica, which denounced the Optional Protocol in 1997, after a number of adverse views adopted by the Committee in relation to cases involving the death penalty. Jamaica was followed in 1998 by Trinidad and Tobago, which then immediately reacceded to the Optional Protocol with a reservation that sought to preclude consideration of any death penalty cases. After the Human Rights Committee took the view that the reservation was contrary to the object and purpose of the Optional Protocol and without legal effect,[4] Trinidad and Tobago denounced the instrument altogether. Guyana remains a party, with a similar reservation yet to be challenged in an individual case.

The Human Rights Committee, created pursuant to Article 28 of the Covenant, consists of eighteen experts of "high moral character and recognized competence in the field of human rights," elected from among nationals of the states parties. They act in their personal capacities, which means that they are not agents or representatives of governments. The Committee normally meets three times each year.

The authority of the Committee to receive and consider communications derives from Article 1 of the Optional Protocol. Although it possesses no formal judicial power, the Committee has established an informal doctrine of precedent and tends to follow its earlier decisions. In addition, the Committee has drafted rules of procedure setting out, *inter alia*, the way in which it undertakes consideration of individual petitions addressed to it.[5]

Substantive Requirements for Complaints

Who may file

Article 1 of the Optional Protocol provides that the Committee may receive communications from "individuals subject to [a state party's] jurisdiction who claim to be victims of a violation by that State Party of any of the rights set forth in the Covenant." The rules of procedure provide that communications may be submitted by the victim directly or by his or her representative. In circumstances in which the victim is unable to submit an application (for example, when it is alleged that the state is responsible for the victim's disappearance), applications may be submitted by a close relative on behalf of the victim, even without formal authorization. The burden rests with the author of a complaint to show that there is a sufficiently close connection to entitle the representative to act on the victim's behalf. Failure to do so renders the application inadmissible.

The Committee has stated that a person can only claim to be a "victim" under the Protocol if she or he is personally affected by a violation of the Covenant. Thus, an individual cannot challenge a law in the abstract by way of an *actio popularis*. However, complainants can exceptionally claim to be victims if the very existence of a law violates their rights; in such a case, one does not need to show that the law has been enforced to his or her detriment. For example, in the context of a law that criminalized homosexual acts but had not been enforced for a decade, the committee stated that "the threat of enforcement and the pervasive impact of the continued existence of these provisions on administrative practices and public opinion had affected [the applicant] and continued to affect him personally."[6] The applicant, an active homosexual, could therefore claim to be a victim even though he himself had never been prosecuted. In its views on the merits, the committee concluded that "the continued existence of the challenged provisions . . . continuously and directly interferes with the author's privacy."[7]

States against whom complaints may be lodged

Only states that have ratified the Optional Protocol may be the subject of a complaint to the Human Rights Committee. An individual need not be a citizen or a resident of the state concerned, as long as she or he was subject to its jurisdiction at the time of the alleged violation.

The phrase "subject to the jurisdiction of" has been considered by the Committee in a number of cases. Normally, an individual must have been present within the territory of the state concerned at the time of the alleged violation. There is some tension, however, between the phrase "subject to the jurisdiction" in Article 1 of the Protocol, and the obligation contained in Article 2(1) of the Covenant to respect the rights of "all individuals within its territory and subject to its jurisdiction." The Committee has tended to adopt a broad interpretation of the territorial requirement, so that it will, in certain circumstances, regard persons as victims who were not physically present within the territory of the state concerned at the time of the alleged violation. For example, the Committee accepted a complaint by a Uruguayan citizen who was living in Canada, concerning the refusal of Uruguay to renew his passport.[8] The Committee also accepted jurisdiction over a complaint against Uruguay in relation to a person who was kidnapped, detained, and mistreated in Argentina by members of the Uruguayan security forces. The committee stated that the words "subject to its jurisdiction, in Article 1 of the Protocol, refer to the relationship between the individual and the state concerned, and not to the place where the violation occurred."[9]

Subject matter

All complaints submitted under the Optional Protocol must allege a violation of one or more rights contained in Parts II and III of the Covenant. Although capital punishment as such is outlawed by the Second Optional Protocol and not the Covenant, many issues pertaining to capital punishment may be addressed under the Covenant itself, including under Articles 6 and 7. The rights protected under the Covenant include the rights not to be tortured or subjected to cruel, inhuman, or degrading treatment or punishment; to life, liberty, and security; to a fair trial; to freedom of expression; to freedom of thought and religion; to freedom of peaceful assembly; to freedom of association; to participate in political life; not to be discriminated against; and to equality before the law and equal protection of the law.

The Covenant covers a large number of those rights contained in the Universal Declaration of Human Rights and is similar in scope to the rights protected by the European Convention on Human Rights. It does not, however, protect the right to property, which is included in the Universal Declaration and in the First Protocol to the European Convention on Human Rights. Equality before the law and the protection from discrimination under Article 26 of the Covenant are substantive rights on their own and need not be linked to the violation of another right guaranteed by the Covenant. For example, in the cases of *Broeks v. Netherlands* and *Zwaan de Vries v. Netherlands*, the Committee found that social security legislation which discriminated against women on the ground of their gender violated Article 26, notwithstanding the fact that the Covenant does not provide a substantive guarantee of the right to social security.[10]

The right to self-determination, which is set forth in Article 1 of the Covenant, cannot be the subject of a complaint under the Optional Protocol. The Committee has consistently held that, since the right to self-determination is conferred on peoples, an individual cannot claim to be a victim of a violation of that right. Peoples, in turn, cannot act as complainants under the Optional Protocol, which requires one or more individual victims. However, in its more recent case law, the Committee has referred to Article 1 in cases decided under other provisions of the Covenant.[11]

The Optional Protocol does not have retroactive effect. Thus, a communication will be declared inadmissible if it alleges a violation which took place prior to the entry into force of the Covenant *and* the Protocol for the state concerned. However, if a violation appears to have continued or has continuing effects after the Covenant and Protocol have entered into force, the Committee will have jurisdiction to consider the complaint. For example, the Committee found a violation when a person was tried under conditions in which fair trial was denied after the entry into force of the Covenant, although he had been detained and tortured prior to its entry into force.[12]

A communication is inadmissible if it relates to a right not protected by the Covenant or is otherwise incompatible with the Covenant. For instance, a communication alleging a violation of the right to property will be declared inadmissible under this ground.

In order to be regarded as admissible, any claim of a violation of the Covenant must be substantiated by facts and arguments. This somewhat discretionary admissibility requirement, derived from Article 2 of the Optional Protocol, allows the Committee also to declare cases inadmissible on substantive grounds whenever it is evident that the communication discloses no violation of the Covenant. As the Committee is not a "fourth instance" in respect of the legal order of a state, it will not reexamine the facts and evidence unless the assessment by domestic courts was arbitrary or amounted to a miscarriage of justice. This principle is of particular importance in cases where the Covenant is part of the domestic law of the country concerned and the domestic courts may have referred to the Covenant and even the Committee's jurisprudence to reach their conclusion. Although the Committee has, in the past, declared inadmissible communications of this type to be incompatible with the Covenant, in recent years it has been more coherent in distinguishing the requirement of "substantiation" from incompatibility *ratione materiae.*

The right to petition may be restricted by a party's reservation to the Covenant or to the Optional Protocol. Reservations can limit the application of a particular provision of the Covenant or Optional Protocol, and, in submitting a communication, a complaint will need to take into account any such reservation. The Committee has taken the position that it has the competence to interpret reservations restrictively and even to disregard reservations that are contrary to the object and purpose of the Covenant or the Optional Protocol.

Under Article 4 of the Covenant, many of the substantive rights guaranteed under the Covenant may be temporarily derogated from if there exists within a state an officially declared public emergency threatening the life of the nation.[13] However, there is no right to derogate from the Optional Protocol itself, so a state may not limit the right of petition other than by a reservation filed at the time of its acceptance of the Optional Protocol. The scope of any derogation is limited, and it is up to the Committee to determine whether or not a particular derogation is "strictly required by the exigencies of the situation," as Article 4(2) of the Covenant requires.

Article 5(2)(a) of the Protocol provides that the Committee cannot consider a communication if the same matter is simultaneously being examined under another procedure of international investigation or settlement. Unless a state has entered a reservation to the contrary, there is nothing to prevent an applicant from using another procedure first and then, upon termination of those proceedings, bringing the case before the Committee. However, several countries have filed reservations to bar consideration of a communication that is or has been considered in another international forum, thus preventing an "appeal" to the Committee.

The concept of the "same matter" refers to identical parties to the complaints advanced and the facts adduced. A two-line reference to the person concerned in a case before the Inter-American Commission on Human Rights, for example, was found not to constitute "the same matter" as that described in detail by the same person in a communication to the Human Rights Committee.[14] Consideration by UN bodies of a "situation" under the "1503 procedure," which governs the examination of gross violations of human rights,[15] also does not prevent an individual complaint from being filed under the Protocol.

Like other international human rights bodies, the Committee may not consider communications unless all domestic remedies have been exhausted, although exhaustion of domestic remedies is required only to the extent that the remedies are effective, available, and not unreasonably prolonged. The burden is upon the complainant to show that all domestic remedies have been exhausted or that no effective remedy exists. If the state concerned disputes the assertion that all remedies have been exhausted, the state must give details of the particular remedies available and proof of their effectiveness. A general description of remedies provided under the law, without linking them to the specific circumstances of the complaint, has been deemed insufficient.

Formal or Procedural Requirements

The Human Rights Committee has produced a model communication to assist complainants, but its use is not compulsory.[16] The essential information to be included in a petition consists of the following: name, address, and nationality of the victim and the author, if different; justification for acting on behalf of the victim; identification of the state against which the complaint is being made; the articles of the Covenant allegedly violated; steps taken to exhaust domestic remedies; a statement on the issue of whether the same matter is being dealt with by another international procedure; and a detailed description of the facts and presentation of the arguments substantiating the allegations, including relevant dates. The more complete the information given in the original application, the faster it will be processed—it is not uncommon for consideration of communications to take three to four years from the date of submission to the adoption of the Committee's final views. The communication must not be anonymous, but it is possible to request the Committee not to reveal the name of the author and/or victim when it publishes its decision. Communications must be signed and dated. Communications may be submitted by e-mail or fax but should be followed by a signed letter.

There is no time limit for the submission of applications under the Optional Protocol, although it is generally in the interests of a complainant to submit a communication in a timely fashion. In some circumstances, the Committee may regard a long delay in the submission of a case as abuse of the right of petition, rendering the communication inadmissible under Article 3 of the Optional Protocol.[17] Unfortunately, there is no provision for legal aid, whether the victim is the author of the communication or is represented by counsel. Communications may, in principle, be submitted in any language. However, the use of languages not comprehended by Secretariat members working in the Petitions Team carries the risk of long delays or even permanent shelving of a communication. Hence, the use of English, French, Spanish, or Russian is strongly preferred.

Means of Investigation

Once a communication has been received by the Committee, it is screened by a member of the so-called Petitions Team at the Office of the High Commissioner for Human Rights (OHCHR), who may contact the author for additional information. On the basis of a summary prepared by the Petitions Team, the Committee's Special Rapporteur on New Communications, who is a member designated by the Committee to act on communications received between sessions, decides about the registration of a communication. If the Rapporteur is satisfied that the communication complies with the preliminary admissibility requirements, then she or he will register the case and instruct the Petitions Team to transmit the communication to the state concerned, with a request for information regarding both admissibility and the merits. The state is given six months in which to respond, after which the author is given six weeks to react to the state's response. If a state insists that a communication is inadmissible, it may demand a decision on admissibility before supplying information pertaining to the merits. Such a request is either accepted or denied by the Special Rapporteur on New Communications.

The Committee's rules of procedure provide that the committee may, prior to forwarding its views on the communication, communicate to the state its "views on whether interim measures may be desirable to avoid irreparable damage to the victim of the alleged violation" (Rule 86). In practice, the Special Rapporteur on New Communications acts on behalf of the committee if urgent communications are received between sessions. The application of this rule does not imply a determination of the merits of the communication. Interim measures are most frequently invoked in cases involving the death penalty, but they also have been requested in cases involving expulsion and extradition, where obtaining medical examination of a prisoner is deemed crucial, and where destructive activities in areas claimed by indigenous peoples are imminent. Requests for interim measures can be made within a very short time after the communication is filed, even if the Committee needs further information from the author on the question of admissibility. Although the provision on interim measures of protection is in the Committee's Rules of Procedure and not in the Covenant, the Committee has taken the position that a state which accepted the right of individual complaint is in breach of the Protocol if it acts in a manner that causes irreparable harm to the complainant, especially in cases where the Committee has indicated a risk of irreparable damage.[18]

After the state has provided its observations on a communication and the author has responded, communications are transmitted in the form of a Secretariat draft to the Working Group on Communications, which consists of at least five members of the Committee. This group meets for one week prior to each of the Committee's sessions and can declare a case admissible if the group is unanimous in its decision. Otherwise, admissibility is considered by the whole Committee. Thus, only the whole Committee can declare a case inadmissible or decide a case on its merits.

Although there is no right of appeal on the question of admissibility, it is possible for the author of a communication to request a review of an inadmissibility decision. Reviews are available on procedural grounds, for example, where domestic remedies have subsequently been exhausted or the matter is no longer being examined by another international procedure.

The Committee is directed by Article 5 of the Protocol to consider the communications it receives "in the light of all written information made available to it by the individual and by the State Party concerned." There is, accordingly, no provision for either oral hearings or on-site investigation of complaints. Unlike many other international procedures, the Committee is not mandated to facilitate a friendly settlement between the parties. Furthermore, there is no possibility for third-party submissions such as *amicus curiae* briefs, unless a third-party submission is sent by one of the actual parties.

Decisions and Implementation

All decisions of the Committee are to be made by majority vote of the members present, but efforts are normally made to arrive at decisions by consensus. After receiving and considering all relevant information on the merits of a case, the Committee adopts what are known as its "views," which it forwards to both the author and the state concerned. The views take the form of a collegiate opinion, but any member of the Committee may request that a concurring or dissenting opinion be appended to the Committee's views. The procedure is confidential, until the Committee adopts its views or otherwise concludes its consideration of a communication. Thereafter, subject to certain limitations,[19] the Committee's decisions on inadmissibility, merits, and discontinuance are published in communiques issued after each session, as well as in the Committee's annual reports to the General Assembly. Despite the fact that the Committee treats the procedure as confidential, the parties are allowed to make public the existence of a pending case and even their submissions, unless the Committee has requested confidentiality.

The Committee goes further than merely stating its views as to whether there has been a violation; in cases of violation, it also reiterates the obligation of a state to provide an effective remedy for any violation, as required by Article 2(3) of the Covenant. Furthermore, the committee usually expresses its view on what would constitute an effective remedy. For example, it has called upon states to take immediate steps to ensure strict observance of the Covenant; to release a victim from detention and ensure that similar violations do not occur in the future; to commute a death sentence in circumstances in which there have been violations of the Covenant; and to provide compensation for the violations suffered.

Technically, the Committee's final views are not legally binding judgments. However, they should not be seen as mere recommendations, either. As the Committee is the international expert body established for the purpose of monitoring compliance with the Covenant, its views are authoritative pronouncements on the legal obligations of a state party, stemming from the legally binding provisions of the Covenant. While it cannot be ruled out that states would resort to other international procedures to obtain another authoritative view of their treaty obligations, it would be unacceptable if a state that has voluntarily ratified the Optional Protocol and participated in the Committee's consideration of a case would simply substitute its own interpretation for the views of the Committee.

During the 1990s, the Committee adopted a number of measures to monitor compliance with its views more effectively. Pursuant to these measures, a Committee member designated Special Rapporteur for the

Follow-Up of Views now monitors the measures taken by states to "give effect" to the Committee's views. Whenever the Committee finds a violation of the Covenant, it now asks the state concerned to inform the Committee of any action it has taken in relation to the case, within a period of ninety days. The Rapporteur's mandate is fairly wide; she or he is permitted to "make such contacts and take such action as appropriate for the due performance of the follow-up mandate." For example, the Rapporteur has contacted the Permanent Representatives to the United Nations of a number of countries, in order to discuss measures which might be adopted to give effect to the Committee's views.

The Rapporteur's mandate also includes the possibility of on-site missions. In 1995, the Rapporteur conducted the first (and, to date, only) such mission, which investigated Jamaica's compliance with the Committee's views, adopted in a number of cases concerning the administration of justice in death penalty cases and conditions on death row. The Rapporteur spoke to government officials and representatives of the judiciary and penitentiary system, as well as the Governor-General of Jamaica. Of course, such a mission can only be carried out with the consent of the state. The main reason for the lack of subsequent missions is lack of available funding.

Follow-up is not restricted to requests for information or on-site investigations. Publicity is an important tool in the Committee's efforts to secure compliance with its views, and the Committee's annual report to the General Assembly includes information on its follow-up activities. The report indicates which states have failed to respond to the Committee's requests or failed to provide a remedy. In addition, the Committee issues press communiques on follow-up activities, usually annually at the end of one of its sessions. Such publicity exposes states that are unwilling to fulfill their obligations under the Covenant and also makes it easier for nongovernmental organizations to monitor the follow-up process. Not only can NGOs bring additional pressure to bear upon governments, but they often are able to furnish the Committee with valuable information which can be used in the Committee's communications with governments. Finally, the Special Rapporteur for the Follow-Up of Views is empowered to "make such recommendations for further action by the committee as may be necessary." This provision allows some scope for the further development of the follow-up procedure, particularly in respect of recalcitrant states.

The Committee does not view the follow-up procedure in isolation from states' general obligations under the Covenant. Thus, information concerning measures taken pursuant to a finding of a violation is now required of states when they submit their periodic reports under Article 40 of the Covenant.[20] When state representatives participate in Committee meetings to discuss the application of the Covenant, they are asked to address the issue of the implementation of the Committee's views adopted under the Optional Protocol.

The International Convention on the Elimination of All Forms of Racial Discrimination

The Convention on the Elimination of All Forms of Racial Discrimination entered into force in 1969, some seven years before the International Covenant on Civil and Political Rights. However, as of late 2003, only forty-two of the 169 parties to the convention had made the optional declaration under Article 14 of the Convention which enables the Committee on the Elimination of Racial Discrimination (CERD) to consider individual communications. By September 2003, CERD had registered twenty-eight cases and concluded twenty-six cases brought against seven countries, finding a violation of the convention in five cases.

CERD is similar in many respects to the Human Rights Committee. It consists of eighteen experts of high moral standing and impartiality, acting in their personal capacities and elected from among nationals of states parties. CERD's rules of procedure include provisions governing the consideration of individual petitions under Article 14.[21] CERD meets twice a year.

Substantive Requirements

Who may file

Article 14(1) stipulates that CERD may consider communications from individuals or groups of individuals within the jurisdiction of a state that has made a declaration under Article 14, if such individuals claim to be victims of a violation by that state of any of the rights set forth in the Convention. The phrase "groups of individuals" does not mean that organizations can raise general allegations of human rights violations. However, membership in a group targeted by a measure allegedly in violation of the Convention is sufficient to create standing.[22] As is true under the Optional Protocol, only victims or their relatives or representatives can initiate the process. In exceptional circumstances, CERD will allow others to submit a communication when it appears that the victim is unable to submit the communication, but the author then has to justify acting on behalf of the victim.

States against which complaints may be lodged

Only states that have made a declaration under Article 14 may be the subject of a complaint to the Committee. The Convention does not include a "same matter" rule preventing CERD from considering a case that has been submitted to another international procedure, but some states have made reservations to the effect that they will only recognize the competence of CERD if the same matter is not being or has not been examined under another procedure of international investigation or settlement, thus preventing CERD from being used as an international appellate forum.

Subject matter

The substantive rights covered by the convention are to a large extent contained in Article 5, which provides that states must guarantee to everyone the right to equality before the law without distinction as to race, color, or national or ethnic origin and to equality in the enjoyment of a number of specified rights. The latter includes the right to equal treatment before tribunals and all other organs administering justice; the right to security of the person and protection by the state against violence or bodily harm, whether inflicted by government officials or others; the right to vote and stand for election; and the right of access to any place or service intended for use by the general public, such as transport, hotels, theaters, and similar establishments. Article 5 also lists a number of civil, political, economic, social and cultural rights which must be guaranteed without discrimination. Article 5, together with Article 6 on the right to effective remedies, has been the basis for most communications submitted under the Convention.

The Convention contains no provision for a state to derogate from protected rights in an emergency, and no such possibility should be implied. It is worth recalling that, under the Covenant on Civil and Political Rights, a state derogating from its normal obligations may not discriminate solely on the ground of race or color, whereas "national origin" is not among the prohibited distinctions during an emergency. This might be compared to the much longer list of prohibited distinctions contained in Article 26 of the Covenant.

The Convention states that CERD shall not consider any communication from an author unless all domestic remedies have been exhausted. As with the Covenant, this rule does not apply if remedies are ineffective or unreasonably prolonged.

Formal Requirements

The same model communication used in submitting cases to the Human Rights Committee can be used in respect of CERD. Communications should contain the fullest information possible, along the lines of a communication under the Optional Protocol. A communication must be submitted to CERD within six months after all available domestic remedies have been exhausted. This condition may be waived, but only when circumstances have been "duly verified" as exceptional. If a state disputes the assertion that domestic remedies have been exhausted, the state must provide details of the remedies available to the victim in the particular circumstances of the case.

Under Article 14 of the Convention, states may establish a national body to deal with complaints under the Convention prior to their consideration by the CERD, but very few states have thus far made use of this possibility.

Means of Investigation

The procedure for considering a communication under Article 14 and the admissibility criteria are very similar to those under the Optional Protocol. A communication which is declared inadmissible for nonexhaustion of domestic remedies may be reviewed upon written request, if the complainant can show that all remaining remedies have been exhausted.

Joint consideration of admissibility and merits is nowadays possible under the Rules of Procedure, with the consent of the parties. If a separate admissibility decision is taken, further submissions on the merits are sought from the state. In the course of considering a case, Rule 94(3) authorizes CERD to request that a state take interim measures to avoid possible irreparable damage to the alleged victim. CERD has the power to invite the parties to an oral hearing, although no such hearing has yet been held. Given the severe financial constraints under which all committees operate, it is unlikely that this provision will be invoked in the near future.

Decisions and Implementation

CERD examines the merits of a communication in light of all the information made available to it by the parties. It may also obtain documentation that "may assist in the disposal of the case" from United Nations bodies or the specialized agencies.[23] CERD then formulates an opinion and makes recommendations and suggestions which are forwarded to the parties. Unlike the Human Rights Committee's pronouncements on the right to an effective remedy, CERD's recommendations and suggestions do not necessarily flow directly from its conclusion on the merits of a case. Thus, CERD often makes recommendations and suggestions even in cases where no violation of the Convention has been established.

All CERD decisions require that two-thirds of its members be present and that a majority of those vote in favor of the decision, but members of the Committee may attach individual opinions to the full Committee's opinion. The state is invited to inform the Committee "in due course" of the action it takes pursuant to the Committee's suggestions and recommendations.

As is true of the other treaty-based procedures discussed in this chapter, CERD's opinions, recommendations, and suggestions have no formally binding legal force as a matter of international law. Nevertheless, the finding of a violation or nonviolation by CERD should be seen as an authoritative interpretation of states' treaty obligations. The Committee's opinions are published in its annual reports to the General Assembly, and press communiques are issued during each session.

The Convention against Torture and Other Forms of Cruel, Inhuman or Degrading Treatment

The Convention against Torture entered into force in 1987. The optional procedure that gives the Committee against Torture jurisdiction over individual complaints is contained in Article 22 of the Convention; as of early 2004, fifty-five out of 134 state parties to CAT had accepted the individual complaints procedure. The Committee's case load gathered momentum in the 1990s, and, as of early 2004, 242 complaints with respect to twenty-two countries had been registered and a decision on the merits had been taken in ninety-three cases (sixty-eight cases of no violation and twenty-five cases of a violation); fifty-one communications were under consideration.

The Committee against Torture consists of only ten experts of high moral standing and recognized competence in the field of human rights, elected from among nationals of the states parties and serving in their individual capacity. The Convention specifically mentions the potential "usefulness" of selecting persons who are also members of the Human Rights Committee; currently, however, there is no overlap between the two committees. Nevertheless, this provision suggests that the framers of the Convention against Torture intended that CAT should draw from the jurisprudence of the Human Rights Committee. The CAT has formulated its own rules of procedure and normally meets twice per year.[24]

Unlike the committees discussed above, CAT has the authority under Article 20(1) of the Convention to initiate its own investigation if it receives "reliable information which appears to it to contain well-founded indications that torture is being systematically practiced in the territory of a State Party." Article 28 of the Convention does give a state the possibility of opting out of the Committee's investigatory jurisdiction under Article 20, but only a few states have done so. Although individual complaints can be lodged only against states which have made a declaration under Article 22, the Committee may act on information regarding a practice of torture concerning any state that is a party to the Convention.

Substantive Requirements for Complaints

Who may file

The Committee may consider applications from or on behalf of individuals subject to the jurisdiction of state which has made a declaration under Article 22, if that individual claims to be a victim of a violation of the Convention. If the victim cannot act on his or her own behalf, a communication can be submitted by relatives or others, so long as they are able to justify acting on behalf of the victim.

Subject matter

Individual complaints must allege a violation of one of the rights protected by the Convention, which include the right to be protected from acts of torture and other forms of cruel, inhuman or degrading treatment or punishment; the right not to be expelled, returned, or extradited to a state where there are substantial grounds for believing that the individual would be in danger of being subjected to torture; the right to have complaints concerning torture and other forms of ill-treatment examined promptly and impartially; the right to compensation for torture; and the right not to have any statement elicited as a result of torture invoked as evidence in any proceeding (except in proceedings against a person accused of torture).

Torture is defined in Article 1 of the Convention; the other forms of ill-treatment covered by the Convention are not defined. It is important to note that the protection afforded by the Convention in relation to torture is greater than that afforded to those subjected to cruel, inhuman, or degrading treatment or punishment. Hence, a complaint based on a claim that extradition or deportation would result in cruel, inhuman, or degrading treatment in the receiving country may be declared inadmissible as incompatible *ratione materiae* with the convention. Such incompatibility would not exist in respect of a case brought to the Human Rights Committee under Article 7 of the Covenant on Civil and Political Rights. This difference is highly important, since a great proportion of all cases sent to CAT concern extradition or deportation.

Like the Human Rights Committee, CAT may declare communications inadmissible as "manifestly ill-founded" if they are not sufficiently substantiated by facts and arguments.

Article 2(2) of the Convention states that "no exceptional circumstances whatsoever . . . may be invoked as a justification of torture," and there is no right to derogate from the prohibition against torture. No explicit mention is made of the possibility of derogation in relation to lesser forms of ill-treatment, but it should be noted that there may be no derogation from the prohibition against torture or the lesser forms of ill-treatment under the Covenant on Civil and Political Rights.

Formal or procedural requirements

The same model communication used by the HRC and CERD may be submitted to CAT, but it is not mandatory. There is no time limit for submitting a communication to the Committee in the text of the Convention, but the Committee may declare an application inadmissible if it is unreasonably prolonged.

Under Article 22(5), a complaint is inadmissible if the same matter has been, or is being, examined under another procedure of international investigation or settlement.

Means of Investigation

The criteria for admissibility and the methods of investigating an individual complaint are similar to those under the Optional Protocol. In 2001, a Rapporteur for New Complaints and Interim Measures was established. The Rapporteur can register complaints, request clarification from the complainant, verify admissibility requirements, request interim measures, and monitor the compliance with a request for interim measures (see Rules 98, 99, 107 and 108). In 2002–2003, a presessional working group for individual communications was established. It consists of four members and meets for five days prior to each session.

Issues of admissibility and merits are usually considered together. The author of a communication is given the opportunity to respond to the state's observations, within specified time limits. If time limits are not respected by either party, the Committee or working group may decide to consider the admissibility of a communication in the light of available information. Once a case has been declared admissible, that decision and any new submissions received from the complainant are sent to the state, which has six months in which to respond in writing.

The Committee examines the merits of each communication in the light of all the information made available to it by the parties. Like CERD, the Committee against Torture may theoretically invite the parties to attend a meeting of the Committee in order to provide further clarification or answer questions concerning the communication; thus far, it has not done so. It also may obtain information from UN bodies or specialized agencies which could assist it in examining a case. All proceedings considering individual communications are confidential.

A case that has been declared inadmissible on grounds of nonexhaustion of domestic remedies can be reviewed at a later date, if evidence is supplied demonstrating that all domestic remedies have, indeed, been exhausted.

At any time during the proceedings, the Committee may request a state to take interim measures to avoid possible irreparable damage to an alleged victim.

Decisions and Implementation

The Committee against Torture formulates its "decisions" on individual communications and forwards them to the complainant and the state concerned. As is the case in the other treaty-based committees, a member of CAT whose views differ from those of the rest of the Committee may attach an individual opinion to the Committee's decision. The state is invited to inform the Committee "in due course" of the action it takes pursuant to the Committee's views. The committee's views are given publicity through press communiques and the Committee's annual reports to the General Assembly.

The Convention for the Elimination of All Forms of Discrimination against Women

The Convention for the Elimination of All Forms of Discrimination against Women entered into force in 1981, but it was only in 1999 that an Optional Protocol permitting individual complaints was adopted. This Protocol entered into force in 2000, and sixty states out of the 176 parties to the Convention had accepted it as of early 2004. Only three cases have been registered so far, and none of them has led to any decision by CEDAW.

The CEDAW consists of twenty-three experts of high moral standing and recognized competence in the field of human rights, elected from among nationals of the states parties and serving in their individual capacity. The Committee has amended its own rules of procedure to include extensive provisions related to the Optional Protocol.[25] Normally the Committee meets twice per year.

Substantive Requirements for Complaints

A complaint under the CEDAW Optional Protocol must include a claim of a violation of any of the rights set forth in the Convention by a state party (Article 2). Like CAT, CEDAW has the authority under Article 8 of the Protocol to initiate its own investigation, if it receives "reliable information indicating grave or systematic violations by a State Party of rights set forth in the Convention."

Who may file

The Committee may consider communications that are submitted by or on behalf of individuals or groups of individuals, under the jurisdiction of a state party. Where a communication is submitted on behalf of individuals or groups of individuals, this must be with their consent, unless the author can justify acting on their behalf without such consent.

Formal or procedural requirements

The admissibility requirements by and large correspond to those under the Optional Protocol to the CCPR, but the Optional Protocol to the Convention on the Elimination of All Forms of Discrimination against Women also draws on the experience of the Human Rights Committee. Communications shall be in writing and must not be anonymous. Domestic remedies must be exhausted, unless they are unreasonably prolonged or unlikely to bring effective relief. The "same matter" rule has been formulated in a way that precludes not only complaints that have been or are being examined under another procedure of international investigation or settlement but also cases that have already been examined by CEDAW itself. Manifestly ill-founded or insufficiently substantiated communications are also inadmissible, pursuant to an explicit provision in the Protocol (Article 4(2)(c)). The *ratione temporis* rule is spelled out in the Protocol, ruling out cases where the facts occurred prior to the entry into force of the Protocol for the state concerned, unless those facts continued after that date. There is no time limit for the submission of communications to CEDAW.

Means of Investigation

The criteria for admissibility and the methods for investigating an individual complaint are similar to those used by the HRC. The amended Rules of Procedure provide for the possibility of working groups and Rapporteurs to assist CEDAW in the consideration of communications, and a unanimous working group of at least five members may declare communications admissible. Admissibility and merits may be dealt with separately or together.

The Committee considers communications in the light of all information made available to it, provided that this information is transmitted to the parties concerned. The Committee's meetings when examining communications under the Protocol are confidential.

The possibility of requesting interim measures of protection to avoid irreparable damage is made explicit in Article 5 of the Optional Protocol itself, rather than merely in the Committee's Rules of Procedure.

Decisions and Implementation

After examining a communication, the Committee transmits its views on the communication, together with any recommendations, to the parties concerned. Under Article 7(4), the state has an obligation to "give due consideration" to the views of the Committee.

Concluding Observations

Of the four procedures described in this chapter, only two have generated sufficient jurisprudence to enable one to analyze their effectiveness. Despite being the oldest of the committees, CERD still has so few final decisions on the merits that it is difficult to draw substantive conclusions about it. Although racial discrimination remains an intractable problem in many countries, relatively few states have accepted the jurisdiction of CERD over individual complaints. This fact may, in turn, account for the lack of visibility of the procedure, whose existence is not well-known to many lawyers and NGOs. Further, many states that recognize the jurisdiction of the Committee are also parties to the European Convention on Human Rights. When faced with a choice between the two procedures, lawyers are more likely to choose the European Convention, which offers the possibility of legal aid and the hope of a binding legal judgment.[26]

The Human Rights Committee has the most highly developed jurisprudence of the committees. Despite the fact that, like the others, it does not possess the power to issue formally binding judgments, there can be no doubt that individual complaints under the Optional Protocol have saved lives, helped people to obtain passports and leave a country, enabled the release from detention of prisoners and detainees, and saved individuals from being returned to a country where they might suffer torture. The incremental development of the follow-up procedure is encouraging, and it is reasonable to assume that maintaining pressure on governments has led some to take remedial action which they might not otherwise have taken. At the same time, however, applicants have the right to expect better efforts to secure the implementation of the Committee's views.

Perhaps the most attractive aspect of the Human Rights Committee as a forum is the broad scope of the Covenant on Civil and Political Rights, compared to other global human rights treaties with complaint mechanisms. In this respect, the most distinctive provisions may be Article 25 (rights of public participation), the free-standing nondiscrimination clause in Article 26, and the minority rights provisions set out in Article 27 (which are also available for indigenous peoples' claims related to lands and natural resources).

The practice of the Committee against Torture is developing quickly, particularly with regard to protecting people from being deported or expelled to states where they are likely to suffer torture. Since many potential receiving states are not parties to the Convention against Torture, such decisions are clearly of great importance to individuals who would otherwise have no recourse to an international procedure capable of addressing their complaints.

As the Committee for the Elimination of Discrimination against Women yet has to decide its first case, it is too early to judge the added value of its complaint procedure. However, the fact that the Convention includes many provisions that pertain to the realm of economic and social rights makes it likely that issues will ultimately arise that could not be adjudicated before the other committees. If successful, the Optional Protocol to the Women's Convention could greatly enhance the prospects for adoption of a complaint procedure to the Covenant on Economic, Social and Cultural Rights.

The procedures described in this chapter are not without their weaknesses; prime among them are the fact that the United Nations has not developed a system under which the UN's political bodies give their systematic and unconditional support to the implementation of the findings of the treaty bodies. Inordinate delays of three or four years from registering an application to a final decision are another weakness, in particular as additional delays have at times occurred at the preregistration stage. However, improvements have been made, and urgent cases, such as those involving the death penalty or possible expulsion to a country where torture is likely, do proceed more quickly. Many states do appear to be taking their obligations under the respective optional complaints systems more seriously, perhaps because of the negative publicity and diplomatic pressure that may result from having been found to have violated human rights, despite the fact that noncompliance remains a serious problem. Individuals, lawyers, and NGOs should therefore not ignore the possibility of filing complaints before any one of these bodies, in addition to considering other available options.

Notes

1. Siân Lewis-Anthony was the sole author of the corresponding chapter in the previous edition of this book. Martin Scheinin is responsible for any changes and updating in the present chapter.

2. The Optional Protocol to the International Covenant on Civil and Political Rights speaks only of "communications," but this chapter will occasionally use the term "complaints," "applications," or "cases" as synonymous.

3. The Convention on the Protection of the Rights of All Migrant Workers and Members of Their Families, which entered into force in 2003, also includes a procedure for individual complaints. However, no state party to the Convention had accepted the right of individual complaint as of early 2004. Discussions of a complaint mechanism under the Covenant on Economic, Social and Cultural Rights have been continuing for some time but seem unlikely to conclude in the near future.

4. Rawle Kennedy v. Trinidad and Tobago (Communication No. 845/1999), decision on admissibility adopted 2 Nov. 1999, Report of the Human Rights Committee, Vol. II, GAOR, Fifty-fifth Session, Supp. No. 40 (A/55/40), at 258–272.

5. The Revised Rules of Procedure may be found in UN Doc. CCPR/ C/3/Rev.6 (2001).

6. Toonen v. Australia, Communication No. 488/1992, reprinted in 1 *Int'l Hum. Rts. Rpt.* 97 (1994), para. 5.1.

7. *Id.* at para. 8.2.

8. Leichtensztein v. Uruguay, Communication No. 77/1980, reprinted in 2 *Selected Decisions of the Human Rights Committee under the Optional Protocol,* UN Doc. CCPR/C/OP/2 (1990) (hereinafter cited as *"Selected Decisions"*), at 102.

9. Lopez Burgos v. Uruguay, Communication No. 52/1079, reprinted in 1 *Selected Decisions,* UN Doc. CCPR/C/OP/1 (1985), at 88.

10. Communications Nos. 172/1984 and 182/1984, reprinted in 2 *Selected Decisions,* at 196, 209.

11. See, e.g., Marie-Hélène Gillot et al. v. France, Communication No. 932/2000, Human Rights Committee, Annual Report, UN Doc. A/57/40 (vol. 2, 2002), at 270.

12. See, e.g., Machado v. Uruguay, Communication no. 83/1981, reprinted in 2 *Selected Decisions,* at 108.

13. Many of the provisions of the Covenant are nonderogable in their entirety, including the right to life; freedom from torture and cruel, inhuman, or degrading treatment or punishment; freedom from slavery; nonretroactivity of criminal laws; the right to recognition as a person before the law; and freedom of thought, conscience, and religion. See General Comment No. 29 (72) of the Human Rights Committee, UN Doc. CCPR/C/21/Rev.1/Add.11.

14. Sequeira v. Uruguay, Communication No. 6/1977, reprinted in 1 *Selected Decisions,* at 52.

15. See chap. 4.

16. A model communication which may be used for all of the treaty bodies is found in Appendix C.

17. See Gobin v. Mauritius, Communication No. 787/1997, decision on admissibility adopted 16 July 2001, Report of the Human Rights Committee, Vol. II, UN Doc. A/56/40 (Vol. II), at 222–227.

18. See Dante Piandiong et al. v. The Philippines (Communication No. 869/1999), paras 5.1 and 5.2, Views adopted 19 Oct. 2000, Report of the Human Rights Committee, Vol. II, UN Doc. A/56/40 (Vol. II), at 181-190.

19. All or part of the submissions, or other information such as the identity of the author, may remain confidential after the Committee's decision on inadmissibility, merits, or discontinuance has been adopted. See Rule 96(4).

20. See chap. 10.

21. The Rules of Procedure of the Committee on the Elimination of Racial Discrimination are found in UN Doc. HRI/GEN/3/Rev.1 (2003).

22. Anna Koptova v. Slovakia, Communication No. 13/1998, UN Doc. CERD/C/57/D/13/1998. Compare with a case declared inadmissible as an *actio popularis,* The Documentation and Advisory Centre on Racial Discrimination v. Denmark, Communication No. 28/2003, UN Doc. CERD/C/63/D/28/2003.

23. Rule 95 (2).

24. The Committee's Rules of Procedure are contained in UN Doc. CAT/C/3/Rev.4 (2002).

25. The Committee's Rules of Procedure are contained in Annex I of the Report of the CEDAW Committee, UN Doc. A/56/38 (2000).

26. See chap. 8.

Chapter 4
United Nations Nontreaty Procedures for Dealing with Human Rights Violations

Nigel S. Rodley and David Weissbrodt

Any evaluation of the United Nation's contemporary role in protecting human rights must understand its actions (or inaction) in an historical perspective. In the early days of the United Nations, the organization generally held that it could not deal with either individual cases or allegations of human rights violations in specific countries. Only since the late 1960s has there slowly developed a complex and sometimes overlapping network of procedures and forums for reviewing state compliance (or lack thereof) with the human rights norms the United Nations has proclaimed. Some procedures relate to general situations in a country and others to individual complaints, while a number consider both. Some are concerned with the whole field of human rights, others with specific types of violation. The procedures vary widely, but each may be used regardless of whether a country is also a party to a relevant international treaty with its own mechanism.

There is now a plethora of political, humanitarian, expert, and even quasi-judicial mechanisms within the UN family that may be useful points of contact for the human rights advocate. This chapter deals with the most significant of those bodies, although it should be borne in mind that the specifics (and politics) of any particular procedure may change with little notice.

The Commission on Human Rights and Its Sub-Commission

The most important procedures have been established within the UN Commission on Human Rights and its Sub-Commission on the Promotion and Protection of Human Rights (formerly the Sub-Commission on the Prevention of Discrimination and Protection of Minorities). The

Commission on Human Rights, which meets annually in Geneva for six weeks beginning in mid-March, consists of fifty-three members elected by the Economic and Social Council (ECOSOC). The Commission reports to ECOSOC which, in turn, reports to the General Assembly. Delegations make statements and vote on proposed resolutions and decisions in the same way as in any other UN body, that is, on behalf of the governments they represent. Most other UN member states send observer delegations that can make statements but have no right to vote.

Governments may give their representatives broad discretion or strict instructions. The more sensitive the issue, the more likely that members will be obliged to seek instructions from their capitals. Often, governments whose human rights practices are under challenge at the Commission will lobby the capitals of Commission members to avoid an adverse vote or action. It has therefore been difficult to condemn or challenge any but the most friendless of countries in the past.

The *Sub-Commission on the Promotion and Protection of Human Rights* also meets annually in Geneva, for three weeks beginning in late July or early August. Formally, the Sub-Commission reports to the following session of the Commission. It is composed of twenty-six individual experts, nominated by their governments and elected by the Commission. In practice, some Sub-Commission members and their alternates are well attuned to the policies of their governments and take positions that are consistent with those policies. It is not unusual for such members to have official positions or to serve in their government's delegation at the Commission, although some quite independent members of the Sub-Commission also may occasionally represent their government elsewhere. On the whole, the Sub-Commission can be expected to act somewhat more on the merits than on the politics of human rights issues—a tendency which was reinforced by the Sub-Commission's adoption of voting by secret ballot on country-related matters since 1989. In 2000, however, the Commission forbade the Sub-Commission from adopting resolutions on country-related matters. The Sub-Commission still debates country situations and undertakes studies or adopts thematic resolutions on issues that impliedly relate to country situations.

A typical cycle of meetings thus starts with the Sub-Commission (July–August), continuing with the Commission (the following March–April), ECOSOC (July), and the General Assembly (September–December). Occasionally, the General Assembly may take up an issue raised during the immediately preceding Sub-Commission session.

Public Discussion of Specific Country Situations

Competence to act on specific country situations is found primarily in ECOSOC Resolution 1235 (XLII). Adopted in 1967, the resolution authorizes both the Commission and Sub-Commission "to examine information relevant to gross violations of human rights and fundamental freedoms." The nature of that examination is undefined, although the Commission alone is allowed to "make a thorough study of situations which reveal a consistent pattern of violations of human rights."

Whatever the initial intent, Resolution 1235 is now interpreted as giving broad authority to the Commission and Sub-Commission to debate particular country situations and, if the Commission chooses, to adopt resolutions on them. The Commission also may authorize appointment of a rapporteur or other mechanism for studying a given country situation or thematic issue, subject to the approval of ECOSOC if there are financial implications.

Even a Sub-Commission resolution that does no more than express concern about a particular issue that may relate to a country's human rights situation can serve three important functions: first, it may give political impetus to further action by the Commission or other human rights bodies; second, even if the Commission is unwilling to act, a Sub-Commission resolution represents the opinion of a formally constituted UN body of human rights experts, which is not without influence; and, third, it may build up an official documentary record by requesting a report by the Secretary-General or a member of the Sub-Commission on the issue. For example, in 2000 the Sub-Commission adopted a resolution on "discrimination based on work and descent" and requested one of its members to prepare a working paper on that subject. The working paper, which contained extensive information supplied by NGOs, discussed, *inter alia*, discrimination based on caste in India, Japan, and Nepal. Adoption of the resolution and the working paper contributed to the adoption by the Committee on the Elimination of Racial Discrimination of a General Recommendation based on descent in 2002, which had considerable political impact.

Machinery on Specific Countries

The Commission has investigated human rights violations in a large number of specific states and territories, beyond simply debating them in plenary sessions. In 2003, for example, there were special rapporteurs or representatives on Burundi, Democratic Republic of Congo (former Zaire), Iraq, Myanmar, and the occupied territories of Palestine. In addition, the Commission adopted resolutions on Belarus, Cuba, the Democratic People's Republic of Korea, Lebanese detainees in Israel, occupied Syrian Golan, Turkmenistan, and Western Sahara. (The General Assembly also may undertake investigations in politically significant cases, as it currently does with respect to the Israeli-occupied territories, the latter through a special committee whose reports are made available to the Commission.) An investigation may be undertaken by a variety of groups or individuals, although the most common designations have become "special rapporteur" or "special representative." The nomenclature may be altered to respond to the political nuances that seem important at the time.

All of these mechanisms have in common fact-finding mandates which are determined by the Commission (subject to ECOSOC approval), to which they report annually (so long as their mandate is renewed) and publicly. In addition, the Commission has authorized the appointment of experts to provide "advisory services" or "technical cooperation" to countries that appear to be in a process of transition to a more democratic or rights-protecting regime; in 2003, such cooperation was being extended to Afghanistan, Cambodia, Haiti, Liberia, Sierra Leone, and Somalia. Although these experts do not report on the human rights situations per se in the countries with which they are concerned, it is generally worthwhile for NGOs to provide them with information about human rights conditions, since this helps prevent their activities being used to camouflage continuing violations.

In general, country mechanisms can take into account information from anyone—individual, group, or government. Even if their mandates limit the sources from which they may actively *seek* information, they tend not to consider themselves to be restricted in the kinds of information that they may receive. They often go out into the field, trying where possible to make on-site visits to "their" countries and to meet any potential sources of information relevant to their mandates.

There are no formalities as regards either written or oral information; it is the responsibility of the working group, rapporteur, or expert to evaluate the information received. Correspondence should be addressed directly to the relevant group or expert, in care of the Office of the UN High Commissioner for Human Rights in Geneva (OHCHR).[1] As a rule, one cannot rely on receiving any response after information is provided, but the information may well contribute to the way in which the situation is described to the Commission.

When providing information, it should be supplied to the rapporteur[2] in a manner that will encourage him or her to take it as seriously as the supplier does. Accordingly, the information should be factual rather than politically polemical or speculative. It should give as much detail as possible, and available documentary corroboration should be furnished. It should also be as up-to-date as possible. National sources of proven reliability are more likely to be approached, if a rapporteur visits the country.

Although country rapporteurs are not generally empowered to take action on individual cases, information on such cases may serve as a basis for concrete contacts and discussions with the authorities of the state in question. If a case is urgent and specific, it is generally best to send information to the relevant thematic mechanism (discussed below) and ask that the information also be brought to the attention of the country-specific mechanism. However, this approach is not essential, as the OHCHR should channel information to the appropriate mechanism.

Confidential Investigations Under the "1503 Procedure"

When ECOSOC Resolution 1235 was adopted in 1967, it was primarily intended to allow the Commission to consider the situations in South Africa, Namibia, Rhodesia, and the African colonies of Portugal. At that time, NGOs were not allowed to make oral interventions or circulate written statements complaining about human rights violations in specific countries. It came as something of a shock to the Commission when, later in 1967, the Sub-Commission recommended that the Commission establish a Special Committee of Experts to consider not only the human rights situations in Southern Africa, but also the situations in Greece (after the 1967 colonels' coup) and Haiti (under the rule of François Duvalier). This initiative goaded the Commission into developing a procedure under which information from nongovernmental sources could be considered in a less directly challenging manner.

The result was the adoption by ECOSOC in 1970 of Resolution 1503 (XLVIII). The "1503 procedure," as it is known, provides that a nongovernmental "communication" (i.e., a complaint) concerning "situations which appear to reveal a consistent pattern of gross and reliably attested violations of human rights" may be dealt with in closed sessions of the Commission.[3]

The communication should be sent to the OHCHR in Geneva. The UN Secretariat acknowledges receipt but usually does not otherwise correspond with the author of the communication. Unless the communication is screened out as "manifestly ill-founded," the OHCHR sends it to the government concerned and summarizes it in a monthly confidential list. A Working Group on Communications composed of five Sub-Commission members (one from each of the UN's five geographic regions) meets in private for two weeks in August immediately following the annual Sub-Commission session to review the confidential lists (the group also has access to the full texts of communications) and any corresponding government replies. Since governments are given a minimum of twelve weeks to reply, a communication transmitted to a government after the third week of May will probably not be considered for another year, unless the Secretariat receives a reply from the government prior to the group's presessional meeting. NGOs should thus submit their communications well before the deadline.

If at least three members of the group agree that a communication appears to reveal a consistent pattern of gross violations of human rights, the group forwards it to the Commission. The Working Group also may keep the matter pending for a year. (Before 2000, the Working Group referred communications to the Sub-Commission, which then decided in closed session which of the situations referred to it by the working group should be forwarded to the next session of the Commission.) The situations in eighty-four different countries have been referred to the Commission since the procedure's creation,[4] although no public announcement is made at this stage about which countries are involved.

A parallel Working Group on Situations, appointed from among the states which are members of the Commission, meets for one week before the Commission's annual session. It examines the country dossiers; determines whether to refer a particular situation to the Commission, keep the matter pending, or discontinue consideration; and makes recommendations to the Commission about how to deal with the situations referred by the Sub-Commission. The Commission is free to accept or reject the Working Group's recommendations.

The Commission considers the "situations" (note that it is no longer dealing only with the forwarded "communications") in closed session. Resolution 1503 empowers it to make a "thorough study" or institute an "investigation by an ad hoc committee." No such ad hoc committee is known to have been created, however, and it would appear (although it has not been publicly confirmed) that only one thorough study has been initiated.

In practice, the Commission has developed a wide range of techniques short of a "thorough study" to investigate a particular situation. The primary ones include (in descending order of their perceived seriousness): (1) referring the situation for consideration by the Commission in public session (this occurred with regard to both Chad and Liberia in 2003); (2) appointing an independent expert/rapporteur (this occurred in 1995, with respect to Chad); (3) asking the Secretary-General to establish direct contacts with the government concerned; (4) asking the government for further information; and (5) and keeping the situation "under review." In each of these cases, the situation is reported on and considered the following year. Of course, the Commission also may simply decide to discontinue consideration.

At the end of the Commission's closed discussions, the Chairperson announces publicly the names of the countries in which situations have been considered and those which have been discontinued. The public is thereby informed of the countries that the Commission is reviewing under the 1503 procedure, but not of the action taken or the nature of the alleged violations. Eventually, the Commission may recommend that ECOSOC put the situation on the public record. ECOSOC has only rarely been called on to do this, either at the request of a new government in the country concerned (e.g., Argentina after democracy was restored under President Raul Alfonsin) or when a country totally refused to cooperate with the Commission (e.g., Equatorial Guinea's refusal to supply any defense to accusations against it). In 1988, ECOSOC failed to act on a Commission recommendation to make the file of Albania public, although it did pave the way for the Commission's public consideration of the situation.

How to Use the 1503 Procedure

The first thing to consider is whether to use the 1503 procedure at all. If the situation has a fair chance of being considered publicly, it might be better to refrain from using the confidential 1503 procedure. Unfortunately, it is difficult to predict the likelihood of public consideration, and it would be wise to consult with an experienced international NGO, such as Amnesty International, the International Commission of Jurists, or the International Federation of Human Rights. The likelihood of progress under the 1503 procedure itself also should be assessed, again by consulting with experienced NGOs. If a country's situation is already the subject of resolution or decision of the Commission, communications with regard to that country will not be considered under the 1503 procedure.

Once a situation is being considered under the 1503 procedure, some Commission members have argued that it is inappropriate to consider the same situation publicly. At the same time, a challenged government might try to exploit the fact that a situation known to have been considered was not taken up, or, if taken up, was discontinued.

The 1503 procedure always should be used if a particular situation is already under consideration in the Sub-Commission Working Group on Communications, the Commission's Working Group on Situations, or the Commission itself, because, in theory, the only way subsequent information can reach the Commission is by going through the whole process from the beginning. In addition, if a situation has been kept under review for a year, a government might argue that the absence of new information is evidence that the situation has improved.

It does not matter whether the information supplier is an individual, an NGO, a victim, or only someone with "reliable knowledge of the violations." There is no restriction on who may submit a communication, although well-known NGOs may be more likely to have their communications considered favorably.

Several *procedural requirements* for the 1503 procedure are laid down in Sub-Commission Resolution 1 (XXIV) of 1971:

- The communication must not be anonymous, although the identity of the author will not be divulged unless confidentiality is not desired. In practice, it should be indicated whether there is any objection to the identity of the communicant being divulged; the government could learn of the authorship of the communication no matter how careful the UN Secretariat might be.
- The communication must not have "manifestly political motivations." While it is not entirely clear, this rule appears to mean that it should not impugn the legitimacy of the government as such. Rather, it should concentrate on factual allegations of human rights violations. Abusive language should be avoided, especially "insulting references to the State against which the complaint is directed"; such language would, in any event, be deleted before the communication would be considered for admissibility.
- The communication must not appear to be "based exclusively on reports disseminated by mass media." Because of the official or semi-official nature of the mass media in some countries, information from such a source could be very strong evidence of the allegations made. Nonetheless, for a communication to be considered admissible, it is necessary to refer to sources additional to, but not to the exclusion of, the mass media.
- The communication must explain how domestic remedies have been exhausted or otherwise demonstrate why such remedies would be "ineffective or unreasonably prolonged." In practice, as long as there is strong evidence of systematic, continuing violations, references to domestic remedies or their inefficacy do not have to be extensively documented.
- The communication must be submitted "within a reasonable time after the exhaustion of the domestic remedies." Indeed, it should be as up-to-date as possible, in order to document the continuing nature of the human rights violations.

There are also some common-sense *substantive requirements:*

- The communication must show the existence of a *consistent pattern* of *gross violations* of human rights. Technically, a series of communications concerning individual violations could be taken together as appearing to reveal a consistent pattern. In practice, however, the communication should provide an overall summary of the human rights violations, refer to any statistics or other indications of the scope of the situation, and then set forth a sufficient number of violations to illustrate the pattern (as few as six or seven cases of prolonged administrative detention have, on rare occasions, sufficed). Gross violations include, but are not limited to, torture, "disappearances," extra-legal executions (killings), other arbitrary or summary executions (e.g., imposition of the death penalty without a fair trial or right of appeal), widespread arbitrary imprisonment or long-term detention without charge or trial, and widespread denial of the right to leave one's country. The more widespread the practice, the less may be the need for the violations to be gross, and vice versa.

- The communication "must contain a description of the facts." All details necessary to show a consistent pattern should be offered, such as names, places, dates, etc.
- The communication "must indicate . . . the rights that have been violated." Often the relevant rights will be obvious, but one should indicate which articles of the Universal Declaration of Human Rights appear to have been violated, because the Working Group on Communications organizes its work on an article-by-article basis.[5]
- The communication should be accompanied by "clear evidence." This proof is required especially if the author is not the victim, but is, for example, a human rights NGO. Direct testimony of victims or their families can be particularly persuasive, both in the text by way of illustration and in annexes.
- The communication "must indicate the purpose of the petition." A sufficient indication would be seeking "UN action to bring an end to the violations of human rights disclosed in this communication." It is unrealistic to expect the Commission to call for such remedies as domestic investigation of the violations, sanctions against individual violators, or compensation for victims or their surviving dependents, once the situation of continuing systematic violations has been brought to an end.

Furthermore, although no special *format* is laid down, a good communication will consist of:

- a covering letter, which should refer to ECOSOC Resolutions 728F and/or 1503, summarize the allegations (to assist the UN Secretariat in drafting the summary for the confidential list), and include a statement of purpose as indicated above;[6]
- the text of the communication (it is generally best to limit the text to twenty–thirty pages, because the Working Group on Communications has many complaints to consider), describing in sufficient detail the consistent pattern of gross violations of human rights; and

- annexes, containing the best available documentary evidence of the allegations, especially in the form of direct testimony. (It should be noted, however, that annexes are generally not translated for the Commission, so the most important substance must be in the communication itself.)

In addition, it is preferable (although not required) to submit the communication in one of the UN's official languages (Arabic, Chinese, English, French, Russian, and Spanish), preferably English, French, or Spanish; enclose any translations into other official languages that are available of the main text or annexes; and send six copies of the communication.

Once the communication has been submitted, there is nothing more required of the submitter. The UN Secretariat will acknowledge receipt, indicating that the communication will be dealt with under the relevant resolutions. If it is not clear whether confidentiality is requested, they may seek to clarify that issue. Otherwise, the communicant will hear nothing more officially.

If it is learned that a situation is being considered (either from the Chairperson's announcement that the Commission is dealing with the situation or unofficially from other sources), a supplementary communication to update the facts may be filed. If a thorough study or similar procedure has been instituted, then the information in the communication may be brought directly to the attention of the person carrying out the study. If there is to be a visit to the country, it may be possible to meet the visiting team (confidentiality becomes illusory here).

In the more likely event that the situation is merely kept under review until the following year, the supplementary communication will be dealt with through the same process as the original one, but with increased chances of its clearing the Working Group on Communications and the Working Group on Situations. Even if there is little prospect of the Commission's doing more than keeping the situation under review, this procedure constitutes a form of pressure, especially in view of the Chairperson's public announcements. If the violations are continuing, one particularly wants to avoid a publicly announced decision to discontinue consideration of the situation.

Either of the Working Groups may decide to keep a communication or situation pending for a year, and updating the information is therefore desirable. If a supplementary communication is submitted, be sure to couch it in language that permits it to be read as a free-standing complaint, so that it may be treated as such if the original complaint was in fact dropped.

Thematic Mechanisms

One of the most positive developments in the UN's work in the past twenty-five years has been the development of thematic machinery to deal with violations of specific types of human rights. Unlike the procedures that deal with general *situations*, the thematic mechanisms can deal with *individual cases* of human rights violations or threatened violations, particularly in countries in which a specific type of violation appears to be widespread.

The most important of these mechanisms which deal with threats to life or physical integrity were among the earliest to be created: the Working Group on Enforced or Involuntary Disappearances (created in 1980), the Special Rapporteur on Summary or Arbitrary Executions (1982), and the Special Rapporteur on Torture (1985). So many thematic mechanisms have been created subsequently that there is some concern at their proliferation, lack of resources to service them, and lack of time on the Commission agenda to consider the results of their work. Among the most significant to direct victims of violations are the rapporteurs or working groups on religious intolerance (1986), arbitrary detention (1991), the sale of children and child prostitution and pornography (1992), internally displaced persons (1993), racism and xenophobia (1993), freedom of opinion and expression (1993), the independence of the judiciary (1994), violence against women (1994), and human rights defenders (2000). Other rapporteurs deal with adequate housing, compensation for victims of human rights violations, education, extreme poverty, food, health, human trafficking, the impact of armed conflict on children, implementation of the Durban Declaration and Programme of Action, indigenous peoples, migrants, racial discrimination faced by people of African descent, the right to development, structural adjustment policies and foreign debt, toxic waste, and use of mercenaries.

To date, these mechanisms have been genuinely impartial. In other words, their annual reports to the Commission indicate that cases and problems are taken up, regardless of the identity of the state whose behavior is called into question. This approach is a radical departure from the practice of some other UN bodies, including the Commission, where actions are partly (if not primarily) determined by political considerations.

The mandates of each of the mechanisms may vary slightly, but their methods of work are sufficiently similar to be described together, along with suggestions for how best to use them.

How the Thematic Mechanisms Work

All of the mandates of the thematic mechanisms require them to "study" the phenomenon in question. This objective has led them to analyze patterns of behavior, factors conducive to violations (e.g., armed conflict), and the relevance of national legal and administrative provisions and structures for the prevention of violations. The various annual reports also offer general recommendations for national and international action.

There is little written guidance on how the rapporteurs/groups should perform their duties. However, most have developed techniques which permit them to act as well as to study. The key element in the mandates is the ability "to respond effectively" to information, and this phrase is now included, for example, within the mandates of the working group on disappearances, special rapporteur on executions, special rapporteur on torture, and special rapporteur on religious intolerance. Although the mandate of the Working Group on Arbitrary Detention does not include this phrase, it does include the explicit and unprecedented authority to "investigate cases."

The activities of the rapporteurs/groups include seeking and receiving information; asking governments to comment on information concerning legislation or official practices; forwarding to governments for clarification allegations about urgent cases that fall within their mandates; in the case of a few mandates, sending government responses to the source of the original information to obtain comments on the responses; seeking and/or responding to invitations to visit countries that seem to have a serious problem which falls within the rapporteur's mandate; undertaking such visits; and reporting annually to the Commission. The annual report of each rapporteur or group contains information on all of the above activities, as well as summaries of correspondence, details of meetings with sources of information and governments, descriptions of visits, and general analyses and recommendations.

Apart from the Working Group on Arbitrary Detention (with its special mandate to "investigate cases "), the thematic mechanisms tend to avoid conclusions as to whether a violation has occurred in the case of a particular individual. Many of them, however, now formulate "observations" in the country entries of their annual reports, which tend to be of a judgmental nature. The conclusions of their reports after country visits are usually unmistakably judgmental.

How to Use the Thematic Mechanisms

The mechanisms may "seek and receive" information from various sources, with slight variations. For example, the Working Group on

Disappearances may gather information from "governments, intergovernmental organizations, humanitarian organizations and other reliable sources." In practice, when dealing with information about individual cases, the Group welcomes information from organizations of families of the disappeared and the families themselves; indeed, when corresponding with nongovernmental sources other than the affected families on such cases, it considers the sources to be acting on behalf of the families, with whom they are expected to share information.

Initially, the relevant resolutions defined permitted NGO sources with varying degrees of precision. Today, however, the thematic mechanisms seek and receive information from individuals, domestic and international NGOs (whether or not they have consultative status with the UN), governments, and intergovernmental organizations, although the assistance of an experienced and careful (and, therefore, known and trusted) NGO may still be valuable.

No particular format is required to submit information,[7] but the information must be as reliable and convincing as possible. Basic information should naturally be included, such as the name of the victim (with identity number, if possible), date and place of the incident, and some indication of the suspected identity of the perpetrators or their official status, as well as information (especially in the case of disappearances) about local remedies, e.g., *habeas corpus*, that have been tried. If the information concerns countries that are being considered under public or private procedures, then there is more likelihood that it will be considered credible. The same applies to countries that have been mentioned in the mechanisms' recent reports, so these materials should be consulted.

In *urgent cases*, a rapporteur or group may not set as high a standard for evidence as in other cases, and the OHCHR has established special fax and e-mail numbers for such cases.[8] But one should not seek action on the basis of unreliable or highly questionable information.

Subsequent developments should always be brought to the attention of the rapporteur or group, whether it tends to remove the concern (e.g., a person has reappeared alive or a death sentence has been commuted), or to confirm it (e.g., medical reports of torture). These updates help the mechanism to act more effectively and avoid mistakes.

Commission on the Status of Women

The Commission on the Status of Women consists of forty-five government representatives elected by ECOSOC and meets annually in New York. Most of the representatives sent by the governments are women.

The Commission has two confidential complaints procedures analogous to ECOSOC Resolutions 728F (individual complaints) and 1503 (communications concerning consistent patterns). Under the individual complaints procedure, established pursuant to ECOSOC Resolutions 76 (V) (1947) and 304I (XI) (1950), the Commission confines itself to "taking note" of the communications received. No individual country situations are known to have been taken up by the Commission under the consistent pattern procedure, which is contained in ECOSOC Resolution 1983/27 (1983) and refers to "a consistent pattern of reliably attested injustice and discriminatory practice against women."

Following the Fourth World Conference on Women, held in Beijing in 1995, the Commission was directed to expand its efforts in addressing the critical areas of concern identified in Beijing. It has identified a number of issues to which it devotes attention each year, but its work remains almost entirely in the realm of discussion, norm-setting, and program proposals, rather than in responding to specific issues or cases of violations of the human rights of women. While the United Nations itself has given women's issues a much higher profile during the 1990s, the Commission on the Status of Women is unlikely to be of great value to the practitioner.

Intervention at the United Nations by NGOs

Most of what follows applies only to NGOs in consultative status with ECOSOC (categories General, Special, and Roster). Such NGOs have certain rights under ECOSOC Resolution 1996/31 (1996), and they are able to play an influential role in all aspects of the public work of relevant UN bodies, in particular the Commission on Human Rights and its Sub-Commission. They often play a key role in the process of drafting new international instruments (particularly in working groups set up for that purpose), and they may take the lead in identifying areas for UN action, such as filling gaps in UN norms and machinery. They also supply information on noncompliance with existing norms.

Effective involvement in drafting international instruments requires a high level of professional expertise, competence in the subject matter at hand, and, preferably, prior experience. Space constraints do not permit a proper description of these processes and how to use them, and NGOs with an interest in a particular drafting exercise are advised either to appoint an experienced representative or one whose professional and substantive competence is sufficient to permit him or her to learn the ropes from older hands.

Here we concentrate on the NGO role in supplying country-specific information to the Commission and Sub-Commission.[9]

Range of Addressable Countries

Until the mid-1970s, country-specific interventions by NGOs were only permitted when the situations appeared specifically on the agenda, i.e., the Israeli-occupied territories, Southern Africa, and Chile. Since the early 1980s, however, oral interventions have been permitted to address any country. Relaxation of the rules relating to written interventions was more gradual, but it is now difficult to identify any concrete limitations on the countries that can be mentioned in written statements.

Choice of Agenda Item

Like other meetings, sessions of the Commission and Sub-Commission follow an agenda that is set in advance, and NGOs are limited in the agenda items on which they may intervene. For example, NGOs are not usually given the opportunity to intervene under procedural items, such as "adoption of the agenda," "organization of work of the session," or "adoption of the draft agenda" for the subsequent session. They may not participate in the substantive debates on draft resolutions and decisions. While the latter, in particular, may be very important, and erroneous or misleading statements may be made during the course of the debates, the only recourse for an NGO is to draw its concern privately to the attention of a member of the body.

There are no clear rules or practices regarding other substantive items, but the rapid increase in NGO country-specific oral interventions (and their repetition under different agenda items) has led to informal proposals to restrict such interventions to only a few items. The latter include the general debate on "the violation of human rights and fundamental freedoms in any part of the world" and items dealing with the human rights of persons in detention. Nonrepetitive and carefully phrased interventions are still permitted under other agenda items, but it is advisable to plan interventions so that they may be accommodated under at least one of the above items. NGOs are still permitted to present country concerns before the Sub-Commission, and their concerns may be answered by governments, discussed by Sub-Commission members, and reflected in thematic resolutions. However, because the Sub-Commission has been forbidden since 2000 from adopting resolutions specifically mentioning countries, there is less incentive to make country-specific interventions in the Sub-Commission.

In any event, NGOs should carefully consult the "preliminary annotated agenda" which is issued a few weeks before each session of the Commission and Sub-Commission. This document explains the background to each item, including references to resolutions and decisions adopted previously, and should be studied carefully to ensure that an intervention is appropriate.

The UN Secretariat may assign a written NGO statement to any agenda item it considers appropriate, if it does not feel that it should be circulated under the item requested.

Working Groups

NGOs are generally able to participate much more effectively and less formally in working groups than in plenary sessions. The Sub-Commission has three such groups, dealing respectively with indigenous populations, minorities, and contemporary forms of slavery. At some point on their agenda, all permit discussion of country-specific situations falling within their scope. Unusually for UN bodies, the working groups on indigenous populations (which meets in July, immediately prior to the full Sub-Commission), minorities (which usually meets in the early months of the year), and slavery (usually in May) permit individuals, interested groups, indigenous or minority representatives, or victims of contemporary forms of slavery to participate on equal terms with NGOs having formal consultative status. Further, the Sub-Commission has established a presessional Social Forum that focuses on economic, social, and cultural rights. The Sub-Commission also has two working groups on the administration of justice and on transnational corporations that meet during the three-week period of the Sub-Commission session.

In addition to the working groups on disappearances and arbitrary detention, the Commission has standing groups on the right to development, problems of racial discrimination faced by people of African descent, and effective implementation of the Durban Declaration and Programme of Action relating to racial discrimination, in addition to standard-setting groups considering a draft declaration on indigenous rights, a convention on disappearances, and the possibility of an optional protocol to the Covenant on Economic, Social and Cultural Rights.[10]

Preparing for Participation

The first decision is to identify which country-specific situation(s) or issue(s) needs to be addressed and whether interventions should be oral or written. This preliminary step may well involve setting priorities, in light of the availability of agenda items, limits on the length of statements, and the desire to achieve maximum impact. Impact tends to decrease in inverse proportion to the number of interventions an NGO delivers, and oral interventions tend to have more immediate impact than written ones.

Written statements

Written statements to the Commission on Human Rights and the Sub-Commission may not exceed 2,000 words (general category NGOs) or 1,500 words (NGOs in the special category or on the Roster).[11] They must be submitted in one of the UN's official languages and "in sufficient time for appropriate consultation to take place between the Secretary-General and the organization before circulation." If the UN Secretariat has comments on the draft text, these must be given "due consideration" before the text is transmitted "in final form." While, as noted above, the Secretariat has become less restrictive as far as country-specific written statements are concerned, it does not consider itself obliged to circulate any particular text; it would be wise to accept suggestions made by a Secretariat member. At the same time, NGO statements have become increasingly direct in their criticisms, and subtlety seems no longer to be required. Written statements may not have as much immediate impact as oral interventions, but they can raise themes that may be considered in greater detail in subsequent sessions. Written statements also are issued as UN documents, which can be distributed and discussed within and outside the United Nations.

Oral interventions

There are no formal rules regarding the content of oral statements.[12] However, perceived problems have led the Commission and Sub-Commission to consider various proposals to restrict NGO interventions, as well as government statements made by way of reply, on an almost annual basis. One of these problems is the increasing number of NGOs making country-specific statements and the tendency of some of them to be repetitive, addressing the same issue under different agenda items, in a working group and then in plenary, or in written as well as oral form. Several NGOs also may make similar statements about the same country or countries.

The following suggestions assume that there will be no radical change in the present system and that NGOs will continue to be essentially self-regulating. They outline what might be termed "best practices," with a view to maintaining the contribution of NGOs to the system and maximizing the impact of each intervention.

- Think strategically. Ask what the NGO is seeking to achieve and formulate a statement that will directly contribute to the objective. NGOs should avoid the temptation, all-too-frequently succumbed to by governments, to intervene simply to play to their own constituency, with only minimal consideration of the impact on the meeting.

- Try to speak to a theme, e.g., a type of human rights violation or conditions which make human rights violations more likely, and use country situations to illustrate the point. Constructive, realistic proposals for action by the body, at least in general terms, are often good concluding passages.
- If concentrating on just one or two countries, consider what specific contribution can be made to redress the situation at issue. Unless the impact is clear, avoid mere repetition and consider collaborating with others in a joint statement. To avoid disruptive procedural challenges or distracting rights of reply by the challenged government (or its supporters), refrain from attacks which seem to be politically motivated or abusive.[13] If a procedural (or other) debate does arise during an NGO intervention, the NGO has no right of reply. If there is reason to fear a challenge to the intervention, the best tactic is to ensure that potentially sympathetic members of the body are briefed so they can defend the NGO. In general, language should be factual and informative, rather than emotional.
- Avoid making more than one statement per session dealing extensively with the same country situation. Multiple interventions may lessen both individual influence and the reputation of NGOs in general. Indeed, in the Sub-Commission "[o]nce an observer has raised a particular issue on a human rights situation under one agenda item, the observer may not raise the same issue under another agenda item."[14]

As far as delivery of the intervention is concerned, there are a number of requirements. An NGO must first accredit its representative, who ideally should be an officer or paid official of the organization. This accreditation is done by a communication from the NGO's headquarters to the NGO Liaison Officer at the OHCHR Office in Geneva. Controversy sometimes arises when NGOs accredit victims of human rights violations or representatives of organizations in the country in question to "testify" before the Commission or Sub-Commission. The problem can be mitigated, but not necessarily eliminated, if the representative is a regular member of the NGO and/or the organization is an affiliate in good standing of the NGO. In case of doubt, this relationship should be made clear at the beginning of the intervention. Placing the "testimony" within the framework of a more general, organizational statement can also help.

The time limit for NGO interventions under the main agenda items has diminished from five minutes to three and one-half minutes for the Commission and from ten to seven minutes for the Sub-Commission, but it may be even less if proceedings are running late. If NGOs give joint statements in either the Commission or the Sub-Commission, they may speak for slightly longer—depending on the number of NGOs that join. In any case, NGO statements are presented under severe time constraints. Since the statement should be delivered at a deliberate, measured pace, to facilitate simultaneous interpretation and increase the impact on the meeting, a ten-minute statement should not be more than approximately 1,200–1,300 words long.

To seek the floor, one approaches the Secretariat conference officer responsible for the speakers' list (usually to the side and below the podium) before the deadline announced by the Chairperson for closure of the list for the agenda item in question. Ask to be put on the list for any agenda item(s) once the session begins. The list is generally called in order of inscription.

It is very difficult to estimate when one might be called to speak. Even after the agenda and timetable have been set, meetings frequently do not run on schedule. In addition, while NGOs often speak after members and observer governments, NGOs may be called on first, if no government or member wishes to take the floor or in order to permit governments to consolidate their rights of reply (this frequently happens at the Sub-Commission). It is not only bad practice for a representative to be absent from the room when his or her organization is called, but the opportunity to intervene may be lost. If, for any reason, the representative cannot be present at a time when the NGO may be called, it may be possible to change places with another NGO (more easily with one lower down the list than with one higher up); it is then essential to inform the Secretariat, so that each NGO is called in the correct order.

Thought also needs to be given to whether to notify the delegation of the country which is the subject of the intervention. Advantages of notification include courtesy, ensuring the delegation's presence, providing it with the opportunity to formulate a considered reply, and possibly increasing the chance for an informal out-of-session dialogue. Disadvantages include the risk of provoking procedural motions aimed at preventing the statement and possible pressure to withdraw or modify the statement.

It is helpful to have copies of the text available before the statement is delivered. A short while before delivery of the statement, the Secretariat will request about twenty copies for the interpreters, précis writers, and press release staff. Other NGOs and governments also may be interested in having a copy of an intervention after it is delivered, so a good rule of thumb is to have thirty–forty copies of every statement for distribution.

Related Activities

A key object of NGO participation is to inform others, especially members of the body and observer governments, of the NGO's concerns. This often can be best achieved by making direct contacts, and a great deal of lobbying is conducted in the coffee lounges or corridors near the meeting rooms (the coffee is good, but expensive). Written materials may not be left on the conference room tables or in pigeon-holes of the members without permission from the Secretariat, but they may be given to delegates personally. Since many Sub-Commission members and most Commission delegations plan their participation in advance, it is better to bring concerns to their attention well in advance of the session, if possible. Often governments will have determined their positions before a session, and it is very difficult to get them to change their approach once the session has begun. Sub-Commission members should be treated as the independent experts they are elected to be, and they should be contacted through the OHCHR or directly.

It is difficult to obtain press coverage of written or oral statements made during UN meetings, but the possibility should be explored if the statements are newsworthy. There is a large press corps at UN headquarters in Geneva, and it may be useful to distribute written statements or copies of oral interventions to some of the press offices, especially the wire services. A covering press release should call attention to the most important points. For a special event, it is possible to organize a news conference at the United Nations, with the approval of the UN Secretariat.

Where to Go for Help

As indicated at several points in this chapter, it is always possible to seek guidance from more experienced NGOs. In addition, the International Service for Human Rights, a Geneva-based NGO, has as an important part of its mandate guiding and assisting NGO representatives unfamiliar with Geneva.[15] The Service will convene meetings of NGOs concerned with particular countries or issues, in order to facilitate planning strategies, distribute substantive work, prepare joint statements, etc. If contacted well in advance of a session, the Service also may be able to help with such practical matters as finding accommodation and, if an NGO without consultative status is being represented, the Service can assist in gaining access to the proceedings.

Good Offices of the UN Secretary-General and High Commissioner for Human Rights

Every Secretary-General has considered himself to have inherent authority to contact governments on matters that fall within the purposes of the Charter of the United Nations. The promotion of human rights is one of those purposes. Successive Secretaries-General have raised serious human rights issues with governments, normally on "humanitarian" grounds, and the more recent occupants of the office have been willing even to raise individual cases.

Since good offices are usually effected privately, there is little public information concerning the kinds of issues the Secretary-General will raise with a government. The key variable seems to be that either a large-scale human rights crisis or an individual case must have a pressing humanitarian element which is seen as more significant than the "mere" violation of human rights. Threats of mass deaths or the ill-health or impending execution of an individual may motivate the Secretary-General to act. A number of General Assembly resolutions have urged him to use his "best endeavors" in cases of summary or arbitrary executions.

The Secretary-General has total discretion in deciding whether and how he may use his good offices. While a visit to the country in question may offer a good occasion to raise humanitarian issues, neither the world at large nor those individuals who provide information to the Secretary-General (through the UN Secretariat) may be informed of any action taken. Sometimes a public initiative may be taken, as when the Secretary-General appeals to prevent the execution in the United States of a person convicted of murder, who was under eighteen at the time he committed the offense.

There is no reliable procedure for initiating the use of good offices. In the most serious cases, it is probably best to communicate via the OHCHR in Geneva or New York. The communication should make it absolutely clear that its purpose is to seek the exercise of the Secretary-General's good offices and not to initiate one of the procedures discussed in the present chapter.

Other senior UN officials may also engage in good offices or analogous activities, often on the Secretary-General's behalf, but appeals should be attempted only in the most serious cases. Since the appointment of a UN High Commissioner for Human Rights in 1994, that official has been increasingly disposed to make public appeals on human rights issues, and the OHCHR has been more willing and open to discussing specific human rights matters in detail with NGOs and others. A "hot line" for reporting human rights violations has been set up in Geneva, to enable the OHCHR to react rapidly to urgent situations.[16] Although one should be careful not to abuse the possibility, direct contact with the Secretariat can be initiated both in urgent cases and for general information about the Office's activities or upcoming meetings. Most such information, including the schedule of upcoming meetings and relatively timely summaries of past meetings, is now available through the OHCHR Website, http://www.unhchr.ch.

Concluding Observations

The United Nations remains the only forum in which human rights violations in *any* country in the world (even those which are not UN members) may be addressed, at least in theory. The 1503 procedure is cumbersome and secret; direct participation in the sessions of the Commission and Sub-Commission in Geneva may be difficult or frustrating; and it is certainly expensive. Engaging one of the thematic rapporteurs or working groups is easier, and such an approach is more likely to lead to success in individual cases. Providing well-founded information to a country-specific rapporteur is one of the most effective means of having an input into the political process of the United Nations, although the impact is necessarily indirect.

Depending on the prevailing political winds and the financial situation of the United Nations, proposals to reform the UN's human rights machinery and to facilitate or limit the access of NGOs to that machinery are put forward frequently. Among the ideas for reform that have been discussed in past years are:

- readjusting the mandates of some of the thematic rapporteurs and ensuring that they receive better support from the Secretariat (which is seriously understaffed);
- ensuring more timely dissemination of rapporteurs' reports and more focussed discussion of the reports at the Commission, including "the extent to which current and relevant past recommendations have been addressed or followed up by concerned parties";
- conducting "regular, focussed and systematic deliberations" at the Commission on situations, if governments fail to cooperate with the Commission or its mechanisms;
- enabling the Bureau (the executive body) of the Commission to review governments' responses to the recommendations of the special mechanisms, including direct confidential dialogue with government representatives and a public briefing prior to the annual human rights debate in the General Assembly;
- involving the Chairperson of the Commission, when necessary, in assisting a rapporteur to obtain "an appropriate response" from governments in urgent cases;
- developing a less politicized means of deciding whether to appoint country-specific rapporteurs, based on better utilization of information from existing UN sources, such as the thematic rapporteurs and the OHCHR; and
- increasing the role of or contact with the author of a communication under the 1503 procedure and authorizing the Chairperson of the Commission to announce not only the names of the countries under

review, but also to identify the main issues of concern and the course of action decided upon by the Commission.

Whatever the result of the continuing efforts to reform the work of the Commission and the Sub-Commission, the advice offered in the present chapter has generally been valid for more than twenty years and is likely to be useful in future. Nonetheless, the practitioner obviously should follow closely any changes in the workings of the Commission, Sub-Commission, or the various procedures.

No matter how many reforms are adopted or procedures amended, no country is required to respond to UN requests for information or to take UN resolutions into account. Nonetheless, diplomatic delegations expend considerable time and energy to avoid criticism (or even inquiry) by the United Nations, and the impact of debates in the Commission on Human Rights on the general human rights situation in a country should not be discounted. Even if only because countries themselves pay so much attention to human rights issues raised at the United Nations, NGOs should be aware of UN forums and procedures and try to utilize them as effectively as possible.

Notes

1. See Appendix D for relevant contact information.

2. For ease of reference, the terms "rapporteur" or "mechanism" are used to describe the activities of all the human rights investigating bodies discussed in this chapter, whether they are technically "rapporteurs," members of working groups, or have some other formal nomenclature.

3. The 1503 procedure amends an earlier procedure contained in ECOSOC Resolution 728F (XXVIII) (1959). That resolution confirmed the traditional position, according to which the Commission had no power to take any action in regard to complaints concerning human rights, but it also mandated the UN Secretariat to circulate to Commission and Sub-Commission members "a confidential list" containing a brief indication of the substance of communications alleging human rights violations. Since this confidential list is never discussed, it is rarely thought of as a "procedure." Nonetheless, since the UN Secretariat does invite governments to reply to any communication alleging human rights violations (even a single case), and since government replies are considered by the Working Group on Communications, a government may respond because it may fear that failure to do so could affect its reputation or result in the communication, in combination with other communications, being held over by the Working Group or even transmitted to the Commission. Hence, submitting a case under Resolution 728F may achieve results, even though the procedure is wholly confidential and voluntary.

4. A list of all countries considered under the 1503 procedure is now posted on the OHCHR Website, http://www.unhchr.ch/html/menu2/8/stat1.htm.

5. In general, it is advisable not to spell out in detail the relevant articles of human rights treaties to which the country is a party that may have been vio-

lated, since this could be used as an argument (spurious though it be) to discourage consideration under the 1503 procedure, on the grounds that the treaty's own machinery should be used.

6. Where the material falls within the mandate of one or more of the thematic mechanisms discussed below, it may be useful to request that the relevant parts of the communication also be forwarded to the mechanism(s) concerned.

7. See Appendix C.

8. See Appendix D.

9. NGOs may occasionally submit written country-specific interventions to the Commission on the Status of Women, but oral interventions are uncommon. Moreover, the public proceedings of that Commission neither lend themselves to country-specific discussions, nor do they attract much public attention. Interventions before it will therefore not be further addressed.

10. In 2000, ECOSOC created a Permanent Forum on Indigenous Issues as an advisory body with a mandate to discuss indigenous issues related to economic and social development, culture, the environment, education, health and human rights. NGOs and indigenous representatives may participate in the Forum's annual meetings, which are usually held in New York in May.

11. This summary is based on the provisions of ECOSOC Resolution 1996/31.

12. There are some procedural rules which the Commission announces at each session, for example: "All NGO representatives shall start their oral statements by saying 'I speak on behalf of . . .' and give the name(s) of their respective NGO(s). The speaker takes the floor as a representative of the NGO that accredited him or her. That NGO takes full responsibility for the contents of the statement. All NGOs are encouraged to make written copies of oral statements available to the conference room officers for the précis-writers, interpreters and press officers. Whenever written copies of NGO statements clearly identify the speaker representing the NGO, the Chair will assume that that person will actually deliver the statement." Main rules and practices followed by the Commission on Human Rights in the organization of its work and the conduct of business, UN Doc. E/CN.4/2002/16 (2002).

13. ECOSOC Resolution 1996/31, para. 57(a), provides for the suspension or withdrawal of consultative status "[f an organization, either directly or through its affiliates or representatives acting on its behalf, clearly abuses its status by engaging in a pattern of acts contrary to the purposes and principles of the Charter of the United Nations including unsubstantiated or politically motivated acts against Member States of the United Nations incompatible with those purposes and principles. . . ." This provision has very rarely been used to suspend or terminate status, but it has been invoked to challenge the content of a statement or the legitimacy of the representative delivering it.

14. Guidelines for the application by the Sub-Commission on the Promotion and Protection of Human Rights of the rules of procedure of the functional commissions of the Economic and Social Council and other decisions and practices relating thereto, Sub-Commission Res. 1999/114, Annex, at 18 (2001).

15. The Service's address is 1, rue Varembé, P. O. Box 16, CH-1211 Geneva 20 cic, Switzerland; telephone (41) (22) 733-5123; fax (41) (22) 733-0826, http:// www.ishr.ch/.

16. See Appendix D.

Chapter 5
Human Rights Complaint Procedures of the International Labor Organization

Lee Swepston

The procedures developed by the International Labor Organization (ILO) form part of what may be the most effective and thorough international mechanism for the protection of human rights. These procedures can be used directly only by a government, a trade union or employers' association, or a delegate to the International Labor Conference, and they are thus not directly available to individual complainants. Nevertheless, they are available indirectly and can be of great use to human rights defenders. To learn how to use the ILO procedures, it is necessary first to understand something about the ILO itself and how it works.

ILO Structure

The ILO was established in 1919 by the Treaty of Versailles. It was the only element of the League of Nations to survive the Second World War, and it became the first specialized agency of the United Nations system in 1945.

The tripartite structure of the ILO (governments, employers, and workers) is unique among intergovernmental organizations. It is the only organization in which governments do not have all the votes. The ILO is composed of three organs: (1) the General Conference of representatives of member states (the "International Labor Conference"); (2) the Governing Body; and (3) the International Labor Office. The Conference and the Governing Body are composed half of government representatives and half of representatives of employers and workers of member states. The presence and voting power of these nongovernmental elements give the ILO a unique perspective on the problems before it and offer possibilities for dealing with practical problems facing ILO members.

The ILO and Human Rights

The ILO has a practical, day-to-day involvement in human rights in many fields, going beyond the limited impression one might have from its name. The ILO's competence includes a wide range of rights in addition to those that might be considered purely "labor" issues. The ILO focuses on the human rights that are perhaps most immediately important to most people: to form trade unions; to protection from child labor, forced labor, and discrimination; to safe and healthy working conditions; and to social security. The ILO has adopted conventions which deal with all these subjects and others, including minimum age for work, vocational guidance and training, protection of wages, occupational safety and health, employment of women, migrant workers, indigenous and tribal peoples, and labor administration.

These rights are implemented principally through the adoption and implementation of international labor standards. The ILO adopts conventions and recommendations at the annual International Labor Conference, requires governments to examine whether conventions should be ratified, and closely supervises and criticizes how countries apply the conventions they do choose to ratify. Member states of the ILO may (but are not obliged to) ratify *conventions* adopted by the Conference; if they do ratify, states become legally obligated to comply with the terms of the conventions and to report regularly to the ILO on how they are complying. By the end of 2003, there were over 7,000 ratifications of the 185 ILO conventions.

Recommendations are intended as guidelines for legislation and policies countries may wish to adopt on certain subjects. They are not subject to ratification, and a state thus undertakes no legal obligation to implement them. They often supplement conventions, which are normally less detailed and lay down only minimum standards of performance.

The ILO completed a review of its standards in 2002, concluding that seventy-one conventions are fully up to date but that ratification of many of the older ones should be supplemented by ratifying more recent instruments.

In 1998, the ILO took another important step in protecting human rights, by adopting a *Declaration of Fundamental Rights and Principles at Work* and a follow-up procedure. This Declaration recognizes that all member states—even if they have not ratified the relevant conventions—have an obligation by the very fact of membership to apply certain basic principles arising from the ILO Constitution: freedom of association and the effective recognition of the right to collective bargaining; the effective abolition of child labor and the elimination of all forms of forced or compulsory labor; and the elimination of discrimination in respect of employment and occupation. Under this Declaration, all member states have to report annually if they have not ratified all of the ILO's basic conventions on these subjects, stating what obstacles to ratification exist. The Office draws up an annual Global Report which spells out progress world-wide in one of these four areas on a rotating basis. After each Global Report, the Governing Body adopts or reviews an action program for the implementation of that right. This program, together with the International Program for the Elimination of Child Labor (IPEC) means that the ILO is unique among development agencies in directing over 50 percent of its technical cooperation towards human rights.

Supervision of Ratified Conventions

It is not the existence per se of conventions and recommendations that makes the ILO effective, but rather the fact that their implementation is regularly and systematically monitored. This supervision is carried out mainly by two bodies, the Committee of Experts and the Conference Committee on the Application of Conventions and Recommendations.

The *Committee of Experts on the Application of Conventions and Recommendations* is composed of twenty independent experts on labor law and social problems, from all the major social and economic systems and all parts of the world. It meets annually to examine reports received from governments, which are obligated to report at intervals of between one and five years on how they are applying the conventions they have ratified. Workers' and employers' organizations in countries that have ratified conventions may also submit comments on how conventions are applied in practice, thus offering a valuable supplement to governments' reports.

If the Committee of Experts notes problems in the application of ratified conventions, it may respond in two ways. In most cases it makes "Direct Requests," which are sent directly to governments and to workers' and employers' organizations in the countries concerned. These are not immediately published,[1] and if governments furnish the information or take the measures requested, the matter goes no further. For more serious or persistent problems, the Committee of Experts makes "Observations," which, in addition to being sent to governments, are published as part of the Committee's annual report to the International Labor Conference.

The Committee's comments are as rigorous as the information it possesses allows. As an example, its Observations, which are less frequent and often shorter than Direct Requests, filled more than 700 pages in 2003. The thoroughness of the Committee's analysis and its reputation for independence and objectivity mean that many problems are resolved at the Direct Request stage. Between 1964 and 2003, the Committee identified over 2,500 cases in which governments took the measures requested of them.

The *Conference Committee on the Application of Conventions and Recommendations* is the next level of supervision. Established each year by the International Labor Conference, it reflects the ILO's tripartite structure of governments and of workers' and employers' representatives. On the basis of the report of the Committee of Experts, the Conference Committee selects a number of especially important or persistent cases and requests the governments concerned to appear before it and explain the reasons for the situations commented on by the Committee of Experts. At the end of each session, it reports to the full Conference on the problems governments are encountering in fulfilling their obligations under the ILO Constitution or in complying with conventions they have ratified. The Conference Committee's report is published in the *Proceedings of the International Labor Conference* each year, along with the Conference's discussion of the Committee's report.

The ILO also employs "direct contacts" as an important method of supervising the application of ratified conventions. This means simply that, when a government encounters problems in applying ratified conventions, the International Labor Office, at the request of the government or with its consent, sends an official or individual expert to discuss the problems with the government and help it resolve them. Since its institution in 1969, this system has been highly successful and is often used by governments to resolve problems in order to avoid public criticism.

Although it is not a supervisory function as such, mention should also be made of the ILO's field structure. Almost all of the ILO's sixteen offices in the developing world have specialists in ILO standards to advise, assist in the ratification and application of these standards, and help acquire whatever technical or financial assistance may be necessary to apply them.

Complaint Procedures

The supervisory mechanism described above is generally an effective way of ensuring that ratified conventions are implemented. However, there are also three basic procedures to consider complaints that ILO conventions or basic principles are not being adequately applied, each of which is discussed in detail below. "Representations" under Articles 24, 25, and 26(4) of the ILO Constitution and "complaints" under Articles 26 to 29 and 31 to 34 of the Constitution must concern *ratified* ILO conventions. The third procedure, which deals with freedom of association, is one of the most widely used international complaint procedures for the protection of human rights. Such complaints, alleging violation of the ILO's basic principles on freedom of association, may be filed *whether or not the state concerned has ratified* any ILO conventions on this subject. Table 5.1 indicates the basic requirements of each of the kinds of complaint procedures.

Discussions of the complaint procedures described below are arranged as follows:

a. Substantive requirements: What may the complaint concern? Against what states may it be submitted? Who may submit a complaint?
b. Formal requirements: To whom must it be submitted? Are there special form and language requirements?
c. Means of investigation
d. Kind of decision reached
e. Implementation of the decision

Representations Under Article 24 of the ILO Constitution

Substantive requirements

Under Article 24 of the ILO Constitution, a representation may be filed if a country "has failed to secure in any respect the effective observance within its jurisdiction of any Convention to which it is a party."

A representation thus may be filed only against a state that has ratified the convention concerned. The state must be a member of the ILO or, if it has withdrawn, still be bound by a convention it has ratified. Representations relating to freedom of association issues will normally be referred to the Committee on Freedom of Association (see below). The ratifications of ILO conventions increase each year, so it is impossible to reproduce them all here; a complete list may be obtained directly from the International Labor Office in Geneva or from its website.

A representation may be submitted by "an industrial association of employers or of workers" (Article 24, ILO Constitution), that is, a trade union or an employers' organization. There is no restriction on which "industrial associations" may file representations, and the determination of what constitutes an industrial association is made by the ILO. They may be local or national organizations, or regional or international confederations, and they need have no connection with the subject of the complaint. However, when the ILO Governing Body is deciding how the representation should be handled, a representation may be given more credence if it is received from an organization that has international standing or some connection with the subject of the complaint. The Governing Body lately has insisted that an organization either have some direct link with the events concerned or that it accept responsibility for the representation and not simply act "as a post box."

TABLE 5.1
Quick Guide to ILO Complaints Procedures

Kind of Complaint	Subject	Ratification necessary?	Who begins the procedure?	Who investigates?
Article 24 "Representation"	Any ILO convention	Yes	Any workers' or employers' organization	ILO Governing Body
Article 26 "Complaint"	Any ILO convention	Yes	1. State that has ratified same convention 2. Delegate to the International Labor Conference 3. ILO Governing Body	Commission of Inquiry
Special procedures for freedom of association	Freedom of association	No	1. Workers' or employers' organization concerned 2. ILO bodies, state concerned, ECOSOC	1. Committee on Freedom of Association 2. Fact-Finding and Conciliation Commission

Formal requirements

The representation should be submitted to the Director-General of the International Labor Office in Geneva. The only restrictions as to form are that the representation must be in writing and must refer specifically to Article 24 of the ILO Constitution and to a ratified ILO Convention.

There are no restrictions as to language. The "official" languages of the ILO are English, French, and Spanish, and the "working" languages are these three plus German, Russian, and Chinese. Most widely used languages can be accommodated.

A representation is receivable or admissible if it fulfills the conditions outlined above: it must come from "an industrial association of employers or workers;" it must concern a member state of the ILO; it must refer to a convention ratified by the state against which it is made; and it must allege that the state "has failed to secure in some respect the effective observance within its jurisdiction of the said Convention." A representation can be filed without anything more, but two of the above items may require further substantiation before a representation is receivable.

First, the filing organization should include some proof of its status, unless it is well known. The Governing Body has stated in the past that it alone will determine whether an organization qualifies, whether or not it is an officially registered trade union or employers' association in its own country.

Second, a representation should contain the best-documented and most complete information available to substantiate the alleged violation. A bare allegation alone will engage the procedure, but it will be slowed down unless the Governing Body has enough facts to make an initial assessment of the situation. It may even declare a representation inadmissible if there is no substantiation.

Means of investigation

After a representation has been declared receivable with regard to form, a special Tripartite Committee appointed by the Governing Body from among its members examines the substance of the representation (except for representations on freedom of association, which are referred to the Committee on Freedom of Association). The Committee communicates with the filing organization, asking for any additional information it may wish to submit, and with the government concerned. The government is asked to comment on the allegations and to "make such statement on the subject as it may think fit." When all the information from both parties has been received, or if no reply is received within the time limits set, the Committee makes its recommendations to the Governing Body.

The Governing Body decides whether or not it accepts the government's explanations, if any, of the allegations. If the Governing Body decides in favor of the government, the procedure is closed, and the allegations and replies may be published. If the Governing Body decides that the government's explanations are not satisfactory, it may decide to publish the representation and the government's reply, along with its own discussion of the case—i.e., to give it wider publicity than simply including the case in its records. This was the case, for example, with respect to a 1977 representation by the International Confederation of Free Trade Unions that alleged the nonobservance by Czechoslovakia of the Discrimination (Employment and Occupation) Convention, 1958 (No. 111).

Kind of decision reached

The decision of the Governing Body that it is or is not satisfied with the government's explanations amounts to a finding of violation of or compliance with the Convention. Publication of a finding of violation constitutes the final decision, although it is also possible for the Governing Body to decide that a case should subsequently be handled under the complaint procedure provided for under Article 26 of the ILO Constitution (see next section).

Implementation of the decision

Whether or not the Governing Body decides that it is satisfied with the government's explanations, the questions raised in the representation are normally followed up by the ILO's regular supervisory machinery, i.e., the Committee of Experts and the Conference Committee on the Application of Conventions and Recommendations. Even if the Governing Body is satisfied that there has been no actual violation, these committees may raise questions that they feel require further examination.

Complaints Under Article 26 of the ILO Constitution

Substantive requirements

As with representations, a complaint must be based on the obligations of an ILO convention that the country concerned has ratified. A complaint may be filed against any state which has ratified the relevant convention and which is a member of the ILO. In fact, even if a state has withdrawn from the ILO but still has obligations under a convention it ratified while a member, a complaint may be filed. Complaints concerning freedom of association will normally be referred to the special procedures created for these questions (see below).

Under Article 26, the complaint procedure may be instituted by:

* *Governments.* Any member state of the ILO that has ratified a convention may make a complaint alleging that the convention is being violated by another state party to the convention. The motive of the state that makes a complaint is irrelevant, and there is no requirement that the state filing the complaint, or any of its nationals, should have suffered any direct prejudice. There have been five cases in which governments have complained under this procedure.
* *Delegates to the International Labor Conference.* During a conference session, any delegate to the Conference may file a complaint against a state that has ratified a convention. It is most common for a group of delegates to institute complaints. A recent example was a complaint against Myanmar (Burma) for violations of the Forced Labor Convention, 1930 (No. 29), the report on which was published in August 1998. In 2003, a complaint was filed against Belarus for violation of the freedom of association conventions.
* *The Governing Body* on its own motion. The ILO Governing Body has the power to begin the complaints procedure at any time, and its standing orders provide that it may decide to convert a representation into a complaint at any time. For example, the Governing Body instituted complaint proceedings and established a Commission of Inquiry following the adoption by the Conference of a resolution concerning Chile in 1974. In another case, it began complaint proceedings at the request of the government concerned, following the examination of a representation (Federal Republic of Germany, 1987). Thus, although the Governing Body does not actually submit a complaint, it may launch the procedure.

Formal requirements

A complaint must be submitted to the Director-General of the ILO. There are no formal requirements as to form or language, except for the substantive requirements set forth in the relevant articles of the Constitution: the complaint must originate from a government, Conference delegate, or the Governing Body; it must refer to a present or former member state of the ILO; and it must refer to a convention ratified by the state against which it is made.

To be receivable, a complaint must allege that a country is not "securing the effective observance" of a convention it has ratified. As noted for representations, a complaint should contain as much substantiation as possible.

Means of investigation

When the Governing Body begins to consider a complaint, it forwards the complaint to the government for its comments. It then normally establishes a Commission of Inquiry, although this is technically a matter of discretion.

In one case, creation of a Commission of Inquiry was deferred in order to allow negotiations between the parties under the ILO's auspices. These were successful, and the Commission was never established (Libya, 1986). When a complaint was filed against Nigeria in 1998, establishment of a Commission of Inquiry was deferred because the situation in the country began evolving rapidly after the complaint was filed, and ultimately the Commission was never established. The Governing Body has been debating for several years whether to establish a commission to investigate complaints against Colombia concerning freedom of association.

Commissions of Inquiry are free to set their own rules and procedures, but certain practices have gradually become established. Written submissions are requested from both parties, often at several stages in the procedure, and submissions from each party are usually communicated to the other for information and comments. A Commission also may request information from other governments (under Article 27 of the Constitution) or from nongovernmental organizations. Commissions of Inquiry usually hear representatives of the parties and witnesses presented by them and sometimes summon witnesses themselves. They also have conducted on-site visits to the countries concerned.

Kind of decision reached

Once the taking of evidence is complete, a Commission arrives at conclusions and may make findings and recommendations to the parties (Article 28 of the Constitution). A report of the case is communicated to the ILO Governing Body and published.

A decision states whether or not the situation in a given country is in conformity with the convention. A recommendation may, for example, suggest changes in national legislation or the adoption of practical measures to give effect to a convention's provisions. A recommendation may even address broader questions, such as the necessity of ending a state of emergency in order to promote civil liberties.

Implementation of the decision

A report of a Commission of Inquiry is normally communicated to the Governing Body and to each of the governments concerned and published in the ILO's *Official Bulletin*; it is also published on ILOLEX and made available on the Internet. In most cases, the Committee of Experts and the Conference Committee on the Application of Conventions and Recommendations will continue to examine implementation of the conventions concerned, with reference to the findings of the Commission of Inquiry, as is done in connection with representations.

Under Article 29(2) of the ILO Constitution, any government concerned in a complaint may refer the complaint to the International Court of Justice, if it does not accept the Commission's recommendations. Although this has never occurred, it remains a possibility. The decision of the International Court of Justice in such cases is final, and the Court may affirm, vary, or reverse the findings or recommendations of the Commission of Inquiry.

Article 33 of the ILO Constitution provides that, if a government does not implement the recommendations of a Commission of Inquiry (or the International Court of Justice) within the time specified, "the Governing Body may recommend to the Conference such action as it may deem wise and expedient to secure compliance therewith." This provision was used for the first time against Myanmar to follow up findings of massive forced labor in that country, when the Governing Body requested all governments, international organizations, and employers' and workers' organizations to review their relations with Myanmar. This kind of continued surveillance of the situation has produced some very slow but steady improvements.

Finally, under Article 34 of the ILO Constitution, a government that has been found to be in violation of a convention by a Commission of Inquiry may request the Governing Body to constitute another Commission of Inquiry to verify that the government has complied with the recommendations made to it. This has never been done.

Special Procedures for Complaints Concerning Freedom of Association

The most widely used ILO petition procedure is the special procedure established for complaints concerning violations of freedom of association. This is not specifically provided for in the ILO Constitution but was established in the early 1950s by agreement between the ILO and the UN Economic and Social Council. By 2003, the Committee on Freedom of Association had considered well over 2,000 cases.

There are two bodies that consider complaints in this area. The Governing Body's *Committee on Freedom of Association* (CFA) receives complaints directly from workers' and employers' organizations. The *Fact-Finding and Conciliation Commission on Freedom of Association* (FFCC) may deal with complaints referred to it by the Governing Body on the recommendation of the CFA or by the state concerned. The FFCC may also examine complaints referred to it by ECOSOC against nonmember states of the ILO.

The Committee on Freedom of Association

Substantive requirements

Freedom of association is codified in ILO conventions such as the Freedom of Association and Protection of the Right to Organize Convention, 1948 (No. 87), and the Right to Organize and Collective Bargaining Convention, 1949 (No. 98), as well as a number of other instruments. However, there is no requirement that a state must have ratified these conventions for a complaint to be filed. The basic authority for examination of such complaints lies in the ILO Constitution itself, which consecrates the principle of freedom of association. A complaint may therefore be made against any member of the ILO.

The CFA is guided by this constitutional principle as well as by ILO conventions in this area. It has gradually developed a set of principles supplementing the conventions and the ILO Constitution, which are summarized in a publication entitled *Freedom of Association: Digest of Decisions of the Freedom of Association Committee of the Governing Body of the ILO*, most recently published by the International Labor Office in 1996.

The principle of freedom of association includes, *inter alia:*

- the right of all workers and employers to establish organizations;
- free functioning of such organizations;
- the right to join federations and confederations and to affiliate with international groupings of occupational organizations;
- the right of organizations not to be suspended or dissolved by administrative authorities;
- protection against anti-union discrimination;
- the right to collective bargaining;
- the right to strike; and
- the right to basic civil liberties, which are a necessary precondition to the free exercise of trade union rights.

Complaints may be submitted either by governments or by organizations of employers or workers. A government may submit complaints to the CFA alleging violations by another government, but no government has ever done so. A complainant government would not itself have to have ratified any of the conventions on freedom of association.

Three categories of employers' and workers' organizations may file complaints:

- national organizations directly concerned with the matter;
- international organizations which have consultative status with the ILO; and
- other international organizations without consultative status, if the allegations relate to matters directly affecting their affiliated organizations.

The CFA reserves the right to determine whether an organization filing a complaint is, in fact, an "organization of employers or workers." It has, for instance, decided that a complaint may be receivable even if a government has dissolved the complainant organization, or if the organization making the complaint was not registered or recognized by the government concerned. However, a complaint will not be accepted from bodies with which it is impossible to correspond, either because they have only a temporary address or because the complaint does not contain an address. The Committee may request the complainant organization to furnish additional information about itself, such as its membership, statutes, or affiliations.

Formal requirements

Complaints must be submitted to the Director-General of the ILO in writing, duly signed by a representative of a body entitled to present them and with the address of the complainant organization. They should be as fully supported as possible with evidence of infringement of trade union rights.

A complaint will be receivable if it is from a proper organization of employers or workers, concerns an ILO member, and alleges a violation of the right of freedom of association. Substantiation of an organization's status should be included, as well as all available proof of the violations alleged.

Means of investigation

Once a complaint is received, the Director-General may allow the complainant time to furnish additional evidence of the allegations. The complaint is communicated to the government concerned, which is asked to comment on the substance of the allegations.

It is normally on the basis of the written documentation received from both parties that the CFA makes its decisions. However, the CFA has recently begun to make more frequent use of oral representations by governments and complainants, contacts with governments during the annual Conference, and on-site visits to gather evidence by representatives of the Director-General.

Kind of decision reached

If the CFA finds that no violation has been committed or that the alleged violation has ceased, it simply halts further examination. If it finds that a violation has occurred, it makes recommendations to the parties to correct the situation. For instance, it may recommend to governments that they institute or refrain from certain actions or that they amend existing legislation. The CFA also may make recommendations to the organization which filed the complaint, if it finds that its activities have contributed to the problem.

Implementation of the decision

If the CFA finds that there are problems in guaranteeing freedom of association, it may ask the government concerned to continue reporting to it, or it may refer the case to the Committee of Experts on the Application of Conventions and Recommendations (if the relevant conventions have been ratified). In exceptional cases, the CFA may recommend referral of the case to the FFCC.

The Fact-Finding and Conciliation Commission

The FFCC is an ad hoc body of independent experts appointed by the Governing Body to examine allegations of infringement of freedom of association. It was established in 1951 at the same time as the CFA, and it has become a forum for examining the more serious cases of violations of freedom of association. It has been convened only rarely, but it has been utilized in cases of particular political delicacy.

Substantive requirements

As in the case for complaints before the CFA, cases before the FFCC deal with freedom of association. A complaint may be submitted against any state, whether or not it has ratified the freedom of association conventions or is a member of the ILO. If a state is not a member of the ILO but is a member of the United Nations, a complaint concerning it may be referred to the FFCC by ECOSOC. In all cases, however, *the state concerned must consent* to the referral of the case to the FFCC. The only exception to this rule is when a complaint under Article 26 of the ILO Constitution concerns ratified freedom of association conventions and is referred to the special procedures on this subject.

Cases may be referred to the FFCC in four ways, each of which requires the participation of a government or international body:

- by the Governing Body, on the recommendation of the CFA;
- by the Governing Body, on the recommendation of the International Labor Conference;
- at the request of the government concerned; or
- by the UN Economic and Social Council.

With the consent of the government concerned, ECOSOC can refer allegations against states that are members of the United Nations but not of the ILO. This was done in cases concerning Lesotho and the United States, both of which had been ILO members but which had withdrawn at the time of the complaint. This process was used most recently with respect to South Africa. In all three cases, examination of a case by the FFCC preceded the country's return to the ILO.

Formal requirements

As this procedure is not directly accessible to individuals or NGOs, the formal requirements need not be noted here. Cases referred to the Commission by the CFA are discussed above.

Means of investigation

FFCCs are free to work out their own procedures, but they usually base their investigations on written evidence furnished by the parties, the testimony of witnesses, and visits to the countries concerned. Representatives of the complainant organizations and the governments against which complaints are made are allowed to participate in proceedings before the FFCC.

Kind of decision reached

The mandate of a Commission is to ascertain the facts and to discuss the situation with the governments concerned, with a view to resolving the difficulties by agreement or friendly settlement. In its dual role of investigator and conciliator, it makes a thorough examination of the facts and formulates recommendations designed to provide a common ground for the resolution of a dispute. Once a decision is reached, it is published in a special report.

Recommendations of the FFCC have concerned the direction in which the trade union movement in a country should be allowed or encouraged to develop, legislative proposals, calls for the ratification of ILO conventions, and even recommendations for the restoration of civil liberties that are essential to the exercise of trade union rights. The FFCC also may make recommendations to other parties, such as the trade unions concerned, as it did in a case concerning Japan.

Implementation of the decision

Like most international complaints procedures, no specific enforcement measures are available to ensure that the FFCC's recommendations are implemented. Since a commission is convened to examine a particular case, it does not itself monitor the effect of its recommendations.

However, compliance with FFCC recommendations is monitored by other ILO bodies. If the country concerned has ratified one of the ILO conventions on freedom of association, the regular supervisory bodies continue to examine the effect given to FFCC recommendations and may refer to the FFCC's conclusions in subsequent comments. The situation also may be followed by the Conference Committee on the Application of Conventions and Recommendations, by the International Labor Conference in plenary session, and by the Governing Body. If the relevant conventions have not been ratified, FFCC recommendations are followed up by the CFA.

Concluding Observations

The procedures outlined above form part of the most comprehensive international system for examining the implementation of international human rights standards. With the exception of the procedures for examining complaints by the Governing Body's CFA, they have not been widely used, although the frequency of complaints has accelerated in recent years, especially representations under Article 24 of the Constitution. Does this mean that they are not effective? The author's experience with the ILO leads him to conclude that, in fact, they have a considerable effect.

If these procedures are used relatively infrequently, it is because they are but one part of a comprehensive and active system of regular supervision. Thus, a situation which violates internationally recognized labor standards rarely reaches the stage that would provoke a complaint; before then, it is dealt with by the Committee of Experts or the Conference which, in turn, may lead to more direct ILO intervention, such as advisory missions and/or technical assistance to resolve problems.

When complaints are filed, however, they signal to the government concerned that the ILO intends to undertake a thorough, objective, and prompt examination of the situation and reach firm and public conclusions on the merits of the case. It is rare, indeed, that governments do not cooperate fully in the ILO's investigations in such cases. Even if a government does not implement the ILO's conclusions immediately, laws and practices may be adopted in the longer term that closely follow the recommendations made. In the recent case of Myanmar and forced labor, the ILO is the only international organization which has been able to establish a human rights monitoring presence in the country, and the threat of further measures has induced the government to cooperate, albeit reluctantly.

The case should not be overstated. Complaints do not invariably result in improvements, and there are sometimes gaps in the information available to the ILO. Situations may arise in which a government feels that it faces such serious internal difficulties that it must postpone taking measures to fulfill its international human rights obligations. Even in such cases, however, the ILO continues to work with the government to attempt to implement the recommendations that result from the examination of a complaint.

Above all, it should be noted that the complaint procedures would not be nearly as effective if they did not form part of the ILO's overall machinery for supervising the implementation of ILO principles and instruments. It is not easy for human rights NGOs to gain access to the ILO machinery, except with the cooperation of trade unions, though they can make an active contribution to the investigations (as in the cases of Myanmar and Haiti). However, NGOs should be aware of the ILO's work in the field of human rights as a valuable source of information and as a defender and promoter of human rights on a daily, working level.

Notes

1. They are made public about a year later in the ILO's data base on standards and supervision, ILOLEX, which is available on-line at http://www.ilo.org, under "International Labour Standards and Human Rights." All other supervisory comments are also published in this manner.

Chapter 6
The Complaint Procedure of the United Nations Educational, Scientific and Cultural Organization

Stephen P. Marks

Introduction

The United Nations Educational, Scientific and Cultural Organization (UNESCO) has included human rights within its mandate since its creation in 1945. Although UNESCO is probably best known for its promotion of teaching and research on human rights, most of the normative instruments (conventions, recommendations, and declarations) adopted by the organization concern human rights. These instruments and UNESCO's constitution provide for reporting procedures and special implementation procedures for certain instruments, such as the appointment of commissioners for cultural property under the 1954 Convention for the Protection of Cultural Property in the Event of Armed Conflict or the Joint ILO/UNESCO Committee of Experts on the Application of the Recommendation concerning technical and Vocational Education, but none of these mechanisms includes a right of individual petition.[1]

The only complaint procedure available to individuals and NGOs is the one described in this chapter. The UNESCO Executive Board adopted this procedure in 1978 in Decision 104 EX/3.3 of the Board [hereinafter "the Decision"]. There are, however, some precedents. In 1952, the Executive Board decided that its chairman could examine communications alleging violations of human rights and submit to the Board those which seemed to call for some action by the organization.[2] Although this decision had the potential to evolve into a procedure for considering complaints, it was never utilized.

It was not until fifteen years later, in 1967, that the Board adopted a rudimentary procedure for considering complaints modeled on and expressly referring to ECOSOC Resolution 728F.[3] Under this procedure, a communication received by the Secretariat was transmitted to the Committee on Conventions and Recommendations in Education (composed of government representatives and formerly called the "Special Committee on Discrimination in Education") if it was found (a) to be addressed to UNESCO by an identifiable author and was not a copy of a communication addressed elsewhere; (b) to concern a specific case of an identifiable victim or victims; (c) to involve human rights; and (d) to relate to UNESCO's fields of competence.

If these conditions were not fulfilled, the author was simply notified that note had been taken of the communication. If the conditions were met, the author was asked if there were any objection to divulging his or her name (or that of the organization submitting the complaint) and transmitting the communication to the government concerned. If there was no objection, which was not always the case, the communication was sent to the government, which was invited to reply. The communication and any reply from the government were transmitted to the Committee, which met in private, reviewed the complaint, and permitted oral statements by the government concerned. The Committee reported on its activities to the full Executive Board, although it did not normally provide details about the cases examined.

The only exception to the confidential nature of this procedure was the case of Chile, during the military dictatorship of Augusto Pinochet. The Board publicly endorsed the conclusions of the Committee's report in 1976 and expressed its "profound disquiet at the continuing infringements, according to the information received, of human rights in the fields of education, science, culture and information."[4] The Board renewed its appeal to the Chilean authorities to take all necessary measures to restore and safeguard human rights and decided that the Committee should continue its examination of appropriate communications. This public decision was highly unusual and reflected a unique political situation, rather than an advance in implementing Decision 77 EX/8.3.

Soon thereafter, the General Conference of UNESCO invited the Director-General and the Executive Board to study ways in which the procedure might be made more effective. This study resulted in the adoption by the Board of Decision 104 EX/3.3 in 1978, which is still applied today.

Handling of Complaints Under the 1978 Procedure

The 1978 procedure permits a victim or anyone with reliable knowledge about a violation to submit either individualized cases or general questions of human rights violations to UNESCO. It is likely that the individual cases will be examined, but it is virtually certain that general questions of systematic violations will not be taken up, as discussed below.

At a minimum, the procedure makes the concerned government aware that the allegations are known outside the country. At best, the procedure may generate sufficient diplomatic or humanitarian pressure to obtain some form of redress.

Most of the communications have concerned release of detained persons before completion of their sentence, authorization to return to their country from exile, or permission to resume employment or other activity. It is unlikely that the UNESCO complaint procedure was the sole or principal reason for the satisfactory outcome of most of these cases, which was often due to a change of regime or other internal factors. However, scrutiny under this procedure contributes to international pressure and in some cases may tip the balance in favor of a positive outcome.

No rules govern the form of communications; they are normally in the form of letters addressed to the Director of the Office of International Standards and Legal Affairs of UNESCO. As long as the author is identifiable and the communication refers to a human rights violation, it will usually be handled in accordance with the procedure outlined in this chapter. The initial letter to UNESCO is not considered to be the "communication" formally examined by UNESCO. Rather, each letter received is acknowledged by the Office of International Standards and Legal Affairs, which assigns a number to the communication and sends the author a UNESCO-prepared form on which information relevant to the complaint must be entered. It also is possible to make a copy of the form and attach the completed form to the initial letter.

The form requests information as to the author's name, nationality, and address; the relationship of the author to the alleged victim; factual information, including the connection between the violation and education, science, culture, or information; and any attempts to exhaust domestic remedies.[5] The form must be signed and returned, with the agreement that it will be transmitted to the government concerned and the name of the author divulged. It is only after the return of this form to UNESCO that a "communication" is formally deemed to exist and a copy is sent to the accused government.

All correspondence between UNESCO and a concerned government is addressed to the government's permanent delegation to UNESCO; in practice, a communication is delivered by hand to the delegation. The letter of transmittal explains that the communication will be brought to the notice of the Committee on Conventions and Recommendations ("the Committee" or "CR") at its next session, together with any reply the government may wish to make. In an emergency, however, the Committee will consider "a communication submitted urgently on account of the seriousness of the matter," even without return of the UNESCO form. Subject to review by the President of the Committee, the Secretariat will not transmit communications not related to UNESCO's competence, manifestly ill-founded, or whose author is mentally unbalanced. It may also exclude portions of a communication that do not relate to UNESCO.

After giving the government at least three months to reply, the communication is placed on the Committee's agenda. Authors should submit communications at least fourteen weeks in advance of scheduled CR meetings to allow the Secretariat sufficient time to process them and send them to the government. The three-month rule may be dispensed with in urgent cases, and the Committee may determine what is a reasonable amount of time for the government to reply.

A summary of each communication is prepared by the Secretariat, giving the communication's procedural status, the identity of the author, the essential elements of the claim, any recourse attempted, and the purpose of the communication. Copies of significant correspondence, including the UNESCO form and any government reply, are part of the confidential dossier given to each Committee member prior to the CR meetings, which take place twice a year, usually during the Executive Board's sessions in April-May and September-October. Special sessions are also possible. All documents and the meetings of the CR, as well as its report on the handling of communications, are confidential, a practice that activists and scholars have severely criticized.

Formal Requirements for Admissibility

The Committee's first task with respect to a new communication is to determine whether it meets all ten conditions for admissibility set out in paragraph 14(a) of Decision 104 EX/3.3. In theory, these are preliminary requirements to enable the Committee to limit its examination on the merits to serious communications and avoid wasting its time on frivolous complaints. In practice, some of the conditions are indeed preliminary, while others engage the Committee prematurely in the substance of the claim.[6]

The conditions contained in sub-paragraphs (i) and (vi)–(x) of paragraph 14(a) of the Decision refer essentially to formal requirements. The condition in sub-paragraph (i) is that the communication *not be anonymous*, which has not been a problem. Sub-paragraph (vi) allows the Committee to declare inadmissible any communication that is "*offensive or an abuse of the right to submit communications.*" This condition is interpreted as referring to attacks against a state's basic social structure or constitution. The Committee can consider the communication "if it meets all other criteria on admissibility, after the exclusion of the offensive or abusive parts," but it does so only after the author submits an amended communication. This may result in a delay of six months until the next session.

Sub-paragraph (vii) requires that a communication "must not be based exclusively on *information disseminated through the mass media.*" This would not seem to exclude press reports as important sources of information, although the credibility of the author may be challenged by a state if these sources are relied on too heavily.

The requirement that a communication must be submitted within a "*reasonable time limit following the facts*" (sub-paragraph 14(a)(viii)) is interpreted according to the circumstances. In practice, this time limit is not considered to run while a victim or organization is endeavoring to obtain redress through domestic or other international channels.

Sub-paragraph (ix) refers to *exhaustion of local remedies,* but the requirement is not one of *prior* exhaustion of those remedies; rather, the author must only "indicate whether an attempt has been made to exhaust" them. The wording of this condition gives the CR considerable flexibility and avoids a detailed examination of local procedures. While in theory an author might merely state that no attempt to exhaust local remedies has been made and thereby attempt to meet the requirement, the Committee is unlikely to admit a communication if it appears that UNESCO is the first or only forum to which the author is appealing. Where local judicial or administrative remedies have been explored without success, this fact should be mentioned in the communication. However, the CR has also indicated to an author that, "should he fail to seek administrative or judicial redress in the country concerned, notwithstanding having been informed of this by the Committee, it would strike the communication from its list *ipso facto* at its next session."[7]

The final formal condition is similar to a rule of *lis pendens.* Sub-paragraph (x) allows the Committee to declare inadmissible any communication that *has been settled, whether under municipal law or international human rights procedures,* as long as the Committee is satisfied that the principles of human rights have been respected in the settlement. For example, the Committee requires confirmation that the alleged victim has been authorized to return to his or her country before removing the case from its agenda. Although the Secretariat requests information from other international organizations on the status of any communication being handled simultaneously by another institution, the fact that the case is before another body is not in itself a cause for inadmissibility.

Substantive Requirements

Most communications declared inadmissible by the Committee fail to meet the substantive conditions set out in sub-paragraphs (ii)–(v) of paragraph 14(a), although the procedure does not itself distinguish between "formal" and "substantive" conditions. The distinction is made here because, in effect, examination of the merits actually begins during the admissibility phase, due to the nature of some of these conditions and the CR's unwillingness to treat the admissibility criteria as originally intended. This "lack of distinction between the two phases has caused the unwarranted rejection of cases and, more commonly, lengthy delays in the consideration of cases."[8] The CR decided more recently to give the government three months to contest admissibility, failing which it would decide on admissibility at its next meeting.

Conditions regarding who may submit a communication are set out in sub-paragraph (ii). A communication must originate "from a person or group of persons who, it can he reasonably presumed, are *victims of alleged violations*," or from "*any person, group of persons or nongovernmental organization having reliable knowledge of these violations.*" There is no definitive interpretation of what constitutes "reliable" knowledge, and the CR has agreed to apply the presumption of good faith in considering whether the author has "reliable knowledge." As already mentioned, a communication must not be based exclusively on information disseminated through the mass media. It is not necessary to demonstrate a connection between the person or organization filing the communication and the alleged victim.

A communication must concern "*human rights falling within UNESCO's competence* in the fields of education, science, culture and information" (sub-paragraph (iii)). There can be no doubt that this formulation includes each of the four rights explicitly mentioning the enumerated fields of competence:

- the right to education;
- the right to share in scientific advancement;
- the right to participate freely in cultural life; and
- the right to information, including freedom of conscience and expression.

Seven other rights are so closely related to the former that they have been included in the interpretation of this sub-paragraph:

- the right to freedom of thought, conscience, and religion;
- the right to seek, receive, and impart information through any media regardless of frontiers;
- the right to protection of the moral and material interests resulting from any scientific, literary, or artistic production;
- the right to freedom of assembly and association for the purposes of activities connected with education, science, culture, and information;
- freedom of movement, when related to activities coming within UNESCO's fields of competence;

- freedom to emigrate, if the profession of the alleged victim falls within UNESCO's fields of competence; and
- the right of children to special protection, insofar as it concerns their education and access to culture and information.

Finally, two collective rights may be relevant, since they both have a cultural dimension:

- the rights of minorities to enjoy their own culture, to profess and practice their own religion, and to use their own language; and
- the right of peoples to self-determination, including the right to pursue cultural development.

Of these thirteen rights, all of which are part of the International Bill of Human Rights, only the first eight have been specifically recognized in official UNESCO documents, the organization's website, and on the form letter sent to complainants. However, all but the right to self-determination have been mentioned in statements by UNESCO before the UN Human Rights Committee or in interpretations by the Committee on Conventions and Recommendations.

The Committee defines these rights according to the International Bill of Human Rights.[9] Authors of communications also should refer, where appropriate, to UNESCO's own normative instruments dealing with human rights, although these are not frequently cited in communications received by UNESCO. The latter would include, *inter alia*, the Convention on the Protection of Cultural Property in The Event of Armed Conflict; the Universal Copyright Convention; the Convention against Discrimination in Education; the Convention on the Means of Prohibiting and Preventing the Illicit Import, Export, and Transfer of Ownership of Cultural Property; the Convention on Technical and Vocational Education; various conventions on the recognition of educational degrees and qualifications; and recommendations and declarations concerning the status of teachers, scientific researchers, and artists; access to culture; race and racial prejudice; and the media.[10]

A complex issue falling between the questions of *what* may be complained about and *who* may submit a complaint concerns the status of the alleged victim. A connection may be presumed if the victim's professional activity falls within the fields of UNESCO's competence, although the Committee may decide that there is not a sufficient link between the right alleged to be violated and the UNESCO-related activity of the victim. For example, a teacher, scientist, writer, musician, or journalist who has been arbitrarily detained or denied the right to emigrate could complain that he or she is being prevented from exercising rights relating to education, science, culture, or information. The Committee may agree, but it might also conclude that the specific right in question, the right to leave one's country, is not a UNESCO right.

The final clause of sub-paragraph (iii), requiring that the communication "*must not be motivated exclusively by other considerations*," suggests that a politically active victim with only the remotest link to UNESCO's concerns may lead the CR to decide that the motivation is "exclusively" other than human rights. The Committee has warned that the presumption of a link with UNESCO's fields of competence is insufficient to justify UNESCO's intervention: "It counts only for the admissibility of the communication. UNESCO's competence is then determined *rationae personae*, according to the status of the alleged victim. Whenever there has been uncertainty as to that status, the alleged victim has always been given the benefit of the doubt."[11]

To the extent that humanitarian considerations prevail over political factors, the CR may be expected to accept such an inclusive interpretation; it has done so in cases of students and teachers who were involuntarily "disappeared," especially in South America during the 1970s.[12] Where the profession is unrelated to UNESCO's fields of competence, such as a manual laborer who has written articles, the activity of the alleged victim is the determining factor for admissibility.

To avoid a decision of inadmissibility because a non-UNESCO right is invoked, authors should stress the relevance of the profession or activity of the alleged victim to UNESCO's competence.

The requirement that communications not be motivated exclusively by non-human-rights considerations, taken literally, would only exclude communications that had nothing but political (or similar) motivations. However, the fact that the author is from a country or organization hostile in some way to the state concerned is usually enough for the representative of that state to claim that the only motivation is political. Authors should therefore avoid characterizing the government concerned and focus instead on facts and legal analysis.

The condition of sub-paragraph (iv)— *compatibility with the principles of UNESCO, the UN Charter, and other basic human rights instruments*—does not appear to be difficult to meet if condition (iii) is fulfilled. It allows the CR to declare inadmissible a communication that, for example, calls for the use of force contrary to the UN Charter or measures contrary to human rights. During states of emergency, one would expect that, where the emergency has been officially proclaimed and measures derogating from rights have been duly notified to the Secretary-General (as required by Article 4 of the Covenant on Civil and Political Rights), the CR would consider the alleged violations of human rights in UNESCO's fields of competence in light of this article. However, the Committee has simply commented that "it is not required to consider communications relating to such situations."[13] Because of the potential confusion created by such language, authors of communications to UNESCO relating to declared states of emergency should take care to explain that the CR *is* required to consider communications to the extent that the rights in question have not been properly suspended in accordance with the interpretation of Article 4.[14]

Sub-paragraph (v) requires that the communication "must appear to *contain relevant evidence*" and "must *not be manifestly ill-founded.*" Taken literally, the first element does not require that any evidence be produced (at least at the preliminary stage of admissibility), only that the matter be presented in such a way that the Committee can expect to examine some evidence at the merits phase of the case. In practice, many accused states assert that a communication is manifestly ill-founded, implying that the state rejects the allegations on the merits and wants the case dismissed immediately. The Committee may accept such assertions without giving the author a chance to rebut the government, and the author may learn of the government's denial of the allegations only when informed that the communication has been declared inadmissible. The Committee has explicitly stated that the Secretariat is "not empowered to transmit [information supplied by the government] upon receiving it" but must wait until the CR has seen it, and then it may transmit it to the author in summary form. Nevertheless, the CR has generally transmitted to the author a record of the discussion of the communication. The important point is that communications that contain only cursory evidence of the allegations, although technically sufficient under sub-paragraph (v), may be declared inadmissible if the government presents detailed counter-evidence to the CR; the author will have no opportunity to rebut the government's evidence.

There is no procedure to appeal or reopen a case, although the author may present "new facts" or an amended communication in subsequent correspondence that the CR may consider as a new communication. This is a roundabout way of overcoming the Committee's tendency to accept assertions by a government and close the case, and it may be worth pursuing when the author has strong evidence that a government has misled the CR.

In theory, the prohibition of "manifestly ill-founded" communications should only bar communications that are obviously outside the scope of the procedure, owing either to a misunderstanding of the rights protected or clearly unsubstantiated allegations. In order to reexamine a communication declared inadmissible on the basis of "new facts," which presumably would include the author's refutation of the government's assertions on which an inadmissibility decision may have been based, the

Secretariat requires the author to fill out a new form and thereby institute a new communication.

A communication should provide the fullest documentation possible, even if, for practical reasons, only a summary will be provided to the CR. It is also helpful to furnish a summary of complex communications, incorporating by reference essential documents annexed to the communication. It should also be noted the CR does not consider potential violations, such as an expected criminal prosecution against a person who wishes to return to his or her country; there must be reliable evidence that the authorities intend to carry out the challenged acts.

A communication may be filed *against any country*. The necessary dialogue with a government would be difficult if the accused country is not a member of UNESCO, but in the past two nonmember states have responded to allegations and participated in CR meetings to answer questions.

Once the Committee is satisfied that the conditions of paragraph 14(a) have been met, a communication is normally declared admissible and the merits considered at the next session. Unlike the "1503 procedure" discussed in chapter 4, the Committee notifies both the author and the government of its decision on admissibility, and this element of transparency clearly appeals to authors of communications. Decisions on admissibility are considered final.

Means of Investigation and Conciliation

As mentioned above, the distinction between the admissibility and merits phases is not strictly adhered to in practice, and the Committee's effort to gather information and reach an amicable solution through cooperation with the concerned government begins with the examination of admissibility and continues throughout the procedure. As is the case in most international investigative procedures, much of the work of analyzing and summarizing the information contained in a communication is done by the Secretariat.

The procedure also provides a direct role for the Director-General of UNESCO. This role, set forth in paragraphs 8 and 9 of the Decision, is often referred to as "humanitarian intercession," and includes "initiating consultations, in conditions of mutual respect, confidence and confidentiality, to help reach solutions to particular problems concerning human rights." Thus, even before a communication is transmitted to the government concerned, the Director-General may consider that it justifies intercession.

While intervening in any way in the internal affairs of member states is expressly prohibited by UNESCO's constitution, the Director-General can draw the attention of a country to a specific human rights problem and seek, confidentially, to obtain a satisfactory solution. Solutions reached in this way, which are not unusual, are naturally preferable to awaiting the outcome of the procedure before the CR.

In addition to initiatives taken by the Director-General, specific measures may be proposed by the CR through the Executive Board. For example, the Executive Board has asked the Director-General to help reach an amicable solution through direct confidential consultations with the government concerned, appeals for clemency, and requests to other international bodies for assistance, particularly financial. During the 2002–2003 biennium, for example, the Executive Board reported, "[i]n line with its humanitarian mission, the Committee requested the Director-General to make representations to the highest authorities of the States concerned on behalf of the alleged victims. The Director-General duly sent letters to them to express concern at the state of the alleged victims' health or to ask that they be given proper medical treatment."[15]

The government concerned is permitted under paragraph 14(e) of the Decision to attend the Committee's meetings "in order to provide additional information or to answer questions from members of the Committee on either admissibility or the merits of the communication." There is also a theoretical possibility that the author of the communication or other witnesses may appear before the Committee. Paragraph 14(g) of the Decision allows the CR "in exceptional circumstances" to seek authorization from the Board to hear "other qualified persons," a provision inserted to open the possibility of allowing the victim or his or her representative to testify. The Committee has not yet taken advantage of this provision, and authors should not expect the CR to use this possibility.

A preambular paragraph of Decision 104 EX/3.3 states that "UNESCO should not play the role of an international judicial body," and the most characteristic feature of the merits phase of the procedure is the search for a dialogue with the government. As long as the government is cooperative, the CR is willing to be patient. Although the Secretariat tends to downplay the quasi-judicial function of the Committee, there is no legal obstacle to the CR finding a violation. However, the Committee does not reach explicit decisions on the merits of many communications and tends to recommend humanitarian measures to redress the situation. All too often, the CR accepts the government's version of disputed facts, rather than deferring its decision on the merits.

The Committee submits confidential reports to the Executive Board at each session, pursuant to paragraph 15 of the Decision. These reports are to contain "appropriate information arising from its examination of the communications which the Committee considers useful to bring to the notice of the Executive Board . . . [as well as] recommendations which the Committee may wish to make either generally or regarding the disposition of a communication under consideration."[16] This provision was intended to allow the functional equivalent of the concluding observations and general comments that may be adopted by the treaty bodies,[17] but the CR has not availed itself of this possibility.

The CR reports on each communication examined at the session, whether it has been declared admissible or not. A report usually includes a brief summary of the facts and the state of the procedure, the views expressed by members of the Committee and by the government concerned, and the decision reached by the Committee. A communication may be admissible, inadmissible, suspended (for further information), or postponed (due to practical or technical considerations). Once the CR deems a communication to be admissible, it may request further information from the government concerned and/or the author of the communication or recommend some other action. It can, for example, request the Executive Board to invite the Director-General to address an appeal to a government for clemency or the release of a detainee.

The outcome on the merits avoids a finding that there has or has not been a violation of human rights. Admittedly, the 1978 procedure notes that UNESCO "should not play the role of an international judicial body" and stipulates, "communications which warrant further consideration shall be acted upon by the Committee with a view to helping to bring about a friendly solution designed to advance the promotion of the human rights falling within Unesco's fields of competence." This is also the approach of many other human rights bodies, which seek friendly solutions when possible as opposed to delivering legal judgments. Unlike the early years of the UNESCO procedure, the Secretariat now stresses to states that the procedure should not result in finding a violation. A recent document noted, "[E]verything has always been done to avoid reaching the conclusion that a State has violated human rights. Such a conclusion would in fact mean a deadlock, preventing the continued search for a solution."[18] The finding of a violation thus remains only a theoretical possibility.

The Board examines the CR report in closed meetings. Members of the Board express their views on the content of the report, and then the Board "takes note" of the report. When the report contains recommendations for action, the record normally shows that the Board has endorsed the wishes of the Committee. Unfortunately, the public record is vague in reporting the Committee's recommendations, and specific countries are not mentioned.

"Cases" and "Questions"

Paragraph 10 of Decision 104 EX/3.3 distinguishes between UNESCO's competence in specific individual "cases" and "questions of massive, systematic, or flagrant violations of human rights which result either from a policy contrary to human rights applied *de jure* or *de facto* by a State or from an accumulation of individual cases forming a consistent pattern." Paragraph 18 further defines such "questions" as including, but not limited to, aggression, interference in internal affairs, foreign occupation, colonialism, genocide, apartheid, racism, and "national and social oppression."

This dual mandate resulted from a compromise among the government delegates who negotiated the Decision in a decidedly Cold War climate. The Soviet Union and its allies felt that only large-scale violations of human rights should be considered, while Western and pro-human-rights developing countries felt that UNESCO should be authorized to respond to individual cases. The former group saw the Decision as an opportunity to allow situations such as Chile under Pinochet, the apartheid regime in South Africa, and Israeli-occupied Palestine to be criticized publicly and be the subject of resolutions adopted by the Executive Board and the General Conference. Western countries wanted individual cases like those of Soviet dissidents and refuseniks to receive redress. The Secretariat and several governments wanted an effective procedure that would build on the precedents that were then emerging from regional human rights bodies and the United Nations. The result was a compromise allowing proponents of all three views to believe they had carried the day.

The essential procedural difference between a "case" and a "question" is that the latter is considered in public by both the Executive Board and, ultimately, the General Conference of UNESCO. If the Committee forwards a question to the Executive Board, the question "should be considered by the Executive Board and the General Conference in public meetings" (paragraph 18). From the beginning of the procedure, however, the Secretariat, the Executive Board, and the Committee have been extremely cautious about considering "questions." The CR adopted a set of rules for considering "questions" which essentially provides that the Committee will determine the existence of a "question" only after a full examination of merits and only as a last resort, if a friendly settlement cannot be reached. In over twenty-five years and after numerous "questions" have been submitted to it, the CR has yet to send "questions" to the Board. Instead, it requires the author to divide the communication into a series of individual cases.

It is unfortunate that the excessive prudence the CR developed in the Cold War atmosphere of the 1980s continues to prevent it from bringing to public attention behavior that makes a mockery of UNESCO's constitution. Until the CR applies the procedure as intended, authors wishing to have a general situation of systematic violation of human rights examined would do well to present it in the form of a series of individual cases.

Concluding Observations

The UNESCO procedure has almost fallen into disuse, although the Secretariat reports some modest results in recent years. According to UNESCO's statistics, the Committee considered 508 communications from 1978 to September 2003, of which 315 were deemed to have been settled.[19] Only forty-eight cases were considered between October 1997 and September 2003, and forty-one cases were considered to have been settled during that period. The average number of cases considered annually over the twenty-five-year existence of the Decision is only twenty; over the last five years, the annual average has fallen to only eight cases considered and 9.6 listed as settled.

One explanation for this situation is that NGOs and the broader public are not adequately informed how to use the procedure effectively. Numerous NGOs have given up on the procedure, and representatives of victims are often unaware of the possibility of appealing to UNESCO. Although information about the procedure does appear on the UNESCO website, it is difficult to find. The fact that the number of communications examined remains small and is even declining suggests that the procedure is not responsive to the needs of victims of human rights violations in UNESCO's fields of competence, although individual complainants may find the procedure helpful in resolving their own cases.

In 2003, the Secretariat proposed to engage in "awareness-raising on the work of the CR Committee in human rights protection, especially among NGOs, human rights activists and other civil society actors" and listed as an expected outcome "more effective reporting and monitoring procedures."[20] Wider use of the procedure would place additional burdens on the small Secretariat staff and the CR, whose mandate was expanded in 2003 to "consider all questions entrusted to the Executive Board concerning the implementation of UNESCO's standard-setting instruments."[21] Of course, a drastic increase in the number of communications examined by the CR at each session would not necessarily be a positive development. It would overtax the Secretariat's resources and might frighten many states to the point where they might seek to dismantle the procedure. However, in the medium term, there is room for at least a doubling of the number of communications examined, which will only occur if there is increased interest by NGOs and wider public awareness of the procedure.

The confidential nature of the UNESCO procedure, its emphasis on friendly settlement, and the lack of strong investigatory or oversight mechanisms suggest that the procedure is relatively weak compared to some of those established by the ILO, the UN Commission on Human Rights, or regional organizations. However, the procedure has some advantages over other international human rights machinery, at least theoretically. It is open to almost any individual or group to complain against any state, and the rule of exhaustion of domestic remedies is less stringent than under other international procedures. Confidentiality is less complete than that imposed by ECOSOC Resolution 1503, since authors are informed of UNESCO's decisions, and there is a theoretical possibility of hearing witnesses and making reports public. The procedure encompasses both individual cases and large scale violations, again, at least in theory. The Committee's role in friendly settlement provides an indirect means for the complainant to seek redress.

Unfortunately, the procedure seems to be growing weaker and to be taken less seriously by states and NGOs, in large part because these comparative advantages on paper are not put into practice. To its credit, the Secretariat has recognized the failures of the reporting procedure to monitor the implementation of UNESCO's standard-setting instruments and proposed that the CR "be recognized as competent to receive and examine communications from individuals or groups of individuals who may reasonably be presumed to be victims of an alleged violation of one of the norms under a convention or recommendation whose follow-up is entrusted to the Executive Board."[22] However, expanding the mandate in this way should not jeopardize the CR's capacity to take on many more complaints under the 1978 procedure.

The time has come to press for the application of the investigatory capacity of the Secretariat and the CR.[23] The Committee can seek authorization to hear witnesses. It can make certain reports public. It can find violations without crossing the line of acting like an international tribunal. It can present questions to the Board for public consideration, when publicity will serve the interests of human rights better than confidentiality and quiet diplomacy; this has happened with respect to two situations in recent years.

The Committee also could embark upon the road of reform and seek Executive Board approval to reduce the number of its members and select them in their personal capacity, so they can act more as experts than as a political body; create a sub-committee to consider admissibility between regular sessions of the Committee as originally intended, rather than delving prematurely into the merits; respond to emergency situations; send fact-finding or conciliation teams to countries where violations are alleged to have taken place; and publicize more than the bare statistics related to its deliberations. The most significant improvement might be to entrust a body that meets more often than every six months with authority to adopt provisional measures in emergency cases and decide on admissibility. The whole Committee would then be able to focus on the merits of cases before it and concentrate on reaching a satisfactory resolution of the situation, in cooperation with the government.

Violations of human rights within UNESCO's fields of competence have not diminished in the twenty-five years since the UNESCO procedure was created. Journalists, editors, artists, writers, performers, and intellectuals are prevented from freely expressing their talents throughout the world. Lack of access to education, discrimination in education, and education not aimed at the full development of the human personality and potential are pervasive. Participation in cultural life and in the benefits of science is unknown to millions of people. People everywhere suffer denials of academic freedom and freedom to assemble and associate for purposes related to education, science, culture, or communication. Many wars and ethnic conflicts are spawned by the denial of freedom of religion and cultural or linguistic expression and identity.

UNESCO's procedure for handling communications alleging violation of human rights in its fields of competence holds the promise of contributing meaningfully to the resolution of such issues on the basis of human rights norms. Unfortunately, that promise has yet to be fulfilled. With the return of the United States to UNESCO in 2003, one may expect many program and staffing changes, although it is uncertain what impact this will have on the human rights procedure. If there is a new climate of cooperation and more governments acknowledge the value of international scrutiny of human rights practices, then some important improvements might be made to toward enhancing the relevance and effectiveness of the procedure.

Notes

1. There is an interstate complaint procedure under the Convention on Discrimination in Education, but it has never been invoked On these implementation procedures, see Stephen P. Marks, "Education, Science, Culture and Information," in Oscar Schachter and Christopher C. Joyner (eds.), 2 *United Nations Legal Order* 620–625 (Cambridge: Cambridge Univ. Press, 1995).

2. UNESCO Doc 30 EX/Decision 11 (1952).

3. UNESCO Doc 77 EX/Decision 8.3 (1977). ECOSOC Res. 728F is discussed briefly in chapter 4.

4. UNESCO Doc 99 EX/Decision 9.5 (1976).

5. The form is reproduced in UNESCO, The Executive Board of UNESCO (2002), at 67–69 and may be downloaded in PDF format from UNESCO's website at http://portalunesco.org/en/ev.php@URL_ID=17501&URL_DO=DO_TOPIC&URL_SECTION=201.html.

6. The Secretariat has acknowledged that "[i]t is not uncommon, during consideration of a communication's admissibility, for the Committee to examine its substance" UNESCO Doc. 169 EX/CR/2 (2004), para. 23.

7. UNESCO Doc 154 EX/16 (24 Feb. 1998), Annex I, at 5, para. 14. This document offers a fuller explanation of the meaning of the Decision's text.

8. David Weissbrodt and Rose Farley, "The UNESCO Human Rights Procedure: An Evaluation," 16 *Hum Rts. Q.* 391–414 (1994), at 398.

9. The International Bill of Human Rights consists of the Universal Declaration of Human Rights; Covenant on Civil and Political Rights; and Covenant on Economic, Social and Cultural Rights

10. These instruments are merely illustrative The full texts of normative UNESCO instruments, which potentially offer considerable support for communications, may be found in UNESCO, *UNESCO's Standard-Setting Instruments* (Paris: UNESCO, 1981, as supplemented), and on the UNESCO Website at http://portal.unesco.org/en/ev.php-URL_ID=12024&URL_DO=DO_TOPIC&URL_SECTION=-201.html. A discussion of these texts may be found in Marks, *supra* note 1.

11. UNESCO Doc 154 EX/16, Annex I, at 1.

12. A special procedure to deal with "disappearances" was adopted in 1979, although it fell into disuse after the creation by the UN Commission on Human Rights of its Working Group on Disappearances in 1980 The Commission's working group is referred to in chapter 4.

13. UNESCO Doc 154 EX/16, Annex I, at 3.

14. See chap 3 for a short discussion of derogations.

15. UNESCO, Report By The Executive Board on its Own Activities in 2002–2003, Including Its Methods of Work, Doc 32 C/9 (2003), para. 78.

16. For a thematic list of wording used in the CR's decisions, see UNESCO Doc 169 EX/CR/2 (2004), at 29–50.

17. See chap 10.

18. UNESCO Doc 169 EX/CR/2 (2004), at 7, para. 39.

19. The breakdown of settled cases in the order of decreasing frequency was as follows: acquittal or release from prison (195, of which nine had completed their sentence); authorization to return to the country (thirty-five); return to employment or activity (twenty-nine); authorization to leave the country (twenty); resumption of a banned publication or broadcast (fourteen); awarding of passports, grants, or diplomas (twelve); changes in discriminatory education laws (seven); and return to "normal life following a cessation of threats" (three). Almost all of the cases added in the last five years relate to release from prison. For a critical analysis of sixty-four cases concerning 190 individuals considered between 1980 and 1991, see Weissbrodt and Farley, *supra* note 8 at 398.

20. UNESCO, Draft Unesco Strategy on Human Rights, UNESCO Doc 32 C/57 (2003), paras. 37–38.

21. 168 EX/Decision 62 (2003), at 6.

22. UNESCO, Proposals by the Committee on Conventions and Recommendation on the Conditions and Procedures Applicable to the Examination of Questions relating to the Implementation of UNESCO's Standard-Setting instruments, UNESCO Doc 164 EX/23 (2002), para. 45.

23. A precedent in this regard could be the decision of the CR in 1984 "to request the Executive Board, after consultation with the government concerned and in agreement with it, to commission one of its members to visit . . . and, with the assistance of the Director-General or his representative, to initiate discussions with the government concerned about the allegations made in the communications." UNESCO Doc. 120 EX/15 PRIV.(1984), para. 69, cited in UNESCO Doc. 169 EX/CR/2 (2004), para. 33.

Part III
Regional Systems for the Protection of Human Rights

Chapter 7
The Inter-American Human Rights System

Dinah L. Shelton

Throughout the Western hemisphere, the Organization of American States (OAS) promotes and protects human rights through a comprehensive system of substantive norms, supervisory institutions, and petition procedures. The constitutional text of the OAS is its Charter, amended by four protocols: Buenos Aires (1967), Cartagena de Indias (1985), Washington (1992), and Managua (1993). The other normative instruments of the regional system are:

- American Declaration of the Rights and Duties of Man (1948)
- American Convention on Human Rights (1969)
- Inter-American Convention to Prevent and Punish Torture (1985)
- Additional Protocol to the American Convention on Human Rights in the Area of Economic, Social and Cultural Rights (1988)
- Protocol to the American Convention on Human Rights to Abolish the Death Penalty (1990)
- Inter-American Convention on Forced Disappearance of Persons (1994)
- Inter-American Convention on the Prevention, Punishment and Eradication of Violence against Women (1994)
- Inter-American Convention on the Elimination of All Forms of Discrimination against Persons with Disabilities (1999)
- Statute and Regulations of the Inter-American Commission on Human Rights
- Statute and Rules of the Inter-American Court of Human Rights

Most of these documents are reproduced in the OAS publication, *Basic Documents Pertaining to Human Rights in the Inter-American System*, and can also be found at the OAS World Wide Website, http://www.oas.org.

The various treaties are binding only on those OAS member states that have accepted them, while the OAS Charter and the American Declaration establish human rights standards for all OAS members. The American Declaration is invoked primarily against states that have not ratified the American Convention, but states that are parties to the Convention must keep in mind that Article 29 precludes any interpretation of Convention rights and obligations that would limit the effect of the American Declaration.

Inter-American Institutions

The Inter-American Commission on Human Rights is the principal organ created under the OAS Charter to promote the observance and protection of human rights and serves as a consultant to the OAS on human rights matters. The Commission also has specific competence over matters relating to the fulfillment of obligations undertaken by states parties to all human rights conventions adopted in the regional framework (with the exception of the Convention on Persons with Disabilities, which creates a separate supervisory committee). Details of the functions and procedures of the Commission are contained in its Statute and Regulations.

The Commission consists of seven independent experts elected to four-year terms by the OAS General Assembly. It is based in Washington, DC, and is assisted by a Secretariat. Commission sessions are normally held in Washington, DC, but they also may be held in other member states. During its sessions, the Commission holds hearings where, upon request, it may hear from individuals and representatives of human rights organizations and states.

The American Convention lists the Commission and the Inter-American Court of Human Right as the organs having "competence with respect to matters relating to the fulfillment of the commitments made by States Parties to [the] Convention." The Court also has some functions that extend to all OAS member states[1] and to parties to the Convention on Violence against Women and the Disappearances Convention. The Court consists of seven judges, nominated and elected for six-year terms by the parties to the American Convention. Judges may be reelected once. The Court's functions and procedures are set forth in the American Convention and its Statute and Rules of Procedure, and its permanent seat is in San Jose, Costa Rica.

The Rights Protected and State Obligations

The OAS Charter contains few references to human rights, although there are provisions specifically devoted to representative democracy, human rights and equality, economic rights, and the right to education. The Declaration and the American Convention protect primarily civil and political rights, with the Convention defining them in more detail. The Declaration also addresses numerous economic, social, and cultural rights, such as the rights to property, culture, work, health, education, leisure time, and social security. Only the first of these rights is guaranteed by the Convention, although Article 26 calls for states to take progressive measures to achieve "full realization of the rights implicit in the economic, social, education, scientific, and cultural standards set forth in the Charter."

The Protocol on Economic, Social, and Cultural Rights obliges parties to it to take progressive action, according to their degree of development, to achieve observance of the right to work and to just, equitable, and satisfactory conditions of work; the right to organize trade unions and to strike; the right to social security; the right to health; the right to a healthy environment; the right to food; the right to education; the right to the benefits of culture; and the right to the formation and protection of families. In addition, special protections are afforded certain vulnerable groups, such as children, the elderly, and disabled persons. The Convention's petition procedures extend to two rights in the Protocol: the right to form trade unions (Article 8(a)) and the right to education (Article 13). Implementation of the remaining rights is supervised through a system of state reports.

Few rights are absolute, and most may be limited under certain circumstances. Both the Declaration and Convention provide that the rights of every person are limited by the rights of others, by the security of all, and by the just demands of the general welfare in a democratic society. In addition, some rights in the Convention are accompanied by specific provisions that permit limitations in the interest of national security, public safety, or public order, or to protect public health or morals or the rights or freedoms of others.

During a period of national emergency, Article 27 of the Convention permits a state party to suspend or derogate from rights under limited circumstances. Any such measure must be nondiscriminatory and "strictly required by the exigencies of the situation." In addition, the state may not suspend the rights to juridical personality, life, humane treatment, freedom from slavery, freedom from *ex post facto* laws, freedom of conscience and religion, family life, a name, nationality, of the child, or to participate in government. The judicial guarantees essential for the protection of human rights, including procedures of *amparo* and *habeas corpus*, must be maintained at all times.[2] The Commission has stated that Article 27 is declarative of general international law, and it thus can be applied to states not party to the Convention, in order to judge the conformity of a state of siege or other emergency with the state's obligation to respect the rights contained in the Declaration.

States are obliged not only to respect the observance of rights and freedoms but also to guarantee their existence and exercise. Thus any act *or omission* by any public authority which impairs guaranteed rights may violate a state's obligations. The Torture Convention and the Convention against Disappearances create a further duty on states parties to establish criminal liability for the commission of or attempt to commit torture or forced disappearance. Other provisions require compensation of victims, training of police and custodial officials, and extradition of those accused of having committed torture or forced disappearance. The Court has held that the practice of forced disappearance constitutes a multiple and continuous violation of many rights protected by the American Convention and is a "radical breach" of a state party's obligations, and the OAS General Assembly has referred to disappearances as a "crime against humanity."

Proceedings Before the Inter-American Commission on Human Rights

Provided that the formal and substantive requirements are met, a petition may be filed with the Commission against any OAS member state. For states that are not party to the Convention, the recognized rights are those contained in the American Declaration. For parties to the American Convention, the rights contained in the Convention are protected in relation to all events which occur after the date of ratification, including continuing violations that may have begun prior to that date. Petitions also may be filed against a state party that violates its obligations under the Disappearances Convention or Article 7 of the Convention on Violence against Women.

The procedures governing complaints are set forth in the Commission's Statute and Regulations. The procedures are identical for all petitions, including criteria for admissibility, procedural stages, fact-finding, and decision-making, but only petitions arising under the American Convention or Disappearances Convention may be submitted to the Court (and then only if the state in question has accepted the Court's jurisdiction).

The Commission is obliged to attempt to achieve a friendly settlement and may undertake an on-site mission, if it deems it necessary and appropriate. The petition process may result in a Commission decision on the merits, together with specific recommendations to the state concerned. The Commission may call for the state to pay "appropriate" compensation when it finds a violation has occurred, but it does not itself set the amount of compensation.

Admissibility Requirements

A petition filed with the Commission must contain information on the person or persons filing the petition, its subject matter, and its procedural posture. The criteria for admissibility of petitions are contained in Articles 44–47 of the Convention and Articles 23 and 27–34 of the Commission's Regulations.

Who may file

Any person, group of persons, or nongovernmental organization legally recognized in one or more of the member states of the OAS may submit a petition to the Inter-American Commission on Human Rights. The petition need not be filed directly by a victim but may be submitted by third parties, with or without the victim's knowledge or authorization. The petition may involve an individual or may indicate numerous victims of a specific incident or practice (a collective petition). Where the petitioners allege the existence of widespread human rights violations not limited to a specific group or event, the Commission tends to use the information in examining the overall human rights situation within the state in question (a country report) or as part of a thematic study, rather than as a specific case. Collective petitions should refer to specific victims, although none of the victims need personally submit or approve the petition. The concept of "victim" includes those who might be affected by legislation that allegedly violates human rights guarantees, even if the legislation has not yet been enforced.

The petition must include the name, nationality, and signature of the person or persons making the submission or, if the petitioner is a nongovernmental organization, the name and signature of its legal representative. The petition must also indicate if the petitioner wishes to have his or her identity withheld from the state concerned. Each petition must include an address for receiving correspondence from the Commission and, if available, a telephone or fax number and e-mail address.

Statement of facts

The petition must describe the act or situation complained of, specifying the place and date of the alleged violation and, if possible, names of victims and officials who were informed of the act or situation. In the latter case, the date, time, and place of the notification should be included. Obviously, the state which is considered responsible for the act or omission constituting the violation, should be identified.

The statement of facts should be detailed, with as much identifying information as possible on the victim or victims. Information linking the government to the act complained of, either through direct commission or through a failure to control private acts, is crucial. The Commission only considers petitions which allege government violations of human rights, not those concerned with purely private conduct. Any known name, rank, or other description of an official responsible for the alleged violation or implicated in the acts complained of should be provided. Statements by any witnesses or persons knowledgeable about the case may be attached, noting, if relevant, that the information should be kept confidential.

Although the regulations do not require it, it is useful to indicate the relevant legal instrument and right or rights alleged to have been violated. If the violation is not obvious, reference may be made to interpretations of the right by the Commission or Court, as evidenced by Commission resolutions, reports, and studies and Court opinions and judgments. Resolutions of other OAS organs also may provide guidance. Even other human rights treaties and their interpretation by UN or regional bodies may assist the Commission in determining the scope of the right at issue.

If the rights allegedly violated have been suspended by the government, the petition may challenge the validity of the suspension or the fact that nonderogable rights were suspended. Even if the rights are subject to derogation, the petition may question the government's compliance with the specific requirements necessary to justify suspension. The measures also may be challenged as being unnecessarily broad, discriminatory, or incompatible with other state obligations under international law.

Exhaustion of domestic remedies

The Commission will not admit a petition unless all available and effective domestic remedies have been exhausted in accordance with general principles of international law. This means that domestic avenues of appeal must be pursued, unless it can be shown that no remedy exists or the purported remedies would be inadequate (i.e., incapable of producing the result sought) or ineffective (available in theory but not in practice). The petition therefore must include information on whether remedies under domestic law have been exhausted or whether it has been impossible or futile to proceed.

If a petitioner cannot prove exhaustion of remedies because of lack of documentation or legal counsel or for any other reason, this should be stated; the burden then may shift to the government to demonstrate which specific remedies remain to be exhausted under domestic law. If the state identifies domestic remedies that have not been exhausted, the burden will shift back to the claimant to demonstrate that one of the exceptions to the requirement of exhaustion applies. The recognized exceptions are: (1) the domestic legislation of the country does not afford effective or adequate remedies to protect the right or rights violated; (2) access to the remedies has been denied; and (3) there has been an unwarranted delay in rendering a final judgment. The petitioner may invoke one of these exceptions by showing, for example, that there exists a consistent pattern of gross violations of human rights which renders theoretical remedies meaningless or that there is no independent judiciary capable of affording redress within the domestic system. In addition, the Inter-American Court has indicated in an advisory opinion that remedies need not be exhausted if a complainant has been prevented from obtaining adequate legal representation due to indigence or a general fear in the legal community and such representation is necessary to ensure a fair proceeding.[3]

The Commission has made clear that it is not a "court of fourth instance." The mere fact that the petitioner lost a case in the national courts is not grounds for bringing a petition to the Inter-American system. The Commission will not substitute its judgment for that of the trier of fact, nor will it substitute its interpretation of a domestic statute or constitutional norm for that of a domestic court. However, the Commission will accept a case if the proceedings in domestic court violated human rights guarantees of due process or fair hearing or were ineffective to remedy the violation, for example, if the domestic court lacks the power to strike down legislation incompatible with the Convention.

Timeliness

Exhaustion of remedies is linked to the time limit within which a petition must be filed. Where domestic remedies have been pursued and exhausted, the petition must be filed within six months of the date on which the party whose rights have been violated was notified of the final ruling. This limit may be extended if the state has interfered with the petitioner's ability to file the complaint within the time period. If the requirement of exhaustion of remedies is excused because no remedies are available or effective, the petition must be filed within a reasonable period of time. If a third party is filing a petition for a victim unable to do so, the reasonableness criterion rather than the strict six-month rule may apply. The petition must include information on compliance with the relevant time period.

Duplication of procedures

The Commission cannot consider a petition if the subject matter is pending in another international governmental organization or "essentially duplicates a petition pending or already examined and settled by the Commission or by another international governmental organization of which the state concerned is a member."4 However, the Commission will consider the matter if the other procedure examines only the general situation on human rights in the state in question, such as the UN's "1503 procedure;"5 there has been no decision on the specific facts in the petition submitted to the Commission; or if the other procedure will not effectively redress the violation. Although the situation is unlikely to arise in practice, the Commission also will consider the petition if the petitioner is the victim or a family member and the petitioner in the other proceeding is a third party acting without specific authorization from the victim.

Precautionary Measures

Precautionary measures are authorized in Article 25 of the Commission's Rules of Procedure, which states that, in serious and urgent cases, the Commission, on its own initiative or upon the request of a party, may request that the state concerned adopt precautionary measures to prevent irreparable harm to persons. If the Commission is not in session, the President, or, in his or her absence, one of the Vice-Presidents, consults with the other members, through the Secretariat, on possible application of precautionary measures. If it is not possible to consult within a reasonable period, the President takes the decision on behalf of the Commission and informs its members. The Commission may request information from the interested parties on any matter related to the adoption and observance of the precautionary measures, which, if adopted, are without prejudice to the final decision.

Requests for precautionary measures may be joined to a petition or filed separately, even prior to the petition being submitted. Petitioners who are seeking precautionary measures should highlight: (1) the seriousness of the matter; (2) the imminence of the danger; and (3) the possible irreparable harm. Such measures have been ordered in the past where there are threats to life or physical injury or prior restraints on freedom of expression.

Finally, the Commission also may request that the Court order "provisional measures" in urgent cases which involve danger to persons, even where a case has not yet been submitted to the Court.

Precautionary measures have become very important in the Commission's practice, in an attempt to protect witnesses and petitioners from violence or to conserve evidence. Petitioners should inform the Commission if the state fails to implement precautionary measures. Information about precautionary measures is published in the annual reports of the Commission and the Court.

Procedure

Petitions are considered in several distinct stages. Initially, petitions are received and processed by the Commission's Secretariat to see if they meet the requirements for consideration in accordance with Articles 26–28 of the Commission's rules. The legal staff begins by verifying the Commission's jurisdiction through examining the nature of both the petitioner and the respondent; the subject matter of the petition; the place where the facts occurred; and the timeliness of the petition. If elements are missing from the petition, a petitioner may be requested to supply further information. If the petition is deemed manifestly groundless or fails to meet the requirements of form, the petitioner may be advised that the Commission cannot process the petition.

Once the petition is complete and the Commission's *prima facie* competence is verified, the petition is registered and given a number, and the relevant parts of the petition are transmitted to the state in question. In transmitting the petition, the Secretariat deletes all details which would tend to identify the petitioner, unless the petitioner has given authorization to have his or her identity revealed. The state is normally given two months from the date the petition is transmitted to respond to it. The state may request one additional month to reply, but it is not automatically entitled to an extension of time and its request must be evaluated by the Secretariat.

The Commission may invite further submissions from either party or may hold hearings prior to making a determination on admissibility. The Commission's regulations provide that, once observations have been received or the relevant time period has passed, the Commission must verify the admissibility of the petition; a working group on admissibility meets prior to each session to examine admissibility and make recommendations to the Commission. Only after the petition is deemed admissible is the petition considered a "case." In exceptional circumstances, where issues of admissibility are tied to the merits, the Commission may join consideration of the two issues and open the case by means of a written communication to both parties. The Commission's decisions on admissibility are published in its annual reports.

The petitioner should seek to be informed about any delays and the reasons therefore. In serious or urgent cases, the Commission can request "the promptest rely from the government, using for this purpose the means it considers most expeditious." If the government fails to respond to the facts alleged, its silence may lead the Commission to presume the truth of the facts alleged in the petition, as provided in Article 39 of its Regulations. The presumption of truth permitted by Article 39 is usually applied after repeated requests for information have met with no response from the government.

The petitioner should always alert the Commission to any failure by the government to respond to an allegation. A merely general denial by the government is inadequate, and the Court has specifically noted that "the State cannot rely on the defense that the complainant has failed to present evidence when such cannot be obtained without the State's cooperation."[6]

Once the case is declared to be admissible, the petitioner is generally given thirty days to submit additional observations on the merits; any submissions by the petitioner are transmitted to the state, which has a similar time period to reply. The Commission may adjust the time limits depending on the difficulty posed by the case. The Commission also must communicate an offer inviting the parties to participate in seeking a friendly settlement.

Given the Commission's inadequate staff and budget, any help a petitioner can give the staff, such as identifying witnesses or documents to be sought, will enhance the effectiveness of the system and the proceedings. Ideally, all documentation should be submitted in the official language of the state in question. Testimony should be transcribed rather than submitted on tape; the reliability of videotape evidence is uncertain. Copies of domestic legal proceedings should be attached. The petitioner may appoint an attorney or representative to assist in this process. Contact with the Commission's legal staff, either orally or in writing, is often helpful, although the Commission is increasingly and rightly concerned with *ex parte* communications from either party to a case.

Hearings and On-Site Visits

The Commission is authorized to hold a hearing to verify the facts, which generally occurs before a chamber of three Commissioners, on its own initiative or at the request of one of the parties. The petitioner should support any request for a hearing by indicating the evidence that will be presented and the information to be requested of the government and witnesses; evidence and facts to be presented should be in addition to those that appear in the written submissions and may concern any matter pertinent to the processing of a petition or case. A request for a hearing must be submitted in writing at least forty days prior to the beginning of the Commission's session and must indicate the identity of the proposed participants. Hearings and working meetings held during hearing week may address friendly settlement issues, precautionary measures, or the general situation of human rights in a specific state.

Parties are notified by the Secretariat one month in advance of the date of any hearing, unless the parties agree to a shorter notice period. During a hearing, the Commission may receive oral and written statements and items of evidence from the parties. Parties are given a rea-

sonable time after the hearing to make observations on any documentary evidence submitted. If the Commission agrees, witnesses may be
heard. The state is prohibited from taking any action or reprisal against
witnesses, experts, or their families because of their appearance before
the Commission. Each party bears its own expenses for appearances and
producing evidence.

In addition to holding hearings on cases, Commission practice now
commonly includes informal visits to a country by the Commissioner
who is the Rapporteur for the country, along with a staff attorney. These
visits typically concern more than one case and are directed at fact-finding, obtaining evidence, or engaging the parties in friendly settlement
discussions. Where appropriate, the full Commission may undertake an
on-site investigation in the country involved, at the request of the petitioner, state, or on its own motion. While on-site investigations are conducted much more frequently in the inter-American system than in
others, they are rarely undertaken solely to investigate a single or individual case. Instead, they are utilized to investigate allegations of widespread human rights violations within the target country, as part of which
individual cases may be examined. No more than one or two such visits
can be undertaken in a year.

Friendly Settlement

The American Convention requires the Commission to place itself at the
disposal of the parties, with a view to reaching a settlement of the dispute grounded in respect for the rights recognized in the Convention.
The friendly settlement procedure requires the consent of both parties,
and either of them may terminate it at any stage. The Commission, which
acts as the moderator of meetings to facilitate agreement, is increasingly
encouraging friendly settlement negotiations. In general, the Commission allows six months to achieve a settlement, although this may be
extended with the consent of the parties.

If a friendly settlement is undertaken, the Commissioner who is
Rapporteur for the country, along with a staff attorney, handles the proceeding. If the Commission finds that either of the parties is not participating in good faith, the procedure may be terminated. If a friendly
settlement is reached, the Commission prepares a report which it transmits to the parties and ultimately publishes.

Final Decisions and Reports

The Commission examines all the evidence in the case and prepares a
report stating the facts, arguments, and its conclusions regarding the
case, including any proposals and recommendations it wishes to make.

If the Commission finds there has been no violation, it states this in the report, which it transmits to the parties and includes in its annual report. When the Commission finds one or more violations, it prepares a preliminary report with its proposals and recommendations and transmits this preliminary report to the state in question. (This is known as the Article 50 report, after the provision in the Convention that mandates it.) The state is given two months to comply with the recommendations and is not authorized to publish the report until the Commission adopts its final decision. The petitioner is notified when the report is transmitted to the state and is given a summary of the findings. The short time limit for compliance and transmittal of information to the petitioner is necessary because the Commission has only three months to decide whether or not to submit a case to the Court. Compliance by the state and the views of the petitioner are important factors in making this decision.

If the state is party to the American Convention and has accepted the jurisdiction of the Court, the petitioner has one month to offer a view on whether the Commission should submit the case to the Court, including any arguments in favor of Court submission, the availability of evidence, claims concerning reparations, and personal information about the victim and the victim's family members.

If the case is not submitted to the Court, the Commission's opinion in the case is published in the Commission's Annual Report to the OAS General Assembly. The Commission also may adopt follow-up measures, including requesting additional information from the parties and holding further hearings, in order to verify compliance with any friendly settlement or recommendations it makes.

Proceedings Before the Inter-American Court of Human Rights

There are a number of arguments in favor of proceeding to the Court. First, the Commission cannot *order* a state to pay compensation, release a detainee, or take other specific action; it can only recommend such measures or other appropriate remedies. (The Commission can, however, negotiate a friendly settlement that includes specific remedial action, including the payment of substantial compensation.) Second, in most member states, Commission decisions and recommendations do not have the force of domestic law and cannot be enforced through local courts. Judgments of the Court, on the other hand, are legally binding and should be directly enforceable. Third, Court judgments are perceived by most states as carrying considerably more political weight than Commission decisions, in addition to the fact that they are final and legally binding.

For the Court to have jurisdiction over an individual case, the state concerned must be a party to the American Convention and have accepted the optional jurisdiction of the Court; proceedings before the Commission must be completed; and the case must be referred by the Commission or the state concerned within three months after the Commission's "Article 50 report" on the matter is transmitted to the state and a summary of it to the petitioner. An individual petitioner cannot invoke the Court's jurisdiction.

Under current rules, there is a presumption that all cases should be submitted to the Court if the Commission has found one or more violations and the responsible state has not complied with the Commission's recommendations within the specified time period. The Commission may nonetheless decide by absolute majority vote not to transmit the case. Factors that the Commission may consider include the nature and seriousness of the violation, the need to develop or clarify case law, the future effect of the decision on member states, and the strength of the evidence. The reasons for the Commission's decision not to proceed with a case to the Court must be set forth in its decision.

Although individual petitioners have no standing to bring cases to the Court, the Court's rules allow them to participate fully in all stages of Court proceedings, in person or through a representative chosen by the petitioner. The representative or petitioner may and should ask the Court for any orders which may be needed to ensure the protection of witnesses and evidence.

Proceedings before the Court are both written and oral. The first stage consists of a written memorial and counter-memorial, submitted according to a time-table set by the Court. The Court also may ask each party for an offer of proof, to indicate the facts that each item of evidence is intended to prove, and how, when, and under what circumstances the party wishes to present the evidence. The 2001 Rules of Court allow the Court to consolidate arguments on preliminary objections, merits, and reparations in a single hearing, in order to expedite the process. The cost of producing evidence is borne by the party requesting its production. The Court's hearings are normally public, but they may be closed if the Court so decides. The Court's deliberations are confidential; its judgments and opinions are published.

If the Court finds a violation of the Convention, it may order that the situation be remedied and award compensation to the injured party. Compensation includes indemnification for actual damage, including emotional or moral injury, but does not include punitive damages. Specific orders for nonmonetary relief also may be awarded, such as the release of wrongfully held detainees. States are legally obliged to comply with a judgment of the Court, and a remedial order may be enforced in the appropriate domestic courts.

Both the Court and Commission permit *amicus curiae* briefs to be filed, and individual petitioners should consider requesting a supporting brief from an NGO if complex legal issues are involved. Such briefs also may be important in regard to requests for advisory opinions of the Court, which can have a significant impact on human rights issues in the system.

The Commission's Country Reports

The Commission has unusually broad authority to prepare reports on its own initiative on the human rights situation in any OAS member state. Individuals and NGOs have no formal role in this process, but it is on the basis of information from these sources that the Commission determines whether a country report is justified. Information on widespread human rights violations in a particular country, whether in the form of a well-documented NGO report or a series of individual cases, should be submitted directly to the Commission. If such a submission is planned, it is advisable to contact the Secretariat lawyer responsible for that country in advance, in order to determine what information might be particularly useful and to obtain information regarding actions the Commission might already be taking or contemplating.

The Commission submits a public annual report to the OAS General Assembly in English and Spanish, which includes resolutions on individual cases, reports on the human rights situation in various states, and a discussion of areas in which further action is needed to promote and protect human rights, such as further codification of human rights standards. Information relevant to any of these items may be communicated to the Commission through its staff.

Concluding Observations

The inter-American system has several advantages over other regional or global petition procedures. Standing to file a petition is virtually unlimited, and other admissibility requirements are less burdensome within the OAS system than elsewhere. The procedures are relatively informal, which theoretically allows the Commission to move more quickly when necessary and to respond flexibly to a variety of situations. The Commission also has the unique option of being able to undertake an in-depth study of the human rights situation in a country, stemming from its consideration of an individual case or general allegations of violations.

The informality and flexibility of the system can also be disadvantageous to individual litigants. Time limits are rarely enforced, and cases may continue for years without resolution. The increasing caseload threatens to exacerbate this problem unless additional staff and resources are forthcoming. The lack of a formal procedure before the OAS General Assembly to review compliance with Commission recommendations and Court judgments also weakens the political impact of the system. Nonetheless, efforts are being made to improve supervision of compliance, and the Court has repeatedly asked the political organs of the OAS to exercise the duty of "collective guarantee."[7] The Commission has created a follow-up mechanism, sometimes holding hearings and then publishing follow-up reports if there is no compliance. Beginning in 2001, the Commission also began including in its annual reports to the OAS General Assembly a chart indicating states' compliance with its decisions.

The inter-American system is undoubtedly stronger than it was a decade ago. Its institutions have achieved legitimacy, have become widely known, and are able to challenge almost any government that violates human rights. But there also are threats to its continued progress, due especially to the lack of resources to process cases quickly and efficiently. Advocates and academics should become more aware of the strengths and weaknesses of the inter-American system and encourage the OAS and its member states to enhance the former and reduce the latter.

Notes

1. Article 64 permits any OAS member state to request an advisory opinion from the Court regarding the interpretation of the American Convention or other treaties concerning the protection of human rights in the American states. Any OAS member also may request an opinion regarding the compatibility of a domestic law with any such international instruments. Because of these wider functions, judges are selected from among the nationals of all member states, although they are nominated and elected only by the parties to the Convention.

2. See Advisory Opinion OC-9/87, Judicial Guarantees in States of Emergency, 9 Inter-Am.Ct.H.Rts. (Ser. A) (1987).

3. Advisory Opinion OC-11/90, Exhaustion of Remedies, 11 Inter-Am.Ct.H. Rts. (Ser. A) (1990).

4. Commission Regulations, art. 33(1)(b).

5. See chap. 4.

6. Velasquez Rodriguez Case, Judgment of 29 July 1988, 4 Inter-Am.Ct.H.Rts. (Ser. C), para. 135.

7. See, e.g., Speech by the President of the Inter-American Court of Human Rights to the Permanent Council of the OAS, 17 Apr. 2002, Appendix XXIV, 2002 Annual Report of the Inter-American Court of Human Rights.

Chapter 8
Council of Europe, OSCE, and European Union

Kevin Boyle[1]

Overview

More than a decade after the fall of the Berlin Wall, ideological confrontation, including over human rights, no longer divides Europe. This is perhaps best illustrated by the fact that almost every country on the continent—including Russia and Ukraine—is now party to the European Convention on Human Rights. However, Europe of the twenty-first century is certainly not devoid of human rights challenges, as the spread of democracy has proved far from being an easy process. Furthermore, violence and tensions associated with a resurgence of nationalism and the accompanying fears of minorities, along with widespread xenophobia towards new immigrants and asylum seekers, present serious long-term challenges. It is the countries with the least experience of democracy which have faced the most serious instability and for whom regional systems of human rights protection are the most important.

The link between the effective protection of human rights and democratic security is now emphasized by all three regional structures discussed in this chapter: the Council of Europe, the Organization on Security and Cooperation in Europe (OSCE), and the European Union (EU). Understanding the role and potential of each of these European structures in human rights litigation and campaigning is essential for the human rights advocate.

The Council of Europe

To practice successfully under the European Convention on Human Rights, lawyers need to understand the body under whose auspices it functions, the Council of Europe. Established in 1949, it is the oldest structure of European integration and has achieved major successes in promoting international human rights standards in Europe.[2] Since 1990, it has grown from a Western European body of twenty-one states to a pan-European system of forty-five states, embracing Eastern and Central European countries and three Caucasian states; Belarus remains the only large European state outside the organization.

The Council has its seat in Strasbourg and has two organs, an intergovernmental Committee of Ministers and an indirectly elected Parliamentary Assembly, drawn from national parliaments. Both are important actors alongside the European Court of Human Rights in now continentwide human rights protection.

In addition to its function of supervising the execution of judgments of the Court, the Committee has since 1996 established a thematic monitoring procedure. All member states may be requested to submit information on issues such as freedom of expression and information, the functioning of democratic institutions, and the judiciary and police. Where specific action is required, on-site visits can be conducted; in recent years, such visits have taken place in nine states. In addition, the Committee monitors compliance with post-accession commitments of all new member states.

A new institution, the Council of Europe Commissioner for Human Rights, was created in 1999. The current Commissioner is Alvaro Gil-Robles, former ombudsman of Spain. He has a wide mandate, intended to give the Commissioner a proactive role in promoting human rights throughout Europe. He works with national human rights bodies and is a key point of contact for NGOs. He has no power to receive individual complaints but can address general situations reflected in individual cases that reach the European Court of Human Rights. The Commissioner also produces an in-depth annual human rights report on Europe.

The Council of Europe's most important achievement has been the *European Convention on Human Rights*, which marked its fiftieth year of coming into force in 2003. It has now been ratified by all of the forty-five member states, representing some 800 million Europeans. A key element of the Convention's system is the right of individual petition to the European Court of Human Rights in Strasbourg, which is discussed in detail below.

Deepened awareness of the Convention in the original Western European member states and the inclusion of Eastern European countries in the Convention have drastically increased the caseload of the European Court, posing a serious challenge to the Convention machinery. Extensive debate about reform led to a radical change in the Convention's institutions in 1998, when a full-time court replaced the previous structure of a European Commission on Human Rights and a part-time court. However, as the workload of the Court continues to grow, further reform of the Convention system is under active consideration.

The *European Social Charter* is a parallel Council of Europe instrument which promotes social and economic rights. It entered into force in 1965 and has been ratified by thirty-four states, sixteen of which have acceded to a revised Charter which provides more comprehensive protection and entered into force in 1999. In 1998, an optional collective complaint mechanism was created, which has been accepted by eleven states. The complaint procedure adds a new element to the earlier jurisprudence of the Committee of Independent Experts of the European Social Charter.

The *European Convention on the Prevention of Torture* (ECPT) entered into force in 1989 and has now been ratified by all of the members of the Council of Europe.[3] It has no complaint mechanism, as such, but is designed to prevent ill-treatment through a regular cycle of visits to places of detention by its monitoring body, the Committee for the Prevention of Torture. Knowledge of the ECPT and awareness of the Committee's reports on particular countries can be an important resource for campaigning and may be useful in individual complaints under the European Convention or in other regional or UN mechanisms.

The *Framework Convention for the Protection of National Minorities* is the first international convention devoted exclusively to minorities; it entered into force in February 1998 and currently has thirty-five parties. The Convention has no complaint mechanism and relies on monitoring of states' periodic reports for its implementation. The practitioner working with other European mechanisms and raising complaints with a minority dimension should be familiar with this convention and the substantive obligations it imposes on states. A *European Charter for Regional or Minority Languages* also entered into force in 1998. It, too, is supervised by a committee of experts, which examines reports filed by states on their compliance with the treaty. At the end of 2003, the Charter had been ratified by seventeen states.

The Organization for Security and Cooperation in Europe (OSCE)

Formerly the Conference on Security and Cooperation in Europe, which adopted the Helsinki Accord in 1975, the OSCE is credited by some with being the catalyst that transformed the political and security face of Europe. The OSCE now embraces fifty-five states, including Canada and the United States. It has become a permanent diplomatic forum for the protection and promotion of human rights and democratic institutions, in addition to its role as a mechanism of conflict prevention and security. A close familiarity with OSCE standards, institutions, and missions is relevant both for international legal work and for implementing such standards in national courts.

The European Community/Union

The European Union (EU) is the unique expression of Western European integration. All twenty-five EU states are also members of the Council of Europe and the OSCE.[4] The EU grew out of the original European Economic Communities (EEC, then EC), which were primarily designed as a political union to be achieved progressively through integrated economic and social policies. However, it has increasingly become a serious institution for advancing human rights both within the EU and externally, through its human rights and development programs. The Treaty on European Union, signed in Maastricht in 1992, introduced the requirement that all three "pillars" of the EU (covering economic and social issues, common foreign and security policy, and justice and home affairs cooperation) must respect human rights in accordance with the standards of the European Convention on Human Rights and national constitutional traditions. However, a proposal to have the European Community, the "first pillar" of the EU, formally accede to the European Convention as a High Contracting Party was dismissed in 1996 by the EU's ultimate court, the European Court of Justice, which held that such a step would require treaty amendment and therefore unanimous ratification by the member states.[5]

The expanding role of the EU in the protection of human rights is only considered briefly below, because, from the perspective of the practitioner, it offers little opportunity for use outside of national proceedings.

The European Convention on Human Rights remains the most important instrument for the human rights practitioner, and this chapter is devoted primarily to that instrument. However, the human rights campaigner should be familiar with all three of these European structures and utilize the potential of each to promote human rights in an increasingly integrated Europe.

The European Convention on Human Rights

The European Convention on Human Rights and Fundamental Freedoms came into force in 1953 and was conceived as a regional implementation of the Universal Declaration of Human Rights. The state parties collectively took primary responsibility for the observance of the Convention in Europe, hence the compulsory acceptance of the possibility of interstate complaints. However, it was the right of individual complaint that became the main vehicle for bringing both individual and large-scale violations under the Convention. Under a 1998 revision of the Convention, the individual complaint procedure is now a compulsory requirement for states, a step that reflects its importance in practice. The dominance of the individual over the interstate procedure is demonstrated by the fact that only one complaint has been lodged by a state against another member state since 1982,[6] while the Court received 38,000 individual complaints in 2003 alone.

Although this chapter will deal only with the practice and procedure of individual applications and not interstate complaints, it would be wrong to assume that the state has been supplanted in significance under the Convention. The cooperation of governments remains crucial for the investigation of individual complaints and for subsequent enforcement of the European Court's judgments. The key to the Court's significance is that states must ensure that their domestic legal order protects the human rights guaranteed under the Convention, including providing domestic remedies, so that the need to have recourse to Strasbourg is significantly reduced. The emphasis on consultation with governments during the handling of complaints, the obligation on the Court to seek a friendly settlement, the confidentiality attached to friendly settlement negotiations, and the "margin of appreciation" doctrine[7] are all components of the Convention that an applicant or lawyer needs to understand.

The ultimate purpose of the Convention is, of course, its full implementation in national law and practice. The Court constitutes a forum of last resort that remains subsidiary to national protection, providing a system of "outer protection" for the range of civil and political rights already protected under the legal and constitutional systems of the state parties. In fact, less than 10 percent of the applications registered under the Convention meet the admissibility requirements. The most frequent reason for the rejection of complaints is that the applicant has no grounds for invoking international remedies, given the degree of protection secured for his or her rights in domestic law.

The practitioner will find it is essential to consult the considerable body of jurisprudence developed by the Convention organs[8] and must be familiar with the Rules of the Court, which regulate all aspects of procedure. Much of the case law is relatively technical, dealing with the edges or limits of rights after their careful consideration by domestic courts. However, more fundamental problems reflecting serious violations (such as forced evictions, arbitrary killings, disappearances, torture, and the lack of internal remedies) have formed a significant dimension of the Court's recent caseload. As one example, more than 120 cases concerning Russia's activities in Chechnya are currently pending before the Court.

The Institutional Framework

The *European Court of Human Rights* has jurisdiction over all matters relating to the interpretation and application of the Convention and consists of a number of judges equal to the number of High Contracting Parties.

The judges, elected by the Parliamentary Assembly, must either have the qualifications required for high judicial office or be jurists of recognized competence. Judges sit in their individual capacity and cannot engage in any activity which is incompatible with independence or the demands of full-time office. Judges can only be dismissed from office by a vote of two-thirds of the other judges.

The Court functions in a number of groupings. The *Plenary Court* elects its President and other officers, establishes other units of the Court, and adopts the Rules of the Court. For all other purposes, the Court functions through Committees, Chambers, Sections, and a Grand Chamber.

Committees of three judges act as a filter for applications. By unanimous vote, they may declare individual applications inadmissible in clear circumstances, and their decision is final.

There are four *Sections*, into which the judges are divided "geographically and gender balanced" (Rule 25.2). The *Chambers*, comprising seven judges each, are drawn from these Sections. The Chambers consider and decide on the admissibility and merits of most applications. Their judgments are final, unless: (1) a Chamber relinquishes jurisdiction to the Grand Chamber; or (2) a party successfully seeks to have a case referred to the Grand Chamber for a rehearing.

The *Grand Chamber*, composed of seventeen judges, has jurisdiction only in cases referred to it by a Chamber or at the request of a party to the case, following a Chamber judgment. It also has an advisory jurisdiction; a request for an advisory opinion can only come from the Committee of Ministers, which availed itself of this possibility for the first time in January 2002.

The *Committee of Ministers* is the political arm of the Convention. Its members serve not as individuals but as government representatives of the members of the Council of Europe. The sole function of the Committee under the Convention is to supervise the execution of the judgments of the Court. If government fails to honor a judgment, the Committee is the vehicle for suspending or expelling that government from the Council of Europe.

Substantive Requirements

Jurisdiction

The Court may only examine an application that alleges a violation of one of the rights and freedoms included in the Convention and its protocols. These cover a wide range of civil and political rights but not necessarily all internationally recognized rights. For example, the Convention is quite weak on issues of discrimination, although an independent equality clause is likely to be approved in the near future as Protocol No. 12 to the Convention. An application must invoke a particular right or rights recognized under the Convention, and one should read the Convention carefully to identify the relevant article that is claimed to be breached. One also should be careful, if the right at issue is found in one of the protocols to the Convention, to ensure that the state against which the application is lodged has ratified the protocol in question; only a minority of states has ratified every protocol. Reservations also have been entered by states to various rights in the Convention and protocols.

Under Article 15, states may derogate from certain (but not all) rights in times of national emergency. Such derogation may extend to all or only part of the national territory, which could be a material issue in an application against that state, and it must be formally filed with the Council of Europe.

Standing

Article 34 provides:

> The Court may receive applications from any person, nongovernmental organization, or group of individuals, claiming to be the victim of a violation by one of the High Contracting Parties of the rights set forth in the Convention or the protocols thereto. The High Contracting Parties undertake not to hinder in any way the effective exercise of this right.

The most important requirement is that the applicant be a victim; the concept of victim has been considered frequently under the Convention. Direct and indirect victims may maintain an application; the latter are generally relatives or others with a close connection to the victim, who may be deceased or a minor. The Convention organs to date have been liberal in interpreting standing, but the Court will not entertain an *in abstracto* application or an *actio popularis* which alleges general human rights violations unconnected to any specific victim applicant.

Article 1 of the Convention imposes an obligation on contracting states to secure the rights and freedoms set out in Section 1 of the Convention to all persons "within their jurisdiction," whether they are nationals or non-nationals. However, the Convention's reach is not limited to acts committed within the national territory. In *Cyprus v. Turkey*, it was held that "the authorised agents of the State, including diplomatic or counsellor agents and armed forces, not only remain under its jurisdiction when abroad but bring any other person or property within that 'jurisdiction' of that State, to the extent that they exercise authority over such persons or property. Insofar as, by their acts or omissions, they affect such persons or property, the responsibility of the State is engaged."[9] However, the essentially territorial basis of jurisdiction was confirmed in the recent case of *Bankovic & Others v Belgium & Others*, which concerned the NATO intervention in former Yugoslavia.[10]

The indirect reach of the Convention is best illustrated by *Soering v. United Kingdom*.[11] In that case, the Court held that the threatened extradition of a German national from Britain to face a capital murder charge in the United States would violate, on the United Kingdom's part, the Convention's prohibition against inhuman or degrading treatment, because of the applicant's exposure to the "death row phenomenon." On similar reasoning, the Court has applied the Convention to protect refugees and asylum-seekers from being deported to countries where they might face torture.[12]

Article 34 requires an applicant to prove that the alleged violation has been committed *by* the state, whether it is a complaint over an act or a failure to act. The state's responsibility is engaged by the acts of its servants and officials, including, for example, the police, military or local authorities, or the courts. But a state is not ordinarily liable under the Convention for the acts or omissions of private individuals or organizations.

Procedural Requirements and Admissibility Criteria

Once it is determined that an alleged violation falls within the scope of the Convention, the most important preliminary consideration is admissibility. The admissibility criteria are set out in Article 35 of the Convention. The Court will consider admissibility at the outset of its consideration of an application, but it can rule an application inadmissible at any stage of the proceedings and may reverse an initial decision on admissibility at a later stage. However, a government must raise any admissibility question at the earliest appropriate stage of the proceedings.

Exhaustion of domestic remedies

Failure to exhaust domestic remedies is the rock on which the majority of applications to the Court fail. What constitutes a remedy, when it is deemed to have been exhausted, and the circumstances in which an applicant may be excused from exhaustion, because a local remedy is "inadequate and ineffective," have all been the subject of numerous decisions, most comprehensively in *Akdivar v. Turkey*.[13] That jurisprudence should be studied carefully before deciding to initiate proceedings under the Convention. In normal circumstances, an applicant should have pursued all normally available domestic civil, criminal, or administrative processes before lodging an application with the Court. The onus of proof is on the state to establish the existence of a remedy and on the applicant to establish why such remedy was inadequate or, if no recourse to it has been attempted, why it would have been inadequate.

Six-months rule

Article 35 stipulates a near absolute rule: the Court may only consider an application which is lodged with the Registry "within a period of six months from the date on which the final [domestic] decision was taken." For purposes of the six-month rule, the relevant date is normally the date on which the Court receives the first communication about an application, even if it sets out the complaint in summary form and even if the complaint is not formally registered on that date. The prudent step, where a speculative or uncertain domestic remedy is being exhausted, is to notify the Court Registry that an application is being pursued, subject to local proceedings. Where an applicant intends to plead that local remedies have not been pursued because they are inadequate and ineffective, then the six-month rule operates from the date of the act or incident which is the subject of the complaint. The one exception to the six-month rule is a complaint concerning a continuing violation, for example, one that arises from the mere existence of legislation or an administrative practice which is alleged to violate the applicant's rights.

Anonymous applications

The Court will not accept an anonymous application. An applicant may ask that his or her identity not be publicly disclosed, although the logic of the Convention requires that it be disclosed to the respondent government. An application must be signed either by the applicant or the legal representative (Rule 45).

Non bis in idem

The Court will not admit an application that is "substantially" the same as an earlier application involving the applicant, nor will it accept an application if the matter is pending before another international judicial mechanism and the complaint to the Court contains no relevant new information.

Incompatibility with the convention

This criterion is addressed to the quite substantial number of applications that are rejected *ratione materiae*, because they allege violations of rights that are not, in fact, protected under the Convention. A complaint may also be rejected *ratione temporis* if it concerns events that occurred before the state ratified the Convention.

Manifestly ill-founded

A manifestly ill-founded application is not one that should never have been brought, as it might seem. Rather, it is an application which, at the admissibility stage, is judged to be one which, even if admitted and if all the facts alleged are true, would not succeed on the merits and should therefore be dismissed.

Abuse of process

This ground of inadmissibility is a matter of common sense. An application which is drafted in an abusive or hostile fashion, or which makes avowedly political arguments against a government, is likely to be dismissed. In the past, proceedings before the Commission were confidential, and inappropriate publicity was a concern. However, all proceedings before the Court are now public, and there is greater latitude for publicity. A prudent lawyer nonetheless understands that the case must persuade the Court, not the press, and the applicant should be circumspect about media comment on or off the record. The best advice is to refer media inquiries to the Council of Europe Press Office.

Power of attorney

A written power of attorney, normally on the form supplied by the Court, must be executed by the applicant (Rule 45). This should be submitted with the application or whenever representation is arranged; failure to provide this authorization will delay registration and consideration of the application.

Other Matters

Language

The question of language, particularly now that 800 million people in polyglot Europe can complain to the Court, is likely to be one of the most important practical questions to be faced in the future.

The official languages of the Court are French and English. The Rules provide that all stages of an application prior to admissibility, including correspondence, can be conducted in either English or French or in an official language of the contracting parties. After admissibility, however, written pleadings and oral hearings must be in English or French.

Nonetheless, the President of a Chamber has discretion to allow the parties to use the same language used in the preliminary stages of the case during the remainder of the proceedings. The representative pleading in any hearing must have a knowledge of one of the official languages, as must an applicant who wishes to present his or her own case. But, again, the President has discretion to allow pleading in a national language.

Practically speaking, a representative should use a language other than English or French only as a last resort. Seeking to persuade a court of the applicant's position through translation, no matter how good, is likely to put the applicant at a disadvantage.

In circumstances where neither the applicant nor the local lawyer speaks English or French, it would be wise either to involve another advocate who does speak one of these languages or enlist the assistance of an NGO that specializes in the advice, preparation, and support of applications under the Convention.[14] The cost of translating local documents (for example, the applicant's own statement or official court decisions) into French or English should be reimbursable as a legitimate cost, if legal aid is granted. In such circumstances, it also should be possible to justify the costs of involving additional lawyers.

Legal representation

Individuals and organizations may initially file applications to the Court themselves, without legal representation. In further stages of the proceedings, however, an applicant must be represented by a lawyer, unless the President of the Chamber exceptionally decides otherwise. An applicant may appoint any advocate authorized to practice in any member state of the Council of Europe or other approved representative.[15]

Legal aid

One of the most innovative and, in practical terms, most important features of the Convention is its provision for legal aid in individual applications. The assistance is paid from Council of Europe funds and is governed by the Court's Rules. The Court may grant legal aid either on the request of the applicant or on its own initiative. In cases where a number of individuals are involved or where the issues are complex, the Court may pay for representation by more than one lawyer; similarly, fees may be increased if one lawyer acts for a group of individuals. Representatives other than an advocate authorized to practice law (for example a law professor) also are entitled to fees and expenses.

Legal aid is based on means, and eligibility is determined by whether an applicant would be entitled to legal aid in the country in question. A legal aid form must be completed, and the appropriate national authority must ratify it. In addition, the respondent government is asked for its comments. The Rules now provide that legal aid will be available at the point when observations on the admissibility of an application are received or are due from the government.

The fees allowed are not generous and are deemed to be only a "contribution" to costs. They cover not only attorney fees but travelling and living expenses and "other out of pocket expenses." But the fact that necessary expenses incurred in preparing a case, as well as travel and subsistence expenses, are paid for by the Council of Europe is extremely important, since it ensures that a case can be adequately prepared without the actual outlay of funds by an applicant.

There are no filing costs associated with an application. Although the Court has power to order that the applicant bear the costs of hearing a witness the applicant has requested to be called, in practice the Court bears the costs. If the application succeeds before the Court, the Court normally awards reasonable legal fees and expenses to the applicant's lawyers to be paid by the government, as discussed below.

Urgent cases

The Court usually hears cases in the order in which they become ready for hearing. However, under Rule 41, the Chamber or its President can give priority to an application in circumstances of genuine emergency or urgency. A request for precedence in the treatment of an application should be made in a covering letter to an application, setting out specific grounds for priority treatment. Such an application should only be made in the clearest cases, for example, where the victim is at risk of continuing ill-treatment in prison or imminent deportation from a country.

Interim measures

Rule 39 provides that a Chamber or its President, at the initiative of the parties or on its own motion, may indicate to the parties any interim measure which appears necessary to avoid irreparable harm being caused to the victim of an alleged violation. A typical situation is when a state is requested not to proceed with a deportation pending the Court's examination of an application. Failure to honor such a request may result in a violation of Article 34 of the Convention, specifically the duty on the state not to hinder the effective exercise of the right of application.

Amicus curiae briefs

Article 36 allows other state parties and NGOs to intervene before the Court, where it is in the interests of the "proper administration of justice." *Amicus* briefs by international human rights NGOs have become fairly frequent in recent years, and the possibility of such briefs is explicitly provided for in the Convention. In addition, Article 36 offers the significant possibility of an NGO addressing the Court orally as well as submitting a written brief. The procedure requires that an intervenor write to the President of the Court and specify which issue the *amicus* brief proposes to address; the President decides on what issue or issues the Court will grant leave for the intervention.

Proceedings Before the Court

Contents of an application

Rule 47 provides that an application is to be submitted on the official application form provided by the registry. It must include:

- the name, date of birth, nationality, sex, occupation, and address of the applicant;
- the name, occupation, and address of the representative;
- the name of the state or states against which the application is lodged;
- a succinct statement of the facts;
- a succinct statement of the alleged violation(s) of the Convention and the relevant arguments;
- a succinct statement regarding the applicant's compliance with the admissibility criteria; and
- an indication of the object of the application.

The applicant has the burden to supply all the evidence on which an application is based. An application should therefore include any relevant documents and copies of all domestic decisions, whether judicial or not, in particular with respect to exhaustion of domestic remedies.

In addition to presenting a detailed account of the facts, an application should include clear arguments which demonstrate how the facts constitute a violation of specific articles of the Convention by the respondent government. The pleadings should refer to the case law of the Convention where possible and appropriate.

Preadmissibility procedure

Once an application has been lodged with the Court, there are a number of stages prior to the determination of whether the application is admissible. These include the introduction of an application, preliminary contacts with the applicant by the Court's Registry, registration, assignment of the application to one of the Chambers, examination by a Judge Rapporteur from the Chamber, and consideration of the Judge Rapporteur's report by one of the Committees or a Chamber. If the case is not dismissed at this stage, it will then be communicated to the government.

Introduction. The application should be addressed to the Registrar of the European Court of Human Rights. As provided in the Rules, all subsequent correspondence in the case is conducted with the Registry of the Court. In practice, the day-to-day handling of applications is the responsibility of the Court's legal Secretariat. A member of the Secretariat opens a provisional file for each application and contacts the applicant to ensure that all information required is assembled. The Registry is empowered to point out to an applicant any obvious ground of inadmissibility, such as failure to appeal to a domestic court or the fact that the applicant's allegation concerns a right not protected under the Convention. The Registry may discourage an application which is plainly inadmissible, but, if the applicant insists, it will be registered. A considerable time may therefore elapse between receipt of an initial communication and its actual registration.

Registration. Registration is the formal process whereby a complaint becomes an application and receives a case number. Once the case is registered, it is assigned to a Chamber and a Judge Rapporteur is appointed. The Judge Rapporteur, assisted by a member of the Secretariat, will prepare a report on admissibility. He or she may refer the case to a three-judge Committee, proposing dismissal, or, if the Judge Rapporteur considers that the application raises a question of principle and is not inadmissible, it may be referred directly to the Chamber. The Committee may reject the application, by a unanimous vote, and that decision is final; most applications are dismissed at this stage. The applicant is sent a short written decision, which does not constitute jurisprudence and is not published.

Communication to the government. If the Committee does not reject the application, it will be referred to a Chamber and communicated to the government for the latter's observations on admissibility. Communication of an application to the government should be the minimum goal of any legal practitioner. Whatever the eventual outcome of an application, communication puts the government on notice that a reasonably serious complaint has been filed, and it may facilitate a resolution of the problem even prior to any formal involvement by the Court in friendly settlement discussions.

Observations on admissibility. The government is normally given six weeks within which to make observations on an application. The Court may ask the government to address a series of questions related to facts (if they are in dispute), domestic remedies, or the merits of the application. It forwards a copy of the government's observations to the applicant for a written response. Once this exchange of pleadings is concluded, the purpose of which is to eliminate or reduce the issues of contention between the parties, a new report on admissibility is drafted by the Judge Rapporteur and discussed by the Chamber. If the case is not rejected at this stage, the Chamber may either adopt a decision on admissibility on the basis of written observations or proceed to hold an oral hearing.

Oral hearings. The Court's heavy caseload dictates that any oral hearing will usually consider both admissibility and the merits of a case, and an oral hearing dealing only with admissibility is highly exceptional. Indeed, it is increasingly the practice for the Court to dispense altogether with any hearing, proceeding to judgment on the basis of the written pleadings. If there is a hearing (which is held in Strasbourg), copies of representatives' statements are requested in advance to facilitate simultaneous interpretation. Members of the Chamber may ask questions, and the parties are given an opportunity for brief replies to each other's submissions. The Chamber deliberates in private. It then communicates immediately and informally its provisional view on admissibility to the parties, which is done, in part, to encourage friendly settlement of the application. The Court's decision on admissibility, without prejudice to its final judgment on the merits, is published.

Fact-finding hearings. In the great majority of cases, the facts are not in dispute, since the application will normally already have been adjudicated upon with regards to issues both of fact and law in the domestic courts. However, in recent years, there have been more cases which involve disputes of fact between the parties and where there has been no domestic consideration of the applicant's complaints. In such situations, the Court may send one or more judges to obtain evidence on-site. Governments must furnish "all necessary facilities" for the Court's investigation.

As an example of fact-finding, three delegates from the former Commission visited Turkey to resolve disputed facts in a number of cases. These investigations included the hearing of witnesses on behalf of the applicant and government, as well as on-site inspections. The applicant and the government were present and able to examine and cross-examine witnesses. The delegates' report on the hearing formed the central evidence on which the Commission reached conclusions as to whether there had been a breach of the Convention. The standard of proof required of an applicant in such proceedings is proof beyond a reasonable doubt, and the new Court has continued the practice of the former Commission.

Friendly settlement. Parallel to its investigation of the merits, the Court is required to "place itself at the disposal of the parties" in order to facilitate a friendly settlement. A friendly settlement may involve a government agreeing to amend existing legislation or to pay monetary compensation. Although the applicant and the government can negotiate directly, they are likely to use the good offices of the Court. The Court may propose a solution, but it cannot insist on a settlement. It can, however, reject one. If a settlement is reached, it must be approved by the Court as consistent with respect for human rights. In a recent landmark case, the Grand Chamber of the Court rejected the request of respondent government to strike a case out following its declaration offering a financial compensation, which had been refused by the applicant.[16] The Court's reasoning suggests that, where there is *prima facie* evidence of a failure of domestic bodies to investigate a serious violation, a unilateral declaration must at least contain an admission to that effect and an undertaking to conduct an investigation. An agreed settlement is binding on the parties, and the case is closed. While the rest of the process of considering an application is public, friendly settlement negotiations and documentation are confidential.

Observations and hearings on the merits. If a settlement is not reached, the Court proceeds to consider the merits of the application. Both applicant and government may be invited to submit written memorials setting out comprehensively their views of law and fact. If there is to be a hearing, then, as noted above, the usual practice is to have only one hearing, encompassing both admissibility and merits. The hearings are likely to be short, perhaps ninety minutes or less. An oral presentation is only likely to be influential if the advocate's statement is focused and confined to key points; any attempt to read a memorial already submitted is likely to receive short shrift from the Court.

Remedies

Article 41 empowers the Court to award "just satisfaction" if it finds a violation of the Convention. It is important for a legal representative to be clear about what is being sought by way of reparation for a violation. First, the finding of a breach of the Convention imposes on the respondent state a legal obligation to put an end to such breach and make reparation for its consequences in such a way as to restore, as far as possible, the situation existing before the breach (*restitutio in integrum*). However, if *restitutio in integrum* is in practice impossible, the respondent states are free to choose the means whereby they will comply with a judgment. This formulation incorporates the general rule of international law with respect to reparation for an international wrong. However, the Court also has consistently held that it has no competence to make consequential orders or declarations; its authority differs significantly in this respect from that of the Inter-American Court of Human Rights.[17]

In practice, therefore, the Court's power is confined to awarding monetary compensation, in addition to costs and expenses. The Court may award both pecuniary and nonpecuniary damages in appropriate cases. Substantial damages have been awarded in both categories, and a practitioner should study awards in other cases in framing claims for just satisfaction. A recent innovation was the appointment of an expert to evaluate pecuniary loss in a complex land case.[18] This could be an important precedent that might avoid disputes over damages when the failure of the parties to agree has resulted in the Court awarding "equitable" sums that can leave the applicant unsatisfied.

Legal costs and expenses also will be awarded where justified, i.e., where they are "reasonable as to quantum and were necessarily incurred." Any claims for legal costs and fees must be set forth in a detailed written claim filed with the Court as required by its Rules. The Court will deduct from any award of legal costs any sums already granted in legal aid.

Rehearing

Either party to a case may, "in exceptional cases," seek referral of the judgment of a Chamber to the Grand Chamber. Article 43 provides that a referral must be lodged within three months of the delivery of a judgment. A panel of five judges drawn from the Grand Chamber considers the request and is to accept it if the case raises a "serious question affecting the interpretation or application of the Convention or the protocols thereto, or [a] serious issue of general importance" (Rule 73(1)). In 2003, the Grand Chamber granted a rehearing in only eight cases out of 64 in which it was requested. It should also be noted that a Chamber has the authority to relinquish jurisdiction in favor of the Grand Chamber if issues of general importance arise at any stage in a hearing, unless one of the parties to the case objects.

Supervision of Execution of the Judgment by the Committee of Ministers

While the procedure before the Committee is confidential, reports of deliberations on implementation of judgments are published. An applicant's representative should not hesitate to submit views through the Committee's Secretariat as to what the applicant considers necessary to ensure full implementation of the judgment. This might include, for example, reform or repeal of a law or a change in administrative practice, as well as the restoration of rights, for example, rights to particular property. If damages and costs are not paid in time (the limit is normally three months from the date of the judgment), then a claim for interest at the rate set by the Court can be made. It is not the practice of the Committee of Ministers to correspond with an applicant or representative, but informal telephone communication should be maintained with the Secretariat to ensure that the judgment is fulfilled. If a state refuses to act in accordance with a judgment of the Court, the Committee of Ministers may publicly condemn such noncompliance.

The European Social Charter

Substantive Rights

The substantive provisions of the Charter comprise a series of Principles (Part I) and a set of articles enshrining social and economic rights (Part II). States undertake to uphold a core number of obligations which includes at least five out of seven specified articles (i.e., the right to work; the right to organize; the right to bargain collectively; the right to social security; the right to social and medical assistance; the right of the family to social, legal, and economic protection; and the rights of migrant workers). States also are required to agree to a specified minimum of other undertakings. This unusual approach was designed to encourage states to progressively increase their commitments to defend social rights.

As noted above, sixteen states have adopted the extended protection provided by a 1996 revision of the Charter, which came into force in 1999. Among the main changes are inclusion of the rights to protection against poverty and social exclusion, decent housing, and protection in cases of termination of employment, as well as a widening of the nondiscrimination provisions.

Implementation

The state reporting process

Parties to the Charter are required to submit reports to a series of oversight bodies on the application of provisions they have accepted. Prior to submission, these reports must be sent for comment to national trade union and employer bodies, whose comments are transmitted along with the reports. Although there is no formal procedure for other NGOs to submit comments on a state's report, they may transmit comments unofficially to the trade unions concerned or to the Secretariat of the Committee of Independent Experts.

The reports are first examined by a Committee of Independent Experts, which is elected by the Committee of Ministers of the Council of Europe and is assisted by an observer from the International Labor Organization. The state's report and the Committee's legal opinion on the degree to which a state has fulfilled its commitments are then transmitted to the Governmental Committee, which is composed of representatives of the parties to the Charter and assisted by European trade union and employer organizations. In light of the findings of the Committee of Independent Experts and on the basis of social, economic, and other policy considerations, the Governmental Committee advises the Committee of Ministers as to what recommendations should be made to a party. Finally, the Committee of Ministers issues recommendations to those states that fail to comply with the requirements of the Charter. Although the Parliamentary Assembly of the Council of Europe no longer takes part in the supervisory process, in practice it may use the conclusions of the Committee of Independent Experts as a basis for social policy debates.

The collective complaint mechanism

Implementation of the Social Charter was given a much needed boost by the adoption of an Additional Protocol in 1995, which provides for a system of collective complaints concerning alleged noncompliance with the Charter. The Protocol entered into force in 1998, but as of early 2004 it has been ratified by only twelve states. Under the Protocol, complaints may be made by three categories of organizations: international organizations of employers and trade unions that participate in the work of the Governmental Committee; other international NGOs that have consultative status with the Council of Europe and have been placed on a list created for this purpose by the Governmental Committee; and national trade union and employer's organizations within the jurisdiction of the state against which they wish to lodge a complaint. By filing a separate declaration, each state also may authorize national NGOs to lodge complaints against it; only Finland has done so.

The Committee of Independent Experts examines collective complaints. It first decides on their admissibility in light of the criteria laid down in the Protocol and its Rules of Procedure. For example, the complainant must fall into one of the categories listed above; the complaint may only address matters regarding which the NGO has been recognized as having particular competence; and the complaint must relate to a provision of the Charter accepted by the state concerned. The official languages are French and English, but the Rules of Procedure permits the third category of complainant to submit a complaint in a language other than one of the official languages.

By the end of 2003, twenty-three complaints had been submitted to the European Committee of Social Rights, leading to eleven decisions on the merits, which are published. Violations have been found in seven cases, concerning a wide range of substantive issues, such as the right to fair remuneration, the prohibition of employment under the age of fifteen, and discrimination in employment.

The European Convention for the Prevention of Torture and Inhuman and Degrading Treatment or Punishment

Unlike the corresponding UN Convention against Torture,[19] the European Convention against Torture includes no mechanism allowing individual complaints; the European Convention on Human Rights already provides such redress. There also is no reporting obligation imposed on states. Instead, the Convention is overseen by a Committee for the Prevention of Torture composed of independent experts, which is entitled to visit any place of detention in a member state where persons are deprived of their liberty by a public authority. This includes prisons, police cells, and psychiatric hospitals, as well as places where asylum-seekers are held. The state is notified about periodic visits by the Committee (usually once every two years), but unannounced, ad hoc visits also may be undertaken if the Committee becomes concerned about the situation in a particular country. During any visit, the Committee can speak privately to detainees and may interview anyone whom it considers may supply relevant information. At the end of a visit, the Committee compiles a confidential report, which is presented to the state, along with any recommendations. If the state fails to implement the recommendations, the Committee may issue a public statement. Although the Convention provides for the continued confidentiality of the Committee's reports, a practice has developed whereby, with the consent of the state in question (which is normally forthcoming), both the Committee's report and the response of the government are published. By January 2004, the CPT had performed 108 periodic visits and sixty-one ad hoc visits and published a total of 120 reports.

Accurate information is the key to the success of the Committee's work, and national and international NGOs have an important role to play in providing information on situations in which detainees are at risk. They also may help by ensuring that information on the Convention and the Committee is available to prisoners and other detainees and that medical, police, and prison professionals learn about the Convention.

The Committee's published reports may, in turn, be of use in individual cases brought under the European Convention, especially where the applicant is claiming that ill-treatment or inhuman conditions of detention are widespread. They also could be used in lobbying initiatives under other European systems, for example in the Council of Europe's Parliamentary Assembly or OSCE meetings or before the European Union Parliament.

The Framework Convention for the Protection of National Minorities

This Convention is the first in the world devoted exclusively to the protection of national minorities, and it entered into force only on February 1, 1998. Thirty-five states are currently party to it. The Convention provides for a wide range of minority rights but has no complaint mechanism. Instead, states submit reports to an Advisory Committee on measures they have taken to give effect to the Convention's principles. The Advisory Committee conducts on-site visits as an element of its oversight, where it meets with both government officials and NGOs. NGOs also can submit written comments on government reports when they are being considered by the Advisory Committee. The Committee submits an opinion on the state report to the Committee of Ministers, which in turn adopts conclusions and, where appropriate, recommendations. During the its first years, this mechanism has led concrete measures aimed at better protection of minority rights in a number of states.

The European Community/Union

The Treaty of Rome, which established the European Economic Community (EEC) in 1957, did not specifically protect human rights, apart from an oblique reference in the preamble to "preserve and strengthen peace and liberty." Article 6 EEC (now Article 12 EC Treaty[20]) prohibited discrimination between EC citizens; Article 48 EEC (Article 39 EC Treaty) established the right to freedom of movement for workers in the Community; and Article 119 EEC (Article 141 EC Treaty) enshrined the principle that men and women are entitled to equal pay for equal work. But, as the EC expanded beyond its original sphere of (mainly economic) activities, it was initially left to the European Court of Justice to develop "general principles of Community law," including fundamental rights, and to protect them through case law.

The Treaty on the European Union (TEU), adopted in 1992 in Maastricht, provided for the first time that the EU must "respect fundamental rights, as guaranteed by the [European Convention] and as they result from the constitutional traditions common to the Member States, as general principles of Community law," thereby codifying the case law of the European Court of Justice. The 1997 Treaty of Amsterdam introduced a new Article 6(1) TEU, which elevated respect for human rights to the status of one of the principles on which the EU is founded: "The Union is founded on the principles of liberty, democracy, respect for human rights and fundamental freedoms, and the rule of law, principles which are common to the Member States."

The European Court of Justice

The European Court of Justice (ECJ),[21] which sits in Luxembourg, was established under the original EEC Treaty and ensures that, in the interpretation and application of the treaties, the "law" is observed. As noted above, the special status of the European Convention on Human Rights was confirmed by the addition of Article 6(2) TEU. Nonetheless, it is clear that the European Convention does not bind the EU institutions or the member states per se when implementing Community law, although the ECJ continues to refer to and rely on European Convention case law in its judgments. However, the fact remains that there is no clear catalogue of rights legally binding on EU institutions.

In addition to the lack of a clear catalogue of rights, it is currently extremely difficult for individuals to bring an action directly to the European Court of Justice, as the Court has interpreted *locus standi* requirements contained in Article 230 EC very restrictively. Most cases that come before the European Court of Justice begin in the national courts and are subsequently referred to the European Court of Justice under Article 234 EC. This so-called "preliminary rulings procedure" entitles national courts to ask questions of the ECJ on the interpretation of the EC Treaty or the interpretation or validity of secondary Community legislation. There are inherent problems associated with this procedure, which have substantially restricted individuals' access to the ECJ—for example, there is no *obligation* on national courts to refer a question to the European Court of Justice.

The EU Charter of Fundamental Rights and the Proposed EU Constitution

More recent developments at the EU political level include the solemn proclamation of the EU Charter of Fundamental Rights in December 2000, which is a catalogue of rights and freedoms which the institutions have declared will, at the very least, constitute a guiding document for their actions. The EU Charter is not yet legally binding,[22] but should current efforts to agree on a constitution for the European Union prove successful, the Charter would be binding and apply to all European Union institutions.

The rights in the Charter include traditional civil and political rights similar to those contained in the European Convention, without mirroring them exactly. For example, Article 2, on the right to life, makes no provision for capital punishment, reflecting the fact that the EU is a death-penalty-free zone. Similarly, Article 9, on the right to marry and to found a family, does not restrict this right to heterosexual relationships, reflecting the fact that some member states of the EU allow same-sex marriage.

In addition, the Charter includes economic, social, and cultural rights, such as the rights of collective bargaining (Article 28); health care (Article 35); and cultural, religious, and linguistic diversity (Article 22). The Charter makes special provisions for the elderly (Article 25) and persons with disabilities (Article 26) and includes a separate section on citizens' rights (Articles 39–46). The last-mentioned includes the right to vote and to stand as a candidate for European Parliament elections, the right of access to documents of EU institutions, and the right to petition the European Parliament and contact the European Ombudsman.

The European Parliament

Within the Parliament, the *Committee on Citizens' Freedoms and Rights, Justice and Home Affairs* monitors human rights within the EU and the implementation of policies such as the elimination of all forms of discrimination and the protection of personal data. The Parliament's *Committee on Foreign Affairs, Human Rights, Common Security and Defence Policy* is mandated to consider human rights outside the EU, and it is an important forum for NGOs. It makes recommendations as to the inclusion of human rights clauses in agreements with third countries and produces an annual report on human rights in the world, which also covers the situation in EU member states.

Right to Petition

In 1987, the European Parliament established a *Committee on Petitions* to which any citizen or resident of the EU, or any company, organization, or association with its headquarters in a member state (i.e. any "natural or legal person" based in the EU), may submit an individual or joint petition regarding a subject which falls within the EU's sphere of activities, including human rights, that affects them directly. As an example of the scale of its work, the Committee declared 744 petitions admissible and 293 inadmissible in 2001–2002.

European Ombudsman

The Ombudsman of the EU was established by the Treaty on European Union to hear complaints about maladministration by EU institutions from any citizen or resident of the EU or company registered in an EU member state, without the requirement of showing that they are directly concerned by the alleged maladministration. The right to apply to the Ombudsman has been confirmed by Article 21 EC Treaty and Article 43 of the EU Charter. Since taking office in 1995, the Ombudsman has dealt with over 11,000 grievances from citizens, companies, organizations, and public authorities. The matters raised have ranged from tax provisions to access to documents, and from competition law to sex discrimination. The Ombudsman has been particularly active in ensuring that the EU Charter of Fundamental Rights is adhered to, reminding institutions of their political commitments under its provisions. The Ombudsman submits an annual report to the European Parliament, and all outcomes of the complaints are available on the World Wide Web.

Organization for Security and Cooperation in Europe

The first meeting of the Conference on Security and Cooperation in Europe (CSCE) led to adoption of the Helsinki Final Act in 1975, "Basket Three" of which concerns respect for human rights, including freedom of movement, thought, conscience, religion, and belief. The CSCE remained a diplomatic process of frequent but irregular meetings rather than a treaty or institution until it was transformed into the Organization for Security and Cooperation in Europe (OSCE) in 1994. The OSCE Secretary-General and the Permanent Council are now based in Vienna, with a documentation and information office in Prague; there is an Office for Democratic Institutions and Human Rights (ODIHR) based in Warsaw; and a Parliamentary Assembly is drawn from the parliaments of participating states. Its fifty-five members include Canada and the United States, in addition to all states in Europe and the former Soviet Union. An OSCE Summit is held every two years; day-to-day operations are overseen by the Permanent Council, which meets weekly, and the Chairman-in-Office, which rotates annually among the participating states. The OSCE's primary focus has evolved into one that works on practical steps to build "human security," a mission that embraces traditional military security and counter-terrorism, human rights, democratization, and the rule of law.

ODIHR

The OSCE Office for Democratic Institutions and Human Rights (ODIHR), based in Warsaw, is the principal institution of the OSCE responsible for the "human dimension" (norms and activities related to human rights and democracy, the term used in the 1975 Helsinki Declaration). The ODIHR assists participating states in building democratic institutions and in implementing their OSCE human rights commitments. An important part of ODIHR's work is election observation missions, and the office is also specifically concerned with human rights issues related to the Roma and Sinti throughout Europe.

High Commissioner on National Minorities

Perhaps the most innovative human rights achievement of the OSCE was the creation in 1992 of the post of High Commissioner on National Minorities. This Office was designed as a conflict prevention mechanism to intervene early in situations of minority tensions and, with the consent of the parties, to seek solutions to potential conflicts. Although not a human rights mechanism per se, the High Commissioner's office may seek and receive information from any source. The Office cannot address individual cases, but it is generally acknowledged that the High Commissioner has contributed significantly to the peaceful resolution of conflicts involving minorities, particularly in the emerging democracies in central and eastern Europe. The High Commissioner's work is confidential, but most of his recommendations to states are published on the Office's website.

Representative on Freedom of the Media

In 1997, the OSCE established a Representative on Freedom of the Media, based in Vienna, to "provide rapid response to serious non-compliance with OSCE commitments and principles in respect of freedom of expression and free media." The Representative may collect and receive information from "all bona fide sources" and is authorized to make direct contacts with states, even if there are national or international proceedings pending concerning alleged violations of freedom of expression. The mandate is conciliatory and advisory, rather than judicial, and it embraces violations in North America as well as in Europe. As is true for the High Commissioner on National Minorities, the ultimate sanction available to the Representative is to report to the political organs of the OSCE.

Human Dimension Mechanism

In 1989, a "Human Dimension Mechanism" was created to give greater political legitimacy to the ability of a state to raise with another state, through diplomatic channels, an individual case or situation concerning human rights. This mechanism is composed of two instruments: the Vienna Mechanism (established in 1989) and the Moscow Mechanism (established in 1991). An individual cannot invoke the Human Dimension Mechanism, but it is possible for an OSCE participating state to invoke the mechanism regarding the case of an individual. The mechanism has become somewhat less important as many OSCE members have become parties to the European Convention and Cold War tensions have disappeared, but it remains available to states that wish to raise issues of noncompliance with OSCE norms in other states.

Distinct from short-term fact-finding missions are the OSCE's "long-term missions," which permit the OSCE to have an active presence in countries that require assistance. Such field presences have emerged as a real strength of the OSCE. Depending on the situation, the emphasis may be on conflict or crisis prevention or conflict resolution. Each mandate is designed to ensure that the mission can address the underlying issues that have generated international concern.

The OSCE remains primarily a diplomatic and political institution to which NGOs have no formal access (except through its "Human Dimension" meetings, the High Commissioner on National Minorities, and the Representative on Freedom of the Media). However, it should not be forgotten by the human rights activist, particularly when the intention is to raise a broader human rights situation, as opposed to an individual violation.

Concluding Observations

During the 1990s, a remarkable expansion of European bodies was set in motion, coupled with the disappearance of divisions between west and east. Today, the Council of Europe is a truly pan-European organization, and the European Union has grown to include much of Central and Eastern Europe. Along with these momentous developments have come critical challenges, as the protection of human rights in the new democracies is put under European scrutiny.

The European Convention on Human Rights remains the most effective international legal mechanism for protecting human rights; in effect, it has become a constitutional court for Europe on human rights. The new implementation system for the European Social Charter has rendered that document more effective and accessible. The possible inclusion of the Charter of Fundamental Rights in the proposed constitution of the European Union would be a significant step within the EU, which, along with the OSCE, has traditionally dealt with human rights issues in a diplomatic or political rather than a legal setting.

More important than new institutions is the new political climate of respect for human rights that one would like to believe has accompanied the development of a deeper and wider European "community" during the past decade. It would clearly be false to conclude that human rights are now universally respected within Europe, but the relevance and acceptance of human rights norms, as well as international responsibility for their implementation, can no longer be doubted.

Notes

1. The author would like to acknowledge and thank Ljiljana Helman, Matias Helman, Karen Silke Hoseman, Essex LLM students, and Estelle Askew Renaut, doctoral student, for their assistance.

2. For an excellent short overview of the work of the Council of Europe, see *Human Rights, a Continuing Challenge* (Strasbourg: Council of Europe Press, 1995).

3. Note also that Protocol No. 1, which entered into force on 1 March 2002, empowers the Committee of Ministers of the Council of Europe to invite any non-member state to accede to the convention.

4. The EU members are France, Germany, Italy, Belgium, the Netherlands, Luxembourg, Ireland, the United Kingdom, Sweden, Austria, Finland, Greece, Denmark, Spain, Portugal, Estonia, Latvia, Lithuania, Poland, Czech Republic, Slovakia, Hungary, Slovenia, Malta, and Cyprus.

5. Opinion 2/94 [1996] ECR I-1759.

6. The European Convention remains the only international mechanism under which any interstate cases have been filed. A total of eighteen often politically sensitive applications have been brought by states concerning human rights violations in Northern Ireland, South Tyrol, Cyprus, Turkey, and Greece.

7. The "margin of appreciation" doctrine was first articulated by the Court in the context of the discretion that should be granted to a state in the context of a declared state of emergency. Later extended to nonemergency situations, it refers to the Court's willingness to grant a certain degree of deference to national authorities in their initial weighing of public versus individual interests.

8. See the works cited in the Bibliographic Essay, Appendix A.

9. Apps. Nos. 6780/74, 6950/75, dec. on admiss., 2 *Dec. & Rep.* 136–137 (1975).

10. Application No. 52207/99, Grand Chamber, 21 Dec. 2001.

11. Soering v. U.K., Judgment of 7 July 1989, Ser. A., No. 161.

12. See Chahal v. U.K., Judgment of 15 Nov. 1996, Ser. A, No. 697.

13. Akdivar et al. v. Turkey, Judgment of 1 Apr. 1998 (art. 50).

14. There are a number of such international organizations, the best known of which are AIRE (Action on Rights in Europe) and INTERIGHTS, the International Centre for the Legal Protection of Human Rights. AIRE's address is Third Floor, 17 Red Lion Square, London WCIR 4QH; tel. 020 7831 4276; fax 0207 404 7760; www. airecentre.org. INTERIGHTS may be contacted at Lancaster House, 33 Islington High Street, London Nl 9LH; tel. (44) (0)20 7278–3230; fax (44) (0) 20 7278–4334; e-mail ir@interights.org.

15. In several cases brought against Turkey, the government objected on the grounds of cost to the applicants being represented by lawyers from the United Kingdom. However, the Court has ruled that an applicant may engage a lawyer from any member state.

16. Tahsin Acar v Turkey, Grand Chamber, 6 May 2003.

17. See chap. 7.

18. Belvedere Alberghiera Srl v. Italy, App. No. 31525/96, 30 Oct. 2003.

19. See chap. 3.

20. The EEC Treaty was amended by subsequent Treaties and renumbered by the Treaty of Amsterdam in 1997. All "new" article numbers refer to the Consolidated Version of the Treaty establishing the European Community, 2002 O.J. C325 (the "EC Treaty").

21. The Single European Act (1987 O.J. L169/1) created a Court of First Instance for the European Communities, which is institutionally part of the European Court of Justice, despite the fact their jurisdiction is split. For further details, see L. Neville Brown and Tom Kennedy, *Brown & Jacobs The Court of Justice of the European Communities* (Sweet & Maxwell, 5th ed. 2000).

22. The Commission has stated before the Court of First Instance that it considers itself bound by the EU Charter (Case T-52/01 R. Jürgen Schäfer v. Commission, Order, [2001] ECR IA-00115; II-00543), and the European Parliament confirmed that the Charter would be the law guiding its actions (Declaration of the European Parliament President at the Nice Summit, 2000). Only the Council has refused to grant the EU Charter more than symbolic significance.

Chapter 9
The African Charter on Human and Peoples' Rights

Cees Flinterman and Evelyn Ankumah

Introduction

The African Charter on Human and Peoples' Rights was adopted in 1981 by the Assembly of Heads of State and Government of the then Organization of African Unity (OAU). The Charter entered into force five years later and has been ratified by fifty-three members of the OAU, now known as the African Union (AU).[1]

The Charter sets forth a wide range of human and peoples' rights. The former include, *inter alia*, nondiscrimination; respect for personal security and liberty; and freedom of conscience, religion, association, expression, and movement. Peoples' rights include the right to self-determination, free disposition of natural resources, development, and a satisfactory environment. There is also a chapter on the duties of the individual to family and society.

The Charter establishes a supervisory mechanism in which the African Commission on Human and Peoples' Rights plays a pivotal role; in 2004, a Protocol establishing an African Court on Human and Peoples' Rights entered into force, but the role of the Court is as yet uncertain. Despite its broad mandate, which is discussed in the following section, the Commission consists of only eleven members. The Commission's Secretariat is also very limited in size, so the Commission cannot undertake many of the tasks entrusted to it.

This chapter focuses on the Charter's provisions relating to the Commission and its procedures. The first section briefly considers some aspects of the substantive provisions of the Charter. The next section describes the procedures relating to complaints by states, individuals, and groups. The third section introduces the new African Court on Human and Peoples' Rights.

At the time of writing, the Commission had been functioning for fifteen years. It has passed its formative stage and is now concentrating on some of the legal issues that arise under the African Charter, interpreting the Charter in a more creative way so as to maximize the protection of human rights. While positive developments have occurred, there remains room for further improvement. It is hoped that, as the Commission continues its work, a better understanding of its mandate and procedures will ensure that individuals and nongovernmental organizations are able to use it in ways that maximize its potential as an effective promoter of human rights. It is further hoped that the African Court on Human and Peoples' Rights will complement and strengthen the role of the Commission.

The Charter's Substantive Provisions

The African Charter sets forth a relatively large number of protected rights, but many are significantly weakened by the inclusion of "clawback" clauses which permit states to act with a great deal of discretion to limit protected rights. Although permissible limitations are common to all international human rights instruments—very few human rights are absolute—the scope of limitations in the African Charter is much broader than that found in other instruments.

For example, the right to express and disseminate opinions under Article 9 can only be exercised "within the law." The right to participate in government, guaranteed by Article 13, "should be exercised in accordance with the provisions of the law." The latter provision might be interpreted as legitimizing compulsory party membership in one-party states, although political reforms in several African countries in the early 1990s suggest that obligatory party membership may soon be a thing of the past.

The fragility of substantive rights guaranteed under the African Charter is underscored by its provisions on the individual's duties "towards his family and society, the State and other legally recognized communities and the international community," set forth in Articles 27–29. For example, Article 27(2) provides that an individual's rights "shall be exercised with due regard to the rights of others, collective security, morality and common interest." Article 29 provides, *inter alia*, that every individual has the duty "[t]o serve his national community by placing his physical and intellectual abilities at its service; . . . [n]ot to compromise the security of the State; . . . [t]o preserve and strengthen social and national solidarity; . . . [and] to contribute to the promotion of the moral well being of society."

Given the extent of the permissible limitations on rights, it is perhaps not surprising that the African Charter contains no article which would permit temporary derogation from any of its provisions in time of national emergency.

If the Commission were to adopt an unduly narrow view of the provisions it was created to promote and protect, the clawback clauses and the duties owed by the individual have the potential to undermine many of the substantive guarantees in the Charter. Fortunately, the practice of the Commission thus far has been encouraging. It has interpreted the clawback clauses restrictively, in favor of human rights, and has held that state legislation which unduly restricts human rights violates the Charter. However, the Commission has so far offered no interpretative statement on clawback clauses generally.

Furthermore, Article 60 of the Charter directs the Commission to "draw inspiration from international law on human and peoples' rights," including not only African instruments but also the Universal Declaration of Human Rights and instruments adopted by the United Nations and its specialized agencies. Article 61 identifies, *inter alia*, other international treaties, rules expressly recognized by OAU members, and customs generally accepted as law "as subsidiary measures to determine the principles of law" to be applied by the Commission. When read together, these two articles underscore the interrelationship between African and other international legal principles, and they reinforce the understanding that nothing in the African Charter should be deemed to diminish human rights obligations that states have accepted pursuant to other international conventions.

From its inclusion of "peoples'" rights to its frequent references to African traditions and civilization, the African Charter can be clearly distinguished from the more individualistic formulations of rights adopted in the European and inter-American systems. That an African regional system for the protection of human rights should reflect African values of community and consensus should not only be expected, it should be welcomed. Of course, there is a danger that fraudulent claims of preserving African traditions may be used to disguise political corruption and dictatorship, but this danger exists in all regions of world—one has only to remember the "national security" claims of Greek colonels and Argentine generals to be reminded that those in power frequently attempt to pervert human rights values to their own ends.

This is not the place to enter into a philosophical discussion of purported distinctions between individual and collective rights. Indeed, the growing demands in Africa for truly effective political participation, pluralism, and increased individual freedoms suggest that the differences may not be as great as some maintain. Therefore, a liberal, rights-protective interpretation of the African Charter is certainly possible, even if the Charter's language does give cause for concern in some respects. If the African Commission continues to interpret the weak, ambiguous provisions of the Charter in a manner that enhances rights, the flexibility inherent in the Charter may contribute to the effective promotion of rights in the context of African policies and culture.

The African Commission on Human and Peoples' Rights

Article 45 of the African Charter grants a broad mandate to the Commission. Four functions may be distinguished: promotion, protection, interpretation of the Charter, and performance of any other tasks which might be entrusted to the Commission by the OAU Assembly of Heads of State and Government.

Promotional Functions

The promotional functions of the Commission are spelled out in detail, but not exhaustively, in Article 45(1)(a)–(c) of the Charter. These functions include such basic activities as collecting documents; undertaking studies and research on African problems in the field of human rights; organizing conferences, seminars, and symposia; disseminating information; and encouraging national and local institutions concerned with human and peoples' rights. The Commission is authorized to formulate principles and rules aimed at solving legal problems relating to human and peoples' rights and fundamental freedoms, upon which African governments may base legislation, and to cooperate with African and international institutions concerned with the promotion and protection of human rights. For example, the Commission has adopted Guidelines and Measures for the Prohibition and Prevention of Torture, a Declaration of Principles on Freedom of Expression in Africa, and a resolution on the Rights of Indigenous Peoples' Communities in Africa.

Promotion is perhaps the least controversial of all possible actions to be taken regarding human rights, as it does not directly call into question the human rights performance of any particular country. Nevertheless, the potential impact of promotional functions should not be underestimated, and, thus far, the Commission has given priority to its promotional tasks. At its second session, the Commission drew up a program of action to promote human and peoples' rights, which has subsequently been updated and expanded. In 1990, with funds granted by the (then) UN Center for Human Rights, the Commission began to publish annual reports and disseminate copies of the African Charter and an informational brochure of the Charter. From 1991 until 2000, a journal, *The Review of the African Commission on Human and Peoples' Rights*, appeared; the *Review* included articles on the Charter and relevant documents. The Commission also mandated each of its members to carry out promotional activities in individual states, on which they report during each session.

The role of nongovernmental organizations (NGOs) in implementing the promotional mandate of the Commission is crucial, and over 300 NGOs have been granted observer status by the Commission.

Protection Functions

Articles 46–49 of the Charter and Rules 88–120 of the Commission's Rules of Procedure (as amended in 1995) set forth the procedures to be followed in considering communications. There are two types of communications, those from states and all others.

Article 46 of the Charter permits the Commission to "resort to any appropriate method of investigation" when considering a communication, an open-ended authorization which is not limited by the immediately succeeding reference to information from the General Secretary of the OAU "or any other person capable of enlightening [the Commission]." Thus, information from individuals, NGOs, and others can be considered by the Commission in the context of communications, even though the requirement of confidentiality might prohibit formal intervention by outside parties in the Commission's consideration of any case.

Communications from states

The state complaint procedure is provided for in Articles 47–54 of the Charter. The Rules of Procedure distinguish between two types of state communications: a "negotiation-communication" (Rules 88–92) and a "complaint-communication" (Rules 93–101), although to date the distinction appears to be of only theoretical interest. In 1999, a communication was filed by the Democratic Republic of Congo against Burundi, Rwanda, and Uganda;[2] as of early 2004, no decision had been taken by the Commission.

"Negotiation-communications" are those filed under Article 47 of the Charter, which provides that a state party which has "good reasons" to believe that another state has violated the Charter may bring the matter to the attention of the latter state. Copies of the communication are sent to the Secretary-General of the OAU and the chairman of the Commission, and the addressee state has three months to respond to the allegations. If the states in question are unable to arrive at a satisfactory solution, either state may submit the matter to the Commission; the issue is also referred to the Commission automatically if the addressee state fails to reply to the communication. Notwithstanding the provisions of

Article 47, a state party may choose to submit a matter directly to the Commission, bypassing the three-month negotiation period.

Referral to the Commission triggers the "complaint-communication" procedure. The Commission is directed first to try "all appropriate means to reach an amicable solution," and it is clear that bilateral negotiations between states are the preferred method of dispute resolution. This provision is equivalent to the "friendly settlement" procedures found in most other international human rights conventions.

The Charter's insistence on negotiation reflects the fact that most African states were (and are) not willing to expose themselves to the possibility of a legally binding judgment being adopted concerning their "domestic" affairs. The search for a mutually acceptable solution to a dispute may also be regarded as consistent with the African tradition of conciliation rather than adjudication. Thus, the Charter did not originally provide for the establishment of a court. (The court created in 2004 is discussed below.)

As is the case under other international procedures, a communication will not be considered by the African Commission until all domestic remedies have been exhausted, "if they exist" and are not "unduly prolonged." Given the problems that exist with respect to the judicial systems in many African states—ranging from lack of an independent judiciary to more practical difficulties, such as a lack of facilities and lawyers—a reasonable interpretation of the exhaustion rule by the Commission should not bar otherwise admissible communications.

There are no other formal requirements for an interstate communication. The Commission may ask the states concerned to produce relevant information, and, if no friendly settlement is possible, it prepares "a report stating the facts and its findings." Pursuant to Article 52 of the Charter, the report may also rely on information "from other sources," from which the Commission may obtain "all the information it deems necessary."

Copies of a report are sent to the states concerned and the Assembly of Heads of State and Government, to which the Commission may make "such recommendations as it deems useful." The report itself and all other measures taken with respect to interstate communications are confidential, unless otherwise decided by the Assembly.

There is no provision for monitoring follow-up on any recommendations that the Commission may make. Responsibility for follow-up activity would seem to rest primarily with the Assembly, although a liberal interpretation of its mandate might enable the African Commission to take steps similar to those adopted by the Human Rights Committee, in order to make it possible to supervise implementation of its recommendations.[3]

Other (individual) communications

The "other communications" referred to in Articles 55–59 and Rules 102–120 are those communications submitted by parties other than states, i.e., individuals, NGOs, or other groups. Complaints must be submitted to the Commission's Secretariat in Banjul, Gambia, which transmits them to the Commission. There is no prior screening for admissibility, but communications are considered by the Commission only if a simple majority of its members agree. In general, however, Commission decisions are taken by consensus, thus providing a *de facto* veto to each member.

Article 56 of the Charter and Rule 116 of the Rules of Procedure spell out in detail the criteria for admissibility of "other" communications. Under the practice of the Commission, one can safely assume that almost anyone can submit a complaint to the Commission, so long as the communication complies with the substantive requirements.

The formal requirements are similar to those found under most other international procedures, although they are more numerous than those applicable to state communications within the African system. A communication must indicate its author (even if anonymity is requested) and be compatible with the OAU Charter and the African Charter. Communications submitted to the Commission must not be written in disparaging language and may not be based exclusively on information from the media (although news reports may provide supporting documentation). Like interstate communications, other communications may be submitted only after exhausting any available domestic remedies which are not unduly prolonged; they must be submitted within "a reasonable period" after the exhaustion of local remedies.[4]

Under the amended Rules of Procedure, there is no barrier to submitting a communication to the African Commission that is also being addressed under a non-African international procedure. The only related restriction is found in Article 56(7), which provides that communications may not deal with cases that have been settled by the states concerned in accordance with the principles of the United Nations, OAU, or African Charter.

The Charter does not clearly distinguish between admissibility and the merits of a communication, although Article 57 does provide that a communication must be sent to the state concerned "prior to any substantive consideration." The 1995 Rules of Procedure, on the other hand, do distinguish between those two stages in the evaluation of communications.

Each communication is assigned to a Commissioner, who may request additional information from the author or the state concerned before making a recommendation to the Commission on the issue of admissibility. During its first few years, the Commission tended simply to follow this recommendation, but it now debates most admissibility decisions. If the Commission declares a communication inadmissible, it notifies the author of the communication and, if the communication has been transmitted to the state concerned, that state.

If the Commission declares a communication admissible, it notifies the state and the author. The state has three months in which to submit any explanation or statement regarding the case, to which the author of the communication may reply. If a state does not respond to three notifications, the facts alleged in the complaint will be deemed proved, pursuant to Rule 119(4). The Commission may review its decision on admissibility in light of information received from the state.

Prior to its consideration of the merits, the Commission may request that a state take interim measures in order to avoid irreparable damage to the victim of the alleged violation, pending examination of the complaint. This important innovation (again, similar to provisions found in other human rights treaties) is found in Rule 111.

If a communication relates solely to individual violations of human rights, the text of the Charter would appear to give the Commission no power to take any action or even to make recommendations to the state concerned. In practice, however, observations by the Commission and any recommendations on a particular communication are submitted to the Assembly of Heads of State and Government, the state concerned, and the author of the communication.

If the Commission finds that one or more communications reveal the existence of "a series of serious or massive violations of human and peoples' rights," the Commission may draw such cases to the attention of the Assembly. Under Article 58 of the Charter, the Commission may "undertake an in-depth study of these cases and make a factual report, accompanied by its findings and recommendations," but only upon the request of the Assembly. In an emergency, the chairman of the Assembly may request an in-depth study.

As noted above, all proceedings under the Charter are confidential. Formally, only the Assembly of Heads of State and Government, not the Commission, may decide to make a Commission report (or other action) public. During the initial stages of its work, the Commission interpreted the principle of confidentiality strictly, to include any action it took. Thus, it published only statistics on the communications it received and those which it declared admissible. This approach was obviously problematic, as publicity is an important means of encouraging states to comply with their obligations. However, there have been some significant improvements in this regard, and the Commission's annual reports to the AU now disclose the status of cases submitted to it and include the Commission's decisions on admissibility and the merits.

The Assembly cannot adopt decisions binding on states, and there is no provision for monitoring recommendations that may be made by the Commission.

Periodic reports

Under Article 62 of the Charter, parties must submit biennial reports "on the legislative or other measures taken with a view to giving effect to the rights and freedoms recognized and guaranteed" by the Charter. These reports are public documents, available from the Commission's Secretariat. Many states, however, do not seem to take the reporting process seriously: as of May 2004, nineteen states to the African Charter had not submitted any report; thirty-one were overdue in submitting periodic reports; and only three states had submitted all of their reports. The Commission publicly calls on states by name to submit overdue reports, but the problem remains.

State reports are examined publicly, and the Commission may put questions to representatives of the state concerned. NGOs and others may submit information on specific countries to the Commission, which may use this information in the examination process. Unfortunately, states frequently fail to send a representative to discuss their reports with the Commission, and the reports are frequently inadequate.

Interpretive and Other Functions

The Commission may interpret the provisions of the Charter at the request of a party to the Charter, an institution of the AU, or any other African organization recognized by the AU. In effect, although it is not a court, the Commission thus has the authority to issue what amount to advisory opinions on human rights matters brought before it. Pursuant to this mandate, the Commission has adopted a number of interpretive resolutions, both on its own initiative and in response to requests and drafts submitted by NGOs. Unfortunately, some of the early resolutions are no clearer than the provisions they seek to interpret (although the same could be said of many of the "general comments" issued by the Human Rights Committee in its early years).[5] Examples of more recent resolutions are the Declaration on Principles on Freedom of Expression in Africa (2002) and the Guidelines and Measures for the Prohibition and Prevention of Torture (2002).

Article 45(4) provides that the Commission shall perform any other task assigned to it by the OAU Assembly of Heads of State and Government, although the Commission's broad mandate would seem to make it unnecessary for it so seek the Assembly's approval for significant initiatives. As already mentioned, Article 46 provides that the Commission "may resort to any appropriate method of investigation," and the Commission has interpreted this authority to permit it to undertake on-site missions. Since 1995, missions have been undertaken to Togo, Mauritania, Senegal, Sudan, and Nigeria, in each case with the consent of the government concerned.

Finally, the Commission has initiated the practice of appointing Thematic Rapporteurs. These rapporteurs have submitted reports on the rights of women; prisons and conditions of detention; and extra-judicial, summary, or arbitrary killing.

The African Court on Human and Peoples' Rights

The African Court on Human and Peoples' Rights will form part of the African regional human rights system, joining the Commission. Since the Commission does not currently posses sufficient protective powers, the Court potentially could have a powerful effect on the system as a whole. Under the Charter, the Commission does not have the authority to issue enforceable judgments, nor has it created a mechanism for encouraging and tracking state compliance with its decisions. The Court, however, will possess the authority to issue legally binding and enforceable decisions.

The Jurisdiction of the Court

The jurisdiction *ratione materiae* of the Court is very broad. According to Article 3 of the Protocol, the Court has jurisdiction over "all cases and disputes submitted to it concerning the interpretation and application of the Charter, this Protocol and any other relevant human rights instrument ratified by the States concerned." The Court applies the provisions not only of the Charter, but of any other pertinent human rights instrument ratified by the states concerned.

The Court has two types of jurisdiction: compulsory and optional. The following are subject to the compulsory jurisdiction of the Court and have the right to submit cases to it: the African Commission on Human and Peoples' Rights, a state which has filed a complaint to the Commission, the state against which a complaint has been filed, any state whose citizen is a victim of a human rights violation, and African intergovernmental organizations. If a state "has an interest in a case," it may request the Court's permission to intervene.

Article 5(3) provides for the possibility of cases being submitted by individuals or NGOs with observer status before the African Commission. However, this possibility is purely optional, and the state against which the complaint has been lodged must first have recognized the competence of the Court to receive such communications, pursuant to Article 34(6) of the Protocol. Without this optional recognition the Court does not have the authority to receive a petition from an individual or NGO. As of early May 2004, no state had accepted the right of individual petition.

The Court may issue advisory opinions at the request of member states, the AU, or any of its organs on "any legal matter relating to the Charter or any other relevant human rights instrument, provided that the subject matter of the opinion is not related to a matter being examined by the Commission." As their name implies, these opinions are not binding; however, they could serve as an important means of interpreting the Charter and other human rights conventions. If there is a dispute as to the jurisdiction of the Court, the Court itself decides the issue.

Organization of the Court

The Court is made up of eleven judges elected by the member states of the AU for six-year terms of office, renewable once. Only state parties to the Protocol may propose candidates; each state may nominate three candidates, at least two of whom must be its nationals. The Court may not include more than one national of the same state. In nominating candidates, states are to give due consideration to adequate gender representation. This gender representation, along with equitable representation of the main regions of Africa and their principal legal traditions, is supposed to be ensured by the Assembly in the election.

The judges are elected by secret ballot by the Assembly of Heads of State and Government. While nonparties to the Protocol are barred from nominating candidates, they participate in the election of the judges.

The Court itself elects its President and Vice-President for a two-year period, renewable once. The Court has a unified structure, without division into chambers or sections.

Judges are elected in their individual capacity and not as representatives of the state parties. After their election, judges must make a declaration that they will discharge their duties impartially and faithfully. They enjoy the diplomatic immunities and privileges necessary for them to discharge their duties. Judges may not hear any case in which they have previously taken part in any capacity and must decline to give an opinion in any case concerning the state of which they are national.

Court Procedure

A number of procedural questions are left by the Protocol to be answered when the Court adopts its rules of procedure, but some issues appear to be clear from the Protocol's text.

Admissibility

When the Court rules on the admissibility of cases, it is to take into account the provisions of Article 56 of the Charter, which sets forth the conditions for admissibility of communications addressed to the African Commission on Human and Peoples' Rights. The Court may request the opinion of the Commission when deciding on the admissibility of cases which fall under the optional jurisdiction of the court. If a case is found to be admissible, Article 6(3) permits the Court either to consider the case itself or to transfer it to the Commission.

Consideration of cases

The hearings of the Court are normally public, although it may decide to conduct proceedings *in camera*. Any party to a case is entitled to be represented by a legal representative of his or her choice. In accordance with international law, any person who appears before the Court, witness or representative, is to be provided with the necessary protection and facilities. The Court may receive all elements of proof that it considers appropriate, whether oral or written. It may examine witnesses and, if it deems it necessary, conduct an enquiry.

In cases of "extreme gravity and urgency" and when necessary to avoid irreparable harm to persons, the Court may adopt such provisional measures as it considers necessary.

Judgments

The Court is required to render its judgment within ninety days of having ended its deliberations. The judgment of the Court is decided by majority vote, and each judge is entitled to deliver his or her separate or dissenting opinion to the Court's judgment. The parties to the case are notified of the judgment, which is read in open court, along with the reasons justifying the judgment. If the Court finds that there has been a violation of a right, it may make appropriate orders to remedy the situation, which may include the payment of fair compensation or reparation. The Council of Ministers of the African Union is responsible for monitoring execution of the judgment on behalf of the Assembly. The judgment is transmitted to the member states of the AU, and the Court will submit an annual report to the regular session of the Assembly of Heads of State and Government. Article 31 of the Protocol directs the Court to specify the cases in which a state has not complied with the Court's judgment.

The judgment of the Court is final and not subject to appeal. However, the Court may interpret its own decision and review it in the light of new evidence, under conditions which will be set out in the rules of procedure.

Relationship Between the Court and the Commission

The Protocol itself does not contain any specific provision on the relationship between the Court and the Commission. It only provides that the Court shall be "complementary to the protective mandate" of the Commission. One inference which might be drawn from this is that the function of the Court is limited to the protective provisions of the Charter, which it will share with the Commission, although broader language in the Protocol's Preamble states that the Court is to "complement and reinforce the functions of the Commission."

There is a potential for duplication of efforts by the Commission and the Court, given that Article 45(3) of the Charter vests the Commission with the power to interpret provisions of the Charter, while the Court has the authority to issue advisory opinions. However, the protective mandate of the Commission is limited to the Charter; the mandate of the Court extends to the interpretation and application of the Charter, the Protocol, and any other relevant human rights instrument ratified by the state concerned. In addition, a dispute relating to any interpretation made by the Commission can be submitted to the Court. There is thus no doubt that the Court will occupy a primary place in the interpretation of not only the provisions of the Charter but also other relevant human rights documents. It is to be hoped that the rules of procedure of the Court will create the necessary practical framework to regulate the relationship between the Court and the Commission. Of course, the effective functioning of the Commission itself will continue to be of paramount importance, if this new arrangement is to be successful.

Concluding Observations

The African Charter on Human and Peoples' Rights entered into force in 1986, and the Commission has been functioning since 1987. Thus far, only one state communication has been filed with the Commission, and only a limited number of initial and periodic reports pursuant to Article 62 of the Charter have been reviewed. However, the Commission has received over 200 communications from individuals and NGOs, the number of which appears to be increasing. Its decisions, while still sometimes difficult to obtain, are publicized and evaluated in various human rights journals.[6] While this record is less than impressive, the Commission's activities are, in fact, comparable to the early years of its counterparts in Europe and the Americas.

Much of the Commission's work thus far has been concerned with institution-building. The necessary infrastructure for future activities is now largely developed, including defining a program of promotional and educational action, developing a wide network of relationships with international and regional human rights bodies, and granting observer status to a very large number of NGOs.

The Commission has used the Charter creatively, by asking states to permit the Commission to conduct on-site investigations. When these requests were initially refused, the Commission sought the assistance of the OAU Secretary-General to persuade states to grant the requested permission. As noted above, several states have now allowed the Commission to conduct on-site investigations.

At the same time, however, the Commission continues to face enormous difficulties in performing its tasks. Some of these are political, flowing from the lackluster support given to the Commission by many African states. Others are more practical; for example, the Commission's Secretariat is small and inexperienced, and it has not been willing or able to suggest initiatives which could be effectively pursued by the Commission. To compensate for this weakness, African, European, and American organizations have supported the Commission by seconding legal officers and interns to the Secretariat.

In addition, Africa is beset by overwhelming economic and social problems and massive political disruptions. These conditions place an even greater burden on the Commission to ensure that human rights are not forgotten in the midst of these upheavals.

The Charter itself places obstacles in the way of an activist Commission, as it ultimately depends on political decisions by the AU Assembly of Heads of State and Government for its authority.[7] Remedies for individual violations of human rights are essentially nonexistent, and the Commission's authority to investigate a nonstate communication still appears to depend on the consent of the Assembly, although, in practice, the Commission investigates every communication which it has declared admissible. African states have been notably reluctant to condemn human rights violations within the region, and they do not appear to be willing to set in motion even the confidential machinery created in the Charter. It is nonetheless encouraging that the Assembly has created a Central Organ for Conflict Prevention, Resolution, and Management, in order to address conflicts *within* African states, thus beginning to weaken Africa's traditionally broad interpretation of what matters fall within a state's domestic jurisdiction.

The wide authority enjoyed by the Commission to receive information from any source and its ability to attempt to influence states during the course of even a confidential investigation should not be ignored. If the Commission draws a "special case" of massive violations to the attention of the Assembly, even confidentially, the diplomatic and political impact could be significant. While it is unfortunate that individual victims cannot force an adjudication of alleged violations, the African

Charter does retain the potential for innovation and meaningful action. One should not undervalue purely promotional activities, and the most important aspect of any international human rights system is its ability to make governments responsive to their own citizens. In this respect, the Commission's authority to make recommendations to the Assembly and to individual states could play an important role.

Cooperation between the Commission and NGOs has been of great significance to the functioning of the Commission, particularly through the NGO workshops that are now regularly held before Commission sessions. NGOs contribute to the substantive work of the Commission by participating in its sessions and assisted in publication of the Commission's *Review*.

Creation of an African Court on Human and Peoples' Rights is a welcome step towards more effective enforcement of the rights protected in the Charter. One can only hope that all African states will support this important initiative by speedily ratifying the Protocol and by recognizing the competence of the Court to consider individual complaints about human rights violations.

It is perhaps fitting to end this chapter in the same way as in the first edition of this book, by emphasizing that "the ultimate success of the Charter and the Protocol on the African Court will rest with the African states themselves, and one can only hope that they are, in the words of the Charter's preamble, 'firmly convinced of their duty to provide and protect human and peoples' rights and freedoms taking into account the importance traditionally attached to these rights and freedoms in Africa.'" In that respect, it is encouraging that the objectives of the newly established African Union explicitly include the promotion and protection of human and peoples' rights in accordance with the Charter and other relevant human rights instruments.

Notes

1. The OAU was replaced by the African Union in 2002, and all references to the OAU in this chapter should be understood also to refer to the AU.

2. Communication 227/99, Democratic Republic of Congo v. Burundi, Rwanda, and Uganda. The communication alleges violations of human rights by the respondent states as a result of their illegal invasion of Congolese territory.

3. See chap. 3.

4. Alternatively, art. 56(6) provides that a communication may be submitted "within a reasonable period . . . from the date the Commission is seized of the matter." It is unclear what "matter" is referred to in this provision, as the Commission obviously cannot be seized of a communication before it is submitted; perhaps the reference is to subsequent communications or information which may relate to a situation already being considered by the Commission.

5. See chap. 3.

6. See the Bibliographic Essay in Appendix A.

7. This situation is not dissimilar from the ultimate authority of the Committee of Ministers of the Council of Europe and the General Assembly of the Organization of American States in their respective regions, before regional courts were established or their jurisdiction widely accepted.

Part IV
Other Techniques and Forums for Protecting Rights

Chapter 10
International Reporting Procedures

Stephanie Farrior

Introduction

The reporting procedures of international human rights treaties offer a useful mechanism for nongovernmental organizations (NGOs) to pressure states into complying with their human rights treaty obligations. By participating at various stages of the reporting process, NGOs have influenced the work of the treaty bodies and have helped bring about changes in state law and practice. Although the results of the reporting procedures have been uneven, NGOs should consider using the procedures as part of their overall advocacy strategy, because of the range of potential benefits at each stage of the process in better protecting human rights.

Implementation of each of the international human rights treaties is monitored by a committee:

- Human Rights Committee (HRC)—monitors implementation of the Covenant on Civil and Political Rights (CP Covenant);
- Committee on Economic, Social and Cultural Rights (CESCR)—monitors the Covenant on Economic, Social and Cultural Rights (ESC Covenant);
- Committee on the Elimination of Racial Discrimination (CERD)—monitors the Convention on the Elimination of All Forms of Racial Discrimination (Racial Discrimination Convention);
- Committee on the Elimination of Discrimination against Women (CEDAW)—monitors the Convention on the Elimination of All Forms of Discrimination against Women (Women's Convention);
- Committee against Torture (CAT)—monitors the Convention against Torture and Other Cruel, Inhuman or Degrading Treatment or Punishment (Torture Convention);

- Committee on the Rights of the Child (CRC)—monitors the Convention on the Rights of the Child (Children's Convention);
- Committee on the Protection of the Rights of All Migrant Workers and Members of Their Families (CMW)—monitors the International Convention on the Protection of the Rights of All Migrant Workers and Members of Their Families, which entered into force on 1 July 2003. (The procedures, practices, and experience reported in this chapter do not include those of this new committee, since its first meeting was only in March 2004.)

The approach all of these committees use in monitoring compliance through the reporting procedure is nonadversarial, and the committees do not act as judicial bodies or issue decisions on whether a state is in violation of its treaty obligations. Instead, the committees seek to establish and maintain a constructive dialogue with states parties, so as to assist states in fulfilling their obligations, make available to them the experience gained from examining other states' reports, and discuss issues related to the enjoyment of treaty rights in their countries. If it is clear that a government is not interested in discussing its human rights record seriously, committee questioning and commentary may be more pointed.

The monitoring process serves to promote a government's accountability to people in its jurisdiction, as well as to the international community. NGOs can contribute substantially to this process by, among other activities, submitting their own reports to the committees on the extent to which the state has complied with treaty provisions, releasing state reports and NGO commentaries to the press, attending treaty body reviews of government reports, helping identify areas for closer scrutiny by the committee, questioning, publicizing committee comments and criticisms, and campaigning for reforms recommended by the committees.

Basic information necessary for effective participation—such as the schedule of upcoming treaty body meetings, a list of the countries to be reviewed and state reports that have been submitted, and texts of the committees' concluding observations—is posted on UN websites[1] and appears in the committees' annual reports. A new Web page on the development of the human rights treaty system has been created, and a detailed overview of the working methods of the treaty bodies also is available.[2]

The report a committee publishes after reviewing a state's submission can be used by NGOs in a number of ways: to create publicity to try to shame a state regarding a human rights situation, to build public pressure both at the national level and with local government authorities, to increase international scrutiny and potential pressure from other states, and to provide benchmarks for use by courts and administrative bodies.

The treaty committees, in addition to supervising the reporting procedure, oversee various other procedures to which states parties may choose to subject themselves, such as the individual complaint procedures discussed in chapter 3.

Why Should NGOs Participate in the Work of Treaty Bodies?

First, and most important, NGOs can make an important difference in a process that has demonstrated concrete results. Governments have changed their laws and practices in response to committee observations. Some governments have acknowledged the direct influence of a particular treaty body; others have attributed changes to their interest in complying with the relevant treaty. There are instances in which NGO participation at a session has directly contributed to a state's decision to take positive action. In addition, national courts have based judgments on pronouncements of the human rights treaty bodies.

Committee members need and use information from NGOs. States often present a glowing picture of the human rights situation in their reports, and NGO reports may be the primary independent source of information committee members receive. Committee members can use the concrete information in NGO reports when developing a list of issues for the government, formulating questions to pose to government representatives, and finalizing their concluding observations. Many committee members have stated that NGO participation is essential to their committee's effectiveness, and one committee chair went so far as to say that the treaty body system functions largely "on the backs of NGOs."

Another reason for NGO participation is to take advantage of government statements made during a committee session that might be used in subsequent campaigns. One example comes from a Human Rights Committee session after Hong Kong's status was changed and it became an autonomous region of China. In its statement to the Human Rights Committee in November 1999, Hong Kong acknowledged the importance of NGO input to the Committee's review of state reports and used the presence of NGOs at the review session to proclaim how free and open a society existed in Hong Kong. This statement was then publicized by the press in Hong Kong, enabling NGOs to refer to it in subsequent advocacy efforts.

A committee's examination of a state's report provides an impetus for national and international NGOs to exchange information and coordinate their work. Coordination among NGOs can also make domestic press coverage more likely, particularly if committee members cite domestic NGO materials or criticize the government, or if a government representative says something unexpected.

A committee's examination of a state's report also provides a useful media peg for publicity about the human rights situation in that country. Journalists who normally would be disinclined to file a story on a government's human rights record might be willing to report on the "news" created by a committee's questioning, especially when the significance of the process is brought to their attention by an astute NGO.

NGO submissions can help a treaty body review a state's compliance with its obligations, even when the state fails to submit its report. NGO pressure also can help prod a state into submitting an overdue report. In 2002, after Brazil finally submitted an overdue report, CESCR took note of a report submitted by a coalition of approximately 300 civil society organizations and public institutions, which encouraged Brazil to present its report. The Committee expressed its appreciation for this NGO participation and opened its list of issues for Brazil with a reference to the group's report. Many of the questions in the Committee's list referred to information in the civil society report that contradicted Brazil's claims or addressed issues raised by the group report but ignored by Brazil.

Finally, producing an analytic human rights report and participating at a committee session can build the internal capacity of an NGO, as well as enhance its visibility and reputation domestically and internationally. For instance, Croatian government officials refused to meet with a Croatian NGO, Be Active, Be Emancipated (B.a.B.e.), until B.a.B.e.'s representatives attended the government's presentation of its first report to CEDAW in 1997. CEDAW's concluding observations were very critical of the government's failure to address violence against women, discrimination against minority women, and obstacles to women's participation in employment. When B.a.B.e. held a press conference in Zagreb to release CEDAW's observations, a government representative attended for the first time; previously, the government had not even acknowledged B.a.B.e.'s requests for a meeting. On the other hand, national NGOs must consider the possibility that participating in a treaty process could result in government retaliation or intimidation. When several Nigerian NGOs attended the 1998 session of CEDAW which considered Nigeria's report, the government urged CEDAW to exclude the NGOs. CEDAW refused, but the atmosphere was ominous.

Common Features of Treaty Bodies

Membership, Staffing, and Schedules

All of the treaty bodies discussed in this chapter are composed of experts who do not represent their governments but instead serve in their personal capacities. All are nominated and elected by states parties to the respective treaties (except members of CESCR, who are nominated by parties but elected by the UN Economic and Social Council [ECOSOC]), with consideration given to equitable geographic distribution and representation of different social and legal systems.

Although committee members are theoretically independent of their governments, the degree of actual independence varies. Some members have also been government officials; others have repeated official positions of their governments during committee sessions. In an effort to promote impartiality, the chairpersons of the treaty bodies have recommended that experts refrain from participating in the review of their own countries. However, only the Human Rights Committee has adopted specific guidelines on the behavior of members, designed to enhance independence and impartiality. Decisions of each committee can be made by a majority or two-thirds vote, but all committees endeavor to reach decisions by consensus; in practice, votes are rare.

The CESCR, CERD, CAT, and CRC meet in Geneva; the HRC meets in New York for one of its sessions and in Geneva for its two other sessions. These five committees are serviced by the Office of the High Commissioner for Human Rights (OHCHR). CEDAW meets in New York and is serviced by the UN Division for the Advancement of Women (DAW). The DAW and OHCHR have increased coordination and information-sharing in recent years, and the OHCHR recently began including the concluding comments of CEDAW in its regular distribution of treaty body recommendations.

The dates and venues of the committees' sessions for the coming year and their schedules for considering state reports are published in their annual reports and on the DAW and OHCHR websites. These sites also post press releases issued by the UN Department of Information both before and after committee sessions, noting the countries scheduled to report, those which did report, and the key issues addressed, including critical remarks by the committees. The following chart sets forth the scheduling and other general practices of the treaty committees.

General Comments

Each of the treaty bodies has issued one or more "general comments" arising out of their review of state reports.[3] These comments are intended to assist states in fulfilling their reporting obligations. Some comments address procedural matters regarding the reporting process; most, however, elaborate the meaning of a provision of the treaty and thus represent one of the few sources of formal (and, arguably, authoritative) interpretations of the various treaty obligations. In recent years, committees have elaborated general comments on such important concerns as the gender-related aspects of racial discrimination, temporary

Figure 10.1
PRACTICE OF THE TREATY COMMITTEES

Name of committee, name of treaty and year adopted by GA	Number of States Parties	Number of Treaty Experts	Meeting places and Session duration	Pre-sessional working groups	Reporting Periods	Individual Communication Procedure	Procedure[1]	Practice of the Committee[2]
Committee on Racial Discrimination (CERD) Racial Discrimination Convention 1965	169	18	Meets in Geneva 2 times a year (March and August) 4-week sessions	None, but appoints Special Rapporteur to report on a country	Within 1 year of ratifying, then comprehensive reports every 4 years and brief updates every 2 years	Article 14 authorizes individual complaints if State Party has agreed to this procedure	No procedure to formally request or receive NGO information	Article 20 authorizes confidential on-site inquiries
Human Rights Committee (HRC) ICCPR 1966	151	18	Meets in Geneva or NY 3 times a year, (March, July & November) 3-week sessions	Meets for 5 days prior to session	Within 1 year of ratifying and every 5 years thereafter	First Optional Protocol	Invites written work from NGOs	Decisions normally based on written submission; follow-up visits with consent of government
Committee on Economic, Social, and Cultural Rights (CESCR) ICESCR 1966	148	18	Meets in Geneva 2 times a year (April & November), 3-week sessions	Meets for 5 days at end of each session	Within 1 year of ratifying and every 5 years thereafter	Currently drafting optional protocol to permit individual complaints	NGOs invited to attend pre-sessional working group and 2-day meeting during opening plenary	May conduct visit upon invitation of host government
CEDAW Women's Convention 1979	176	23	Meets in NY 2 times a year (January & June), 3-week sessions[3]	Pre-sessional working group	Within 1 year of ratifying and every 4 years thereafter	Optional Protocal	No formal procedure but welcomes information from NGOs	No on-site visits to date

				Pre-sessional working group		Article 22 / complaints	NGOs	Visits
Committee Against Torture (CAT) Torture Convention 1984	133	10	Meets in Geneva 2 times a year (May & November), 2-week sessions	Pre-sessional working group	Within 1 year of ratifying and every 4 years thereafter	Article 22 authorizes individual complaints if State Party has agreed to this procedure	Invites written work from NGOs	May conduct on-site, confidential inquiries
Committee on Children's Rights (CRC) Children's Convention 1989	192	18	Meets in Geneva 3 times a year (January, May & September), 4-week sessions	Meets for 1 week at end of each session to prepare questions for next session	Within 2 years of ratifying and every 5 years thereafter	None	Officially encourages NGO participation. Also, NGO Group facilitates NGO participation	May conduct consultations and visits
Committee on the Protection of Migrant Workers (CMW) Migrant Workers Convention 1990	25	10	Meets in Geneva 1 time a year	[To be determined]	Within 1 year of ratifying and every 5 years thereafter	Art. 77 authorizes individual complaints if state Party has agreed to this procedure (procedure will not enter into force until after 10 states have accepted it; none has to date)	[to be determined]	Visits not mentioned in the Convention

1   NGOs may submit written information to committees and also participate informally by meeting individually with committee members.

2   All treaty bodies have the authority to issue "General Comments" regarding their interpretation of both the procedure and substance of the treaty obligations. Additionally, all bodies issue some form of individualized remarks to State Parties, designated by terms such as "Concluding Observations."

3   According to the text of the Convention, CEDAW is authorized to meet once a year for two weeks; a General Assembly resolution authorized the increase in meetings.

special measures (affirmative action), HIV/AIDS and the rights of the child, descent-based discrimination, the right to water, minority rights, and the right to health.[4]

Because of the potential importance of general comments, NGOs should contribute when possible to help shape the content of a comment. There is no formal mechanism for doing so, but NGOs can always contact individual committee members directly. The committees' annual reports announce the subject matter of any general comments that are under consideration, which are usually discussed over several sessions. Although it appeared in the past that some committees did not wish to be seen to be lobbied or unduly influenced by NGOs, NGO input has been actively invited by committees in recent years, including CERD (regarding descent-based discrimination) and CEDAW (regarding affirmative action). The HRC even posted its draft general comment on Article 2 of the CP Covenant on the OHCHR Website, in order to solicit comments.

Consultation among treaty bodies also occurs. The HRC, CRC, and CESCR have circulated draft general comments to the other treaty bodies for review. It is possible that treaty bodies might adopt joint general comments in the future. The CESCR, for example, has approached CEDAW about the possibility of adopting what would be the first such joint general comment, on Article 3 of the ESC Covenant and comparable Article 3 of the Women's Convention.

Meetings of Chairpersons of Treaty Bodies and Other Joint Meetings

In order to discuss issues of common concern, including issues relating to the methods of work of the treaty bodies, the chairpersons meet annually; as of 2002, annual intercommittee meetings now take place as well, in which two to three members of each treaty body participate. These meetings address substantive issues, in addition to administrative and procedural matters. The chairpersons have encouraged all committees to exchange information regarding women's rights, integrate gender perspectives in their examination of reports and formulation of concluding observations and general comments, request that data provided to them by states parties be disaggregated by gender, and address issues of human rights education.

NGOs may attend and make submissions to the chairpersons meetings and intercommittee meetings. In 2003, for example, the IRWAW Asia Pacific attended both meetings and submitted information highlighting the link between the reporting process and implementation of treaty obligations at the national level, sharing their experience with the NGO involvement in the process of reporting and follow-up, and offering proposals in that light.

Members of other UN bodies also participate in these meetings, to strengthen ties among them and to exchange information and ideas. Treaty body members have often urged other UN bodies to make use of their concluding observations, and these other bodies now also recommend areas of questioning for the committees to undertake. For example, at the 2002 meeting of treaty body chairpersons, the UNAIDS representative indicated that stronger conclusions from the bodies were needed in order to take more effective action to follow up their conclusions. The representative also criticized the HRC, CAT, and CERD for rarely mentioning HIV/AIDS in their reports.

The committees also hold consultations involving UN, NGO, and other experts. In 1997, for example, the chairpersons invited UNAIDS and other experts to address the relevance of AIDS to the mandates of the various committees. In 1996, the UN Population Fund (UNFPA) hosted a meeting of members of the treaty bodies to discuss approaches to women's health, focusing on reproductive and sexual rights. In 2001, UNFPA held a follow-up meeting to assess progress and elaborate further measures and strategies to be used by the treaty bodies. The following year, it reported that one of the recommendations that had emerged from that meeting—that members of the treaty bodies should be given briefings on reproductive and sexual health—had already been implemented. In 2002, the chair of CESCR met with members of the International Monetary Fund and the World Bank, as the committee worked toward developing new guidelines for a human rights approach to poverty reduction strategies.

The chairpersons also meet jointly with UN special rapporteurs, experts, and chairpersons of working groups of the special procedures of the Commission on Human Rights (described in chapter 4) to improve collaboration and the exchange of information and to discuss specific human rights issues. The focus of the joint meeting in 2003, for example, was the impact of globalization on human rights.

Finally, the treaty bodies have convened or participated in joint meetings with NGOs to examine specific human rights issues and themes. In 2000, for example, CESCR and the International NGO Committee on Human Rights in Trade and Investment organized a workshop on the relationship among international trade; investment and finance; economic, social and cultural rights; and the possible role of the committee with regard to developments in these areas.

Form and Content of State Reports

States are required to submit an initial report to the treaty body within one or two years after becoming a party to the treaty. Thereafter, they are to submit periodic reports every four or five years and such additional information as a committee may request.

The initial report is the first contact between the reporting state and the committee and establishes the base line against which subsequent progress (or regression) is measured. Periodic reports are intended to update information provided in previous reports, respond to questions which were not fully answered at a state's previous appearance, and explain in detail how treaty obligations are actually being implemented. Both initial and periodic reports are supposed to discuss all constitutional, legal, administrative, judicial, and other measures the state has taken to promote and protect the rights specified in the respective treaties, as well as any factors which may impede practical realization of those rights.

Because of concerns regarding the workload for states that have ratified several treaties, the committees have adopted consolidated guidelines for the introductory section of both initial and periodic reports and invited states to submit the same core document to all of them.[5] The guidelines request information on demographic characteristics, political structure, the general legal framework within which human rights are protected, and information on efforts to promote public and governmental awareness of relevant rights. Most of the treaty bodies are developing additional recommendations to simplify reporting burdens, but proposals to have states submit a single report to all committees monitoring treaties to which it is a party has not been supported by the committees or by most NGOs.

Examination of State Reports

All committees examine state reports in meetings that are open to the public. Most governments send representatives to respond to questions when their report is considered, although their attendance is not required by the treaties.

Committees follow similar procedures in their consideration of initial and periodic reports. First, the state's representative makes a short introductory statement of generally no more than thirty minutes. Committee members then make comments and ask questions, and the state representative is given a short period of time to prepare answers. If the representative is unable to answer a question, additional information may be submitted later in writing.

After listening to the representative's answers and explanations, committee members offer their own observations on the report and the state's efforts to comply with the treaty; the representative then makes a short concluding statement. Committees usually request that any questions that remain unanswered be dealt with in the next periodic report, but, if answers are particularly inadequate, they may ask for written answers to be submitted within a shorter time. On average, the committees devote between six and nine hours of meetings to each initial report and a somewhat shorter time to periodic reports.

As of 2002, when CAT first adopted the practice, all committees except CERD convene presessional working groups to develop in advance a list of questions that will serve as the focus of the dialogue with the government representatives during the review of a state's report. The list of questions is sent to the government ahead of the meeting, in order to facilitate more focused discussion. CERD still maintains its practice of designating one member to serve as rapporteur for each country under review; this person assumes primary responsibility for examining materials and formulating questions. NGOs wishing to submit information regarding a state report should make every effort to have that information before the committee at the preceding session, so that the information may be considered as the working group develops its list of questions for the government.

Early transmittal of questions from the committee to governments tends to enhance the quality of the dialogue and hence the effectiveness of committee scrutiny, and it prevents governments from attempting to excuse their failure to respond to questions by claiming inadequate notice. On the other hand, it presents a challenge to NGOs, as few national NGOs are able to attend both a presessional meeting and the meeting itself. However, NGOs can at least identify issues of concern in writing in advance of the presessional discussion.

All of the committees issue "concluding observations" or "concluding comments" after reviewing each country's report. Although committee practice varies slightly, members generally meet in private after the dialogue with a country's representative to discuss the concluding observations. A member of the committee (usually the country rapporteur) drafts the observations, which are considered, perhaps modified, and then adopted by the committee as a whole. The committee chairpersons have agreed that the concluding observations should emphasize specific recommendations and actions to be taken, which enhances their usefulness to NGOs campaigning for implementation of treaty obligations.

The HRC, CERD, CEDAW, and CAT submit annual reports to the General Assembly; the CRC is required to do so only every other year. The CESCR transmits its annual report to ECOSOC. These annual or biennial reports are the most readily available summaries of the work of each committee and should be regularly consulted by interested NGOs. Annual reports previously included detailed summaries of discussions, but financial constraints have reduced their length; they now only highlight issues raised by committee members, the replies given by state representatives, and any concluding observations made by the committee.

Treaty bodies may receive information for the review process from sources other than governments and NGOs. For example, the CRC has developed a strong relationship with UNICEF, and the CESCR meets regularly with the ILO. The CESCR has also contacted relevant special rapporteurs, e.g., those concerned with the right to adequate housing and the right to food, with respect to specific country situations. In 2003, the CESCR formed a joint expert group with UNESCO on monitoring the right to education.

Consultations and exchanges of views with other bodies also are increasing. A member of the UN Security Council's Counter-Terrorism Committee (CTC), for example, briefed the Human Rights Committee on the work of the CTC in March 2003. In turn, the Vice-Chair of the HRC briefed the Security Council three months later, urging the Council not to leave the protection of human rights only to those parts of the UN system that have a specific human rights mandate.

NGO Participation

CESCR, CRC, and CAT permit NGOs to make formal written interventions to their sessions, and all of the treaty bodies accept written material from NGOs. However, the practice of the committees varies considerably with respect to oral interventions. Some allow NGOs to make oral presentations at the beginning of each session; others limit opportunities for oral intervention to presessional working groups; and others schedule informal sessions with NGOs outside their regular meetings. The UN usually does not provide simultaneous translation for informal meetings and does not produce written records or translate NGO submissions. Some committees refer to NGO interventions in their summary reports of sessions; others do not. The committee chairpersons have indicated their interest in increasing NGO participation and making committee practice with respect to NGOs more consistent, but marked differences remain.

The CRC actively welcomes NGO participation, both oral and written; NGOs were actively involved in drafting the Children's Convention, and the CRC has interpreted the Convention as inviting input from NGOs, even on matters unrelated to the consideration of state reports. The HRC, CAT, and CESCR encourage NGO written submissions by inviting NGOs to submit information to them in advance of the session at which a state report is to be considered. HRC members regularly participate in informal meetings organized by NGOs during lunch and other breaks, and the HRC has held closed sessions for briefings by NGOs during presessional meetings. CESCR permits NGOs to make oral interventions on any matter during the first afternoon meeting of the opening plenary; Committee members often refer to these interventions, but they are not reflected in the summary record. CESCR also invites NGOs to attend one meeting of its presessional working group. CEDAW now holds a formal session with NGOs during its regular meeting time. CERD has convened informal meetings with NGOs outside of its regular meetings, and its work with NGOs generally is facilitated by the Anti-Racism Information System. CAT, in contrast, has not met with NGOs in any organized way.

It may be helpful for NGOs to coordinate their efforts so as to increase their effectiveness. The NGO Group for the Committee on the Rights of the Child, for example, is a coalition of international NGOs that work together to facilitate implementation of the Convention on the Rights of the Child. However, such coalitions should not operate to restrict NGOs that wish to approach committees directly.

Common Problems and New Strategies

Backlogs, Delinquent Reports, and Inadequate Resources

The growing number of parties to the six human rights treaties has led to a crisis of success: almost all of the treaty bodies experience backlogs, several of up to several years, and all experience late reporting by dozens of countries.[6] The HRC and CAT have begun to meet representatives of states whose reports are overdue and, since 1996, they now identify long overdue reports at concluding press conferences. CERD and CESCR notify the most delinquent governments (from seven to fifteen years overdue) that, unless the committees receive more timely information, they will consider their compliance with the treaty based upon their last report and relevant summary records. This approach has been modestly successful in encouraging delinquent governments to submit information. The chairpersons of the treaty bodies have recommended that all of the committees adopt this procedure when other remedies, such as provision of technical assistance, have been exhausted.

Another problem is the backlog of reports to be reviewed. To address this problem, meeting times of committees have been occasionally extended. Two extraordinary sessions held by CESCR in 2000 and 2001 allowed it to clear up its backlog of reports, and the Committee has resumed its usual schedule of two sessions per year. An exceptional session to reduce its backlog was also held by CEDAW in 2002. CAT recently stated that its backlog is exacerbated by its small size (ten members).

Despite the fact that the work of all of the treaty bodies has increased dramatically, there has been insufficient growth in the resources available to support and service them. In the 1990s, several CERD sessions were canceled due to lack of funds,[7] and UNICEF has provided funds to the CRC to assist it with some of the additional tasks it has undertaken.

The treaty body chairpersons have called for an examination of whether similar voluntary funding strategies could be developed for other committees, without endangering core funding from the UN regular budget.

An annual appeal has been instituted to raise extrabudgetary funds to provide additional resources to the Secretariats servicing the treaty bodies. These funds have been used, among other things, to provide research support, process complaints, assist in implementing treaty body recommendations, and establish a system for maintaining information about the best means of implementing recommendations. A new document-processing unit has been created in the OHCHR to streamline the process of document delivery and improve the normal functions of the treaty bodies.

Implementation of Recommendations

The treaty bodies have no punitive or enforcement powers, and countries routinely fail to implement committee recommendations. Individual country rapporteurs can monitor countries' responses to committee recommendations, but there are no sanctions for noncompliance. The treaty bodies must rely on the political will and self-interest of states themselves to comply with their obligations and avoid criticism, as well as the direct efforts of NGOs (particularly national NGOs) to hold governments accountable.

A Treaty Body Recommendations Unit (TBRU) was established in 2002 within the OHCHR to provide assistance to states and civil society in implementing treaty body recommendations, although it is perhaps too early to reach conclusions about its effectiveness. This unit has established direct contacts with the Secretariats of the Inter-American Commission on Human Rights and the African Commission on Human and Peoples' Rights and organized training sessions with UN Country Teams, governments, and members of civil society, to promote a "rights-based approach" to development issues. The OHCHR has stated that field presences will be providing national-level support for ratification, reporting, and follow-up activities. To enhance awareness of treaty body recommendations, the TBRU distributes them automatically at the end of each treaty body session through an automated public listserve, to which any one may subscribe via a link on the OHCHR Website.

Other UN offices that have contacts with the countries under review could contribute to implementation of treaty body recommendations by referring to the concluding observations in their dialogues with governments. Unfortunately, many UN agencies are reluctant to discuss human rights concerns, even those highlighted by the UN treaty bodies, because they want to have good relations with governments and believe that raising human rights concerns could jeopardize those relations.

The OHCHR and some treaty bodies have recently initiated steps that have included NGOs in an effort to strengthen national follow-up measures to treaty body concluding observations. In August 2002, for example, a pilot workshop on the concluding observations of the HRC took place in Quito, Ecuador. NGOs participated, along with representatives of eight states in the Americas, and representatives of national human rights institutions, UN agencies, and the Inter-American Commission on Human Rights. They adopted a set of recommendations aimed at each of these sectors.[8] A similar workshop on follow-up to concluding observations of the CRC for three countries in the Arab region, also involving NGOs, was planned in 2003. These examples underscore the important role that NGOs can play in implementing treaty body recommendations in their countries.

Early Warning and Urgent Procedures

The treaty bodies are limited by their rigid timetables, but human rights crises obviously do not happen on schedule. However, the committees have begun to explore how to identify and respond to signals that imminent and massive violations are likely to occur. Cognizant of the potential for racial and ethnic hatred to erupt into mass violence, the CERD adopted early warning procedures in 1994, by adding to its agenda a review of urgent situations, assigning country rapporteurs, and issuing urgent recommendations. Since 1991, the HRC has requested special reports from countries when it receives allegations of potentially grave situations.

Despite these steps, the ability of the treaty bodies to take urgent actions is limited. As yet, the committees have not been able to contribute effectively to preventing the deterioration of threatening situations, except by offering a forum for NGO participation during regularly scheduled sessions.

Specific Reporting Procedures

Human Rights Committee

The CP Covenant sets out a broad range of fundamental rights that states must respect and ensure, including freedom from slavery, torture, arbitrary deprivation of life, discrimination, and violations of private and family life; rights to a fair trial; freedom of expression, religion, association, and assembly; equality under the law; and rights of citizens to political participation.

The HRC has issued thirty general comments concerning both the CP Covenant's substantive norms and various procedural issues. Its influential commentary on discrimination, for example, expressly incorporates the content of the tests for discrimination adopted by CERD and CEDAW. Its general comment on the equality of rights between men and women calls upon states to report on measures taken or data relating to a broad range of areas, including pregnancy-related and childbirth-related deaths of women; dowry killings; domestic violence; regulation of clothing to be worn by women in public; and equality in education, feeding, and health care. The HRC also has reminded states that rights to liberty and security of the person apply in the contexts of education and immigration, as well as criminal justice, and it has explored the rights of aliens under the Covenant.

The HRC has recently tried to become more systematic in its consideration of country reports. It has established Country Report Task Forces to improve its preparation of the lists of issues that it sends the government in advance of review sessions, to take the lead in conducting the dialogue with the state party, and to assist the rapporteur who follows up on state compliance with the committee's concluding observations. The Special Rapporteur on Follow-Up identifies priority recommendations from among the Committee's concluding observations and requests the state party to provide additional information on their implementation. This information, along with information from other sources (including NGOs), is the basis on which further action might be based.

Committee on Economic, Social and Cultural Rights

Parties to the ESC Covenant undertake, pursuant to Article 2(1) "to take steps . . . to the maximum of [their] available resources, with a view to achieving progressively the full realization of the rights recognized" in the Covenant. Thus, the treaty's principal obligation of *result*—to achieve progressively the full realization of the rights recognized—is subject to the availability of resources.

Nonetheless, some obligations have immediately binding effect. First, under Article 2(2), states "undertake to guarantee" that relevant rights "will be exercised without discrimination of any kind." Second, the obligation "to take steps" under Article 2(1) requires that states adopt measures within a reasonably short period of time after the Covenant's entry into force that are "deliberate, concrete and targeted as clearly as possible towards meeting the obligations recognized in the Covenant." The CESCR has stated that "a minimum core obligation to ensure the satisfaction of, at the very least, minimum essential levels of each of the rights is incumbent upon every State party." While any assessment of whether a state has discharged its minimum core obligation must take account of resource constraints, a state may justify its failure to meet its minimum obligation only if it can demonstrate that "every effort has been made to use all resources that are at its disposition in an effort to satisfy, as a matter of priority, those minimum obligations."[9]

The CESCR has adopted fifteen general comments, including substantive comments on the rights to adequate housing, health, adequate food, education, and water. The Committee also adopts statements to clarify its position with respect to major international developments and issues that bear on implementation of the Covenant. For example, the CESCR submitted a formal statement to the preparatory committee for the 2002 World Summit on Sustainable Development on matters related to the ESC Covenant.

The Committee holds a five-day working group meeting at the end of each session, in order to prepare the lists of questions to which states are to respond when they present their report at the following session. NGOs are invited to submit relevant information to this working group in person or in writing. In addition, the Committee sets aside part of the first afternoon at each of its sessions to enable representatives of nongovernmental organizations to make oral statements.

Its follow-up procedures are similar to those of the HRC. Any new information from the state concerned and/or NGOs is considered at the next meeting of the working group and may lead to the adoption of additional concluding observations, a request for further information, or authorization to the Committee chair to take up the issue with a delegation of the state party at the next Committee session. NGOs can play an important role in this procedure by providing to CESCR their own assessments of how the state has implemented the Committee's recommendations.

The Committee devotes one day each session, usually the Monday of the third week, to a general discussion of a particular right or a particular aspect of the Covenant, in order to develop its understanding of the issues and encourage input to its work from interested parties. In 2003, the day of general discussion was devoted to the right to work, laying the foundation for the development of a draft general comment on this right.

With respect to overdue reports, the CESCR may negotiate as to when the report will be presented. However, if the state fails to submit a report, the Committee designates one of its members to report on the country even without state input.

Committee on the Elimination of Racial Discrimination

The CERD is the oldest treaty supervisory body. Although in many respects it has been fairly conservative, as in its relations with NGOs, in other respects it has been path-breaking, e.g., in developing an "early warning" role and in dealing with delinquent reports.

Parties to the Racial Discrimination Convention pledge to pursue "by all appropriate means and without delay a policy of eliminating racial discrimination in all its forms" (Article 2(1)). Racial discrimination is defined in Article 1 to mean treatment of someone because of their "race, colour, descent, or national or ethnic origin" that limits, whether intentionally or not, the person's human rights.

The Convention specifies that it does not apply to exclusions or restrictions on rights "between citizens and non-citizens." However, CERD has made it clear that the protection of rights in the convention is fully applicable if the discrimination a person faces is on the basis of race or ethnic origin rather than on noncitizen status. CERD has also issued a general comment on discrimination against refugees and displaced persons.

CERD has frequently urged states to develop training programs for law enforcement officials on protecting against human rights violations, such as the arbitrary arrest and detention of persons because of their race or ethnic origin. It has also emphasized the importance of the obligation under Article 7 of the treaty to adopt measures aimed at the root causes of discrimination, particularly through teaching and education, cultural programs, and the media.

CERD has adopted twenty-nine general comments to date, the most recent of which address gender-related aspects of racial discrimination, the right to seek just and adequate reparation, and descent-based discrimination, the latter adopted in part to affirm that caste-based discrimination falls within the purview of the convention.

CERD country rapporteurs propose conclusions about the progress made by states in implementing the Convention, which are then discussed and may be modified by the Committee. NGOs have made a substantial contribution to this process. For instance, conclusions following the 1998 review of the report of the Czech Republic drew attention to the condition of the Roma population, based on information supplied by a regional Roma rights NGO. NGOs planning to provide information to CERD should contact the country rapporteur assigned by the Committee to prepare the examination of that particular country situation, via the CERD Secretariat in the OHCHR in Geneva.

Committee on the Elimination of Discrimination against Women

The Women's Convention requires states to take steps to eliminate discrimination against women in a broad range of areas and requires full equality between women and men. Article 1 defines discrimination as "any distinction, exclusion, or restriction made on the basis of sex, which has the effect or purpose of impairing or nullifying the recognition, enjoyment or exercise by women, irrespective of their marital status, on a basis of equality of men and women, of human rights and fundamental freedoms in the political, economic, social, cultural, civil or any other field." CEDAW has interpreted inclusion of the phrase "or any other field" to give it jurisdiction over discrimination not just in public life but in private life as well, where women have faced some of the greatest obstacles to equality.

Unfortunately, many states have included crippling reservations to one or more of the Convention's substantive provisions, and progress in achieving actual implementation has been slow. CEDAW has tried to persuade states through dialogue to review and limit their reservations, rather than criticizing them directly.

CEDAW has issued twenty-five general comments, one of the most influential of which considers violence against women as a form of discrimination covered by the Convention. Other recent general comments address women and health, and the meaning of "temporary special measures"—what some states call "affirmative action" or "positive discrimination."

A presessional working group prepares questions for state representatives prior to consideration of periodic reports, but lack of time and the large number of questions posed means that there is often little opportunity for follow-up questions or serious dialogue. Some experts focus on certain rights, thus permitting a degree of specialization, but overly detailed questioning on occasion detracts from the impact of the reporting process. CEDAW devotes one of its formal three-hour sessions to interventions from NGOs, and it is open to receiving information from NGOs in advance of its consideration of state reports.

In addition to the presessional working group, CEDAW has established two working groups that meet during its sessions, one to suggest ways to expedite the Committee's work and the other to prepare drafts of general recommendations. While working groups have their advantages, especially for a committee as large as CEDAW, one unfortunate consequence is that the Committee's limited time is diverted from its consideration of country reports. In order to deal with time constraints, CEDAW revised its methods of work in 2002 to set a time limit for presentation of the report by the state party (forty-five minutes for initial reports and thirty minutes for subsequent reports), and a time limit of five minutes per intervention by a Committee member. At the same session it also adopted revised guidelines on reporting, setting a page limit of 100 pages for initial reports and seventy pages for subsequent reports.

Thus far, all the members of CEDAW since its creation in 1982 have been women, with the exception of one man elected in 2001, one in 2003, and one who served from 1982–1984. This, as well as the fact that

CEDAW is the only treaty body not serviced by the OHCHR in Geneva, impedes one of CEDAW's important tasks, the integration of gender issues in the work of the other treaty bodies and the UN generally.

An Optional Protocol to the Women's Convention, adopted in 1999, allows for individual complaints as well as investigations by CEDAW; it is discussed in chapter 3.

Committee Against Torture

The questioning of state representatives by CAT has been inconsistent. At times it is rigorous, but there are also occasions on which CAT has ignored even its own previous recommendations and concerns in reviewing a state's subsequent report. Some members have been especially deferential to governments and dismissive of NGO participation.

CAT is the only treaty body expressly authorized by the treaty it monitors to comment on individual state reports, which it forwards to the state concerned. The state may respond by sending observations to the Committee, and the Committee may then include its comments and the government's observations in its annual report to the General Assembly. These "concluding observations" on each state report are included in CAT's annual reports.

In 2003, the CAT instituted a practice of following up on its concluding observations, similar to that adopted by the HRC. It selects a number of priority concerns and requests further information from the state party, to be submitted within one year, on measures taken by the government to implement those priority recommendations.

Because several other treaties and instruments also prohibit torture and other ill-treatment or punishment, one of CAT's major challenges has been to clarify the scope of the prohibition for purposes of the Torture Convention. CAT's mandate also overlaps with that of the Special Rapporteur on Torture, who is appointed by the Commission on Human Rights (discussed in chapter 4). The Committee and the Rapporteur have discussed ways of coordinating their work on specific countries, as well as on thematic issues, such as the definition of torture. When an appeal is urgent and concerns an individual case, it should be addressed initially to the Special Rapporteur. Nonurgent requests for information, country visits, or the formulation of recommendations should be addressed to both the Special Rapporteur and CAT, making clear to each that both have been contacted; the Rapporteur and CAT can then consult in order to ascertain what action is most appropriate.

Once it enters into force, an Optional Protocol to the Convention against Torture, adopted by the UN General Assembly in December 2002, will create a Sub-Committee on Prevention with authority to visit places of detention in states parties.

Committee on the Rights of the Child

The Convention on the Rights of the Child has nearly universal ratification; 192 states (all states but the United States and Somalia) are parties. The size of the Committee has been expanded from ten to eighteen in light of the large number of reports to be reviewed, and the General Assembly has expanded the time the Committee is authorized to meet to three annual sessions of four weeks each. During the first three weeks, the Committee examines state reports; during the fourth week, which is closed to the public, the Committee prepares for its review of reports at the next session.

The Convention has a wide range of substantive articles, some of which confer new rights not explicitly addressed in the other human rights treaties, such as rights concerning the treatment of children by the justice system, intercountry adoption, elimination of various exploitative practices, and facilitation of rehabilitation. Other provisions make clear that rights owed to everyone—such as freedom of expression, religion, and association—also attach to children. Perhaps the Convention's most important innovation is the recognition that children are entitled to human rights in their own right, and that a child's best interests may differ from the wishes or best interests of his or her parents or other legal guardians.

The Committee has given special priority to four rights: the rights of children to nondiscrimination (Article 2); to life, survival, and development (Article 6); to participate in decisions that affect them (Article 12); and to have their best interests be a "primary consideration" in all actions concerning them undertaken by public authorities or private social welfare institutions (Article 3). These rights, in addition to requiring protection in and of themselves, are considered in analyzing government progress in implementing other rights. While the Committee has declared that reservations to any of these four rights are unacceptable, more than sixty governments have entered reservations to the treaty, some of which are so broad that they might undermine the state's commitments to protecting these core rights.

The CRC has issued five general comments, which address issues such as the aims of education, HIV/AIDS and the rights of the child, and adolescent health and development.

Two optional protocols to the Children's Convention entered into force in 2002, one on the involvement of children in armed conflict, and one on the sale of children, child prostitution, and child pornography. Both contain a reporting mechanism and will therefore increase the CRC's already heavy workload.

The decision by UNICEF to incorporate the Children's Convention into the agency's mandate illustrates how a rights-based framework can enhance the work of a UN agency. This decision has also benefited the Committee, since UNICEF provides it with considerable financial support, including assistance to some governments and NGOs in their preparation of reports and commentaries.

Concerns relating to overlap between the CRC and other human rights bodies are similar to those mentioned in relation to CAT, although the overlap in the case of the CRC is even greater. All of the human rights treaties recognize various rights to which children are entitled, and the special rapporteurs on torture, summary or arbitrary executions, violence against women, and the right to education, as well as the working groups on forced disappearances and arbitrary detention, may consider violations committed against children. NGOs should submit information to these bodies as appropriate, making sure that each is aware if another body also has been contacted.

NGOs were more involved in drafting the Children's Convention than in the drafting of any other human rights treaty, and they play a significant role in its implementation. Before the Committee's first session in 1991, members met informally with NGOs to receive their suggestions about procedures. Moreover, the drafters agreed that the reference to "competent bodies" in Article 45 (which authorizes the committee to invite "the specialized agencies, UNICEF and other competent bodies . . . to provide expert advice on [the Convention's] implementation") includes NGOs. Article 44, which requires states to make available to the general public in their own countries their reports and the CRC's concluding observations, also has contributed to greater public awareness of the CRC's activities.

The CRC relies on a coordination mechanism created by a group of thirty-seven NGOs concerned with children's issues, which includes a full-time liaison officer whose job it is to enhance cooperation among coalitions of national and other NGOs. As other committees explore the benefits of this kind of coordination, however, some NGOs have raised concerns over the "gatekeeping" function of such a coordinating group and the potential problems that may arise if some NGOs acquire the ability to affect the access of other NGOs to the treaty bodies.

Committee on the Protection of the Rights of All Migrant Workers and Members of Their Families

The ten members of this Committee were elected by states parties in December 2003, the Convention having entered into force on 1 July 2003. As of March 2004, there were twenty-five states parties. The Treaty does not create new rights but rather emphasizes that migrants are also human beings and therefore entitled to respect for their rights. It contains provisions aimed at preventing and eliminating the exploitation of migrant workers throughout the entire migration process, such as ending the illegal recruitment and trafficking of migrant workers and discouraging the employment of irregular or undocumented migrant workers. The Convention sets out binding standards on the treatment, welfare, and rights of both documented and undocumented migrants, and it creates obligations for both sending and receiving states.

NGO Contributions to the Oversight Process

There are three broad areas in which NGOs can contribute in significant ways to the work of the human rights treaty bodies: (1) by supplying information to committee members in advance of the review of a state report; (2) by drawing a committee's attention to particular issues during consideration of state reports; and (3) by ensuring that national NGOs are promptly informed about the reporting process, so that they can use the committees' work as part of their own advocacy activities.

Providing Information

In formulating their questions to state representatives, committee members need not rely only on information submitted by the reporting state but may also refer to other materials, including information from NGOs, the press, international organizations, and specialized agencies. Although CERD has made it clear that it will only use information received from governments when it formulates suggestions and general recommendations, its members may use NGO and other information in preparing questions for government representatives.

The staff of the OHCHR and DAW will send government reports to NGOs, if the NGO cannot obtain them by other means. Although much information is available on the OHCHR and DAW websites, the committees' calendars are constantly subject to change, and the websites are not always up to date. As many NGOs do not have access to the sites, direct phone or fax contact with the OHCHR and DAW is recommended.

The OHCHR will forward NGO reports to committee members if an adequate number of copies is provided, and DAW appears willing to do the same. Usually, an NGO must provide one copy for each committee member plus one for the staff, at least one week and preferably three weeks before the session begins; it is best first to confirm arrangements with a UN staff member. Since CERD designates country rapporteurs in advance, an NGO need send only one copy of its materials to the OHCHR for forwarding. An NGO should not generally send reports directly to committee members, unless they are serving as country rapporteurs or the NGO has had direct dealings with them previously.

If an NGO plans to submit a report or critique on a particular country, it should organize its information by article of the treaty under consideration. It is usually helpful if the NGO refers to specific paragraphs in the government's report, so that committee members may easily compare the government's claims with those of the NGO. The report should not be too long: some committees have suggested a maximum of ten–fifteen pages, with annexes detailing key areas of concern.

Because NGO reports are not considered official UN documents, the UN will not translate them. In most cases, English is the preferred language, although some experts prefer Spanish or French. If an NGO submits a report in a language other than English, it should also try to submit a summary in English; similarly, if the report is in English, summaries should be provided in other languages whenever possible. If an NGO is unable to get a report to a committee before the beginning of a session, there are usually a few members on each committee willing to consider NGO information they receive during the session.

NGOs may propose specific questions to be asked by committee members, but they should be aware that some committee members do not like NGOs to frame questions for them. For this reason, NGOs should instead highlight areas of concern and suggest concrete recommendations, unless invited by members to submit specific questions.

Information about individual cases should be included in reports only to illustrate a pattern of violations. Although individual cases may be considered under individual complaint procedures, individual case work does not fall within the committees' monitoring function. Therefore, a few thoroughly documented cases, grouped together to show a pattern of violations, will have a greater impact than lists of names with varying degrees of documentation.

There is no harm in submitting the same information to more than one committee or to other UN bodies, but the fact that information has been submitted elsewhere should be clearly stated. If information about a particular case has been submitted to one body and the government has not provided an adequate response, that fact should be mentioned when submitting the information to another body. In that way, the bodies can reinforce one another's efforts and will not be susceptible to a government's claim that it has addressed the alleged violation via another mechanism.

The UN Secretariat encourages governments to involve national groups and independent experts in the preparation of their reports, and some have done so. Norway, for example, has an Advisory Committee on Human Rights, which includes NGO representatives and human rights researchers, one function of which is to comment on draft reports to international human rights bodies. Government invitations to NGOs provide welcome opportunities for timely input; of course, NGOs that respond should also feel free to offer public criticism when warranted. NGOs also may contribute to state reports by submitting suggestions and raising concerns with governments in writing or informal meetings.

Focusing Committee Attention

Having an NGO representative present at a committee session can help to focus the committee's attention on certain issues and makes it possible to supply additional information to support follow-up questions to government representatives. While most committee members are pleased to have short meetings with NGOs during breaks or at day's end, NGOs should be aware that committee members naturally dislike being hounded. NGOs will generally be more persuasive if they are not insistent, and they should be careful not to duplicate unnecessarily the work of other NGOs concerning the same situation. Once a member has expressed support, he or she is likely to be more helpful if left to meet with colleagues than if pressed with additional details.

Promoting Cooperation Among NGOs and UN Agencies

One of the most important aspects of working with treaty bodies is to ensure that the process of reporting involves a full cycle of information flowing from national to international venues, and then back to national and local groups that can publicize highlights of the reporting process domestically. A government is rarely motivated to improve its human rights record solely by the comments of members of a UN committee meeting far away in New York or Geneva. In countries that are represented at treaty bodies only by a diplomat from their UN missions, government officials in the capital may not even be aware of a committee's comments.

NGOs that attend committee sessions play a vital role in ensuring that information about what transpires in Geneva or New York reaches the country concerned. The stronger the links between international and national NGOs, the more effective will be the treaty bodies' supervision. The activities of many UN oversight bodies occur in obscurity, and only publicity can increase their impact. International NGOs should increase their efforts to help national NGOs find out about, submit information to, and attend relevant sessions of treaty bodies, as well as to publicize committee comments and recommendations when a session has concluded.

NGOs also can facilitate the exchange of information between the treaty bodies and other UN entities. As appropriate, NGOs with links to development or humanitarian UN agencies or programs should consider urging them to transmit relevant information to treaty committees, disseminate committee recommendations, and incorporate treaty-based obligations and committee recommendations in their activities. UN agencies may be approached in-country as well as at their headquarters to make them more aware of, and responsive to, resource problems that governments may face in fulfilling their treaty obligations.

Concluding Observations

Participation in the treaty monitoring process can be frustrating. It requires attention to the activities and timetables of several committees, analysis of sometimes difficult-to-obtain government reports, and (ideally) a personal presence in Geneva or New York. Listening to a lackluster discussion between marginally interested committee members and evasive government representatives is a far cry from the more "activist" initiatives which NGOs (and many funders) seem to prefer.

Nonetheless, the reporting and oversight process offers one of the few opportunities for formal international scrutiny of the human rights records of most governments. Although the treaty bodies do not attract the same amount of attention as do the UN Commission on Human Rights and its Sub-Commission, many countries successfully avoid criticism by those latter bodies. The treaty-based committees offer a particularly good forum for examining countries whose human rights records are not among the worst or whose political influence protects them from close scrutiny in more diplomatic forums.

Notes

1. See the Bibliographic Essay for a listing of the most important Websites.

2. See http://www.unhchr.ch/html/menu2/system.htm and UN Doc. HRI/ICM/2002/2.

3. Technically, HRC and CESCR adopt "general comments," while CERD and CEDAW adopt "general recommendations"; the present chapter refers to both as "general comments."

4. The UN periodically issues a Compilation of General Comments and General Recommendations from all of the committees. The most recent is UN Doc. HRI/GEN/1/Rev.7 (2004); subsequent general comments may be found on the OHCHR Website.

5. The consolidated guidelines are published in UN Doc. HRI/GEN/2/Rev.2 (2004), available on the Internet by inserting this document number into the "Treaty bodies database search" box on the UNHCHR home page.

6. For a detailed study of the United Nations human rights treaty system, See Anne Bayefsky, *The UN Human Rights Treaty System: Universality at the Crossroads* (Ardsley, NY: Transnational Publishers, 2001). For a more current statistical examination of the reporting system, see Recent Reporting History under the Principal Human Rights Instruments, UN Doc. HRI/GEN/4/Rev.4 (2004).

7. The CERD and CAT are unusual in that their activities are funded wholly by the parties to each treaty rather than, as is the case for the other treaty bodies, from the UN's regular budget. The General Assembly adopted interim measures to assure funding for CERD on a temporary basis; however, the state parties have not yet amended the treaty in order to make the reforms permanent.

8. UN Doc. HRI/TB/FU/1 (2003).

9. See CESCR, General Comment No. 3 (1990).

Chapter 11
Quasi-Legal Standards and Guidelines for Protecting Human Rights

Jiri Toman

Introduction

Standards, guidelines, and principles constitute a form of "soft" law with
notable influence and utility in protecting human rights. As expressions
of policy and ideals rather than binding or "hard" law, such standards
set forth basic principles which have been agreed upon and elaborated
by the United Nations or other organizations in the form of guidelines
for international action and national legislation. Although these instruments are not directly legally binding, they are more appropriately considered to be quasi-legal rather than nonlegal in their effect.

Standards provide recommendations and guidance for governments
in developing national legislation, allowing governments to assess their
own systems and to contribute to the further development of the norm.
International standards also constitute important interpretative tools,
for they are often based on or lead to the adoption of other internationally binding instruments.

Quasi-legal international human rights standards may constitute elements of state practice and thus contribute to the formation of customary international law, although, standing alone, they are insufficient to
create binding legal obligations. But the cumulative enunciation of the
same guideline in numerous nonbinding texts may contribute to expressing the *opinio juris* of the world community, which is necessary to the
development of customary law.

One of the first examples of this "soft" law was the Standard Minimum
Rules for the Treatment of Prisoners, adopted by the United Nations in
1957. In the mid-1970s, new standards began to appear, and since the
1980s they have proliferated, particularly in the field of criminal justice.
The present chapter cannot deal with all such international standards
in detail, so it is limited to a general overview and focuses on norms in
the field of criminal justice and its administration.[1]

Implementation of Human Rights Standards, Guidelines, and Principles

On the Domestic or National Level

Unimplemented standards are of little use. Therefore, at the national level, standards must be implemented either by direct incorporation into national legislation or by indirect use as nonbinding norms or goals. In the United States, for example, principles of the UN Standard Minimum Rules for the Treatment of Prisoners have been embodied in documents such as the American Law Institute's 1962 Model Penal Code, the American Correctional Association's 1970 Declaration of Principles of Prison Discipline, and the correctional standards developed in 1973 by the National Advisory Commission on Criminal Justice Standards and Goals.

Once standards are adopted, their implementation must be supervised. Some countries have a central authority which exercises general supervision and is responsible for implementation of standards regarding, for example, prison administration. Others may rely on legislative, executive, or judicial institutions. Perhaps the most common vehicle for legislative supervision is a parliamentary ombudsman, often associated with the Scandinavian countries but also established in many other countries. In a 1990 survey on the implementation of the Standard Minimum Rules, three-quarters of the countries responding indicated that prisoners have access to an ombudsman or a similar system, or that they are able to appeal to the courts for redress.

If there is no central authority responsible for supervising implementation of guidelines, it may be more difficult to ensure their uniform application. An administrative body is often powerless to take action except in institutions under its direct control, and its authority to change regulations or procedures may be limited to recommending actions to higher administrative or legislative bodies. In other cases, administrative measures may be amended by local authorities or even by individual administrators.

Judicial oversight of prison conditions may be the responsibility either of courts of general competence or special courts, which may take international standards into account. Even where standards are not directly binding, they may "inform" the interpretation of domestic laws and regulations, and thereby exert considerable influence.[2]

On the Regional Level

The Council of Europe updated and adapted the Standard Minimum Rules to European conditions in 1973. While the European rules retain the basic wording and format of the Standard Minimum Rules, new provisions expand the UN Rules in several respects and also introduce the principle of vesting control in a judicial authority or other duly constituted body outside the prison administration. In 2004, the Council of Europe's Parliamentary Assembly and the EU's European Parliament called for drafting a new European Penitentiary Charter.

The procedures of the European Convention on Human Rights play an important role in this field, as more than half of the individual applications under the Convention are filed by prisoners. Many complaints concern prison conditions, and, while the European rules are not directly binding, the standards they set may influence the interpretation of the Convention by the European Court of Human Rights.

Conditions of detention and the protection of detainees are also important facets of the work of the Inter-American Commission on Human Rights, although there is no regional set of standards equivalent to the European Standard Minimum Rules.

On the International Level

Reporting mechanisms are central to the promotion and implementation of human rights standards at the international level. Many standards contain recommendations that they be acted upon nationally, regionally, and internationally; implemented through national law; and broadly disseminated among law enforcement officials, judges, lawyers, executive and legislative branches, and the public. States are usually invited to submit periodic reports to the Secretary-General or another UN body on the progress achieved in implementing the standards, so that the United Nations can gauge the effectiveness of the standards and identify areas where further guidance is needed. In most cases, the body receiving and analyzing the reports is the Commission on Crime Prevention and Criminal Justice, an intergovernmental organ that replaced an earlier group of independent experts in 1992. The Commission meets annually and has tried to approach the issue of monitoring the implementation of criminal justice norms more systematically.[3]

A reporting requirement not only enhances international accountability in relation to the rights set forth in a given instrument, but it also may prompt states to review policies and programs affecting human rights and make appropriate adjustments. Occasionally, reports may lead to the development of new standards. For example, suggestions on the use of force and firearms by law enforcement officials contained in country reports on implementation of the Code of Conduct for Law Enforcement Officials served as the basis for a new instrument in this area adopted in 1990.

Unless otherwise indicated, the standards discussed in this chapter all contain some form of implementation-reporting language. Unfortunately, reporting is much easier than implementation, and serious gaps remain in many parts of the world between standards and reality. UN reports have identified lack of coordinated action, shortage of funds, low priority, inadequate human and professional resources and lack of political will or public apathy as major obstacles to implementation.

Proposals for the Improvement of Implementation Mechanism on International Level

It has long been difficult to assess compliance with the various criminal justice norms, which has been measured primarily through a confusing system of questionnaires and reporting to the Commission and/or Congresses.[4] For example, the 2003 session of the Commission on Crime Prevention and Criminal Justice received responses to questionnaires regarding penal reform from only fifteen states; regarding the administration of juvenile justice, seven states; sexual abuse or exploitation of children, thirty-two states; crime prevention, five states; and restorative justice, two states.

The most recent proposal suggests periodic reporting on the crosscutting aspects of all or several instruments at once, although it is not yet clear exactly how this new procedure will work. A special working group of experts has recommended discussing issues according to "clusters," in the following priority: juvenile justice and prison reform; the conduct of law enforcement and criminal justice practitioners, including the integrity of the judiciary; public security and crime prevention; the treatment of victims and witnesses; and international cooperation through model treaties.[5]

Rights of Prisoners and Detainees

Standard Minimum Rules for the Treatment of Prisoners

In 1955, the First UN Congress on the Prevention of Crime and Treatment of Offenders adopted a landmark set of rules for inmates, the Standard Minimum Rules for the Treatment of Prisoners. The culmination of efforts that began in 1926 at a meeting of the International Penal and Penitentiary Commission in Bern, Switzerland, the Rules were later approved by the Economic and Social Council (ECOSOC), which invited governments to adopt and apply them and arrange for their widest possible dissemination. The ECOSOC resolution also requested the Secretary-General to review, every five years, the progress made in applying the Rules, which were to serve as a model for future standard-setting.

The Rules do not describe a model system of penal institutions. Rather, they establish minimum guidelines, which may be adapted to the political, economic, social, and legal circumstances of individual countries. The Rules reflect the modern approach of reform-minded penologists who emphasize rehabilitation and restraint of a prisoner rather than retribution and deterrence.

The Rules are not concerned with the reasons for or manner of detention but are addressed solely to the conditions of detention. They are thus complementary to the substantive protections against arbitrary detention provided in other human rights instruments. According to the Rules, "imprisonment and other measures which result in cutting off an offender from the outside world are afflictive by the very fact of taking from the person the right of self-determination by depriving him of his liberty. Therefore, the prison system shall not, except as incidental to justifiable segregation or the maintenance of discipline, aggravate the suffering inherent in such a situation" (Rule 57).

The Standard Minimum Rules are divided into two main parts: "Rules of General Application" and "Rules Applicable to Special Categories." They also contain provisions on the selection and training of personnel and on open penal and correctional institutions. The basic principle underlying the Rules is that they are to be applied impartially, without discrimination on grounds of "race, color, sex, language, religion, political or other opinion, national or social origin, property, birth or other status," but with due respect for religious and moral beliefs.

Part I sets out the minimum conditions for the detention of "all categories of prisoners, criminal or civil, untried or convicted, including prisoners subject to security measures or corrective measures ordered by the judge." Subsequent provisions deal with the formalities of registration; separation of different categories of prisoners; and regulation of a prisoner's daily life, including accommodation, personal hygiene, clothing, bedding, food, exercise, and sport. The detailed provisions relating to medical services include a recommendation that a prison medical officer have at least some knowledge of psychiatry and that every prisoner be seen and examined by a medical officer "as soon as possible after his admission and thereafter as necessary."

The provisions on discipline and punishment include an absolute prohibition on the use of corporal punishment; punishment by placing a prisoner in a dark cell; cruel, inhuman, or degrading punishment; and the use of instruments of restraint, such as handcuffs, as punishment. Rules 46–54 include restrictions on the use of force, which must be "no more than is strictly necessary" and which must be immediately reported to the director of the institution. Other provisions offer guidelines, *inter alia*, on contacts between prisoners and the outside world, the right to receive information, the right to practice a religion, and the right to make requests or complaints to the prison administration.

The "special categories" of prisoners covered in Part II of the Rules consist of prisoners under sentence (Part A), insane and mentally abnormal prisoners (Part B), prisoners under arrest or awaiting trial (Part C), civil prisoners (Part D), and persons arrested or imprisoned without charge (Part E). Part A is the most detailed and is equally applicable to category B, C, and D prisoners, "provided they do not conflict with the rules governing those categories and are for their benefit."

The provisions concerning mentally abnormal prisoners are cursory and only require that such persons be specially treated and be under the care of a medical officer. They do not consider the standards under which a person may be determined to be mentally ill and, therefore, are not relevant to the possible abuse of psychiatry in detaining persons for political purposes. In 1991, the UN General Assembly adopted the Principles for the Protection of Persons with Mental Illness, which also consider rights and conditions in mental health facilities, including guidelines for determining whether adequate grounds exist for detention.[6]

Part E, which pertains to persons arrested or detained without charge, consists of a single provision and was added to the Standard Minimum Rules in 1977, perhaps reflecting the increasing use of detention without trial and the concomitant increase in human rights violations during such detention. The Rule provides that, "without prejudice to the provisions of article 9 of the International Covenant on Civil and Political Rights, persons arrested or imprisoned without charge shall be accorded the same protection" as that accorded under Part 1 of the Rules (rules of general application); Part II, section C (prisoners under arrest or awaiting trial); and the relevant provisions of Part II, section A (prisoners under sentence), "provided that no measures shall be taken implying that re-education or rehabilitation is in any way appropriate to persons not convicted of any criminal offence."

Implementation of the Standard Minimum Rules at the national level was examined in several surveys conducted by the United Nations between 1967 and 1994. Almost all responding countries indicated that the Rules had been embodied in their laws or prison regulations. Of course, state responses to such surveys tend to be self-serving, and the Rules may be cited as having influenced laws or practice even where such influence is difficult to identify. Nevertheless, the Rules have had an impact. In the United States, for example, at least six states have administratively adopted the Standard Minimum Rules. The U.S. Supreme Court has cited the Rules as evidence of "contemporary standards of decency" in a case involving the definition of "cruel and unusual punishment" under the U.S. Constitution.[7] A lower federal court cited the Standard Minimum Rules in support of its decision in a prisoners' rights and prison conditions case, not only on the basis of the state's administrative adoption of the Rules, but also on the ground that UN adoption of the Rules constituted "an authoritative international statement of basic norms of human dignity and of certain practices which are repugnant to the conscience of mankind. The standards embodied in this statement are relevant to the canons of decency and fairness which express the notions of justice embodied in the Due Process Clause."[8]

At the international level, efforts to implement the Rules seek not to expand the text but rather to improve the dissemination and application of the Rules as they now stand. At the same time, however, concern with the conditions of prisoners and detainees has led to the adoption of several new international instruments and guidelines, which are mentioned below. In 1984, ECOSOC adopted the Procedures for the Effective Implementation of the Standard Minimum Rules for the Treatment of Prisoners, which affirm that "all States whose standards for the protection of all persons subjected to any form of detention or imprisonment fall short of the Standard Minimum Rules for the Treatment of Prisoners shall adopt the Rules." In 1990, the UN Crime Congress proposed, and the General Assembly adopted, the Basic Principles for the Treatment of Prisoners, in the belief that articulating the spirit and basic principles underlying the Standard Minimum Rules would facilitate their full implementation.[9]

Obviously, standards of living and availability of resources vary considerably in different countries. While most countries apply the Standard Minimum Rules to a large extent, lack of sufficient funds causes severe problems in meeting minimum standards for prisoners in many countries. In addition, owing to the limited use of noncustodial measures, prison overcrowding remains a major problem in many countries. As a consequence, separation of different categories of prisoners was reported to be a challenge for prison management in a number of countries. That situation has also hindered educational activities and working conditions in many prisons and reduced the availability of adequate facilities for leisure activities. In some countries, not even beds and bedding could be guaranteed to every prisoner. In addition, social services and projects aimed at resocializing the offender upon release were available to only a limited number of prisoners.

Body of Principles for the Protection of All Persons under any Form of Detention or Imprisonment[10]

The pronounced increase in the use of torture by states during the early 1970s led the UN Sub-Commission on Prevention of Discrimination and Protection of Minorities (now the Sub-Commission on the Promotion and Protection of Human Rights) to begin work on a set of principles that would protect not only imprisoned persons (as do the UN Standard Minimum Rules), but all detainees, from abuses such as arbitrary detention, coercive interrogation, torture and other ill-treatment, and "disappearance." The General Assembly did not adopt the Body of Principles until 1988, and the lengthy drafting process testifies to the political and practical difficulties encountered in developing standards of criminal procedure to be applied in a wide variety of legal systems.

The Body of Principles supplements the protections contained in the Standard Minimum Rules and is directed more specifically toward safeguarding the physical safety of detainees and prisoners. The Principles were derived primarily from existing instruments and stress the importance of access to the outside world and independent supervision of detention conditions.

Principle 1 affirms that persons in detention or imprisonment must "be treated in a humane manner and with respect for the inherent dignity of the human person." Detention and imprisonment must be carried out strictly in accordance with law, and any measure that affects detainees' human rights must be under the effective control of a judicial or other authority. Torture and cruel, inhuman, or degrading treatment are prohibited, and a footnote states that this prohibition is to be "interpreted so as to extend the widest possible protection against abuses, whether physical or mental," including deprivation of "the use of any of [the detainee's] natural senses, such as sight or hearing, or of his awareness of place and the passing of time."

A record is to be kept and made available to a detainee and the detainee's counsel of the names of all law enforcement personnel involved in arrest and/or interrogation; immediately after arrest and after any transfer to another place of detention, a detainee's family is to be notified of the detainee's whereabouts; communication with legal counsel is to be provided "without delay" and in full confidentiality; access is to be given to a medical officer; and noncompliance with the Body of Principles in obtaining evidence "shall be taken into account in determining the admissibility of such evidence against a detained or imprisoned person."

In an important guarantee that supplements the Convention against Torture, an inquiry into a death or disappearance that occurs during detention must be held by a judicial or other authority, either on its own motion or at the request of family members or others with knowledge of the case.

The Body of Principles does not contain any implementation procedure or even a reporting system. Nevertheless, it serves as a model for national legislation and practice and provides standards for nongovernmental bodies to invoke when pressuring governments to cease the abuse of detainees.

Safeguards Guaranteeing Protection of the Rights of Those Facing the Death Penalty[11]

Since its creation, the United Nations has continuously expressed its concern over the issue of capital punishment. The General Assembly and ECOSOC adopted several resolutions on this important issue, and ECOSOC adopted the present Safeguards in 1984. In 1989, the UN General Assembly adopted the Second Optional Protocol to the Covenant on Civil and Political Rights, aimed at the abolition of the death penalty.

Approved on the understanding that they would not be invoked to delay or prevent the abolition of capital punishment, the Safeguards set forth basic guarantees to be respected in criminal justice proceedings and stipulate that the death penalty may be imposed "only for the most serious crimes, it being understood that their scope should not go beyond intentional crimes with lethal or other extremely grave consequences." They cover, *inter alia*, the right to benefit from lighter penalties under certain conditions, to appeal, and to seek pardon; exemptions from capital punishment for persons below eighteen years of age, pregnant women, new mothers, and persons who have become insane; necessary evidentiary requirements; and criteria for staying executions.

The Safeguards reiterate portions of Article 6 of the Covenant on Civil and Political Rights and elaborate on provisions prohibiting the arbitrary deprivation of life. Capital punishment may only be imposed "when the guilt of the person charged is based upon clear and convincing evidence leaving no room for an alternative explanation of the facts" and only after a legal process "which gives all possible safeguards to ensure a fair trial, at least equal to those contained in article 14" of the Covenant. When an execution does occur, it should be carried out "so as to inflict the minimum possible suffering."

To implement the Safeguards, ECOSOC invited states to facilitate the efforts of the Secretary-General to gather information about implementation of the Safeguards and the death penalty in general. Reports on the question of capital punishment have been submitted to ECOSOC at five-year intervals since 1975. However, only one-third of UN members have responded to the questionnaire, mostly those who support abolition of the death penalty. As might be expected, there was a relatively poor response from retentionist countries, especially those in which capital punishment was most frequently applied. One major conclusion to be drawn is that, since 1994, the rate at which countries have embraced abolition remained unchanged. The observations of the United States, for example, stated that "[i]mplementation of the death penalty in the United States has been and continues to be reviewed by judicial, legislative, and executive officials to both state and federal governments. Our highest state and federal courts have upheld capital punishment subject to the heightened procedural safeguards required under our state and federal constitutions and statutes, which generally meet or exceed those provided under international standards and the laws of most other nations."[12]

Principles on the Effective Prevention and Investigation of Extra-Legal, Arbitrary, and Summary Executions[13]

Adopted by the Economic and Social Council in 1989, these Principles establish standards for implementing Article 6 of the Covenant on Civil and Political Rights, which proclaims that everyone has the right to life.

In addition to preventing extralegal, arbitrary, and summary executions, governments are to guarantee effective protection to individuals and groups in danger of such executions, including those who receive death threats. Governments also must ensure that accurate information on custody and the whereabouts of detainees is made available promptly to the detainees' relatives.

The Principles require a thorough, prompt, and impartial investigation of all suspected cases of extralegal, arbitrary, and summary executions. Governments are to maintain investigative offices and procedures to undertake such inquiries, and the investigative authority is to have the power to obtain all information necessary to the inquiry. The Principles provide details regarding both the legal and the medical aspects of investigatory procedures. It was on the basis of these Principles that, for example, a Royal Commission of Inquiry was established in Australia to investigate reports of deaths of aborigines in Australian prisons.

The Principles also impose on governments a duty to bring to justice, or cooperate in the extradition of, persons identified by an investigation as having participated in arbitrary executions.

Administration of Juvenile Justice

Standard Minimum Rules for the Administration of Juvenile Justice (Beijing Rules)[14]

The UN Standard Minimum Rules for the Treatment of Prisoners were not intended to regulate the administration of institutions set aside for young persons or correctional schools, although Part 1 (Rules of General Application) is applicable in such institutions. To address the specific conditions of young offenders and their treatment, the UN General Assembly adopted in 1985 what became known as the Beijing Rules, "to serve as a model for national justice systems in the administration of juvenile justice."

The Beijing Rules provide that juveniles may be deprived of their liberty only if they are found to have committed "a serious act involving violence against another person or of persistence in committing other serious offences and unless there is no other appropriate response." They emphasize that "[t]he placement of a juvenile in an Institution shall always be a disposition of last resort and for the minimum necessary period and, that juveniles in institutions are to be kept separate from adults."

Children's privacy is protected by the provision that no information about juvenile offenders may be published and that formal trials should be avoided wherever possible. Special police units or special training for police officers dealing with juveniles are recommended.

States are to report every five years to the Commission on Crime Prevention and Criminal Justice on implementation of the Rules. Initial reports indicated that the Rules have inspired significant changes in juvenile justice systems in many parts of the world, including raising the minimum age of criminal responsibility to between seven and eighteen years, with most countries setting this limit between twelve and sixteen years. A 1998 analysis indicated that so-called "status offences" (e.g., truancy and school and family disobedience) exist in thirteen countries; separate juvenile courts are in place in twenty-nine countries; and, in twenty-four countries, authorities consider dealing with juvenile offenders without resorting to a formal trial, when appropriate. Detention pending trial was avoided if there was an alternative measure that could be applied, although some countries reported considerable delays in their juvenile justice proceedings.

United Nations Guidelines for the Prevention of Juvenile Delinquency (Riyadh Guidelines)[15]

Adopted by the UN General Assembly in 1990, the Riyadh Guidelines set forth standards for the prevention of juvenile delinquency, including measures to protect young persons who are abandoned, neglected, abused, or in marginal circumstances. They concern the preconflict stage (i.e., the stage before juveniles come into conflict with the law) and are based on the premise that society must try to eliminate conditions that adversely influence the healthy development of a child. The Guidelines focus on early preventive and protective intervention and encourage an active role on the part of various social agencies, including the family, the educational system, the mass media, and the community, as well as the young persons themselves.

Rules for the Protection of Juveniles Deprived of Their Liberty[16]

While the Beijing Rules apply in cases of detention and imprisonment, the Rules for the Protection of Juveniles Deprived of their Liberty apply in all cases involving the deprivation of liberty by order of any public authority. The Rules advocate the minimum use of deprivation of liberty, especially in prisons or other closed institutions, and they call for the separation of juveniles from adults in detention and the classification of juveniles according to their sex, age, personality, and type of offense, with a view to ensuring their protection while in custody. The major part of the Rules deals with the management of juvenile facilities, an area not covered by the Beijing Rules; the 1990 Rules also deal with juveniles under arrest or awaiting trial.

States are invited to inform the Secretary-General of implementation efforts and to report "regularly" to the Commission on Crime Prevention and Criminal Justice on progress achieved in implementation, but no specific reporting dates are set.

In order to improve implementation of the international standards and norms on juvenile justice, an expert group adopted a set of Guidelines for Action on Children in the Criminal Justice System in 1997. The Guidelines were welcomed by ECOSOC Resolution 1997/30, and states were asked to consider the Guidelines in implementing the provisions concerning juvenile justice found in the Convention on the Rights of the Child. The Guidelines also should facilitate the provision of assistance to states to implement the Children's Convention and related instruments. A coordination panel will provide a framework for cooperation between specialized agencies and NGOs in technical assistance projects and provide advice on juvenile justice matters.

The Committee on the Rights of the Child has given considerable attention to the subject of juvenile justice during its review of state reports that it receives, including the basic principles reflected in the three UN instruments described in this section.

An analysis by the Max Planck Institute for Foreign and International Criminal law in Freiburg, Germany, in collaboration with the UN International Center for Crime Prevention, evaluated the practical relevance of standards and norms in the area of juvenile justice, focussing on South Africa. About 400 correctional officers and 800 children/juveniles participated in the survey. The study concludes that the "facilities do not comply with the Rules on some sensitive issues, although the scope and ideals . . . are clearly considered. To improve the use and application of the Rules, a comprehensive reforms strategy is necessary which would focus on more than one aspect of its implementation. . . . A lack of financial resources will be the biggest obstacle to its realization."[17]

Alternatives to Imprisonment

Standard Minimum Rules for Non-Custodial Measures (Tokyo Rules)[18]

The Tokyo Rules, adopted by the UN General Assembly in 1990, encourage alternatives to incarceration and declare that detention is considered justifiable "only from the viewpoints of public safety, crime prevention, just retribution and deterrence." Judges are urged to imprison people only "if it can be shown that there are reasonable grounds for believing that community sanctions would be inappropriate." The Rules aim to reduce the use of imprisonment and rationalize criminal justice policies, taking into account observance of human rights, the requirements of social justice, and offender rehabilitation.

States are to balance the rights of individual offenders, the rights of victims, and the concern of society for public safety and crime prevention. Other provisions deal with the implementation of noncustodial measures (supervision, duration, conditions, treatment process, discipline); staff (recruitment and training); use of volunteers and other community resources; and research, planning, policy formulation, and evaluation.

States are to report on implementation of the Rules to the Commission on Crime Prevention and Criminal Justice every five years. The Secretary-General submitted a commentary on the Rules to the Commission in 1998, emphasizing legal safeguards, implementation of the Rules, and development of similar guidelines at the regional level.[19]

Principles to Be Applied by Persons Involved in the Administration of Justice

Code of Conduct for Law Enforcement Officials[20]

The need to ensure that law enforcement officials fulfill their duties without resorting to torture or other cruel, inhuman, or degrading treatment or punishment led to the adoption of the Code of Conduct for Law Enforcement Officials by the UN General Assembly in 1979. Based on drafts submitted by professional law enforcement associations and other experts, the Code of Conduct stipulates that the actions of law enforcement officials should be subject to public scrutiny, although it does not prescribe the kind of reviewing agency. It underscores the fact that the standards it sets will have practical value only if they are incorporated into the training, education, and supervision of law enforcement officials.

The Code contains eight articles, with commentaries that are intended to facilitate domestic implementation. The commentary to Article 1 defines "law enforcement officials" as "all officers of the law, whether appointed or elected, who exercise police powers, especially the powers of arrest or detention," which clearly includes military authorities and other security forces. Any violation of national law or the Code is to be reported through the chain of command, or outside the chain of command "when no other remedies are available or effective." Law enforcement officials should serve the community and protect all persons against illegal acts, consistent with the high degree of responsibility required by their profession.

The use of force by officers is authorized "only when strictly necessary," and the extent of force permissible is governed by the principle of proportionality. The use of firearms is considered an extreme measure, and, in general, "firearms should not be used except when a suspected offender offers armed resistance or otherwise jeopardizes the lives of others, and less extreme measures are not sufficient to restrain or apprehend the suspect offender."

The Code stipulates that confidential matters in the possession of law enforcement officials shall be kept confidential, unless the needs of justice require otherwise. No law enforcement official may inflict, instigate, or tolerate any act of torture or other cruel, inhuman, or degrading treatment or punishment. Law enforcement officials should protect the health of persons in their custody and should take immediate action to secure medical attention whenever required.

Article 7 of the Code of Conduct stipulates that law enforcement officials may not commit any act of corruption. Subsequent instruments, such as the UN Declaration against Corruption and Bribery in International Commercial Transactions[21] and the International Code of Conduct for Public Officials,[22] have expanded this principle.

ECOSOC subsequently adopted Guidelines for the Effective Implementation of the Code of Conduct for Law Enforcement Officials, which encourage states to incorporate the principles into national law and request governments to report to the Secretary-General at least every five years on implementation of the Code; the Secretary-General submits periodic reports to ECOSOC and the Commission on Crime Prevention and Criminal Justice.

Basic Principles on the Use of Force and Firearms by Law Enforcement Officials[23]

The Basic Principles elaborate on the principle contained in the Code of Conduct for Law Enforcement Officials that force should be used only as a last resort and only to the extent required. Specific restrictions are placed on the use of force and firearms; the development of nonlethal incapacitating weapons is encouraged; and governments are required to punish arbitrary or abusive use of force and firearms as a criminal offense. Internal political instability or other public emergency may not be invoked to justify any departure from the Principles. The Principles also contain provisions on controlling unlawful gatherings and persons in custody or detention; qualifications, training, and counselling (including stress counselling); and reporting and review procedures.

Principles of Medical Ethics Relevant to the Role of Health Personnel, Particularly Physicians, in the Protection of Prisoners and Detainees against Torture and Other Cruel, Inhuman, or Degrading Treatment or Punishment[24]

Reflecting its concern over violations of the human rights of detainees, the UN General Assembly asked the World Health Organization (WHO) in 1974 to prepare a draft set of principles of medical ethics, in order to remove health personnel from any involvement whatsoever in torture or other ill-treatment of detainees. Based on a study by the Council for International Organizations of Medical Sciences and the 1975 Declaration of Tokyo, adopted by the World Medical Assembly, the Principles of Medical Ethics were adopted by WHO and the UN General Assembly in 1982.

The Principles declare it to be a "gross violation of medical ethics, as well as an offence under applicable international instruments," for medical personnel "to engage, actively or passively, in acts which constitute participation in, complicity in, incitement to or attempts to commit torture or other cruel, inhuman and degrading treatment or punishment." There are several more specific prohibitions, such as the prohibition against assisting in interrogation or certifying detainees as fit for any form of punishment which could adversely affect their physical or mental health. No derogation from the Principles is allowed, even in time of public emergency.

Although the Principles contain no monitoring mechanism, it is hoped that their impact as a set of professional standards, largely based on norms developed by doctors themselves, will deter physicians who might presently be participating in unlawful interrogations, as well as provide meaningful international support for those who refuse to participate in such actions. In cooperation with WHO and NGOs, the Office of the High Commissioner for Human Rights is taking steps to ensure that physicians and other health professionals are familiar with the Principles.

Basic Principles on the Independence of the Judiciary[25]

The bedrock of these Principles, which were adopted by the UN Congress on Prevention of Crime and Treatment of Offenders in 1985 and subsequently endorsed by the General Assembly, is the requirement that judicial independence be guaranteed by the state and be respected by all government and other institutions.

Independence of the judiciary should be enshrined in the constitution or law of the country. The Principles point out, *inter alia*, that justice requires that everyone is entitled to a fair and public hearing by a competent, independent, and impartial tribunal. The judiciary "shall decide matters before them impartially, on the basis of facts and in accordance with the law, without any restrictions, improper influences," or other pressure, "direct or in direct, from any quarter or for any reason." The judiciary is to have jurisdiction over all issues of a judicial nature and exclusive authority to decide whether an issue is within its competence. The Principles also include provisions on freedom of expression and association; qualifications, selection, and training; conditions of service and tenure; professional secrecy and immunity; and discipline, suspension, and removal.

Basic Principles on the Role of Lawyers[26]

These Principles have a limited but focused approach and contain pragmatic suggestions for the day-to-day operation of the legal profession, with emphasis on criminal justice. Attention is given to the following issues: the right of all persons arrested, detained, or imprisoned to have access to a lawyer within forty-eight hours; effective access to legal services for all, including the indigent; the right of accused persons to counsel and assistance of their own choosing; the right of lawyers to represent clients or causes without threat of prosecution or other sanction; educating the public on the role of lawyers in protecting fundamental rights and liberties; and the obligation of lawyers to keep communications with their clients confidential, including the right to refuse to give testimony.

Guidelines on the Role of Prosecutors[27]

The Eighth UN Crime Congress also adopted guidelines on the role of prosecutors, completing its adoption of standards for all those directly involved in the administration of criminal justice: law enforcement officials, doctors, judges, lawyers, and prosecutors. The Guidelines on the Role of Prosecutors address qualifications, selection, and training of prosecutors; status, conditions of service, and tenure; the discretionary power of prosecutors; the prosecutor's role in criminal proceedings; alternatives to prosecution; relations with the police and other public institutions; and disciplinary proceedings.

International Code of Conduct for Public Officials[28]

Concerned about the seriousness of the problem posed by corruption, the General Assembly adopted the International Code of Conduct for Public Officials in 1996. According to the Code, public officials may not use their official authority for their improper advancement or financial interest; may not engage in any transaction, acquire any position or function, or have any financial, commercial, or other comparable interest that is incompatible with their office; and shall declare business, commercial, and financial interests or activities undertaken for financial gain that may raise a possible conflict of interest. Public officials may at no time improperly use public moneys, property, services, or information that is acquired in the performance of, or as a result of, their official duties for activities not related to their official work.

Similar prohibitions are contained in the General Assembly's Declaration against Corruption and Bribery in International Commercial Transactions, also adopted in 1996.[29] A Global Program against Corruption was launched by the UN Office on Drugs and Crime in 1999.

Victims of Crime

Declaration of the Basic Principles of Justice for Victims of Crime and Abuse of Power[30]

This obvious complement to other criminal justice instruments was adopted by the UN General Assembly in 1985. According to the Declaration, "victims" are persons who, individually or collectively, have suffered harm, including physical or mental injury, emotional suffering, economic loss, or substantial impairment of their fundamental rights through acts or omissions that violate criminal laws, including those laws proscribing criminal abuse of power. All victims should be treated with compassion and respect for their dignity. The Declaration examines the questions of restitution, compensation, and assistance.

Part B of the Declaration deals with abuse of power and victims who suffer from acts or omissions that do not yet constitute violations of national criminal law but do violate internationally recognized human rights norms. States are to consider formally proscribing abuses of power and providing remedies to victims of such abuses; they also should consider negotiating multilateral treaties relating to victims.

Two important guides were published in 1999 by the United Nations Center for Crime Prevention: *Guide for Policy Makers on the Implementation of the Declaration of Basic Principles of Justice for Victims of Crime and Abuse of Power* and *Handbook on Justice for Victims on the Use and Application of the Declaration of Basic Principles of Justice for Victims of Crime.*[31]

Model Strategies and Practical Measures on the Elimination of Violence against Women in the Field of Crime Prevention and Criminal Justice[32]

The Model Strategies adopted in 1998 recognize the need for a policy of "integrating a gender perspective into all policies and programmes related to violence against women and of achieving gender equality and equal and fair access to justice." They examine issues of criminal law, enforcement by police, sentencing and correction, victim support and assistance, health and social services, training, research and evaluation, crime prevention measures, international cooperation, and follow-up activities. The Model Strategies are aimed at deterring and preventing all types of criminal violence against women and girls. They promote the fair treatment and rights of women, gender equality, equal access to justice, and integrating a perspective of gender fairness within justice administrations. The Model Strategies are built upon the measures included in the Platform for Action adopted by the Fourth World Conference on Women, held in Beijing in 1995.[33]

The Commission on Crime Prevention and Criminal Justice

The Commission plays an essential role in the development and applications of the standards and norms mentioned in this chapter. Created in 1992, it consists of forty government representatives elected by the Economic and Social Council and is a subsidiary body of the Council. The Commission offers nations a forum for exchanging information and agreeing on ways to fight crime on a global level.

The Commission's main functions are to

- provide policy guidance to the United Nations in the field of crime prevention and criminal justice;
- develop, monitor, and review implementation of the UN Crime Prevention Program;
- facilitate and help to coordinate the activities of interregional and regional institutes on the prevention of crime and the treatment of offenders;

- mobilize the support of member states;
- prepare the UN Congresses on the Prevention of Crime and the Treatment of Offenders, which are held every five years;
- undertake international action to combat national and transnational crime, including organized crime, economic crime and money laundering;
- promote the role of criminal law in protecting the environment; and
- develop crime prevention in urban areas, including juvenile crime and violence.

Other Standards and Principles

While a plethora of international principles and guidelines has been developed in recent years in the area of criminal justice, other issues have been the topic of similar initiatives. In most instances, these initiatives have come first from NGOs concerned with a specific issue; sympathetic governments then have led the UN's political bodies to adopt relevant texts.

While an exhaustive listing is impractical, the following General Assembly declarations are illustrative of instruments adopted outside the realm of criminal justice and the rights of detainees.

Declaration on the Elimination of Intolerance and Discrimination Based on Religion or Belief[34]

The UN General Assembly adopted the Declaration in 1981, nineteen years after the United Nations announced its intention to develop standards to eliminate religious intolerance. The long drafting process resulted both from political conflicts within the United Nations and the sensitive nature of the issues involved. The final document, however, represents a significant advance over the rather vague norms previously accepted with respect to this issue and represents international standards on the issue.

Article 1 of the Declaration parallels the Covenant on Civil and Political Rights and proclaims the right to freedom of thought, conscience, and religion, including the right to manifest one's religion or belief "in worship, observance, practice, and teaching." Article 6 elaborates on ways in which one may manifest one's religion, all of which are subject to rather broad limitation by measures "necessary to protect public safety, order, health or morals or the fundamental rights and freedoms of others." Some degree of proselytizing is permitted, based on the freedom of teaching, worship and observance, but the question of when proselytizing becomes "coercive" is problematic; "coercion" is prohibited but undefined.

Discrimination on the ground of religion or belief is prohibited. States are to take positive measures to prevent or eliminate discrimination, but there is no requirement that states make remedies available for harm suffered from discrimination.

The Declaration itself contains no reporting or implementation mechanism, but separate means of considering the issues addressed by the Declaration have been adopted. Since 1986, a Special Rapporteur appointed by the Commission on Human Rights has examined incidents of religious intolerance and discrimination and reports annually to the Commission on Human Rights.[35] The Special Rapporteur has interpreted his mandate broadly and has identified a wide range of human rights violations based on religion and belief. He examines incidents of religious intolerance, reports on violations or compliance with the Declaration, and recommends remedial measures. If necessary, the Rapporteur also transmits urgent appeals to governments. The Special Rapporteur has also initiated studies on *Racial discrimination and religious discrimination: identification and measures* and *Racial discrimination, religious intolerance, and education.*

Persons with Disabilities

Several instruments dealing with disabled persons have been adopted by the UN General Assembly. They include the Declaration on the Rights of Mentally Retarded Persons,[36] the Declaration on the Rights of Disabled Persons,[37] Principles for the Protection of Persons with Mental Illness and for the Improvement of Mental Health Care,[38] and the Standard Rules on the Equalization of Opportunities for Persons with Disabilities.[39] The Declaration on the Rights of Disabled Persons sets forth thirteen rights that are to be "used as a common basis and frame of reference" for governments to improve the quality of life for people with disabilities. The Declaration promotes measures to enable people with disabilities to enjoy the rights set forth in the Universal Declaration of Human Rights, stating that people with disabilities "have the same fundamental rights as their fellow citizens of the same age" and "the same civil and political rights as other human beings." They are to be protected against discriminatory or degrading treatment and are entitled to measures to enable them to become as self-reliant as possible. The Declaration has been invoked in support of barrier-free access to buildings, availability of reading materials in braille, and measures to benefit the hearing impaired.

To further the Declaration's goal of full and equal access to society, the UN General Assembly has taken several additional actions. The International Year of Disabled Persons was proclaimed in 1981, inspiring some countries to improve access and transportation for the disabled. In the United States, for example, the government requested that the National Council of Architectural Registration Boards include more information and questions about barrier-free designs in the certification exam for architects. In addition, all U.S. embassies were made accessible to people with disabilities, and the government undertook studies on improving accessibility.

In 1982, the General Assembly adopted the World Program of Action concerning Disabled Persons, which declared the years 1983–1992 as the UN Decade of Disabled Persons, made a variety of recommendations for national and international action to enable disabled persons to participate fully in social life, and invited states to submit reports to the Secretary-General on their implementation of the recommendations.

The Standard Rules were adopted at the end of the Decade in 1993 and gave greater specificity to the Declaration. "Disability" is defined as any functional limitation, including physical, intellectual, or sensory impairment, or medical condition or mental illness, whether permanent or transitory. In 1998, the Commission on Human Rights urged governments "to implement the Rules, having particular regard for the need of women, children and persons with development and psychiatric disabilities in order to guarantee their human rights and dignity."[40] States have begun to address disability in their periodic reports to treaty bodies, which have begun to refer more frequently to disability.

In 2002, the General Assembly established an Ad Hoc Committee to consider proposals for a Comprehensive and Integral International Convention on Protection and Promotion of the Rights and Dignity of Persons with Disabilities. A working group of this Committee adopted a draft convention in 2004, which will form the basis for subsequent negotiations and ultimate adoption by the General Assembly. The draft covers broad issues, such as general principles and obligations; equality and nondiscrimination; the right to work; and equal recognition before the law. It also addresses more specific issues, such as living independently; children with disabilities; education; accessibility; personal mobility; social security; and adequate standards of living, as well as issues related to the inclusion of the disabled in society, including the promotion of positive attitudes to persons with disabilities; participation in political and public life; and participation in cultural life, recreation, leisure, and sport.

Declaration on the Human Rights of Individuals Who Are Not Nationals of the Country in Which They Live[41]

Inspired to some extent by the world's negative reaction to the expulsion of Asians from Uganda in 1972, this Declaration on the rights of aliens began with a report prepared by a member of the UN Sub-Commission on Prevention of Discrimination and Protection of Minorities. Among other provisions, the Declaration requires that an alien lawfully within a state "may be expelled therefrom only in pursuance of a decision reached in accordance with law and shall, except where compelling reasons of national security otherwise require, be allowed to submit the reasons why he or she should not be expelled." There should be a right of appeal from any expulsion order, and "[i]ndividual or collective expulsion of such aliens on grounds of race, colour, religion, culture, descent or national or ethnic origin is prohibited." No implementation machinery was included when the Declaration was adopted, and it has not been the subject of much political or scholarly commentary.

Declaration on the Rights of Persons Belonging to National or Ethnic, Religious or Linguistic Minorities[42]

Unlike its predecessor, the League of Nations, the United Nations paid little attention to minority rights during its early years, preferring to emphasize individual human rights and the right of "peoples" to self- determination. Between 1945 and 1990, the only substantive reference to minority rights in an international instrument was the minimalist formulation found in Article 27 of the Covenant on Civil and Political Rights.[43]

At the initiative of Yugoslavia, a working group of the UN Commission on Human Rights began drafting a declaration on minority rights in 1979, but a final text could not be adopted until 1992—ironically, at the time that Yugoslavia itself was disintegrating. The Declaration addresses a number of substantive issues, including the right of members of minorities to enjoy their own culture; use their own language; practice their own religion; establish their own educational and other associations; "participate effectively" in national and regional decision-making that concerns them; and maintain free and peaceful contacts across borders with other members of their group. Wherever possible, states should enable minorities to be educated in or learn their mother tongue.

In 1995, a working group of the Sub-Commission on Prevention of Discrimination and Protection of Minorities was created to "review the promotion and practical realization of the Declaration . . . examine possible solutions to problems involving minorities . . . [and] recommend further measures, as appropriate, for the promotion and protection" of the rights of minorities. The group meets for one week annually in sessions in which minorities may participate, even if they are not NGOs in consultative status with ECOSOC. The group engages in general thematic discussions and reports annually to the Sub-Commission. A *United Nations Guide for Minorities*, which describes ways in which minorities can raise concerns before various UN institutions, was published by the Office of the UN High Commissioner for Human Rights in 2001.[44]

Draft Declaration on the Rights of Indigenous Peoples[45]

An ambitious attempt to define the rights of indigenous peoples began in 1982, with the creation of a working group of the Sub-Commission on Prevention of Discrimination and Protection of Minorities. Indigenous representatives participated actively in the group's annual sessions, and a draft declaration on indigenous rights was finally approved and forwarded to the Commission by the Sub-Commission in 1993. Many issues within the draft remain controversial, and the text has been under consideration by an open-ended intersessional working group of the Commission since 1995.

In 2000, a Permanent Forum on Indigenous Issues was created to serve as an advisory body to the Economic and Social Council, with a mandate to discuss indigenous issues relating to economic and social development, culture, the environment, education, health and human rights. In 2001, the Commission on Human Rights appointed a Special Rapporteur on the situation of the human rights of indigenous peoples. Although neither of these institutions is specifically tasked with monitoring the draft declaration, the draft has already acquired a certain political relevance, despite the fact that it has not yet been adopted by any intergovernmental (as opposed to expert) body.

Guiding Principles on Internal Displacement[46]

In 1992, the UN Secretary-General appointed a Representative on internally displaced persons. The Representative initially focused on normative issues and in 1996 prepared a Compilation and Analysis of Legal Norms relating to internal displacement. The Guiding Principles based on these norms were presented to the UN Commission on Human Rights in 1998. A subsequent resolution of the Commission illustrates precisely the quasi-legal status of instruments such as the Principles. The Commission

[e]xpresses its appreciation of the Guiding Principles on Internal Displacement as an important tool for dealing with situations of internal displacement, welcomes the fact that an increasing number of States, United Nations agencies and regional and non-governmental organizations are applying them as a standard, and encourages all relevant actors to make use of the Guiding Principles when dealing with situations of internal displacement; [and]

Welcomes the dissemination, promotion and application of the Guiding Principles on Internal Displacement and the fact that the Representative of the Secretary-General continues to use the Guiding Principles in his dialogues with Governments, intergovernmental and non-governmental organizations and other pertinent actors, and requests him to continue his efforts in disseminating and promoting them, inter alia through supporting and initiating their publication and translation, participation in training, and, in consultation with governments, regional organizations, intergovernmental and non-governmental organizations and other relevant institutions, the holding of national, regional and international seminars on displacement, as well as in providing support for efforts to promote capacity-building and the use of the Guiding Principles.[47]

The principles apply to different phases of displacement and are intended to protect against arbitrary displacement, ensure that displaced persons have access to protection and assistance, and guarantee the safety of displaced persons during their return or alternative settlement and reintegration.

Concluding Observations

The value of international standard-setting instruments varies in direct proportion to the extent they are publicized, utilized, and taken seriously by those affected by them. Much of human rights practice consists of persuasion rather than coercion, and the existence of agreed-upon international norms can assist that process of persuasion while avoiding (where appropriate) the adversary situation created where "violations" of human rights are alleged.

The quasi-legal nature of these international standards should not obscure the fact that they often interpret and implement fundamental human rights, such as the right to be free from torture, to receive a fair trial, to have the assistance of legal counsel, and other related rights. In this sense, they might be viewed as the international equivalent of administrative regulations, whose implementation will ensure that basic rights are effectively guaranteed.

The administration of criminal justice traditionally has been considered to lie exclusively within the domestic jurisdiction of states, but the United Nations has discovered a reasonably effective method of encouraging national improvements through "soft law" standard-setting. Although the sometimes self-serving periodic reports that states submit to the Commission on Crime Prevention and Criminal Justice are often bland, they can provide the basis for further, more specific, action at both the national and international levels. The most recent UN Congress on the Prevention of Crime and the Treatment of Offenders (2000) adopted the Vienna Declaration on Crime and Justice, which recognizes the importance of UN standards and norms and their contribution to dealing with crime more effectively. The Declaration also committed the participating states to endeavor, "as appropriate, to use and apply the United Nations standards and norms in crime prevention and criminal justice in national law and practice."

As noted above, nonbinding principles and guidelines may presage the subsequent adoption of legally binding treaties, as did, for example, the Universal Declaration on Human Rights, the Declaration of the Elimination of All Forms of Racial Discrimination, and the Declaration on the Rights of the Child. Standards which have achieved the degree of consensus necessary to be adopted by the UN General Assembly or other organs can have more impact than a poorly ratified treaty, and human rights activists should be alert to the possibilities of utilizing these instruments whenever appropriate.

Notes

1. Additional instruments relating to the administration of justice but not discussed in the present chapter include the Naples Political Declaration and Global Action Plan against Organized Transnational Crime (UN Doc. A/49/748 (1994), Annex), Guidelines for Cooperation and Technical Assistance in the Field of Urban Crime Prevention (ECOSOC Res. 1995/9 (1995), Annex), UN Declaration on Crime and Public Security (G.A. Res. 51/60 (1996), Annex), and Declaration against Corruption and Bribery in International Commercial Transactions (G.A. resolution 51/191 (1996), Annex). Several model treaties also have been developed under the auspices of the UN Crime Prevention and Criminal Justice Program, addressing issues such as the transfer of foreign prisoners, preventing crimes infringing on the cultural heritage of peoples in the form of movable property, extradition, mutual assistance in criminal matters, the transfer of proceedings in criminal matters, the return of stolen or embezzled vehicles, and the transfer of offenders conditionally sentenced or conditionally released. Many of these instruments may be found in Compendium of United Nations Standards and Norms in Crimes Prevention and Criminal Justice, available on the Website of the UN Crime and Justice Information Network at http://www.uncjin.org/Standards/Compendium/compendium.html.

2. See chap. 13 for a discussion of the impact of international law in domestic courts.

3. Until 1990, the Secretary-General submitted quinquennial reports on implementation of the Standard Minimum Rules to the UN Congresses on the Prevention of Crime and the Treatment of Offenders. Since then, information gathering has been based on state responses to various questionnaires sent out by the Secretary-General.

4. On implementation generally, see Roger S. Clark, *The United Nations Crime Prevention and Criminal justice Program* (Philadelphia: Univ. of Pennsylvania Press, 1994), at 229–283.

5. Report of the Meeting of Experts on the Application of United Nations Standards and Norms in Crime Prevention and Criminal Justice, UN Doc. E/CN.15/2003/10/Add.1 (2003).

6. G.A. Res. 46/119 (1991).

7. Estelle v. Gamble, 429 U.S. 97, 103–04 & n.8 (1976).

8. Lareau. v. Manson, 507 F. Supp. at 1177, 1188 n. 9; Detainees of Brooklyn House of Detention for Men v. Malcolm, 520 F.2d 392, 396; Sterling v. Cupp, 290 Ore. 611, 622; Carmichael v. United Technologies Corp., 835 F.2d 109, 113; Williams v. Coughlin, 875 F. Supp. 1004, 1012; Taylor v. Perini, 431 F. Supp. 566, 606; Jones v. Wittenberg, 440 F. Supp. 60; Austin v. Hopper, 15 F. Supp. 2d 1210, 1260. By the late 1990s, however, U.S. courts seemed to be more reluctant to invoke the Rules to guide their interpretations. See generally chap. 13.

9. G.A. Res. 45/111 (1990).

10. G.A. Res. 43/173 (1988).

11. ECOSOC Res. 1984/50 (1984).

12. UN Doc. E/CN.15/2001/10, para. 84.

13. ECOSOC Res. 1989/61 (24 May 1989), Annex, endorsed in G.A. Res. 44/162 (1989).

14. G.A. Res. 40/33 (1985).

15. G.A. Res. 45/112 (1990).

16. G.A. Res. 45/113 (1990).

17. See http://www.unodc.org/unodc/crime_cicp_standards.html.

18. G.A. Res. 45/110 (1990).

19. UN Doc. E/CN.15/1998/CRP.3 (1998).

20. G.A. Res. 34/169 (1979), Annex.

21. G.A. Res. 51/191 (1996).

22. G.A. Res. 51/59 (1997).

23. Eighth UN Congress on Crime Prevention and Control, UN Doc. A/CONF.144/28 (1990), at 112.

24. G.A. Res. 37/194 (1982).

25. G.A. Res. 40/32 (1985) and 40/146 (1985).

26. UN Doc. A/CONF.144/28/Rev. 1 (1990), at 118.

27. *Id.* at 189.

28. G.A. Res. 51/59 (1996).

29. G.A. Res. 51/191 (1996).

30. G.A. Res. 40/34 (1985).

31. Available from the website of the Office on Drugs and Crime, http://www.unodc.org/unodc/en/crime_cicp_publications.html.

32. G.A. Res. 52/86 (1998).

33. Also relevant to these issues are two recent treaties which entered into force in 2003 and 2004, respectively, as supplements to the UN Convention against Transnational Organized Crime: Protocol to Prevent, Suppress and Punish Trafficking in Persons, Especially Women and Children; and Protocol against the Smuggling of Migrants by Land, Sea and Air. See G.A. Res. 55/25 (2000).

34. G.A. Res. 36/55 (1981).

35. See the discussion of thematic mechanisms in chap. 4.

36. G.A. Res. 2856 (XXVI) (1971).

37. G.A. Res. 3447 (XXX) (1975).

38. G.A. Res. 48/96 (1993).

39. G.A. Res. 46/119 (1991).

40. Comm. H.R. Res. 1998/31 (1998).

41. G.A. Res. 40/53 (1985). The final report, by Baroness Elles of the United Kingdom, is found in UN Doc. E/CN.4/Sub.2/392/Rev.1 (1980).

42. G.A. Res. 47/135 (1992).

43. Since 1990, several instruments on minority rights have been adopted, most of them under the auspices of the Council of Europe or the Organization on Security and Cooperation in Europe. See chap. 8.

44. Available online at http://www.unhchr.ch/minorities/publications.htm.

45. The draft declaration is contained in Report of the Working Group on Indigenous Populations on Its Eleventh Session, UN Doc. E/CN.4/Sub.2/1993/29, Annex 1 (1993), reprinted in 34 Int'l Legal Mat. 541 (1995).

46. Human Rights, Mass Exoduses, and Displaced Persons, Report of the Representative of the Secretary-General, Mr. Francis M. Deng, UN Doc. E/CN.4/1998/53/Add.2 (1998).

47. Comm. H.R. Res. 2003/51 (2003), paras. 7 and 8.

Chapter 12
The International and National Protection of Refugees

Maryellen Fullerton

Historical Background

Since ancient times people have been forced to flee their homes and seek refuge in other lands. The Bible describes places of asylum for those who are persecuted. The Greeks and Romans similarly set aside certain areas to provide refuge to individuals fleeing for their lives. In medieval times, history records that whole populations sometimes were forced to flee and seek refuge. Religious intolerance led to the expulsion of thousands of Jews from Spain in 1492, followed ten years later by the expulsion of thousands of Muslims. Protestants fled France after the Saint Bartholomew Day massacres in 1572 and again after the repeal of the Edict of Nantes in 1685. More Protestants were expelled from Salzburg in 1731; thousands of Jews were forced out of Bohemia in 1744.

Religious persecution was not the sole force that generated large groups of refugees. Political persecution also played a part. For example, the British Governor of Nova Scotia, suspicious of the political sympathies of French-Acadian farmers, deported thousands from their homes in 1755. The expansionist policy of the U.S. government in the nineteenth century resulted in mass deportations of Native Americans from their ancestral lands to government reservations on the other side of the continent. In the early twentieth century, the Balkan Wars generated forced migrations of large populations of Greeks, Bulgarians, and Turks. The Russian Revolution triggered successive waves of refugees. The Nazi regime in Germany reached new depths in the expulsion of national groups and the forced transfer of whole populations from lands their families had inhabited for centuries.

Despite the international consensus, codified in the Charter of the International Military Tribunal at Nuremberg, that forced deportation of civilian populations constitutes a crime against humanity, refugee movements have continued unabated in the post-World War II era. The victorious allies expelled millions of Germans from densely populated territory that was awarded to Poland. Huge national groups were deported from the European portion of the Soviet Union to Central Asia. Millions of Muslims fled to Pakistan and Hindus fled to India at the time of the partition of British India in 1947. The Hungarian revolt in 1956 triggered many refugees, as did the overthrow of Salvador Allende in Chile in 1973 and the fall of Saigon in 1975. Africa witnessed the expulsion of large numbers of noncitizens from Ghana in 1969, Asians from Uganda in 1972, Egyptians from Libya in 1976, Rwandans from Uganda in 1982, and nearly two million individuals from Nigeria in 1983. The civil wars in Sudan and Sri Lanka generated substantial numbers of refugees throughout the 1980s and 1990s, as had the civil war in East Pakistan, now Bangladesh, in the 1970s.

At the century's close, widespread violence in the 1990s produced millions of refugees and displaced persons in the Middle East, Europe, and Africa. The conflict in the Persian Gulf was followed by the dissolution of former Yugoslavia, where war and "ethnic cleansing" in Croatia and Bosnia-Herzegovina displaced more than three million people. Several years later, nearly one million fled from Kosovo to Montenegro, Macedonia, Albania, and other countries. In Africa, the genocide in Rwanda and Burundi forced millions more to flee, an exodus of biblical proportions, and the violence and refugee movements spread to other countries in the Great Lakes region of Central Africa. West Africa was not spared, as armed conflict engulfed Sierra Leone, Liberia, and the Ivory Coast, and created many more refugees.[1]

The beginning of the twenty-first century brought some positive developments. More than two million refugees returned to Afghanistan; close to one million ethnic Albanians returned to Kosovo; and 400,000 Bosnians returned to their homeland. Due to these and other repatriations, the world-wide refugee population numbered roughly twelve million in 2002, compared to fifteen million in 1995. This was offset, however, by a huge rise in the number of internally displaced people. These individuals, forced from their homes by persecution, armed conflict, and other violence, numbered almost twenty-five million in 2003, approximately twelve million of whom were in Africa. Although they did not cross an international border, they suffered the age-old fate of refugees: they were uprooted, dispossessed, and vulnerable.

Although this abbreviated overview shows that refugees are an age-old phenomenon, societal responses to refugees during the past century have differed substantially from those in earlier times. Before the emergence of industrialized societies and the rise of the welfare state, rulers often welcomed refugees into their realm, anticipating that artisans would benefit the society they joined, while others seeking refuge would increase the taxpayer rolls and enlarge the pool of those who could be conscripted for military service. There was no corresponding public duty to care for refugees from another land. Private charity might sustain refugees for a short time, but quasi-permanent government-supported refugee camps were unknown. Refugees became self-supporting fairly quickly or perished.

During the nineteenth and twentieth centuries, governments grew more wary of refugees. The growth of "nation-states" and the creation of national identities led to the view that refugees and other outsiders threatened a society's security and cultural cohesion by introducing disease, subversive ideas, and foreign traditions. Simultaneously, post-Enlightenment societies gradually assumed greater responsibility for the poor but did not want to see their numbers swelled by large groups of outsiders. The ironic result was that, as governmental obligations to assist the helpless and indigent became a fundamental tenet of society, states began to impose extremely restrictive conditions on those who sought to enter the national territory. This tension between generosity toward those at home and wariness of those from abroad still persists and, in many ways, characterizes the responses of developed nations to the millions of refugees in the world today. The turn of the century has been characterized by a sense of "compassion fatigue" in the industrialized world, with many nations enacting laws to restrict the access of refugees to their territory and to reduce the legal and social protections available to those already within their territory.

International Protection of Refugees

The disintegration of the Turkish, Russian, and Austro-Hungarian empires in the early twentieth century emphasized the international scope of refugee movements. Millions of refugees fled in all directions. International organizations dedicated to refugee assistance were created; with them came attempts to define legally who is a refugee. Early definitions tended to describe refugees in terms of their nationality, implicitly recognizing that political events had triggered the flight of certain groups of people. The cataclysm of World War II and the streams of humanity that it displaced gave impetus to the 1951 Convention Relating to the Status of Refugees (referred to throughout this chapter simply as the Convention), which defined a refugee as follows:

> any person who . . . owing to well-founded fear of being persecuted for reasons of race, religion, nationality, membership of a particular social group or political opinion, is outside the country of his

nationality and is unable, or owing to such fear, is unwilling to avail himself of the protection of that country, or who, not having a nationality and being outside the country of his former habitual residence as a result of such events, is unable or, owing to such fear, is unwilling to return to it.

This definition diverged from earlier definitions in several important respects. It took a more universal approach by specifying five different bases for persecution that can occur in any society, rather than listing specific national or religious groups at risk in certain societies. It also has been interpreted as rejecting a group determination approach, indicating instead that refugee status should be decided on an individual basis. The definition's World War II origin is revealed in its implicit vision of persecution as actions by a totalitarian state systematically oppressing individuals deemed undesirable due to their personal characteristics and in its restriction to refugee situations caused by events which occurred prior to 1951. This last restriction, however, was removed by the 1967 Protocol Relating to the Status of Refugees, which has been ratified by most of the countries that ratified the 1951 Convention.

In 1969, the Organization of African Unity (OAU), now known as the African Union (AU), promulgated the Convention Governing the Specific Aspects of Refugee Problems in Africa, which adopted the 1951 Convention definition and then expanded it:

[t]he term "refugee" shall also apply to every person who, owing to external aggression, occupation, foreign domination or events seriously disturbing public order in either part or the whole of his country of origin or nationality, is compelled to leave his place of habitual residence in order to seek refuge in another place outside his country of origin or nationality.

This formulation better reflects the reality of contemporary refugee movements. Nonetheless, it, too, has been criticized as unduly restrictive, and it has not been adopted by any non-African country.

In contrast to the 1951 Convention, the African Convention addresses the issue of receiving and resettling refugees. States are required to "use their best endeavors consistent with their respective legislations to receive refugees and secure [their] settlement." While this language represents an advance over the 1951 Convention, which does not require state parties to admit refugees, it falls far short of an enforceable individual right of asylum.

In 1976, the Council of Europe publicly acknowledged that the 1951 Convention definition was too limited. The Council asked member governments to "apply liberally the definition of 'refugee' in the Convention" and to refrain from expelling *de facto* refugees, those who have not been formally recognized as refugees under the terms of the Convention but are "unable or unwilling for . . . other valid reasons to return to their countries of origin." However, concerns about inadequacies in the 1951 Convention have not led to adoption of a broader legal definition of refugee in Europe.

In 1984, a group of Latin American states adopted the Cartagena Declaration on Refugees, which encompasses the Convention refugee definition and expressly expands it to include the following people:

> [those] who have fled their country because their lives, safety, or freedom have been threatened by generalized violence, foreign aggression, internal conflicts, massive violations of human rights or other circumstances which have seriously disturbed public order.

This definition suggests that, in some instances, group determination of refugee status is appropriate and that the harm refugees fear may be indeterminate. Thus, it moves beyond the individual determination based on one of five specified bases of persecution that has become the hallmark of refugee status decisions under the 1951 Convention. The General Assembly of the Organization of American States approved the Cartagena definition, but this definition has been formally adopted by only a relatively small number of countries. It is therefore appropriate to turn our attention from these regional agreements of limited application to the more universally accepted 1951 Convention.

The Convention and Protocol Relating to the Status of Refugees

The 1951 Convention, as modified by the 1967 Protocol, contains the most widely accepted refugee definition. More than 135 countries have ratified the Convention and its 1967 Protocol. Although this indicates that there is a consensus concerning who qualifies as a refugee, the Convention and Protocol contain major weaknesses. Neither provides a mechanism under which individuals who squarely fit the refugee definition can protest the denial of refugee status by a ratifying state. Even more significantly, neither imposes an obligation to allow refugees to enter and reside in the territory of a state. Despite these flaws, the Convention and Protocol remain the most significant international instruments for the protection of refugees. Accordingly, it is useful to examine the components of the Convention refugee definition, as interpreted by the Office of the United Nations High Commissioner for Refugees (UNHCR).[2]

Well-founded fear of persecution

To gain Convention refugee status, individuals must show that they subjectively fear persecution and that their fear is rational or reasonable, based on objective facts. Thus, both subjective and objective elements must be considered in determining the existence of well-founded fear. Past persecution, or credible threats of future persecution, directed at an individual or at similarly situated persons would support a conclusion that a well-founded fear exists.

A refugee must fear *persecution*, as opposed to conditions such as poverty or natural disaster. The concept of persecution is flexible. Threats to life, bodily harm, torture, prolonged detention, repeated interrogations and arrests, internal exile, and other serious human rights violations constitute persecution. Discrimination generally does not rise to the level of persecution unless it entails serious restrictions on important rights, such as the right to practice a religion, earn a living, or receive an education. Similarly, criminal prosecution normally does not constitute persecution, unless the offense is a political crime, the punishment is excessive, or the law violates accepted human rights standards. Persecution typically stems from action by government authorities, but it also may include action by private individuals if government officials cannot or will not protect the victims. A few states have interpreted the Convention to apply to persecution by nonstate forces only when they effectively control large swaths of territory or when there is no central government at all, but this is definitely a minority view.

Bases of persecution

Recognition as a refugee is predicated on persecution based on one of five grounds: race, religion, nationality, membership in a particular social group, or political opinion. Any combination of these reasons suffices, but persecution based solely on a different ground, such as purely personal dislike, does not.

Race is used in the broadest sense and includes ethnic groups and social groups of common descent.

Religion also has a broad meaning, including identification with a group that tends to share common traditions or beliefs, as well as the active practice of religion.

Nationality obviously includes an individual's citizenship, lack of citizenship, or former citizenship. In many parts of the world, though, nationality refers not to formal citizenship, but to the language, culture, and ethnic background of a group. For these reasons, persecution of ethnic, linguistic, and cultural groups within a population also may be deemed persecution based on nationality.

A *particular social group* refers to people who share a similar background, habits, or social status. Added to the refugee definition to provide flexibility in responding to new bases of persecution, this category often overlaps with persecution based on one of the other four grounds. It has been applied to families of capitalists, landowners, entrepreneurs, former members of the military, students, tribal groups, and individuals who violate the caste system. Recently, some refugee authorities have recognized certain groups defined by gender and sexual orientation as protected social groups. Specific examples have included women threatened with female genital mutilation, women facing domestic violence who have no recourse to government protection, men persecuted for their homosexuality, and individuals ostracized as AIDS victims.

Political opinion refers to ideas not tolerated by the authorities, including opinions critical of government policies and methods. It includes opinions attributed to an individual by the authorities, even if the individual does not, in fact, hold that opinion. Persecution based on political opinion presupposes that the authorities are aware—or will become aware—of the opinion. Individuals who conceal their political opinions until after they have fled their countries may be eligible for refugee status, if they can show that their views are likely to subject them to persecution if they return to their homeland.

Outside the country of nationality or former habitual residence

Applicants for refugee status must be outside the country of their nationality. Applicants who are stateless must be outside the country of their former habitual residence. If they do not satisfy this requirement, they are ineligible for protection under international law. For purposes of the 1951 Convention, refugees who have sought asylum in a foreign embassy located within the refugees' homeland are not deemed to be outside the country of their nationality or, if stateless, their country of habitual residence. Certain Latin American countries do, however, extend diplomatic asylum to political dissidents who seek shelter in foreign embassies.

The 1951 Convention does not require that refugees must be outside their countries due to persecution. Individuals may have left their country for purely private reasons, such as to study abroad, but circumstances may have changed since departure so that the individuals now fear persecution if they return.

Unable or unwilling to return to the former country

Refugee applicants are unable to return to their former country when the country denies passport facilities or refuses to accept the individuals or when the absence of diplomatic relations prevents their return.

Refugees also may be unable to avail themselves of the protection of the country of their nationality if a war or other serious disturbance prevents the country from offering effective protection.

Individuals who are able to return to their former country, but are unwilling to do so, may qualify for refugee status in certain instances. Their unwillingness must be due to a well-founded fear of persecution based on race, religion, nationality, membership in a social group, or political opinion. Other reasons for unwillingness to return do not satisfy the refugee definition. Situations involving a well-founded fear of persecution in one region, but not all, of a country are complicated. In general, authorities must review all the circumstances, such as language, family ties, ability to earn a living, and the existence of genuine protection, to determine if it would be reasonable to send individuals who have a well-founded fear of persecution in particular areas of their homeland to seek refuge in a different part of their country.

Loss of refugee status

The Convention and Protocol list six circumstances under which individuals recognized as refugees may lose that status because they no longer need international protection. The first four result from acts voluntarily taken by the refugees in question; the last two concern changes in the country of origin. A refugee may lose his or her status in the following situations:

- A refugee has voluntarily accepted the protection of the country of nationality. Obtaining passports or entry permits in order to return are indications that refugees may have sought and received protection from their country. Merely acquiring documents from the country of nationality or making a brief emergency visit is not regarded as voluntarily reavailing oneself of protection.
- A refugee has voluntarily reacquired his or her nationality, which had previously been lost. The granting of nationality by operation of law does not constitute voluntary reacquisition.
- A refugee has acquired a new nationality and enjoys the protection of the country of new nationality.
- A refugee has voluntarily "reestablished" in the country where persecution was previously feared. Temporary return visits by refugees traveling on travel documents issued by another country do not constitute reestablishment.
- The reasons for becoming a refugee have ceased to exist. The circumstances that impelled a refugee to fear persecution at home must have changed in a fundamental, not transitory, way.

- The reasons for a stateless person to seek refuge have ceased. Again, circumstances must have changed in a fundamental way, and, in addition, a stateless refugee must be able to return to the country where he or she formerly resided.

Persons excluded from refugee status

The Convention and Protocol explicitly exclude from refugee status those individuals who, despite satisfying the refugee definition, fall into the following categories:

- Persons who already receive protection or assistance from UN agencies other than the UN High Commissioner for Refugees. This currently applies to Palestinian refugees who fall within the mandate of the UN Relief and Works Agency (UNRWA).
- Persons who have been granted the rights and obligations of nationals in the country in which they have gained residence. This would include, for example, ethnic Germans from other lands who have the right to resettle and exercise the rights of citizens in Germany.
- Persons who have committed crimes against peace, war crimes, or crimes against humanity, as defined in international instruments such as the Nuremberg Charter and the Statute of the International Criminal Court.
- Persons who have committed a serious nonpolitical crime outside the country of refuge prior to admission as a refugee. A serious crime means a capital offense or a grave act punishable by a severe sentence. To determine whether a crime is nonpolitical, it is necessary to examine the nature and purpose of the act, as well as the relative weight of the political and nonpolitical elements of the crime. Heinous acts that are out of proportion to the alleged political objective rarely will be deemed political crimes.
- Persons guilty of acts contrary to the purposes and principles of the United Nations. This includes criminal acts undertaken by persons in positions of power in their states.

With respect to the last three categories, there is no requirement of proof of criminal prosecution and conviction; it is sufficient that there are serious reasons for believing that the refugee applicant committed the proscribed acts.

Recently, former child soldiers pressed into service by insurgent groups or by government security forces have faced challenges during asylum proceedings because the groups of which they were members persecuted others or committed acts contrary to UN principles. These cases can be quite complicated, raising evidentiary questions concerning the age, maturity, level of responsibility, voluntary participation, etc., of the particular individual. In general, though, mere membership in such a group should not disqualify an individual from refugee status; evidence of the asylum seeker's participation in the proscribed activities is required.

Nonrefoulement and other limitations on rejection and expulsion of refugees

Although the Convention and Protocol do not expressly require state parties to admit refugees to their territory, they do contain specific provisions that limit the discretion enjoyed by a state. Article 33 contains the most significant limitation, the principle of *nonrefoulement*, which explicitly prohibits a state from expelling or returning a refugee "in any manner whatsoever to the frontiers of territories where his life or freedom would be threatened on account of his race, religion, nationality, membership of a particular social group or political opinion." There are only two exceptions: refugees who are reasonably believed to be a danger to the security of the receiving country and refugees who have been convicted by a final judgment of a particularly serious crime and are a danger to the receiving country. The duty of states not to return those who face threats to their life or freedom implies a duty to provide at least temporary refuge, although not full-fledged asylum. Many now view *nonrefoulement* as a principle of customary international law that is binding on all states, even those that have not ratified the Convention and Protocol.

Article 31 prohibits states from penalizing refugees who enter or remain illegally, provided that (1) the refugees have come directly from a land where their lives or freedom were threatened, and (2) the refugees present themselves to the authorities without delay and show good cause for their illegal entry or presence. Article 32 prohibits states from expelling a refugee lawfully present in a country, unless there are compelling reasons of national security or public order.

Although they do not guarantee refugees the right to permanent lawful residence, these three articles, taken together, have effectively provided protection to millions of refugees who have crossed frontiers in search of safety.

Rights of those granted refugee status

The Convention and Protocol require that states grant certain substantive rights to individuals that the state has recognized as refugees. All refugees must be granted *identity papers and travel documents* that allow them to travel outside the country.

Refugees must receive *the same treatment as nationals of the host country* with regard to the following rights: free exercise of religion and religious education; free access to the courts, including legal assistance; protection of industrial property, such as inventions and trade names; protection of literary, artistic, and scientific work; access to elementary education; access to public relief and assistance; access to rationed goods; protection provided by labor legislation; protection provided by social security; and equal treatment by taxing authorities.

Refugees must receive the *most favorable treatment provided to nationals of a foreign country* with regard to the following rights: the right to belong to trade unions; the right to belong to other nonpolitical nonprofit organizations; and the right to engage in wage-earning employment. Restrictions applicable to foreign nationals regarding wage-earning employment do not apply to refugees in the following circumstances: (1) the refugee was exempt from such restrictions when the Convention entered into force in the host country; (2) the refugee has resided in the host country for three years; or (3) the refugee's spouse or child is a national of the host country.

Refugees must receive the *most favorable treatment possible, which must be at least as favorable as that accorded foreigners generally in the same circumstances,* with regard to the following rights: the right to own movable and immovable property; the right to practice a liberal profession; the right to self-employment in agriculture, industry, handicrafts, and commerce, including the right to establish commercial and industrial companies; access to housing; and access to higher education, including eligibility for scholarships and fee waivers.

Refugees must receive the *same treatment as that accorded to noncitizens generally* with regard to the following rights: the right to choose their place of residence; the right to move freely within the country; and all other rights not explicitly provided in the Convention.

Role of the United Nations High Commissioner for Refugees

In 1950, the United Nations General Assembly established an international agency to assist refugees, the Office of the United Nations High Commissioner for Refugees (UNHCR). Initially, the mandate of the UNHCR was generally co-extensive with the refugee definition adopted by the 1951 Convention, although it was not restricted to refugee-producing events that occurred in Europe prior to 1951. The UNHCR acted to provide material assistance and legal protection to individuals with a well-founded fear of persecution based on race, religion, nationality, membership in a social group, or political opinion.

Refugee movements do not always correspond to legal definitions, however, and in 1959 the General Assembly authorized the UNHCR to use its "good offices" to assist refugees who did not fall strictly within the Convention definition. Gradually, the UNHCR's mission grew to include people who flee their home country "due to armed conflicts, internal turmoil and situations involving gross and systematic violations of human rights."[3] In pursuing its expanded mandate to help refugees, the UNHCR eschewed the individualized approach generally adopted by parties to the Convention. This enabled the UNHCR to respond quickly and effectively to large-scale refugee movements. This approach also allows the UNHCR to assist groups of refugees without explicitly or implicitly criticizing the political conditions in the refugees' country of origin.

The UNHCR is active in all phases of refugee work. It provides the institutional framework for coordinating international refugee efforts. It organizes material assistance to refugees around the globe, establishing refugee camps, delivering food, and arranging for medical care. In addition to responding to emergency conditions, the UNHCR undertakes longer-term assistance, such as education and training programs. The UNHCR is particularly active in countries of first asylum, i.e., countries such as Thailand and Tanzania that have received refugees from nearby lands and allowed them to remain on a temporary basis. This aspect of the UNHCR effort has led to serious dilemmas in recent years, as refugee camps administered by UNHCR in countries of first asylum have sometimes been effectively controlled by militias who obstruct resolution of the crisis and use the refugees as tools to further their political and military goals.

The UNHCR's primary mission, the voluntary repatriation of refugees, requires it to focus much of its energy and resources on arranging the return of refugees from countries of first asylum to their homelands and monitoring their safety and welfare after their return. When repatriation is not possible, the UNHCR works to integrate refugees into the local community and its economy. As a last resort, the UNHCR coordinates efforts to resettle refugees in other countries. The difficulties that can accompany these tasks were highlighted in the mid-1990s in Central Africa. Many agreed with UNHCR that the peaceful repatriation of the refugees would have been the best solution, but armed militia members who controlled many of the camps of Rwandan refugees prevented those willing to return home from doing so. The stalemate ended in disaster, as warfare engulfed refugee camps in Central Africa and soldiers hunted down the militias hiding among the refugees, driving both militia members and refugees deep into rainforests, where many were massacred.

In addition to providing direct assistance to refugees, the UNHCR spearheads the development of international and national legislation and policies to improve the legal protection of refugees. The UNHCR offers training programs on international law for immigration officials, lawyers, and refugee advocates; actively participates in the refugee determination process in some countries; helps asylum seekers locate *pro bono* legal counsel; occasionally intervenes in domestic cases that raise important issues of refugee law; and, in some cases, provides information in support of individual refugee applications. The UNHCR has offices around the world, and UNHCR staff members can call on their colleagues in other countries to obtain up-to-date information on recent political and legal developments or to help locate family members of refugees.

In short, UNHCR staff members can be extraordinarily helpful to refugee advocates both in developing policies attuned to national and international concerns and in providing support for individual refugee applicants. Because the formal role the UNHCR plays in the refugee process varies so much from state to state, it is impossible to provide specific advice about when and how to seek UNHCR assistance concerning particular issues. However, UNHCR offices in each country should be consulted directly whenever possible.

National Protection of Refugees

As the Convention does not require states to grant asylum, legal protection for refugees is generally found in national laws. It is significant, then, that many of the states that have ratified the Convention and Protocol have not adopted domestic legislation to implement these agreements. This is not to say that all of these countries have turned their backs on refugees. Many states without refugee legislation have provided refuge to tremendous numbers of individuals fleeing persecution, and this humane response has been essential in saving the lives of millions. However, it has rarely resulted in legal protection, and refugees in these countries often remain in limbo, unable to regularize their status and proceed with a normal life.

Those states that have enacted domestic legislation to implement the Convention and Protocol have created a wide variety of measures concerning refugees. Although the details of refugee legislation vary enormously from state to state, there are certain themes that recur. Some elements are derived from the Convention itself; others reflect issues highlighted by the procedures recommended by the UNHCR. Still others reflect more recent legislative efforts by many developed countries to erect new barriers to stem the influx of refugees.

Almost all states with national legislation regarding refugees have adopted the basic Convention refugee definition, although variations exist with respect to the bases for exclusion from or loss of refugee status. Generally, national legislation entitles those individuals recognized as refugees to official identification documents and to lawful residence.

A recent worrying trend, often referred to as the "safe third country" principle, is the denial of refugee status and the residence permits associated with it to individuals who satisfy the refugee definition but who passed through a state in which they did not fear persecution en route to the state in question.

Procedures for Determining Refugee Status

The Convention and Protocol require no particular procedure for determining refugee status. Instead, each state establishes its own procedures for evaluating applicants who request recognition as refugees. In an attempt to assure minimal standards of fairness, the UNHCR recommends the following basic guidelines:

1. The competent official (e.g., immigration officer or border police officer) to whom applicants address themselves at the border or in the territory of a state should have clear instructions for dealing with cases that might come within the purview of the relevant international instruments. The official should be required to act in accordance with the principle of *nonrefoulement* and to refer such cases to a higher authority.
2. Applicants should receive necessary guidance as to the procedure to be followed.
3. There should be a clearly identified authority—whenever possible a single central authority—with responsibility for examining requests for refugee status and taking a decision in the first instance.
4. Applicants should be given all facilities necessary, including the services of a competent interpreter, to submit their cases to the appropriate authorities. Applicants should also be given the opportunity, of which they should be duly informed, to contact a representative of UNHCR.
5. If applicants are recognized as refugees, they should be so informed and issued documents certifying their refugee status.
6. If applicants are not recognized, they should be given a reasonable time to appeal from the decision, either to the same or to a different authority, whether administrative or judicial, according to the prevailing system.
7. Applicants should be permitted to remain in the country pending a decision on their initial request by the competent authority referred to in paragraph (3) above, unless it has been established by that authority that the request is clearly abusive. Applicants should also be permitted to remain in the country while an appeal to a higher administrative authority or to the courts is pending.[4]

Although these standards are not part of a legally binding international instrument, they can be extremely useful politically in encouraging states to improve their refugee determination procedures.[5] These standards also might be considered to constitute the minimum norms of due process, which, according to other international instruments, must be extended to all persons.

States that have enacted national legislation to implement the Convention and Protocol generally have designated a central authority with jurisdiction over requests for refugee status, although the details vary significantly from state to state. Some states assign this function to a law enforcement department, such as the Ministry of Justice or Ministry of the Interior; others delegate refugee matters to the Ministry of Foreign Affairs or to independent refugee or immigration agencies; and, in several others, jurisdiction over refugee matters is shared jointly by designated agencies—typically law enforcement departments and departments dealing with foreign relations.

Many countries provide some role for the UNHCR in their refugee determination process. Often, a UNHCR representative is a regular observer or advisor to the government body that decides refugee cases, and UNHCR representatives may assist individual refugee applicants. In other instances, the UNHCR role is more limited and may be restricted to activities such as providing letters in support of selected individual applications.

In a majority of the states with implementing legislation, the authorities must provide reasons for negative decisions, and rejected refugee applicants have a right to seek a reconsideration or appeal of the decision. The grounds for pursuing an appeal vary, as do the bodies to which an appeal can be made. Some states allow appeals based on factual or legal contentions; others will reconsider a decision only if newly discovered facts are alleged. Some states provide no judicial review; others allow appeals to both administrative and judicial tribunals. National legislation also varies widely as to whether a refugee applicant may remain in the country while an appeal is pending.

Learning these details, as well as others pertaining to the refugee procedure, is crucial to providing effective assistance to refugees and asylum seekers. The UNHCR website provides country-specific information on legislation and other legal documents that affect refugees. It is a useful starting point for understanding the national refugee law framework, although it is no substitute for learning about the legal protections afforded refugees in a particular nation from refugee advocates working there.

De Facto Refugees

Although, as mentioned earlier, national implementing legislation generally adopts the 1951 Convention refugee definition, a number of states have concluded that this definition does not provide sufficient protection. As a result, some states have created additional categories of persons that deserve protection. *De facto*, or humanitarian, refugees are those who do not meet the Convention definition but nonetheless have a compelling need for protection. For example, persons fleeing generalized violence or internal turmoil may not be able to demonstrate that they are likely to be targeted for persecution, but they may be able to show that their lives would be at great risk if they were to return to their homeland. They might be permitted to remain in states that recognize *de facto* or humanitarian refugees.

This concept takes many different forms. Some legal systems distinguish between *de facto* refugees and humanitarian refugees, using the first term to denote applicants whose cases are quite similar to, but not as compelling as, those that fall within the 1951 Convention definition, and using the second term to denote applicants who are at serious risk but whose fear is based on conditions not enumerated in the Convention definition. Other countries make further distinctions. For example, German legislation recognizes multiple refugee categories: Convention refugees who have not passed through a safe country en route to Germany (asylum status), Convention refugees who have passed through a safe country but cannot be returned there (lesser asylum status), refugees who do not satisfy the Convention definition but would face torture or serious threats to their life or freedom if returned (humanitarian residence permit status), and war refugees (temporary protection status granted for periods of six months).

In other states, there are fewer gradations. Thus, Sweden recognizes both Convention refugees and persons otherwise in need of protection, which includes individuals fleeing internal armed conflict, environmental disasters, capital punishment, torture or inhuman treatment, and several other categories. The United Kingdom grants "exceptional leave to remain" to those who are authorized to remain despite denial of refugee status, and the United States has relied on "extended voluntary departure" and "temporary protection status." The distinctions can be dizzying, and it behooves refugee advocates to master the details of this concept in their country.

The development of the concept of *de facto* refugee has been controversial. Many believe that its existence encourages governments to apply the Convention definition in an excessively strict manner, thus denying traditional refugee status to many who deserve it. Since national laws typically grant fewer rights to *de facto* refugees than to Convention refugees, this is a serious concern. Nonetheless, it is useful to remember that the purpose behind the *de facto* or humanitarian refugee concept is a benevolent one, and, as this concept is strongly entrenched in some states, it is crucial for all those dealing with refugees to be aware of it.

Recent Developments

The waning years of the twentieth century witnessed a growth in restrictive measures affecting refugees. In the early 1990s, as Eastern Europe and other areas were suddenly transformed from refugee producing to refugee receiving countries, new refugee policies bloomed. However, the initially progressive refugee efforts that accompanied the dissolution of communist regimes have gradually changed to more restrictive policies, as the newly emerging democracies have followed the developed countries' lead in adopting measures to limit and deter refugees and asylum seekers.

During the 1990s, Western European countries joined together in several efforts that have had major impacts on refugees. Under the Schengen Convention, most of the European Union (EU) countries worked to abolish internal borders and simultaneously raise external barriers to entry to the region. Most EU countries also ratified the Dublin Convention, which sets forth guidelines to determine which state is responsible for examining an asylum application. As the twenty-first century dawned, the EU expanded its membership from fifteen to twenty-five states and simultaneously began to develop a common EU policy on asylum and migration. EU officials drafted directives on minimum standards for asylum procedures and for qualification of non-EU nationals as refugees or persons in need of protection. Hotly debated and criticized as diluting refugee law principles, the proposals were mired in multiple rounds of consultations and discussion as this text went to press.

Imposing advance visa requirements on nationals from many refugee producing countries has become commonplace in the EU and elsewhere in the industrialized world. Refugees and asylum seekers who lack a valid entry visa are prevented from even boarding an airplane or ship heading for safety. Carrier sanctions have also become common, and airline and shipping companies face fines if they board asylum seekers without entry documents for the destination.

Those who manage to travel to developed countries increasingly face an array of devices that turn them away at the border either immediately or within a matter of days: The development of the "safe third country" principle, an expanding network of readmission agreements, the growth of the "manifestly unfounded" concept, accelerated hearings, and curtailed judicial review all play a role. Under the "safe third country" rubric, some states turn away asylum seekers, no matter what countries they fled or what persecution they fear, if they passed through a country en route to the destination state that the destination state considers to be "safe." There is no examination of the merits of the asylum claims and, generally, no examination of whether the so-called "safe" country will admit the asylum seekers under its own refugee procedures. As more countries adopt this "safe" third country approach, each applying it own notions of what is "safe" and each party to different bilateral readmission agreements, the chances of chain deportation leading to *refoulement* increases dramatically.[6]

Asylum seekers not rejected on "safe third country" grounds may find their claims denied as "manifestly unfounded." An elastic concept in many national systems, the "manifestly unfounded" notion provides decision-makers with great discretion. Those whose claims are deemed to fall into this category generally have far fewer procedural protections and may face curtailed administrative hearings, shortened deadlines, fewer (if any) rights to challenge the decision in court, and deportation pending any appeal.

Expedited proceedings held at airports, as in the United States, Germany, and Spain, are another measure devised to turn away asylum seekers quickly and to deter potential future applicants. To accomplish similar goals, the five largest EU states (Germany, France, Italy, Spain, and the United Kingdom) banded together in early 2004 to develop a "safe country of origin" list. Citizens of such "safe" countries will not be eligible to seek refugee status in any of the five states.

Asylum seekers allowed to enter and remain during the refugee determination process often face harsh treatment designed to make their stay so unpleasant that others, in turn, will hesitate to come. Many countries have reduced social support for asylum seekers during the asylum process, and most prohibit asylum seekers from working. Thus, refugees and asylum seekers who can barely make ends meet are prevented from helping themselves, which can easily lead to people becoming increasingly dysfunctional. At the same time, negative public perceptions that refugees and asylum seekers are lazy and unwilling to contribute to society are reinforced.

More draconian yet is the increasing use of detention as a response to asylum seekers. The United States now detains all who request asylum at the border, although thus far the number of asylum seekers has outstripped available detention facilities and overwhelmed the policy. Australia, too, detains all noncitizens, including asylum seekers, if they lack authorization to enter, and keeps them in detention for the length of the refugee determination procedure. Various European countries have begun to use detention at the end of the asylum process, incarcerating those whose applications are denied. Whether detention occurs at the beginning or the end of the asylum process, it poses major problems. The conditions of the detention facilities are often deplorable. Even worse, asylum seekers who have not been charged with a crime often are housed with those convicted of serious criminal acts.

The repercussions of the September 11, 2001, attacks on the United States have been widespread and negative. The United States has enacted multi-faceted anti-terrorist legislation, which has had negative impacts on many noncitizens, including asylum seekers.[7] A heightened concern with controlling the borders and preventing future terrorist attacks has led to expanded government authority to detain suspected terrorists, including those who have been granted asylum. Special registration requirements were imposed on adult males from designated countries, mostly Arab and Muslim states. Although the asylum system within the United States has not been noticeably disrupted, the annual resettlement of refugees from abroad has declined precipitously, from 76,000 per year in the five years preceding 2001 to 29,000 per year since then.

This post-September-11th phenomenon has not been confined to the United States. The discovery of terrorist cells in Europe has led Germany, France, and the United Kingdom, among other countries, to adopt anti-terrorist laws and administrative measures that impose new burdens on asylum seekers and other migrants. Some members of these governments have proposed transferring their refugee determination procedures to regional centers, outside the EU and closer to the refugee producing areas. Successful applicants would then be resettled in EU countries, saving the EU states the costs of accommodating asylum seekers in the EU during the procedures and sparing the applicants the dangers and costs of long journeys to reach the EU. Although these proposals are not likely to become reality, they reveal the current fear of foreigners, frustration with attempts to create effective and efficient asylum procedures in EU states, and awareness of the increasing role of professional human smugglers.

Such measures also indicate that the atmosphere in Europe has increasingly become focused on managing migration, and the rhetoric has often confused immigration and asylum. This has led to criticism of the 1951 Convention as outmoded, because it does not provide a workable framework for migration in the twenty-first century, a task it was never designed to achieve.

Although many recent legal developments concerning asylum seekers have been retrogressive, there have been some positive steps. Refugee authorities in Canada, followed by those in the United States, Australia, and the United Kingdom, have developed guidelines concerning female asylum seekers which recognize and work to overcome many of the difficulties that have been experienced by women who claim asylum. Other countries are studying similar guidelines, and an increased awareness of the impact that gender has on claims to refugee status and on cultural presumptions that influence the refugee determination procedure itself has begun to develop.

In addition, refugee advocates in many countries are becoming more knowledgeable about the potential of other international human rights instruments to protect refugees and asylum seekers in certain instances.

For example, after recourse to national asylum procedures, refugees may turn to the complaint procedures provided under UN human rights treaties or regional human rights institutions. In particular, the Convention against Torture has been a genuine source of protection against *refoulement* of rejected asylum seekers, although it dos not afford the social and legal benefits that accompany refugee status. Article 3 of the European Convention on Human Rights offers another powerful tool for rejected asylum seekers in Europe, since its prohibition against torture and inhuman or degrading treatment also protects against *refoulement* in many instances. Additional provisions of this and other human rights instruments can sometimes provide crucial safeguards for individuals, although they are clearly no panacea.

It is impossible in this chapter to describe the details of specific countries' refugee legislation and other human rights laws. It is clear, though, that human rights practitioners at the start of the twenty-first century must understand the basic international and regional human rights framework, in addition to knowing the sources of international refugee law and the national refugee laws in the states where they work. A list of important reference resources may be found in Appendix A.

Concluding Observations

The 1951 Convention refugee definition, as modified by the 1967 Protocol, remains a mainstay of refugee law. Over 135 states have agreed not to return Convention refugees to lands where their lives or freedom are threatened due to their race, religion, nationality, membership in a particular social group, or political opinion. Many countries also have adopted national legislation that incorporates the Convention definition and entitles those who satisfy it and have managed to enter their territory to lawful residence. Many national systems also provide lawful residence to *de facto* or humanitarian refugees who have a compelling need for asylum, even if they do not satisfy the Convention definition.

Human rights practitioners working on behalf of refugees should know the international refugee definition, regional formulations, and the pertinent national legal system. Informal networks of lawyers and refugee advocates in each country can provide valuable insight and assistance to newcomers to the refugee field. The UNHCR staff, both locally and through their world-wide network, can also be helpful allies in the never-ending work of refugee assistance and protection.

Notes

1. For a brief review of many of the refugee movements described in the text, see A. De Zayas, A Historical Survey of Twentieth Century Expulsions, in Anna

C. Bramwell, ed., *Refugees in the Age of Total War* (London and Boston: Unwin Hyman, 1988).

2. See Office of the United Nations High Commissioner for Refugees, *Handbook on Procedures and Criteria for Determining Refugee Status under the 1951 Convention and the 1967 Protocol relating to the Status of Refugees* (Geneva: UNHCR, rev. ed. 1992). The *Handbook* is widely accepted by practitioners and most governments as an authoritative interpretation of the Convention and Protocol.

3. Executive Committee of the High Commissioner's Program, Report on the 36th Session, Note on International Protection, UN Doc. A/AC.96/660 (1985), para. 6.

4. These standards were recommended by the Executive Committee of the High Commissioner's Program, Report on the 28th Session, Conclusions on International Protection, UN Doc. A/32/12/Add.1 (1977), at 12–16.

5. See chap. 11 for a discussion of the use of quasi-legal standards and guidelines.

6. A simple example illustrates the danger. Suppose an Armenian family fled persecution in Azerbaijan by making its way first to Moscow, then to Ukraine, Poland, and Germany. Without examining their claim of persecution, Germany would reject them at the border and turn them back to Poland, a country Germany deems safe. Poland has readmission agreements with many countries, including Ukraine, and might return the family there, even though German law does not deem Ukraine safe and Germany has no readmission agreement with Ukraine. Ukraine might push the family back to Russia, which, if the situation is unstable and no functioning refugee system exists, might push them back to Azerbaijan. No country would have evaluated the claim, but *refoulement* to the place where persecution is feared could easily occur.

7. The USA Patriot Act of 2001, Pub. Law 107–56, is perhaps the best known of the recent anti-terrorist laws adopted by the United States. It addresses a wide variety of issues, including enhanced surveillance procedures, improved intelligence gathering, border control measures, and other topics that have an impact on asylum seekers, other noncitizens, and U.S. nationals.

Chapter 13
The Role of Domestic Courts in Enforcing International Human Rights Law

Ralph Steinhardt[1]

Introduction

In addition to the international and regional mechanisms canvassed elsewhere in this book, the domestic courts of the various nations offer an essential means of articulating and enforcing international human rights law. "Domestic courts" are not a single institution, of course, and they potentially introduce elements of decentralization, idiosyncracy, and redundancy into the enforcement picture. But when they work as designed, domestic courts provide an effective mechanism that stands between two more visible modes of enforcement: *internationalization*—i.e., the operation of international institutions, nongovernmental organizations, and tribunals for the protection of human rights—and *internalization*—i.e., the incorporation of human rights standards into training and disciplinary regimes for government agents, such as the police and the military.

Effective human rights protection by domestic courts does not necessarily require explicit consideration of international norms. In many democratic states, for example, provisions of the constitution, statutes, and regulations track the guarantees of the major human rights instruments and present few conflicts with customary human rights norms. In these circumstances, the domestic courts will at least implicitly reinforce international standards in the very process of enforcing domestic law. By contrast, where national law is deficient compared to international obligations, or where reference to international standards by national enforcement bodies may strengthen the protection of fundamental rights, the direct incorporation of treaty and customary norms and their utility in interpreting constitutional and statutory text may substantially improve the practical enjoyment of international human rights.

Over the last quarter century, various domestic courts have developed an international human rights jurisprudence in civil, criminal, and administrative proceedings that broadly fall into two categories: (1) cases that arise *within* the forum state, in particular those challenging that state's official acts or policies (e.g., the treatment of refugees, prisoners, and minorities) or a particular official's misconduct; and (2) transnational cases involving violations of human rights *outside* the forum state and involving parties who are not necessarily citizens of that state.

Not surprisingly, states deal differently with cases in both of these categories. For example, with high-profile but rare exceptions involving criminal prosecutions for human rights violations in other countries, domestic courts in the member states of the Council of Europe tend to be stronger in the first category, routinely securing the territorial state's own treaty obligations.[2] By contrast, U.S. courts tend to assess the legality of the government's conduct under purely domestic constitutional and statutory standards, but they have developed an exemplary jurisprudence for the transnational enforcement of human rights through civil actions brought by aliens against foreign officials present in the United States for abuses that occurred abroad.[3]

This chapter addresses three questions that arise in the enforcement by domestic courts of international human rights law in both the internal and the external case categories:

First, by what authorization do domestic courts invoke or apply international human rights law in the first place? There may be matters of doctrine, practice, and logistics that limit the legitimacy or justiciability of international standards in domestic courts, or constrain the invocation of international law by individual litigants, or distinguish between the domestic enforceability of treaties and customary international law.

Second, to what evidence do the domestic courts turn in defining international norms? As the line blurs between the "soft" law of *lex ferenda* and the "hard" law of *lex lata*, or between treaty and custom, or between states and nonstate actors, domestic judges increasingly seek guidance in defining the relevant norms—frequently an exercise in comparative law no less than in international law.

Third, what are the defenses that are likely to be raised in civil cases with elements of international human rights law? The civil prosecution of human rights cases tends to trigger certain recurring defenses, especially immunities (e.g., foreign sovereign immunity, head-of-state immunity and diplomatic immunity) and objections based on the standing of the plaintiff, the political posture of the case, and the inconvenience or unfairness of the forum. These defenses tend to be highly fact-dependent, meaning that they pose no prophylactic barrier to a domestic court's enforcement of international human rights standards, but counsel must nevertheless anticipate and address them.

The Incorporation of International Standards into Domestic Law

Treaties

Recognizing that international enforcement typically plays a subsidiary role to implementation by domestic bodies, the framers of many human rights treaties inserted specific provisions obligating states parties to provide effective remedies at the national level for a breach of the agreement.[4] In some states, such as Austria and the Netherlands, ratified treaties occupy a superior position in the hierarchy of legal norms, prevailing even over inconsistent provisions of the national constitution. In other states, such as the United States, Germany, and Japan, treaties have a status equivalent to that of statutes, meaning that the later in time prevails to the extent of any unavoidable conflict.

Although some states automatically incorporate ratified treaties into domestic law (the "monist" tradition), others require specific legislative implementation (the "dualist" tradition). In the latter, the nation may have an international treaty obligation enforceable by other parties to the treaty at the international plane, but it is not automatically transformed into a domestically enforceable obligation in the absence of explicit legislation to that effect.

The domestic enforcement of human rights treaties also may be limited or blocked by a state's failure to ratify a treaty or by reservations that remove certain noncomplying national practices from the treaty's scope.[5] As noted by Judge Thomas Buergenthal, the consequence of these state-to-state variations is paradoxical: as the global order becomes increasingly dominated by international treaty law, it is increasingly dependent on each state's domestic law, especially "the domestic normative rank treaty provisions enjoy in the States parties to them."[6]

United States practice

Under the Supremacy Clause of the U.S. Constitution, "All treaties made, or which shall be made, under the authority of the United States, shall be the supreme law of the land; and the judges in every state shall be bound thereby, any thing in the constitution or laws of any state to the contrary notwithstanding." As a result, international agreements trump the laws of the various states of the union and can, in principle, provide a rule of decision in both federal and state cases, much as federal statutory law can. Congress has explicitly (if selectively) incorporated certain human rights treaties into domestic criminal law, allowing criminal prosecutions for torture, genocide, and war crimes at a minimum.[7]

In addition, certain civil claims arising under human rights treaties may be litigated under the Alien Tort Claims Act (ATCA),[8] the Torture Victim Protection Act of 1992,[9] and general federal question jurisdiction.[10] Such litigation is not common, and its applicability to agents of the U.S. government has been limited.[11]

The direct enforcement of human rights treaties in U.S. courts—especially in civil or administrative actions against U.S. officials or agencies—is complicated by the failure of the United States to ratify major treaties or its tendency to subject them to limiting reservations, understandings, and declarations. Unfortunately, the Supreme Court has frequently undermined the impact of treaties by interpreting them simplistically and with an implausible literalism.[12]

Direct enforcement also may be barred if the treaty is deemed "non-self-executing," i.e., if its terms require additional legislative implementation or are too vague or aspirational to be judicially enforceable.[13] Regrettably, the U.S. Senate has recently adopted a practice of attaching declarations of non-self-execution to its ratification of human rights conventions, such as the Covenant on Civil and Political Rights, the Convention on the Elimination of All Forms of Racial Discrimination, and the Convention against Torture. In these circumstances, a human rights treaty may be of greater value as an interpretive guideline in the interpretation of constitutional or statutory text than as a directly enforceable obligation.[14] For example, a successful challenge based on the Covenant to a death sentence imposed on a juvenile offender would require convincing a U.S. court both that the relevant U.S. reservation to the Covenant is invalid and that the Senate's declaration that the Covenant is non-self-executing does not prevent criminal defendants from asserting rights under the treaty defensively in proceedings commenced by the state.

Early in the modern human rights era, the "self-executing treaty" doctrine derailed efforts to combat *de jure* racism in the United States through litigation based on the nondiscrimination clauses of the United Nations Charter.[15] Courts also have rejected claims that the Charter of the Organization of American States contains sufficiently explicit human rights provisions to provide a cause of action for persons challenging certain U.S. policies (for example, exclusion of undocumented alien children from public education).[16] But the self-executing treaty doctrine is not fatal to all categories of human rights litigation. One relatively successful line of treaty-based cases has involved persons resisting extradition when it would violate provisions of bilateral extradition treaties, such as clauses requiring dual criminality between the requesting and the rendering state, specialty clauses that limit the charges upon which an extradited defendant may be tried, or clauses adopting the political offense exception.[17] Other criminal litigation has raised questions concerning the enforceability of humanitarian law treaties[18] or the proper remedy for noncitizen capital defendants who were denied their treaty-based right to consular services prior to their conviction.[19]

Practice in other states[20]

The direct application of international human rights treaties to domestic events is far more common in other developed democracies than in the United States, although many domestic courts struggle to define the place of human rights treaties within their legal system. In *Austria*, for example, the European Convention was given special constitutional status in 1964 and is frequently invoked to invalidate contrary domestic legislation, even if the legislation is later in time. Austrian courts rely upon the jurisprudence of the Council of Europe human rights bodies in interpreting the provisions of the European Convention. In contrast, the two Covenants do not have special constitutional status, and enforcement of their terms hinges upon the provisions of implementing legislation.

The situation in *Italy* is somewhat more complex, as the Court of Cassation initially denied direct effect to the European Convention but in more recent years has found that its terms should prevail even over later-enacted domestic law. Other human rights treaties have been specifically implemented in Italian law and, while treaties generally have a status equivalent to statute, Italian courts recognize the principle that human rights treaty norms should have a special resistance to abrogation by later-enacted domestic laws.

In *Germany*, treaties have a status equivalent to that of statutes, prevailing over the laws of the Länder and earlier-adopted federal provisions. However, under Article 33(5) of the Basic Law, constitutional norms will prevail over contrary terms of treaties ratified by Germany. German courts have generally recognized that the provisions of the European Convention and the Covenant on Civil and Political Rights are self-executing, but they have resisted giving direct effect to the programmatic rights of the Covenant on Economic, Social and Cultural Rights or the Convention on the Elimination of All Forms of Discrimination against Women.

Article 98 of the Constitution of *Japan* requires that ratified treaties be faithfully observed, even in preference to the terms of later-enacted statutes, as long as those treaties have legally binding character. A 1994 revision to the Constitution of *Argentina* confers supremacy on certain human rights treaties over national law, although human rights treaties are generally relied upon for interpretive purposes, rather than directly enforced, in domestic litigation.

The courts of the *United Kingdom* and *Canada* do not directly enforce treaties that have not been legislatively incorporated into national law. Suits to enforce treaty rights in such jurisdictions thus arise under the implementing legislation rather than under the treaty. However, the interpretation of a treaty's provisions by competent international bodies may influence the domestic courts' understanding of the relevant national law.

Customary International Law

In both civil and common law systems, customary international law is generally incorporated automatically as domestic law, although the direct enforcement in domestic courts of customary human rights norms against officials of that state remains rare. More common is judicial recognition of immunities or jurisdictional limits derived from customary international law. While there are significant practical barriers to the direct enforcement of customary human rights law, which are addressed below, the primary obstacle appears to be the unfamiliarity of judges with this elusive and complex body of legal norms.

United States practice

Customary international law (or "the law of nations") is not explicitly included in the Supremacy Clause, but the Supreme Court has held repeatedly that customary international law is to be treated as federal common law. "International law is part of our law," the Supreme Court declared in *The Paquete Habana*, "and must be ascertained and administered by the courts of justice of appropriate jurisdiction, as often as questions of right depending upon it are duly presented for their determination."[21] From the beginning of the Republic, U.S. courts have episodically enforced the criminal prohibitions of international law,[22] and the 1789 Alien Tort Claims Act (ATCA) opened the federal courts to civil suits by aliens "for a tort only, committed in violation of the law of nations or a treaty of the United States." As a result, the United States allows expansive civil jurisdiction over violations of international human rights law in foreign countries, even as it lags behind other democracies in asserting jurisdiction over international crimes committed outside the United States.

The touchstone in ATCA litigation is *Filartiga v. Peña-Irala*,[23] in which Paraguayan nationals successfully sued the Inspector General of Police in Asuncion, who had tortured one of their relatives to death in Paraguay. The Second Circuit Court of Appeals ruled that the ATCA was fully satisfied on the grounds that: (1) the plaintiffs were aliens in the

United States; (2) wrongful death by torture is a tort; and (3) deliberate torture perpetrated under color of official authority violates the law of nations. To reach that latter conclusion, the court examined, *inter alia*, treaties, national constitutions and codes, United Nations declarations, and the position of the executive branch to establish that the contemporary law of nations no longer allowed governments to torture their own citizens. To the contrary, the modern-day torturer had become—like the pirate of the eighteenth century—the enemy of all mankind, and ATCA jurisdiction would be proper whenever the torturer could be served within the United States.

Since 1980, numerous cases that fit the *Filartiga* paradigm have been brought successfully (at least on the issue of jurisdiction), alleging a variety of customary law violations, against a variety of defendants: police officers and concentration camp guards for torture, genocide, and rape; commanders and superior officers who bore command responsibility for abuses on their watch; and political leaders, including the former president of the Philippines, for human rights abuses during their regimes.[24] Cases have also been filed against corporations allegedly complicit in human rights violations.[25] However, plaintiffs rarely invoke customary international human rights law in litigation arising out of events occurring in the United States.[26]

In *Sosa and the United States v. Alvarez-Machain* (2004), the Supreme Court confirmed the well-established rule that the ATCA not only provides jurisdiction, but also requires no additional statutory cause of action before an alien can sue for a tort in violation of the law of nations or a treaty of the United States. In 1992, Congress endorsed the post-*Filartiga* trajectory of the ATCA and extended *Filartiga* to U.S. citizens by adopting the Torture Victim Protection Act (TVPA).[27] The courts have repeatedly found it significant that Congress had a clear opportunity to revise or restrict the ATCA and did the opposite.

Practice in other states

The dominant approach to customary international law in other countries is automatic incorporation. In some states, the national constitution explicitly establishes the enforceability (and in some cases the superiority) of customary norms. In the *United Kingdom* and *other Commonwealth states*, customary international law is absorbed into the common law, subject to the general qualification that it is incorporated "only so far as is not inconsistent with Acts of Parliament or prior judicial decisions of final authority."[28] Although other nations have not replicated the specific practice of the United States under the ATCA, there have been criminal investigations of gross human rights violations committed in foreign states, especially where nationals of the forum state have been victims, in which ATCA-like compensation of victims or survivors is a possibility.[29] Differing theories concerning the proper exercise of jurisdiction over extraterritorial acts affect the availability of these forms of relief.

The Interpretation of Domestic Law in Light of International Standards

The incorporationist argument just discussed is one way to advance international human rights law in domestic courts, but it is not the only or even the dominant approach. In virtually all legal systems, courts are obliged to interpret domestic law in conformity with international law whenever possible. As a result, international human rights law—in both conventional and customary form—provides potentially potent constraints on a court's interpretation of constitutional provisions and statutes. Because many fundamental rights provisions of domestic law are vague or ambiguous, substantial scope exists for promoting conformity with international human rights norms by mobilizing the interpretive powers of domestic judges. This interpretive approach has proven to be vitally important in ensuring the full implementation of international human rights law by domestic courts.

United States Practice

For two centuries, U.S. courts have adhered to Chief Justice John Marshall's admonition in *The Charming Betsy* that acts of Congress "ought never to be construed to violate the law of nations if any other possible construction remains."[30] When Congress clearly manifests its intent to override international law and the resulting statute cannot be reconciled with prior international obligations, the legislative will prevails. But in the absence of such clear repudiation, the courts are obliged to adopt that interpretation of the statute that best conforms to international obligations of the United States under customary international law and treaties.

The logic of *The Charming Betsy* principle requires the courts to undertake a three-step analysis in construing a statute before assuming that Congress has actually exercised its constitutional authority to legislate in derogation of international standards. First, they must determine the meaning and the status of any relevant international norms, using the traditional standards adopted by the Supreme Court for proving the content of custom or the meaning of a treaty. Second, if an international norm is relevant and nothing in the legislation overrides it, or if an inconsistency between the norm and the statute can be resolved fairly through interpretation, the court should adopt the interpretation that preserves maximum scope for both. Third, if the conflict between the international norm and the statute is unavoidable, then and only then may the court resort to the supremacy axioms of American dualism to resolve the case according to the domestic norm.

Thus, for example, in the field of refugee law, the Supreme Court conformed U.S. practice to international standards of refugee eligibility in *INS v. Cardoza-Fonseca*, relying in part upon the UNHCR *Handbook on Procedures and Criteria for Determining Refugee Status* and rejecting the executive branch's interpretation of an asylum applicant's burden of proof. The UNHCR *Handbook*, though not binding did offer "significant guidance" to the court.[31] The "evolving standards of decency" embodied in the Eighth Amendment have similarly been interpreted in light of instruments such as the Universal Declaration of Human Rights, the Standard Minimum Rules for the Treatment of Prisoners and the Body of Principles for the Protection of All Persons under Any Form of Detention or Imprisonment.[32] The due process guarantees in the Fifth and Fourteenth Amendments might also be informed by the procedural rights guaranteed by treaties and customary law, such as Articles 9 and 14 of the Covenant on Civil and Political Rights.

If federal statutes are subject to the *Charming Betsy* principle, *a fortiori* state statutes must be similarly constrained, and provisions of state constitutions should be construed in light of international standards.[33] The interpretive use of international law also may add precision to a common law tort claim or suggest the invalidity of a claimed defense. For example, in a tort suit against medical personnel who conducted experiments upon indigent hospital patients without the patients' consent, the court rejected defendants' claims that no duty to secure informed consent existed at the time of the experiments, citing the recognition of such a duty in the Nuremberg Code.[34] State tort law may also be interpreted in light of humanitarian law principles.[35]

Practice in Other States

The *Charming Betsy* principle has explicit analogues in the jurisprudence of other states and is repudiated in none. Even states that require domestic implementation of treaties, such as *Canada* and the *United Kingdom*, recognize and regularly give effect to a similar interpretive principle. In *Germany*, the evocatively named principle of *Volkerrectsfreundlichkeit* ("friendliness toward international law") requires domestic courts to interpret ambiguous domestic law in conformity with Germany's international obligations. Even the provisions of the Basic Law must be interpreted, where possible, not to fall below the requirements of the European

Convention. In *South Africa*, the Constitution itself requires the courts to construe the Bill of Rights and domestic legislation in light of international law.

Determining the Content of Conventional and Customary International Law

Treaties

The basic rule for construing an international agreement is that "a treaty shall be interpreted in good faith in accordance with the ordinary meaning to be given to the terms of the treaty in their context and in the light of its object and purpose."[36] The "plain meaning" rule means that questions about the scope or meaning of a conventional obligation are resolved by reference to the text of the agreement, unless that literal approach "leaves the meaning ambiguous or obscure; or leads to a result which is manifestly absurd or unreasonable."[37] In these latter circumstances, recourse may be had to the legislative history of the treaty, or *travaux préparatoires*, as a supplementary means of interpretation.

In both civil and common law jurisdictions, deference to the executive is a powerful corollary to the ideal of "plain meaning" interpretations. In the United States, for example, "[a]lthough not conclusive, the meaning attributed to treaty provisions by the Government agencies charged with their negotiation and enforcement is entitled to great weight."[38] Executive submissions may be decisive if the court must identify an authoritative text or articulate the mutual understanding of the parties.

The general rules of international treaty law may also affect the determination of a state's substantive obligations under a treaty. Thus for example, under the Vienna Convention on the Law of Treaties, a state may unilaterally modify its international obligations under a treaty through reservations, understandings, and declarations, but these unilateral modifications may not violate the object and purpose of the treaty. The Vienna Convention also recognizes the existence of peremptory norms of international law, or *jus cogens*, which no treaty may contravene.

Custom

Customary international law arises not out of an explicit agreement but out of a "general practice accepted as law."[39] Advocates seeking to base a claim on customary international law must demonstrate both that (1) there is a general practice among states, i.e., that states behave in a consistent pattern, and (2) states behave in these consistent ways out of the conviction that the behavior is required by law (*opinio juris*). Proving both of these elements can be problematic, because there is no single "legislative moment" when custom comes into existence and no easily accessible or authoritative compendium of customary international human rights law. Certainly, where national law or enforceable treaty provisions would provide a basis for equivalent relief, there is little incentive to select the more challenging course of proving customary law.

Determining the existence and meaning of custom is an intrinsically impressionistic process. The evidentiary standard adopted by the U.S. Supreme Court in *The Paquete Habana* reflects the dominant approach:

> [W]here there is no treaty, and no controlling executive or legislative act or judicial decision, resort must be had to the customs and usages of civilized nations, and, as evidence of these, to the works of jurists and commentators who by years of labor, research, and experience have made themselves peculiarly well acquainted with the subjects of which they treat. Such works are resorted to by judicial tribunals, not for the speculations of their authors concerning what the law ought to be, but for trustworthy evidence of what the law really is.[40]

In *Paquete Habana*, the humanitarian norm protecting domestic fishing vessels from seizure as prize in wartime existed "independently of any express treaty or other public act" and independently of the litigation position of the Executive branch, which had argued that the norm was strictly a matter of courtesy or humanitarianism and was distinctly not law.

In attempting to give content to customary law, advocates may offer evidence in a variety of forms, including: the laws, constitutions, and high court decisions of different countries; diplomatic exchanges, in which states define their legal expectations of one another; unilateral declarations evincing wide agreement on legal principles; treaties, especially to the extent that they enjoy near universal support or if the parties understand that the treaty is declaratory of customary law; consistent resolutions and declarations legal subjects adopted by intergovernmental organizations such as the United Nations; decisions of international tribunals and arbitral panels; the writings and expert testimony of legal scholars; authoritative statements of customary law, like the American Law Institute's *Restatement of the Foreign Relations Law of the United States*; and submissions from the executive branch or foreign ministries.

In essence, proof of custom resides in the history and repetition of state practice in multiple forms. Widely accepted norms, such as the prohibitions on torture, summary execution, and genocide, may be established with relative ease to the extent that they are "specific, universal, and obligatory," while emerging norms present difficult and sometimes insoluble problems of proof.[41]

Anticipating Immunities and Other Defenses in Civil Cases

Even if a domestic court is convinced that it is authorized to apply or consult international law, and even if it has determined the content of the relevant international obligation, certain issues can obstruct or complicate private, civil litigation. The precise details of these potential difficulties vary from jurisdiction to jurisdiction, but their general outlines can be anticipated. In countries other than the United States, civil suits for human rights violations committed outside the forum state have been rare, especially where both plaintiff and defendant are noncitizens. However, an increasing number of criminal investigations or prosecutions of gross human rights violators have been instituted in recent years, and they potentially create the basis for civil suits against the perpetrators.

Foreign Sovereign Immunity

Suing a foreign state directly for human rights violations may be foreclosed by the doctrine of foreign sovereign immunity, even though the traditionally absolute principle of sovereign immunity has been largely superseded by statutes codifying a more restrictive principle. The restrictive principle differentiates between immune sovereign acts and nonimmune acts. The latter typically include a government's commercial activity, certain torts within the jurisdiction of the forum, and, at least in the United States, state-sponsored terrorism. Human rights claims will occasionally fall within these exceptions to the immunity, as, for example, when the abuse takes commercial form,[42] but there is no generally accepted exception to foreign sovereign immunity for human rights violations per se.

Significant controversy exists over the definition of the "sovereign" and, in particular, whether individual government officials are entitled to a derivative form of sovereign immunity. To date, many successful human rights suits have been brought against individual government officials, rather than against a foreign state or one of its agencies or instrumentalities on the grounds that those who commit gross human rights violations are acting beyond the scope of their official authority.[43] Similarly, when a successor regime repudiates the acts of the deposed official, foreign sovereign immunity (along with head of state or diplomatic immunity) will generally not be a barrier to suit. If the official serves a government still in power, however, and is not deemed to have acted outside the scope of his or her authority, the foreign state's statutory immunity typically extends to the individual.

Head of State and Former Head of State Immunity

Under customary international law, especially the traditional rules of foreign sovereign immunity, a sitting head of state is generally regarded as immune from prosecution or civil suit in the courts of a foreign state. Head of state immunity is lost if the foreign state repudiates the leader or if executive officials of the forum state do not recognize his or her claim to be head of state. In the Pinochet case, the British House of Lords held (in a three to two decision) that the UK State Immunity Act did not extend immunity to former heads of state for crimes against humanity and gross human rights violations.[44]

Forum Non Conveniens and the Exhaustion of Local Remedies

An important principle of comity recognized in transnational litigation is that of *forum non conveniens*. If the cause of action arises in a foreign state, the defendant would be prejudiced by having to litigate in a remote forum, and an adequate judicial remedy exists in a state with closer contacts to the dispute, the case may be dismissed or stayed pending foreign proceedings. The collapse or corruption of the court system in the state where the violation occurred should preclude the application the *forum non conveniens* doctrine. In similar circumstances, the failure to exhaust local remedies—which might otherwise render a case unripe for international adjudication—may be waived.

The Political Question Doctrine

A human rights advocate must anticipate the defense that adjudicating human rights claims may cause a domestic court to interfere inappropriately with the policies of the government or the foreign policy objectives of the forum's government. In the United States, the "political question" doctrine forecloses judicial inquiry into the propriety or wisdom of political decisions based on executive discretion. Therefore, the more it can be shown that legal and not just political standards guide the court's decision, the less likely it is that the doctrine will apply.[45] The doctrine may also be foreclosed if the government files a "statement of interest" indicating that the foreign relations of the United States might be more compromised if the litigation were stopped than if it went forward. Statements of interest may also be used defensively.[46] The doctrine is most likely to apply when a case implicates the explicit and exclusive constitutional powers of the executive.

The Act of State Doctrine

Under this common law doctrine, courts will not judge the legality of a public act by an extant and recognized foreign government within its own territory, unless there is a controlling domestic or international standard for the court to apply. Because human rights litigation tends to involve violations of incontestible international norms, the Act of State Doctrine has not been a serious practical barrier to U.S. jurisdiction in cases brought under the ATCA or the TVPA. The prospect that a foreign government will be embarrassed by revelations of improper behavior by its officials is not a sufficient basis for invocation of the doctrine. While the general reluctance of non-U.S. courts to entertain transnational human rights litigation may be attributable to concerns similar to those underlying the act of state doctrine (perceived judicial incompetence or fears of interference with foreign relations), little case law exists outside the United States on this particular doctrinal barrier to human rights litigation.

Logistical Concerns

It is not possible in this space to anticipate all of the procedural and logistical issues that may arise in human rights litigation in the domestic courts of all nations. But experience in the United States under the Alien Tort Claims Act and the Torture Victim Protection Act illustrates the range of concerns that human rights advocates must anticipate.

Establishing Personal Jurisdiction

Because the United States attracts many immigrants and visitors, including a substantial number of persons allegedly complicit in serious human rights violations, plaintiffs have succeeded on a number of occasions in effecting personal service of process on defendants in ATCA and TVPA claims. While some defendants reside in the United States, others have been served during brief visits. The due process clause of the Fifth Amendment permits U.S. courts to exercise personal jurisdiction over persons who are only briefly present, so long as they are properly served and the court possesses subject matter jurisdiction over the cause of action.

Establishing Subject Matter Jurisdiction

Alien plaintiffs who successfully allege that the defendant committed a tort in violation of customary international law will establish subject matter jurisdiction in federal court under the ATCA. Under the TVPA, subject matter jurisdiction in federal court is established by alleging a violation of the prohibitions against torture or extrajudicial killing, when the violation was committed under color of foreign law. Other statutes, like the Foreign Sovereign Immunities Act and the Federal Question Statute, may also establish subject matter jurisdiction in narrow circumstances. In addition, state courts of general jurisdiction may hear claims arising under customary international law and the transitory tort doctrine.

Choice of Law and the Presumption Against Extraterritoriality

In every transnational human rights case, the court is required to make a choice of law for each issue that arises—everything from standing and the elements of the claim, to the burden of proof, the measure of damages, and evidentiary privileges. When there is no controlling statute, courts are generally not required to find a single law that resolves all issues in a case but can instead engage in *dépeçage*—a splitting process in which different issues in a single case may be resolved by reference to the laws of different jurisdictions.[48] Generally, courts will presume that domestic law does not apply to extraterritorial events or persons, but comity does not inevitably require the application of foreign law to cases with contacts in both the United States and foreign nations.[49] The application of international standards by domestic courts is not generally considered to constitute the extraterritorial application of domestic law.

Managing Discovery

One characteristic of civil litigation in the United States is that the litigants themselves have nearly unlimited access to all information that might be relevant in the case. Rule 26(b) of the Federal Rules of Civil Procedure gives the parties to a civil action broad authority to "obtain discovery regarding any matter, not privileged, which is relevant to the subject matter involved in the pending action." The breadth of this authority is confirmed by the fact that "[t]he information sought need not be admissible at the trial if the information sought appears reasonably calculated to lead to the discovery of admissible evidence." These discovery rules, and the court's sanction powers behind them, can lead to significant international conflict, especially with those legal systems in which the gathering of pretrial evidence is an exclusively judicial function. In an effort to reduce these conflicts, many countries have become parties to the Hague Convention on the Taking of Evidence Abroad in Civil or Commercial Matters, which obliges parties to designate a "Central Authority" to provide judicial assistance in the completion of official acts, including the execution of letters of request. When the treaty is not applicable, courts must determine how best to obtain evidence located abroad, recognizing that some cases may ultimately turn on evidence in the United States only, including the testimony of the parties.

Establishing a Defendant's Legal Responsibility

Some ATCA and TVPA suits may involve a defendant's responsibility for human rights torts inflicted by persons under his or her command or supervision; in other cases, defendants may be accused of having personally inflicted the harm. Where responsibility is indirect, an advocate must prove lines of command or organizational hierarchy, in light of recognized international norms (largely derived from humanitarian law) and general tort doctrines.[50]

Protecting the Plaintiffs from Retaliation

Where the human rights violations are on-going, and especially where plaintiffs or their relatives remain in the state of origin or are otherwise vulnerable, advocates must protect their clients' anonymity through the use of pseudonyms (John or Jane Doe pleading) and through protective orders. The measures to protect witness anonymity adopted by the ad hoc international criminal tribunals for the former Yugoslavia and Rwanda offer instructive guidance on this delicate point, which requires balancing the safety of plaintiffs against the due process rights of the defendant.

Establishing the Liability of Nonstate Actors

Increasingly, human rights cases are being brought against nonstate actors for violations of international human rights law in ways that trigger legal responsibility under the ATCA and TVPA. These nonstate actors may be insurgent or dissident leaders;[51] they may be complicit in a government's human rights violations;[52] or they may be corporate entities engaged in violations of international law or as joint venturers with repressive governments.[53] These cases require careful proof that specific norms of international law bind nonstate actors or that the nonstate defendant is acting under color of law with government officials in depriving plaintiffs of their legal rights.

Class Actions

There are circumstances in which human rights abuses may be viewed as mass torts—cases in which a class of plaintiffs can establish that they were the victims of a single orchestrated and illegal policy. In the United

States, a class action may be available if the case satisfies the criteria in Rule 23 of the Federal Rules of Civil Procedure or its state law cognates. In the human rights cases against former Philippine President Ferdinand Marcos, for example, the Marcos estate was found liable to a class of roughly 10,000 Filipinos and twenty-three named plaintiffs for torture, summary execution, disappearance, and prolonged arbitrary detention. The propriety of class actions in certain circumstances should not lead counsel to underestimate the procedural and ethical complexities that such actions may involve.[54]

Enforcing Judgments

Human rights defendants often do not have significant assets in the United States, with the result that the actual recovery of damages under the ATCA and the TVPA has been rare. Some defendants keep their assets offshore, and, although it is conceivable that a U.S. judgment might be enforced abroad pursuant to treaty or comity, U.S. judgment-creditors do not compete on a level playing field: U.S. courts are relatively liberal in recognizing and enforcing foreign judgments, while foreign courts are not. Techniques for enforcing judgments vary widely, but they can work and should be attempted, even if the primary motivation for bringing such actions is not the expectation of compensation.[55]

Concluding Observations

In the last quarter century, a substantial human rights jurisprudence has emerged from domestic courts. This body of law is a natural consequence of the Nuremberg experience, which established that any person who commits an international wrong bears personal responsibility for it. Now a second, equally axiomatic proposition has emerged from the proliferation of international human rights tribunals, each with its own principle of subsidiarity to domestic jurisdiction: Domestic courts—operating through civil, criminal, and administrative proceedings—offer meaningful mechanisms for the enforcement of international human rights. The next stage in the evolution of this domestic jurisprudence-of-accountability will be surviving both the post-9/11 terrorist challenge and governments' responses to it.

Notes

1. This chapter is dedicated to the memories of Joan Fitzpatrick and Richard Lillich, who wrote the chapters on this topic in prior editions of this book. Richard and Joan inspired generations of students, activists, and colleagues

during the formative period of contemporary international human rights law and practice, and they are deeply missed.

2. See, e.g., in Belgium, In re Vincent Ntezimana, et al., Brussels Court of Assizes, 8 June 2001, available at http://www.asf.be/Assises Rwanda1/fr/fr_VERDICT_verdict.htm (genocide); the Netherlands, Prosecution of Bouterse, HR 18 Sept. 2001, available at http://www. rechtspraak.nl (LJN NO AB 1471) (torture); Switzerland, Niyonteze v. Public Prosecutor, 96 *Am. J. Int'l L.* 231 (2002).

3. See generally Beth Stephens and Michael Ratner, International Human Rights Litigation in U.S. Courts (Irvington-on-Hudson, NY: Transnational Publishers, 1996); Kenneth Randall, Federal Courts and the Human Rights Paradigm (Durham, NC: Duke University Press, 1990).

4. See generally U.N. Commission on Human Rights, Basic Principles and Guidelines on the Right to a Remedy (rev. Oct. 24, 2003), UN Doc. E/CN.4/2004/57 (2004); Right to Restitution, Compensation, and Rehabilitation for Victims of Grave Violations of Human Rights and Fundamental Freedoms, Final Report of the Special Rapporteur, UN Doc. E.CN.4/2000/62, at §§ 2(b), 2(c), 3(d). Steven R. Ratner and Jason S. Abrams, Accountability for Human Rights Atrocities in International Law (New York: Oxford University Press, 2d ed. 2001); International Law Association, Final Report on the Exercise of Jurisdiction in Respect of Gross Human Rights Offences (2000), available at http://www.ila-hq.org/pdf/Human%20Rights%20Law/HumanRig.pdf.

5. The number and scope of reservations to the Convention on the Elimination of All Forms of Discrimination against Women is especially notorious. See Rebecca Cook, Reservations to the Convention on the Elimination of All Forms of Discrimination Against Women, 30 *Va. J. Int'l L.* 643 (1990). The Human Rights Committee issued a General Comment stating that reservations are invalid, as contrary to the object and purpose of the Covenant, if attached to treaty provisions that represent customary norms, especially those of a peremptory character. General Comment No. 24, UN Doc. CCPR/C/21/Rev.1/Add.6 (1994).

6. Thomas Buergenthal, Self-Executing and Non-Self-Executing Treaties in National and International Law, 235 Receuil Des Cours 304, 313 (1992-IV).

7. See, e.g., the Torture Convention Implementation Act, 18 U.S.C. § 2340A, and the Genocide Convention Implementation Act, 18 U.S.C. § 1091. The War Crimes Act of 1996, 18 U.S.C. § 2441 (2001), as amended, explicitly incorporates a treaty-based definition of "war crimes," including, *inter alia*, the grave breaches regime of the 1949 Geneva Conventions and its protocols and certain violations of the 1996 Landmines Convention.

8. 28 U.S.C. § 1350. The ATCA, discussed in greater detail below, establishes jurisdiction over claims brought by aliens for "torts . . . in violation of . . . a treaty of the United States," and was intended, at least in part, to provide an avenue of redress against tortfeasors who violate international norms within U.S. territory, e.g., by assaulting a diplomat on U.S. soil.

9. 28 U.S.C. § 1350 note. The TVPA, which incorporates a treaty-based definition of torture, permits suits by U.S. citizens as well as aliens for acts of torture or extrajudicial killing, so long as the defendants act under color of foreign law, a precondition that may be satisfied by proving that they engaged jointly in tortious activity with foreign officials.

10. 28 U.S.C. § 1331. General federal question jurisdiction opens federal courts to lawsuits against U.S. officials for violations of the U.S. Constitution, under the theory of Bivens v. Six Unknown Named Agents, 403 U.S. 388 (1971), and under remedial statutes providing causes of action against state officials, such as 42 U.S.C. § 1983. Aside from substantive reservations to the relevant treaty provisions and the problematic effect of a declaration that the treaty is non-self-executing, there should be no barrier against using Section 1331 as the jurisdictional basis for a suit to enforce human rights treaty provisions with regard to events occurring in the United States.

11. Sosa and United States v. Alvarez-Machain, __ U.S. __, 2004 U.S. LEXIS 4763 (June 29, 2004).

12. See, e.g., Sale v. Haitian Centers Council, 509 U.S. 155 (1993); Société Aérospatiale et al. v. United States District Court, 482 U.S. 522 (1986); United States v. Alvarez-Machain, 504 U.S. 522 (1992); and Breard v. Greene, 523 U.S. 371 (1998).

13. Foster v. Neilson, 27 U.S. (2 Pet.) 253, 314 (1829). See generally, Restatement (Third) Foreign Relations Law of the United States § 111 (1987).

14. See, e.g., Thompson v. Oklahoma, 487 U.S. 815, 831 n.34 (plurality opinion), 851 (O'Connor, J., concurring) (1988) (finding unconstitutional the imposition of the death penalty on offender aged fifteen at time of crime and referring to the International Covenant on Civil and Political Rights for interpretive purposes). But see Hain v. Gibson, 287 F.3d 1224 (10th Cir. 2002).

15. Sei Fujii v. California, 97 A.C.A. 154, 217 P.2d 481 (1950), aff'd, 38 Cal.2d 718, 242 P.2d 617 (1952).

16. See Plyler v. Doe, 628 F.2d 448, 453–54 (5th Cir. 1980), aff'd, 457 U.S. 202 (1982); In re Alien Children Education Litigation, 501 F. Supp. 544, 590, aff'd unreported mem. 5th Cir. 1981, aff'd sub nom. Plyler v. Doe, 457 U.S. 202 (1982).

17. See generally John Dugard and Christine Van den Wyngaert, Reconciling Extradition with Human Rights, 92 Am. J. Int'l L. 187 (1998) (noting cases in U.S. and other national courts implementing rights-protective provisions of extradition treaties and also giving priority to human rights treaty provisions over terms of extradition agreements and national law).

18. United States v. Noriega, 808 F. Supp. 791, 794 (S.D. Fla. 1992) (concerning provisions of 1949 Geneva Conventions on treatment of prisoners of war). See generally, Ralph G. Steinhardt, International Humanitarian Law in the Courts of the United States: Yamashita, Filartiga, and 911, 36 George Washington Int'l L. Rev. 1 (2004).

19. To some extent, the Vienna Convention on Consular Relations has been implemented through federal regulations. 28 CFR § 50.5(1) et seq. Judicial decisions have been somewhat more equivocal; see Breard v. Pruett, 134 F.3d 615 (4th Cir. 1998), cert. denied sub nom., Breard v. Greene 523 U.S. 371 (claim under treaty defaulted by failure to raise it in state court); United States v. Jimenez-Nava, 243 F.3d 192, 198–99 (5th Cir. 2001) (Vienna Convention does not create a judicially enforceable exclusionary rule). The International Court of Justice has ruled that the consular notification practices of the United States in capital cases violate the Vienna Convention. Case concerning Avena and Other Mexican Nationals (Mexico v. United States of America), [2004] I.C.J. Rep. __ (31 Mar. 2004).

20. Much of the material in this and other sections concerning practice and jurisprudence outside the United States is drawn from Benedetto Conforti and Francesco Francioni, eds., Enforcing International Human Rights in Domestic Courts (Cambridge, MA: Martinus Nijhoff, 1997), and Craig Scott, Torture as Tort: Comparative Perspectives on the Development of Transnational Human Rights Litigation (Portland, OR: Hart Publishing 2001).

21. The Paquete Habana, 175 U.S. 677, 700 (1900). Accord, Talbot v. Janson, 3 U.S. (3 Dall.) 133 (1795); Banco Nacional de Cuba v. Sabbatino, 376 U.S 398 (1964); Sosa and United States v. Alvarez-Machain, *supra* note 11.

22. See, e.g., United States v. Smith, 18 U.S. (5 Wheat.) 153 (1820) (piracy); Respublica v. DeLongchamps, 1 U.S. (1 Dall.) 111 (1784) (assault on foreign consul); Henfield's Case, 11 F. Cas. 1099 (C.C.D. Pa. 1793) (breach of neutrality).

23. Filartiga v. Peña-Irala, 630 F.2d 876 (2d Cir. 1980). This body of case law is examined in detail in Stephens and Ratner, *supra* note 3. Advocates wishing to keep up to date on this litigation should consult the websites of the Center for Justice and Accountability (www.cja.org) and the Center for Constitutional Rights (www.ccr.org).

24. See, e.g., Hilao v. Estate of Marcos, 25 F.3d 1467 (9th Cir. 1994), *cert. denied,* 513 U.S. 1126 (1995) (torture, summary execution, arbitrary detention); Kadic v. Karadzic, 70 F.3d 232 (2d Cir. 1995), *cert. denied,* 518 U.S. 1005 (1996) (torture, genocide, war crimes); Abebe-Jira v. Negewo, 72 F.3d 844 (11th Cir. 1996), *cert. denied,* 519 U.S. 830 (1996) (torture, sexual assault); Mehinovic v. Vuckovic, 198 F. Supp. 2d 1232 (N.D. Ga. 2002) (genocide); Mushikiwabo v. Barayagwiza, No. 94CIV3267 (JSM), 1996 WL 164496 (S.D.N.Y. Apr. 9, 1996) (genocide); Cabello v. Fernandez-Larios, 157 F. Supp. 2d 1345 (S.D. Fla. 2001) (summary execution, war crimes); Xuncax v. Gramajo, 886 F. Supp. 162 (D. Mass. 1985) (summary execution); Paul v. Avril, 901 F. Supp. 330 (S.D. Fla. 1994) (arbitrary detention).

25. See Presbyterian Church of Sudan v. Talisman Energy, 244 F. Supp. 2d 289 (S.D.N.Y. 2003); Wiwa v. Royal Dutch Shell, 2002 WL 319887 (S.D.N.Y. Feb. 28, 2002); Bowoto v. Chevron Texaco Corp., No. C 99-2506 SI, __ F. Supp. 2d __ (N.D. Cal., Mar. 22, 2004).

26. But see Jama et al. v. U.S. I.N.S. et al., 22 F.Supp. 2d 353 (D.N.J. 1998) (finding jurisdiction under the ATCA for claims of cruel, inhuman, and degrading treatment brought by detained asylum-seekers against U.S. immigration officials and private detention agency providing contract services to U.S.).

27. A plaintiff filing an action under the ATCA must be an alien, but the defendant may be either an alien or a citizen. The TVPA permits suits by both alien and U.S. citizen plaintiffs, but only for torture or extrajudicial killing and only against defendants acting under color of foreign law.

28. Ian Brownlie, Principles of Public International Law 41 (New York: Oxford University Press, 6th ed. 2003).

29. See Beth Stephens, Translating Filártiga: A Comparative and International Law Analysis of Domestic Remedies for International Human Rights Violations, 27 *Yale J. Int'l L.* 1 (2002).

30. Murray v. The Schooner Charming Betsy, 6 U.S. (2 Cranch) 64, 118 (1804).

31. INS v. Cardoza-Forseca 480 U.S. 421 (1987), at 439 n.22. In 1980, Congress implemented the 1967 Protocol to the 1951 Convention relating to the Status of Refugees, by incorporating its terms into the U.S. Immigration and Nationality

Act. Refugee Act of 1980, Pub. L. No. 96-212, 94 Stat. 102. As a result, the terms of the Refugee Protocol, especially the *nonrefoulement* obligation of Article 33(1), are recognized as binding on U.S. administrative officials and judges.

32. See, e.g., Estelle v. Gamble, 429 U.S. 97, 103–04 n.8 (1976) (reference to Standard Minimum Rules); Lareau v. Manson, 507 F. Supp. 1177 (D. Conn. 1980), *aff'd in part and modified and remanded in part,* 651 F.2d 96 (2d Cir. 1981) (same). *Cf.* Wilson v. Seiter, 501 U.S. 294 (1991) (holding that a prisoner must demonstrate that prison officials acted with "deliberate indifference" in imposing abusive conditions). International human rights standards and decisions were recently consulted by the Court in invalidating Texas criminal sodomy laws. Lawrence v. Texas, 123 S. Ct. 2472, 2481 (2003).

33. One such attempt is Moore v. Ganim, 233 Conn. 557, 638, 660 A.2d 742, 781 (Conn. 1995) (Peters, C.J., concurring) (interpretation of Connecticut Constitution in light of Universal Declaration of Human Rights and Covenant on Economic, Social, and Cultural Rights).

34. In re Cincinnati Radiation Litigation, 874 F. Supp. 796, 819–21 (S.D. Ohio 1995). *Cf.* Abdullahi v. Pfizer Inc., 2002 WL 31082956 (S.D.N.Y. Sept. 17, 2002), vacated in part, 77 Fed. App. 48, 2003 WL 22317923 (2d Cir. Oct. 8, 2003). In Pfizer, aliens who allegedly received an experimental antibiotic during an epidemic in Nigeria sued the drug manufacturer which had administered the antibiotic, claiming that its practices violated the Nuremberg Code and other international norms. The lower court dismissed on grounds of *forum non conveniens,* but the court of appeals reversed and remanded on that issue. As of this writing, the plaintiffs' international law claims remain in the case.

35. Linder v. Calero-Portocarrero, 963 F.2d 332, 336–37 (11th Cir. 1992).

36. Vienna Convention on the Law of Treaties, art. 31.

37. *Id.*, art. 32.

38. Sumitomo Shoji America, Inc. v. Avagliano, 457 U.S. 177, 184–85 (1982).

39. I.C.J. Stat., art. 38(1).

40. The Paquete Habana, 175 U.S. 677, 700 (1900). The definition of a "controlling executive act" remains unclear, though the analysis in *The Paquete Habana* suggests that only the President and potentially his cabinet have the power to override customary international law as the law of the united States. See, e.g., Barrera-Echavarria v. Rison, 44 F.3d 1441 (9th Cir. 1995), *cert. denied,* 116 S.Ct. 479 (1995); Agora: May the President Violate Customary International Law?, 80 *Am. J. Int'l L.* 913 (1986); 81 *Am. J. Int'l L.* 371 (1987). *Cf.* Opinion 6/1997, Report of the Working Group on Arbitrary Detention, UN Doc. E/CN.4/1998/44/Add.1 (1997). Where the challenged acts are attributable to state officials, the likelihood that inconsistent federal law or policies may insulate the practice from challenge is diminished. See, e.g., Gonzalez Martinez v. City of Los Angeles, 141 F.3d 1373 (9th Cir. 1998).

41. In litigation under the ATCA, for example, the courts routinely dismiss cases in which plaintiffs fail to meet the stringent criteria for proving a norm of customary international law. See, e.g., Flores v. Southern Peru Copper Corp., 343 F.3d 140 (2d Cir. 2003) (environmental torts are not in violation of customary international law); Guinto v. Marcos, 654 F. Supp. 276 (S.D. Cal. 1986) (full First Amendment freedoms do not exist in international law); Zapata v. Quinn, 707 F. 2d 691 (2d Cir. 1983) (international law does not address claims

for loss of money from state lottery distribution system); Hamid v. Price Waterhouse, 51 F.3d 1411 (9th Cir. 1995) (fraud is not a violation of the law of nations); Maugein v. Newmont Mining Corp., No. CIV.A.02-204, 2004 WL 73279 (D. Colo. Jan. 15, 2004) (defamation is not a violation of international law). On the requirement that the norms be "specific, universal, and obligatory," see Sosa and United States v. Alvarez-Machain, *supra* note 11.

42.   Siderman de Blake v. Republic of Argentina, 965 F.2d 699 (9th Cir. 1992).

43.   See, e.g., Hilao v. Marcos, *supra* note 24, at 1470–71; Trajano v. Marcos (In re Estate of Ferdinand Marcos, Human Rights Litigation), 978 F.2d 493, 497 (9th Cir. 1992), *cert. denied*, 508 U.S. 972 (1993); Xuncax v. Gramajo, *supra* note 24; Cabiri v. Assassie-Gyimah, 921 F. Supp. 1189, 1197–98 (S.D.N.Y. 1996).

44.   Re: Augusto Pinochet Ugarte; Ex parte Augusto Pinochet Ugarte (High Court of Justice, Queen's Bench Div. 28 Oct. 1998; House of Lords, 25 Nov. 1998).

45.   See, e.g., Republic of the Philippines v. Marcos, 862 F.2d 1355 (9th Cir.1988) (*en banc*).

46.   See, e.g., Letter from William H. Taft, Legal Adviser to Judge Louis Oberdorfer, Doe et al. v. Exxon-Mobil, et al., No. 01-CV-1357 (D.D.C. July 29, 2002).

47.   The classic U.S. articulation of this doctrine is found in Banco Nacional de Cuba v. Sabbatino, *supra* note 21.

48.   See generally, Tachiona v. Mugabe 234 F. Supp. 2d 401 (S.D.N.Y. 2002). On remand in *Filartiga*, the court concluded that it was "appropriate to look first to Paraguayan law in determining the remedy for the violation of international law." Filartiga v. Peña-Irala, 577 F. Supp. 860, 864 (E.D.N.Y. 1984). But the court was unwilling to apply Paraguayan law to the extent that it "inhibit[ed] the appropriate enforcement of the applicable international law or conflict[ed] with the public policy of the United States," explicitly concluding that the interests of the global community trump those of any one state. *Id.*

49.   See Hartford Fire Ins. Co. v. California, 509 U.S. 764 (1993).

50.   See Stephens and Ratner, *supra* note 3, at 339.

51.   See Kadic, *supra* note 24; Doe v. Islamic Salvation Front, 993 F. Supp. 3, 9 (1998) (finding individual defendant capable of violations of Common Article 3 of the 1949 Geneva Conventions and the prohibitions on slavery and hijacking).

52.   See Belance v FRAPH, Civ. 94-2619 (E.D.N.Y.); Mushikiwabo v. Barayagwiza, 1996 WL 164496 (S.D.N.Y.).

53.   See e.g., Presbyterian Church, *supra* note 25; Wiwa, *supra* note 25; Estate of Rodriquez v. Drummond Co., Inc., 256 F. Supp. 2d 1250 (N.D. Ala. 2003); Doe v. Unocal, 963 F. Supp. 880 (C.D. Cal. 1997), 110 F. Supp. 2d 1294 (C.D. Cal. 2000), *aff'd in part, rev'd in part*, 2002 WL 31063976 (9th Cir. 2002), *reh'g en banc*, __ F.3d __, 2003 WL 359787 (9th Cir. 2003). The Ninth Circuit Court of Appeals has suspended further proceedings pending the Supreme Court's disposition of Alvarez-Machain v. Sosa, *supra* note 11. See Anita Ramasastry, Secrets and Lies? Swiss Banks and International Human Rights, 31 *Vand. J. Transnat'l L.* 325 (1998). Corporations that proclaim a commitment to human rights as part of their marketing campaigns could face liability for deceptive advertising if that commitment is violated in fact. Kasky v. Nike, Inc., 119 Cal. Rptr. 2d 296 (Cal. 2002), *cert. dismissed as improvidently granted*, 123 S. Ct. 2554 (2003). In September 2003, Nike agreed to pay $1.5 million to settle the case.

54. Depending on the facts of each case, these include the potential confusion of causation issues and the consequent impairment of the jury function; the extrapolation from the experience of a few victims to the experience of thousands; and the potential distortion of the relationship between counsel and client (especially if the class attorney has taken the case on a contingent fee), to name a few.

55. See Stephens and Ratner, *supra* note 3, at 218–224; Beth Van Schaack, In Defense of Civil Redress: The Domestic Enforcement of Human Rights Norms in the Context of the Proposed Hague Judgments Convention, 42 *Harv. Int'l L.J.* 141 (2001).

Appendix A: Bibliographic Essay*

Introduction

The literature of human rights is vast and varied, ranging from philosophical works on the nature of rights to reports on specific human rights abuses in individual countries. The quality is as variable as the content. Many materials are not indexed anywhere, and, once identified, are difficult to obtain, since they are not issued by major commercial publishers. Only a few large academic law libraries have extensive collections, although these holdings are now supplemented by a number of electronic resources available on the World Wide Web or Internet.

Much of the human rights literature has little direct relevance for practitioners. Even when the title seems relevant, one should exercise some judgment. International human rights remains a rapidly developing field, and the information in many books and articles may be outdated even before it is published; it is essential to check the publication date before placing any reliance on a particular text. In addition, the political orientation of governments and some smaller human rights organizations, in particular, should be taken into account in evaluating reports.

This brief survey aims not to provide comprehensive coverage of the international human rights literature, but to offer suggestions for finding books, articles, and documents on various human rights institutions and mechanisms. The emphasis is on reference materials, international and regional documentation systems, and means of obtaining the most up-to-date information. The sources in the section on Bibliographies and Research Aids should be consulted for works on specific rights or categories, such as women's rights, children's rights, minority issues, torture, etc.

---

* This essay is the product of the work of many people through several editions of this book, including Rachel Guglielmo Waters, Jennifer Sisk, Marie-Noelle Little, the late Diana Vincent-Daviss, and the editor.

All regional materials concerning Africa, Europe, and the Americas are listed separately, whether they are texts, teaching materials, or other sources of documentation.

Sources for Texts of International Instruments and Documents

Print Resources

Major international treaties may be found in the United Nations Treaty Series, and the status of ratifications, reservations, and objections may be found in the publication, Multilateral Treaties Deposited with the Secretary-General, UN Doc. ST/LEG/SER.E/20 (last updated in 2001); there is a regional equivalent for official texts of existing human rights instruments adopted at the regional level. However, these collections are often subject to long delays before entries are made and are not always easy to locate. There are a number of unofficial compilations of international instruments, which vary in comprehensiveness of coverage and in timeliness of publication. Among the most useful and easily available are:

Brownlie, Ian and Guy S. Goodwin-Gill, Editors. Basic Documents on Human Rights. London: Oxford University Press, 4th ed. 2002.
    Texts for 99 international human rights documents; available in paperback.
Ermacora, Felix et al., eds. International Human Rights: Documents and Introductory Notes. Vienna: Manz, 1993.
    Broad selection of the basic texts, with brief commentary.
International Labor Organization. ILOLEX. Geneva: International Labor Office.
    CD-ROM collection of major ILO materials, including resolutions and recommendations; updated biannually. Available in English, Spanish and French at http://www.ilo.org/public/english/support/publ/pindex.htm. Available on-line at http://www.ilo.org/ilolex/english/ilolexhelpEng.htm#cd; updated continuously (in English only; French and Spanish in preparation).
Martin, J. Paul, Editor. 25+ Human Rights Documents. New York: Columbia Univ., 2001.
    Twenty-seven key global and regional instruments. This basic collection has been supplemented by two additional compilations: Women and Human Rights: The Basic Documents (1996) and Religion and Human Rights: Basic Documents (1998). All are moderately priced paperbacks and are available directly from the Center for the Study of Human Rights, School for International and Public Affairs, Columbia University, New York, NY 10027 (http://www.columbia.edu/cu/humanrights/).
Rights International. International Human Rights Law and Practice, Cases, Treaties. Kluwer Law International, 1997.
    Provides a comparative analysis of the jurisprudence of international tribunals with U.S. and foreign law. It presents extracts from cases for use in

pleadings. A documentary supplement volume includes the full text of all relevant treaties, conventions, procedural rules, case flow charts, and model pleadings.

Symonides, Janusz, ed. The Struggle against Discrimination: a collection of international instruments adopted by the United Nations system. Paris: UNESCO, 1996.

Print version can be ordered free of charge at http://www.unesco.org/shs/human_rights/pubfree.htm (on-line version also available).

Symonides, Janusz and Vladimir Volodin, eds. Access to Human Rights Documentation. Documentation, Bibliographies, and Data Bases on Human Rights. Paris: UNESCO, 1997.

Includes numerous human rights instruments—conventions, covenants, declarations, and resolutions. Print version can be ordered free of charge at http://www.unesco.org/shs/human_rights/pubfree.htm (on-line version also available).

UNESCO. Resolutions and Decisions: 1987–1997. Paris: UNESCO, 2d ed. 1998.

CD-ROM collection of General Conference resolutions and Executive Board decisions, in English, French, and Spanish.

Symonides, Janusz and Volodin, Vladimir. UNESCO and Human Rights: standard-setting instruments, major meetings, publications. Paris: UNESCO, 1996.

The texts of UNESCO instruments linked directly or indirectly with human rights, and the final documents of major meetings related to human rights organized by UNESCO in recent years. Print version can be ordered free of charge at http://www.unesco.org/shs/human_rights/pubfree.htm (on-line version also available).

United Nations. Human Rights: A Compilation of International Instruments. New York: United Nations, 2002 (vol. I, parts 1 & 2), 1997 (vol. II). U.N. Sales Nos.: E. 02.XIV.4, E.97.XIV.1.

A good selection of treaties, declarations, and other instruments adopted under UN auspices; the second volume includes regional instruments.

United Nations. Human Rights and Disability: the Current Use and Future Potential of United Nations Human Rights Instruments in the Context of Disability. New York: United Nations, 2002. U.N. Sales No.: E. 02.XIV.6.

Analysis of current use and future potential of UN human rights instruments in the specific field of disability.

United Nations. International Legal Instruments Relevant to Women. New York: United Nations, 1995.

UN High Commissioner for Refugees. Collection of International Instruments and Other Legal Texts Concerning Refugees and Displaced Persons. Geneva: United Nations, 1995. 2 vols.

Volume I includes universal instruments and Volume II regional instruments.

UN High Commissioner for Refugees. REFWORLD. Geneva: UNHCR, 1996– .
See entry under refugees.

Wallace, Rebecca. International Human Rights, Text & Materials. London: Sweet & Maxwell, 1997.

Excerpts from international instruments are collected by subject matter, including the right to development, women, minorities, indigenous people,

children, persons with disabilities, refugees, migrant workers, protection of
civilians during hostilities, and prisoners.

International Human Rights Reports. Nottingham, U.K.: Univ. of Nottingham
Human Rights Law Centre, v.1, 1994– . 4/yr.

> Decisions, judgments, general comments, and other documents from UN
> and regional human rights bodies. Most documents are reprinted within a
> few months of issuance. On-line version also available to subscribers.

International Legal Materials. Washington, D.C.: American Society of
International Law, v.1, 1962– . bi-monthly.

> Major international and regional instruments and court decisions are
> reprinted in full text. Each issue lists new ratifications to treaties and con-
> ventions. An excellent source for recent instruments and judicial decisions
> not available on the World Wide Web.

Electronic Resources

For those with access to it, the Web has become one of the best sources
for official documentation and the texts of various international instruments. The following sites are particularly useful for the texts of international instruments; additional information on the UN system in
general is noted below.

United Nations system

Human rights and related treaties may be found in the United Nations
Treaty Collection, http://untreaty.un.org/, the United Nations Dag
Hammarskjöld Library, http://www.un.org/Depts/dhl/resguide/spechr.
htm, and at two sites maintained by the Office of the High Commissioner
for Human Rights: http://www.unhchr.ch/html/intlinst.htm (treaties
and other instruments) and http://www.unhchr.ch/tbs/doc.nsf (documentation from the various treaty bodies). An up-to-date list of ratifications of the major treaties is found at http://untreaty.un.org/ENGLISH/
bible/englishinternetbible/bible.asp and on the OHCHR website. UN
High Commissioner for Refugees documentation may be found at
http://www.unhcr.ch/cgi-bin/texis/vtx/home?page=PROTECT&id=
3c0762ea4.

Regional organizations

Most treaties and the current status of ratifications may be obtained from
the respective organizations. The home page of the African Union (the
former Organization of African Unity) is: http://www.africa-union.org/
(in English and French); Council of Europe treaties may be found at
http://conventions.coe.int/Default.asp (in English, French, German,

Italian and Russian); and the Organization of American States home page is http://www.oas.org (in English, Spanish, French and Portuguese).

Nongovernmental sources

There are several excellent Internet sites maintained by academic institutions, which contain both treaties and other documentation. These include:

The American Society of International Law (ASIL) maintains an extremely comprehensive website, offering access to primary international and regional documents and related websites, indexed according to a wide range of specialized human rights topics, at http://www.eisil.org/.

Bayefsky.com, http://www.bayefsky.com/, is based at York University in Toronto and is a well-organized resource for a wide range of instruments, data, jurisprudence, and other documentation concerning the UN human rights treaty system, including a detailed presentation of complaint procedures.

Netherlands Institute of Human Rights Treaty Database, http://sim.law.uu.nl/SIM/Library/HRinstruments.nsf/%28organization%29?OpenView.

Project Diana is a consortium for the establishment of an international human rights database to commemorate the pioneering work of the late Diana Vincent-Daviss. Participants in Project Diana include Yale University, which maintains a library of historical documents as well as current human rights cases and documents at http://www.yale.edu/lawweb/avalon/diana/index.html; the University of Minnesota Human Rights Library, which includes a wide range of UN and regional documents, committee reports, etc. at http://www1.umn.edu/humanrts/ (in English, Arabic, French, Japanese, and Spanish); and the Bora Laskin Law Library at the University of Toronto, which offers an extremely comprehensive library of women's human rights resources at http://www.law-lib.utoronto.ca/Diana/.

Tufts University, The Fletcher School of Law and Diplomacy Multilaterals Project, http://fletcher.tufts.edu/multilaterals.html, provides the texts of international multilateral conventions and other instruments.

The University of Connecticut Human Rights Institute includes a listing of international human rights organizations, http://www.humanrights.uconn.edu/reso_gen_links_dir.htm.

The University of Iowa, Center for Human Rights, http://www.uichr.org/resources/guides.shtml.

Bibliographies and Research Aids

Print Resources

Human Rights Internet. Masterlist: A Listing of Organizations Concerned with Human Rights and Social Justice Worldwide. Ottawa: Human Rights Internet, 5th ed. 1994. Supplement to Human Rights Internet Reporter, vol. 15.
  Also see entry under Serial Publications.

Langley, Winston E., ed. Women's Rights in International Documents: A Source-book with Commentary. Jefferson, N.C.: McFarland, 1991.

Lawson, Edward H. Encyclopedia of Human Rights. London: Taylor and Francis, 2d ed. 1996.

A potpourri of information, including country-specific entries, bibliography, and a good selection of human rights texts.

Minority Rights Group. World Directory of Minorities. Chicago; London: St. James Press, 2d ed. 1997.

Redman, Nina and Lucille Whalen. Human Rights: A Reference Handbook. Santa Barbara: ABC-CLIO, 2d ed. 1998.

Skurbaty, Zelim. Human Rights Training Materials: a bibliography of existing human rights teaching and training materials. Lund: Raoul Wallenberg Institute, 2000.

Tobin, Jack and Jennifer Green. Guide to Human Rights Research. Cambridge, MA: Harvard Law School Human Rights Program, 1994. Also available at http://www.law.harvard.edu/programs/HRP/guide/rgtoc.html.

UNESCO. World Directory of Human Rights Research and Training Institutions. Paris: UNESCO, 5th ed. 2001 (in English, French and Spanish).

United Nations. Human Rights on CD-ROM: Bibliographical References to United Nations Documents and Publications. New York: United Nations, 1999.

This CD-ROM contains bibliographic references to UN documents from 1980 to 1998, as well as the full texts of ninety-five international instruments. Searches can be conducted in English, French or Spanish.

United Nations. Implementation Handbook for the Convention on the Rights of the Child. New York: United Nations, 2002.

Includes an article-by-article analysis of the Convention, drawn from the work of the Committee on the Rights of the Child up to 2001, and references to relevant provisions of other international instruments.

United Nations. Index to United Nations Documents and Publications [CD-ROM]. New Canaan, Conn: Newsbank/Readex, 1990.

Covers 1951–present, updated monthly. Will eventually cover the period from 1945.

Walters, Gregory J. and Denise Derocher. Human Rights in Theory and Practice: a selected and annotated bibliography. Metuchen, NJ: Scarecrow Press, 1995.

Wiseberg, Laurie S. Human Rights Information and Documentation, in Manual on Human Rights Reporting. Geneva: United Nations, 1997. UN Doc. HR/PUB/91/1/Rev. 1, UN Sales No. E.GV.97.0.16 (1997).

Electronic Resources

American Society for International Law, http://www.asil.org/resource/humrts1.htm.

A comprehensive guide to the electronic resources available on international human rights law, including CD-ROM, the Web, and commercial on-line services. Also includes tips for doing research as well as for locating necessary documents and materials.

Consortium of Minority Resources (COMIR), http://lgi.osi.hu/comir/db/index.htm.

Contains numerous links to reports on minorities, arranged by subject matter, ethnic group, geographic area, and type of document.

Harvard University. Guide to Human Rights Research, http://www.law.harvard.edu/programs/HRP/projects.htm and Getting Started in Human Rights Research: On-Line and Off-Line Resources, http://www.law.harvard.edu/programs/hrp/getting_started.html.

Harvard University. Foreign and International Law Resources: An Annotated Guide to Web Sites Around the World, http://www.law.harvard.edu/library/ref/ils_ref/annotated/index.php.

Islam and Human Rights, Emory School of Law, http://www.law.emory.edu/IHR. With articles, databases, journals and bibliographies on topics related to Islam and human rights.

Lacabe, Margarita. Concise Guide to Human Rights on the Internet. Derechos Humanos, 2d ed. 1998, http://www.derechos.org/human-rights/manual.htm.

Minority Rights Database, http://www.uel.ac.uk/law/mr/min.html
The UEL Minority Rights Database is a legal database which contains international documents on minorities, judicial decisions by international fora on minority rights in different states, a recommended reading list on the area of minority rights, and some information on the related topics of self determination, equality, and discrimination under international law, as well as a set of links to other related websites.

Minority Rights Group International, http://www.minorityrights.org.
Offers links to other organizations concerned with minority rights, as well as a listing of MRG's numerous publications.

Parker, Penny. UN Human Rights Documentation: A Guide to Country-Specific Research, http://www1.umn.edu/humanrts/bibliog/guide.htm.
Intended as a guide for persons representing refugees in political asylum claims and other human rights advocates.

Perkins, Steven C. Researching Indigenous Peoples Rights under International Law, http://www.ogiek.org/sitemap/researching-indigenous-peoples.htm#note2.

Perkins, Steven C. International Human Rights Law and Article 38(1) of the Statute of the International Court of Justice, http://intelligent-internet.info/law/icjart.html.

UNESCO Social Science Database (includes periodicals), http://databases.unesco.org/dare/.
Provides access to approximately 10,000 references on social science, peace, and human rights research and training institutes, social science specialists, and social science periodicals.

United Nations Department of Public Information. Human Rights Today: a UN Priority, UN Briefing Papers, http://www.un.org/rights/HRToday/ (also available in French and Spanish).
On-line version of publication outlining the UN's efforts to strengthen its human rights programming and work more effectively with its partners in government and civil society; includes links to websites of the relevant substantive offices in the UN system as well as to the full texts of the international human rights treaties and declarations.

United Nations High Commissioner for Human Rights. Indigenous Peoples
Website, http://www.unhchr.ch/indigenous/main.html.
   The portal to UN activities on indigenous peoples; includes references to
   UN materials and an extensive list of indigenous organizations and NGOs.
United Nations High Commissioner for Refugees. Select Bibliography of Refugee
Literature, http://www.unhcr.ch/cgi-bin/texis/vtx/research.
United Nations Dag Hammarskjöld Library. United Nations Documentation
Research Guide, http://www.un.org/Depts/dhl/resguide/spechr.htm.
University of Berkeley Institute of International Studies. Bibliography on Issues
in Human Rights, http://globetrotter.berkeley.edu/humanrights/bibliogra-
phies/.
University of Chicago Law Library Guide to Researching International Law using
the Internet, http://www.lib.uchicago.edu/~llou/forintlaw.html.
University of Minnesota Human Rights Library Bibliography Page, http://
www1.umn.edu/humanrts/bibliog/biblios.htm and http://www1.umn.edu/
humanrts/bibliog/BIBLIO.htm
   Comprehensive listing of human rights bibliographies and guides and bibliography for research on international human rights law.
University of Toronto. International Law Guide IV: International Women's
Human Rights and Humanitarian Law, http://www.law-lib.utoronto.ca/res-
guide/women2.htm.
   Provides an outline of the major documents and a brief research guide.
Yale University United Nations Scholars' Workstation, http://www.library.
yale.edu/un/.
   A collection of texts, finding aids, data sets, maps, and pointers to print and
   electronic information. Subject coverage includes disarmament, economic
   and social development, environment, human rights, international relations,
   international trade, peacekeeping, and population and demography.

Serial Publications

Much of the most useful information for international human rights
practitioners can be found in law review articles and other serial publications. There are several good legal indices for periodical literature.
Both the *Index to Legal Periodicals* (http://www.hwwilson.com/Databases/
legal.htm) and the *Gale Group Legal Resource Index* (http://library.dia-
log.com/bluesheets/html/bl0150.html) are available on-line and on CD-
ROM as well as in printed versions; they provide the most current
information but are limited to English language materials. Wider coverage is provided by the *Index to Foreign Legal Periodicals* (http://www.
law.berkeley.edu/library/iflp/) and *Public International Law* (http://www.
virtual-institute.de/en/hp/e-pil.cfm); the latter has an excellent subject
index to law reviews world wide and is published by the Max Planck
Institute in Heidelberg, Germany. Unfortunately, it comes out only twice
a year and is somewhat slow in entering information. On-line access to
a wide range of legal periodicals is provided by commercial services, such
as LEXIS and Westlaw.

Helpful information in journals may appear in a number of different forms. Most international law journals, which can be located through the indexes listed above, publish articles, notes, and comments on human rights; almost every issue of the *American Journal of International Law* and the *International & Comparative Law Quarterly* contains some reference to human rights. In addition, there are a number of specialized human rights journals, including the following:

African Human Rights Law Journal. Pretoria: University of Pretoria, v.1, 2001– . 2/yr.
> Aims to publish contributions dealing with human rights topics of relevance to Africa, Africans, and scholars of Africa. http://www.up.ac.za/chr/centre_publications/ahrlj/ahrlj.html.

Australian Journal of Human Rights. Sydney: University of New South Wales, v. 1, 1994–. 2/yr.
> The first journal of its kind in Australia to be devoted exclusively to the publication of articles, commentary, and book reviews about human rights developments in Australia and the Asia-Pacific region. Back-issues available on-line at http://www.austlii.edu.au/au/journals/AJHR/.

Canadian Human Rights Reporter, Human Rights Digest, Vancouver: CHRR Inc., 1980– . 8/yr.
> Provides summaries and digests of recent tribunal and court human rights decisions from all jurisdictions in Canada. Also available in hard copy and on disk: Revised Consolidated Index to the Canadian Human Rights Reporter, Volumes 1–41, 1980–2001. Subscriptions can be ordered at http://cdn-hr-reporter.ca/frame-aboutchrr.htm.

Columbia Human Rights Law Review. New York: Columbia University, v.1, 1972– . 2/yr. http://www.columbia.edu/cu/hrlr/.

European Human Rights Law Review. London: Sweet & Maxwell, v.1, 1995–. 6/yr. http://www.sweetandmaxwell.co.uk/index.html.

Harvard Human Rights Journal. Cambridge, Mass.: Harvard Law School, starts with v.3, 1990–. Annual. [Continues Harvard Human Rights Yearbook. v. 1, 1988; v. 2, 1989.]
> Full text of all articles, book reviews and book notes of the current issue and back issues (starting with Volume 12, 1999), tables of contents of earlier issues and general information about the Journal available at http://www.law.harvard.edu/students/orgs/hrj/.

Human Rights Brief. Washington, DC: Center for Human Rights and Humanitarian Law, Washington College of Law, American University. v.1, 1994–. Irreg.
> Short articles on human rights topics by Center students, updates on activities of global and regional intergovernmental bodies, and information on US legislative initiatives related to human rights.

The Human Rights Journal. Bordeaux: l'Institut des Droits de l'Homme de l'Union des Avocats Européens (European Lawyers' Union). v.1, 1999–. 12/yr.
> The European Lawyers' Union (UAE) is an Association of lawyers established in the European Community. Its monthly on-line publication is available in English and French to members only at http://www.uae.lu/en/

10.html. Back issues available in French only at http://www.uae.lu/en/droit-shomme5.html.

Human Rights Law Journal. Kehl am Rhein: Engel, v.1, 1980–. [Continues Human Rights Review.] Quarterly.

Human Rights Law Review. Nottingham, UK: University of Nottingham Human Rights Centre, v.1, 1996–. Quarterly. http://www.nottingham.ac.uk/law/accessweb/hrlc/hrlc_law_review.htm.

Human Rights Quarterly: A Comparative and International Journal of the Social Sciences, Humanities and Law. Baltimore: Johns Hopkins University Press, v.1, 1979–. Quarterly.

> The leading English-language journal that specializes in human rights issues. Recent volumes are available on-line to subscribing institutions at http://muse.jhu.edu/journals/human_rights_quarterly/.

International Journal of Human Rights. London: Frank Cass, v. 1, 1997–. Quarterly.

> Contents and abstracts of previous volumes available at http://www.frankcass.com/jnls/hr.htm.

Kóãǧa Roñétã. Equipo Nizkor and Derechos Human Rights. Ongoing.

> An on-line journal in English and Spanish. Posts articles on a range of human rights topics, http://www.derechos.org/koaga/main.htm.

Netherlands Quarterly of Human Rights. Utrecht, Netherlands: Intersentia, v.1, 1989–. Quarterly.

> Contents and abstracts for volumes since 1993 available at http://www.uu.nl/uupublish/homerechtsgeleer/onderzoek/onderzoekscholen/sim/english/publications/nqhr/articles/20480main.html.

New York Law School Journal of Human Rights. New York: New York Law School, v.1, 1983–. 2/yr. http://www.nyls.edu/pages/312.asp.

South African Journal on Human Rights. Braamfontein: Ravan Press, v.1, 1985–. 3/yr. http://wwwserver.law.wits.ac.za/sajhr/sajhr.html.

United Nations Diplomatic Times. Vol. 1– , 1999– . Teaneck, NJ. v. 1–10, No.5; 1990–99. [Continues International Documents Review, the Weekly Newsletter on the United Nations.]

> Dedicated to covering the entire range of the UN's activities, including economic and social issues, UN reform, budgetary and personnel matters, and political-security issues. It often contains relevant current information, documentary references, and summaries of important human rights issues.

United States Department of State, Bureau of Democracy, Human Rights and Labor. Country Reports on Human Rights Practices. Washington, D.C.: Government Printing Office. Annual.

> This annual publication, which began in 1978, compiles information gathered from a number of sources, predominantly U.S. embassies, on the human rights situation in all UN member states. While it should be read with the understanding that it is a U.S. government publication that may reflect U.S. foreign policy concerns, particularly in regions in which the United States is actively involved, the *Country Reports* remain a worthwhile source of information. Reports available on-line at http://www.state.gov/g/drl/hr/c1470.htm.

Yale Human Rights and Development Law Journal. New Haven: Yale Law School,
v. 1, 1998–. 1/y4. http://www.yale.edu/yhrdlj/index_enhanced.htm.

A number of nongovernmental organizations publish journals, annual reports,
and newsletters which are excellent sources for current information and reports
on specific countries' human rights practices. Since many of these materials are
produced on very tight budgets and often under difficult circumstances, some
are issued irregularly, suspend publication for periods of time, or cease publication altogether. The most substantial, substantive, and permanent of these
NGO serial publications include:

Amnesty International. Annual Reports and Monthly News. London. Available
at http://web.amnesty.org/shop/all.
For the Record (Bilan Des Droits de la Personne). Ottawa: Human Rights
Internet, 1997– . Annual.
   Electronic annual report of human rights developments at the UN.
   Published in English and French, and available at as well as on CD-ROM,
   with links to all UN official source documents available electronically. The
   website allows on-line comparison of human rights developments between
   countries both in the UN system and the European system (see *For the
   Record: The European Human Rights System*, 2000 and 2001).
For the Record: the European Human Rights System. Ottawa: Human Rights
Internet, in partnership with Netherlands Institute of Human Rights,
2000–2001.
   On-line version contains links to all Council of Europe "official" source documents available electronically. English and French versions available at
   http://www.hri.ca/fortherecord2001/euro2001/bilan2001/index.htm.
Freedom House. Freedom in the World. New York. Annual.
HRI Reporter. Ottawa: Human Rights Internet. Annual.
   The Reporter systematically abstracts and indexes thousands of the publi-
   cations received at HRI. Recent editions focus on such themes as ethnic
   conflict and women's rights. HRI also publishes the Human Rights Tribune
   (see below); an occasional paper series; and an electronic newsletter,
   "Human Rights Eye," at http://www.hri.ca.
Human Rights First (former the Lawyers' Committee for Human Rights).
Critique: Review of the Department of State's Country Reports on Human
Rights Practices. Occasional.
   Published from 1983 through 1996, discontinued through 2001, and restarted
   in 2002, this is a comprehensive review and critique of the U.S. State
   Departments Country Reports on Human Rights Practices, mentioned above.
Human Rights Tribune. Ottawa: Human Rights Internet, v.1, 1993–. Quarterly.
   News and reports from the human rights NGO community and the United
   Nations; includes calendar of upcoming events, feature articles, and reports
   on recent meetings.
Human Rights Watch. Annual World Report and weekly and monthly on-line
bulletins. New York, http://www.hrw.org/.
International Geneva Yearbook. United Nations. Annual.
   Information on the organization and activities of international institutions
   in Geneva, including lists of NGOs.

International Helsinki Federation for Human Rights. Reports. Vienna. Irreg.
The International Helsinki Federation for Human Rights is a self-govern-
ing group of nongovernmental, not-for-profit organizations that act to protect human rights throughout Europe, North America, and Central Asia. A
primary goal is to monitor compliance with the human rights provisions of
the Helsinki Final Act and its Follow-up Documents. A full listing of Helsinki
reports and publications can be found at http://www.ihf-hr.org/docu-
ments/?sec_id=3.

International Service for Human Rights. Human Rights Monitor. Geneva.
Quarterly.
Perhaps the most timely and analytical review of UN activities, including
summaries of the UN Commission on Human Rights, Sub-Commission on
Promotion and Protection of Human Rights, and treaty-monitoring bodies.
Address is case postale 16, 1 rue de Varembé, CH-1211 Geneva 20, Switzer-
land. Also in French and occasionally in Spanish and Arabic. Also available
on-line at http://www.ishr.ch/About%20UN/Reports%20and%20Analysis/
HRM.htm.

Human Rights First (former the Lawyers' Committee for Human Rights). Rights
Wire. Electronic Newsletter. New York. Bi-weekly.
Analysis of current human rights issues. Free subscription available at
http://www.humanrightsfirst.org/rights_wire/rightswire.htm.

Interights. Interights Bulletin. London. Quarterly.
Substantive articles on issues of international human rights law, news and
comment on significant developments, as well as reviews of important new
publications and summaries of major recent decisions of international tribunals applying international human rights law. Selected or composite issues
of the Bulletin also available in Hungarian, Bulgarian, Russian, and French.
Subscriptions and back issues available at http://www.interights.org/pubs/
bulletin1.asp.

Minority Rights Group. Reports. London. Irreg.
Each report normally considers a particular minority situation; occasional
regional or legal focus. Complete listing of publications available at http://
www.minorityrights.org/.

Physicians for Human Rights. Reports. Boston. Irreg.
Reports on issues related to health and human rights, including medical
ethics, discrimination in access to health care, women's health and reproductive rights, and land mines. Complete listing of publications available at
http://www.phrusa.org/publications/index.html.

Oneworld Network. http://www.oneworld.net/article/frontpage/10/3.
An on-line network that posts a wide range of news, articles and reports
selected by its partner centers all over the world, in eleven different languages. OneWorld is dedicated to harnessing the democratic potential of
the Internet to promote human rights and sustainable development.

Practice Oriented Materials

Ball, Patrick. Who Did What to Whom? Planning and Implementing a Large
Scale Human Rights Data Project, American Association for the Advancement
of Science, available at http://shr.aaas.org/www/cover.html.

Bayefsky.com.
    An on-line guide to the UN treaty system developed by Canadian law pro-
    fessor Anne F. Bayefsky; available at http://www.bayefsky.com.
Cooper, Jonathan and Roisin Pillay. Auditing for Rights: developing Scrutiny
    Systems for Human Rights Compliance. London: JUSTICE, 2001.
English, Kathryn and Adam Stapleton. The Human Rights Handbook: A
    Practical Guide to Monitoring Human Rights. Colchester: University of Essex
    Human Rights Centre, 1995.
Foley, Conor. Combating Torture: a Handbook for Judges and Prosecutors.
    Colchester: University of Essex Human Rights Centre, 2003.
        Available free of charge at http://www.essex.ac.uk/combatingtorturehand-
        book/feedback.htm.
Giffard, Camille. The Torture Reporting Handbook: How to document and
    respond to allegations of torture within the international system for the pro-
    tection of human rights. Colchester: University of Essex Human Rights
    Centre, 2000.
        Available free of charge at http://www2.essex.ac.uk/human_rights_cen-
        tre/publications/trh.shtm.
Human Rights Information and Documentation Systems International (HURI-
    DOCS), http://www.huridocs.org/about.htm.
        HURIDOCS provides access to documents and training on monitoring,
        information handling and document control and facilitates networking and
        cooperation among human rights documentation centers.
Human Rights Resource Center. The Human Rights Education Series. University
    of Minnesota, 2000.
        Provides resources for the ever-growing body of educators and activists work-
        ing to build a culture of human rights in the United States and throughout
        the world. Includes a handbook on effective practices in human rights edu-
        cation, available at http://www1.umn.edu/humanrts/edumat/hreduseries/
        hrhandbook/toc.html.
Norwegian Agency for Development Cooperation. Handbook in human rights
    assessment. Oslo: NORAD, 2001.
        Aims to provide the user with a practical tool for enhancing the human
        rights profile of development programs.
O'Flaherty, Michael. Human Rights and the UN: Practice Before the Treaty
    Bodies. Nijhoff. 2002.
Orentlicher, Diane F. Bearing Witness: The Art and Science of Human Rights
    Fact-Finding. Harvard Human Rights Journal, vol. 3 (Spring 1990).
        A comprehensive analysis of the professional standards and institutional
        imperatives of international nongovernmental organizations.
Thompson, Kate and Camille Giffard. Reporting Killings as Human Rights
    Violations. Colchester: University of Essex Human Rights Centre, 2002.
        Available free of charge at http://www.essex.ac.uk/reportingkillingshand-
        book/.
United Nations. Centre for Human Rights. Human Rights Fact Sheets. Geneva:
    Office of the High Commissioner for Human Rights, 1998–. Irreg.
        These short pamphlets contain useful information on various aspects of the
        United Nation's human rights activities; they are available on-line, and

copies may also be ordered free of charge at http://www.unhchr.ch/html/menu6/2/PUBLISTe.pdf. Twenty-eight booklets had been issued through 2003, addressing a wide variety of substantive and procedural issues.

United Nations. Office of the High Commissioner for Human Rights. United Nations Guide for Minorities. 2001.

A looseleaf collection of pamphlets in all of the official UN languages outlining mechanisms and institutions available to promote and protect minority rights. Available online at http://www.unhchr.ch/minorities/publications.htm.

United Nations. Manual on Human Rights Reporting. Geneva: UNOHCHR/UNITAR/UN Staff College Project, 1997. UN Sales No. E.GV.97.0.16 (1997).

This manual includes consolidated guidelines for state reports under various international treaties (including the two Covenants, Convention on the Elimination of All Forms of Racial Discrimination, and Convention against Torture), and articles related to the reporting process. While primarily designed for use by states, it is an excellent source of information about the manner in which oversight bodies perform their supervisory functions. Available in English and Spanish at http://www.unhchr.ch/html/menu6/2/training.htm. An updated set of the consolidated guidelines has been published as UN Doc. HRI/GEN/2/Rev.2 (2004).

United Nations. The United Nations and Human Rights 1945–1995. New York: United Nations 1996.

A part of the UN's "Blue Book" series, this volume provides a summary of many of the UN's primary human rights activities and references to relevant documents.

Velin, Jo-Anne. Reporting Human Rights and Humanitarian Stories: a Journalist's Handbook. Human Rights Internet and the International Centre for Human Rights Reporting, 1997.

A resource for journalists who report stories with human rights or humanitarian components. Available at http://www.hri.ca/doccentre/docs/handbook97/, with updated version expected in Winter 2004.

Teaching Materials and Resources

Courses and Programs

A number of NGOs and universities offer short (usually four to eight weeks) courses on human rights law and practice, in addition to their regular course offerings. Among those institutions offering courses on a reasonably regular basis are:

Andean Commission of Jurists, Los Sauces, 285, Lima 27, Peru, http://www.cajpe.org.pe/.

Limited to those from the Andean region of South America, this course is offered every June.

Columbia University Center for the Study of Human Rights, 1108 International Affairs Building, Columbia University, New York, NY 10027, http://www.columbia.edu/cu/humanrights/training/training.htm.

Runs the "Initiative on Human Rights Advocacy and the Global Economy," a four-month, intensive training program in New York for up to ten activists each year to advance human rights thinking and activism with respect to the global economy.

George Washington University School of Law and Oxford University Program on International Human Rights Law.

Offers a one-month summer course in Oxford, UK, that includes both a general human rights course and specialized seminars. Information and application forms available at http://www.gwu.edu/~specprog/abroad/oxford.html.

Instituto Interamericano de Derechos Humanos, San Jose, Costa Rica, http://www.iidh.ed.cr/.

Offers free access to the "Inter-American Virtual Classroom," with Spanish-language courses on the inter-American human rights protection system; utilization of the inter-American system for the protection of women's human rights; and the universal human rights protection system.

International Institute of Human Rights, 1, quai Lezay-Marnésia, 67000 Strasbourg, France, http://www.iidh.org/pages_a/sess_ann_a.html.

The Institute has offered summer courses in human rights, emphasizing both substantive norms and teaching methods, for over three decades; basic courses are offered in English, French, Spanish, and Arabic. A text reproducing lectures and outlines is produced for each course.

International Service for Human Rights, 1, rue Varembé, P.O. Box/Case 16, CH-1211 Geneva 20 cic, Switzerland, http://www.ishr.ch/.

The Service offers a short training course prior to sessions of the UN Commission and Sub-Commission, in addition to a number of training sessions offered throughout the year in various countries.

University Human Rights Consortium (Consorcio Universitario pelos Direitos Humanos), São Paulo, Brazil, http://www.consorciodh.org.br/ .

Sponsors the annual Human Rights Colloquium for two weeks every May in São Paulo, Brazil, for young professionals and activists engaged in the promotion of human rights in developing countries. In Portuguese and Spanish. Some fellowships available.

World Association for the School as an Instrument of Peace (Association mondiale pour l'école instrument de paix [E.I.P.]), 5, rue du Simplon, CH-1207 Geneva, Switzerland, http://www.eip-cifedhop.org/english/training/ index.html.

This Geneva-based NGO organizes an annual training session directed at teachers and specialists in human rights education, evaluates educational programs, and maintains a variety of materials related to human rights and peace education, in English and French.

Texts and Teaching Materials

Print resources

Buergenthal, Thomas, Dinah Shelton and David Stewart. International Human Rights in a Nutshell. St. Paul: West, 3d ed. 2002.

Claude, Richard Pierre. Methodologies for Human Rights Education. People's Decade for Human Rights Education, 1998.

Devine, Carol, Carol Rae Hansen and Ralph Wilde. Human Rights: the Essential Reference. Phoenix: Oryx Press, 1999.
  Excerpts available at http://www.humanrightsreference.com/index.html.

Eide, Asbjorn, Catarina Krause and Allan Rosas, Editors. Economic, Social and Cultural Rights: a textbook. Dordrecht: Martinus Nijhoff, 2d ed. 2001.

Lillich, Richard B. and Hurst Hannum. International Human Rights: Problems of Law and Policy. Boston: Little, Brown, 3d ed. 1995.

Weissbrodt, David, Joan Fitzpatrick and Frank Newman. International Human Rights: Law, Policy and Process. Cincinnati, Ohio: Anderson, 3d ed. 2001.

Robertson, Arthur H. and J.G. Merrills. Human Rights in the World: An Introduction to the Study of the International Protection of Human Rights. Manchester: Manchester University Press, 4th ed. 1996.

Steiner, Henry J. and Philip Alston. International Human Rights in Context. Oxford: Clarendon Press, 2d ed. 2000.

Symonides, Janusz. Editor. Human Rights, New Dimensions and Challenges: Manual on Human Rights Teaching. London: Dartmouth/Ashgate, 1998 (vol. I), 1999 (vol. II).
  A collection of articles organized by substantive issue, published under the auspices of UNESCO.

UNESCO. World Directory of Human Rights Research and Training Institutions. Paris: UNESCO, 5th ed. 2001 (in English, French, and Spanish).

United Nations High Commissioner for Human Rights. ABC: Teaching Human Rights, Practical Activities for Primary and Secondary schools. Geneva: United Nations, 1999.
  Available in English at http://www.unhchr.ch/html/menu6/2/abc.htm.

Electronic Resources

United Nations CyberSchoolbus, http://www.un.org/Pubs/CyberSchoolBus/cur.html.

United Nations High Commissioner for Refugees Teaching Materials, Teaching Tools at http://www.unhcr.ch/cgi-bin/texis/vtx/publ and Learning For a Future: Refugee Education in Developing Countries, http://www.unhcr.ch/cgi-bin/texis/vtx/publ.

AIUSA Human Rights Educators Network, http://www.amnestyusa.org/education/.

Canadian Human Rights Foundation, http://www.chrf.ca/.

Columbia University Center for the Study of Human Rights, http://www.columbia.edu/cu/humanrights/.

Human Rights Education Associates Human Rights Education Library, http://erc.hrea.org/Library/index.php.
  Contains over 1,000 full-text guides, curricula, textbooks and other documents that can be used for both formal and non-formal education in human rights.

Human Rights Internet Education Resources, http://www.hri.ca/doccentre/.
  Includes syllabi, programs, and textbook profiles.

University of Ottawa, Human Rights Research and Education Centre, http://
www.cdp-hrc.uottawa.ca/index_e.html.
University of Minnesota.
>A rich site with varied human rights materials, including a number of edu-
cational materials, http://www1.umn.edu/humanrts/education/materi-
als.htm, and a list of human rights centers, http://www1.umn.edu/humanrts/
links/program.html.

Works on the Human Rights Activities of Nongovernmental Organizations

Publications by NGOs themselves are the best source of information,
and a number of comparative or other works also are available.

The Inter-African Network for Human Rights and Development (Afronet). The
Human Rights Resource Directory.
>Relatively comprehensive listing of human rights NGOs, with links, http://
afronet.org.za/directory/hr-ngo.html#Amnesty .
Human Rights Internet. HRI Reporter. Ottawa: Human Rights Internet. Annual.
>The *HRI Reporter* and *Human Rights Tribune* are one of the best sources of
information on NGO activities. A *Master List* of human rights NGOs is pub-
lished irregularly as a supplement to the *Reporter.* See entry under Serial
Publications for address.
Human Rights Internet. Funding Human Rights: an international directory of
funding organizations and human rights awards. Ottawa: Human Rights
Internet, 3d ed. 1999.
International Service for Human Rights. Human Rights Monitor. Geneva:
International Service for Human Rights. Quarterly.
>Focuses on NGO activity related to UN human rights organs. See entry
under Serial Publications for address.

United Nations

UN documents are organized by a system of code numbers and letters,
with a different code assigned to each organ and sub-organ within the
UN system. In addition to identifying the body which issued the document, the code also identifies the type of document, e.g., resolution,
summary record, NGO statement, etc. While the entire system appears
complex, a knowledge of the basic codes relevant to human rights makes
understanding the material available within the UN system much easier.
Documentation issued by the various human rights bodies is available at
UN Headquarters in New York and Geneva while the body is in session;
it is mailed to NGOs in consultative status and available to others who
request it a few weeks after the end of the session. Unfortunately, printed
compilations (such as the jurisprudence of the treaty bodies) is often

badly delayed, although this problem has been remedied by generally excellent UN websites, for those with access to the Internet.

Some important documents, such as major reports of committees, commissions, and sub-commissions, are also issued as sales publications by the United Nations. Sales numbers consist of a letter designating the language of publication, followed by the last two numerals of the year of publication, roman numerals indicating the UN subject classification for the document (human rights documents are in category XIV), and an arabic numeral issued chronologically by date of publication within the calendar year. An example of a document issued in both formats, with a UN document code and a sales number is: Sub-Commission on the Prevention of Discrimination and the Protection of Minorities. Study on the Rights of Persons Belonging to Ethnic, Religious and Linguistic Minorities. Special Rapporteur: Francesco Capotorti. UN Doc. E/CN.4/Sub.2/384/Rev.1, UN Sales No. E.78.XIV.1 (1979); this study was later reprinted in the UN's *Human Rights Study Series*, thereby acquiring a new sales number (E.91.XIV.2) which does not indicate that the report was originally published in 1978.

UNDOC is the *United Nations Index*, which indexes UN documents by subject matter. While it is quite comprehensive, it can be somewhat confusing to use. If documents of particular organs are sought, it can be easier to find a document simply by leafing through the organ's documents for the time period in question. This process also may identify other relevant materials which might not have been retrieved through UNDOC.

Each of the major UN bodies concerned with human rights produces an annual report of its activities. This report is submitted to the parent body—most often the General Assembly or Economic and Social Council—and is issued as a supplement to the parent body's Official Records. The annual report of each body generally receives the same supplement number each year, so locating the report for one year makes it easy to find other annual reports by the same body. For example, the 1998 annual reports of the following committees have the UN document number A/52/xx, where "52" denotes the General Assembly's fifty-second (1998) session and "xx" is the number of the supplement: CERD (18), CEDAW (38), Human Rights Committee (40), Committee on the Rights of the Child (41), and Committee on Torture (44).

The Office of the High Commissioner for Human Rights issues a number of publications useful to human rights practitioners, under a variety of often confusing titles; many do not have document codes or sales numbers. In addition to the *Human Rights Fact Sheets* (mentioned above), these include *Special Issue Papers*, whose titles have concerned, *inter alia*, human rights and disability, reproductive and sexual health, guidelines on HIV/AIDS and human rights, protecting the heritage of indigenous peoples, and the right to adequate housing; a *Professional Training Series*, which includes shorter handbooks that attempt to translate legal standards into practical guidelines in specific areas, such as social work, elections, pretrial detention, national human rights institutions, and police training; a *Guide Series* providing information on relevant UN operations and procedures for special groups such as minorities and indigenous peoples; a *Series on the United Nations Decade for Human Rights Education (1995–2004)*; and ad hoc publications, such as reports of occasional seminars. The Office's publications website is http://www. unhchr.ch/html/ menu6/2/index.htm.

The *Official Records* (formerly *Yearbook*) *of the Human Rights Committee* generally take three to five years to be published, but each two-volume annual publication reprints the full texts of reports submitted by states under Article 40 of the Covenant on Civil and Political Rights, summary records of the Committee's discussions of the reports, and the Committee's annual report to the General Assembly. These reports are available in full on the Internet within months of each Committee sessions at http://www.unhchr.ch/html/menu2/6/hrc/hrcs.htm.

For relatively current information on human rights activities in the United Nations, agendas and reports of meetings of human rights bodies, new and draft instruments, and listings of new ratifications of human rights treaties, see the serial publications listed above or, where possible, the UN's various websites. *U.N. Chronicle* is an informative quarterly magazine that reports on meetings of major UN human rights bodies as well as other UN organs.

Despite all the research tools and compilations, there is no substitute for the documents themselves. The following is a partial list of the UN document codes that are likely to be most useful in human rights work:

General Assembly (GA)

A/	Documents for plenary
A/INF	Information papers for the GA
A/RES	GA Resolutions
A/C.1–C.6	GA Main Committees, issued only during Assembly sessions; the Third Committee considers human rights issues, and the Sixth Committee deals with legal matters
A/AC.109	Special Committee on Colonialism
A/AC.115	Special Committee on Apartheid
A/AC.160	Committee on International Terrorism
GAOR	General Assembly Official Record

Human Rights Bodies Reporting to the General Assembly

CAT	Committee against Torture
CCPR	Human Rights Committee
CEDAW	Committee on the Elimination of Discrimination against Women
CERD	Committee on the Elimination of Racial Discrimination
CMW	Committee on the Protection of the Rights of All Migrant Workers and Members of their Families
CRC	Committee on the Rights of the Child
UNHCR	High Commissioner for Refugees

Economic and Social Council (ECOSOC)

E/	Documents for plenary
E/C.2	Committee on Nongovernmental Organizations
E/C.12	Committee on Economic, Social and Cultural Rights
E/CN.4	Commission on Human Rights
E/CN.4/Sub.2	Sub-Commission on Promotion and Protection of Human Rights
E/CN.4/Sub.2/AC.4	Working Group on Indigenous Populations
E/CN.4/Sub.2/AC.5	Working Group on Minorities
E/CN.5	Commission for Social Development
E/CN.6	Commission on the Status of Women
E/CN.15	Commission on Crime Prevention and Criminal Justice
E/CN.19	Permanent Forum on Indigenous Issues

General Codes for Subsidiary Bodies

A subsidiary body is assigned an arabic number which usually indicates the order in which is was established. The documents of some subsidiary bodies bear a symbol consisting of the basic series symbol of the parent body followed by the initials or acronym of the body itself.

-/AC.	Ad hoc committee or similar body
-/C.	Standing, permanent or main committee
-/CN.	Commission
-/CONF.	Conference
-/PC.	Preparatory Committee
-/SC.	Sub-committee
-/Sub.	Sub-commission

-/WG.	Working group
-/WP.	Working party

Codes Indicating Nature of the Document

-/CRP.	Conference room paper (usually an informal working document available only during the meeting)
-/DEC.	Texts of decisions
-/INF.	Information series
-/L.	Limited distribution (usually available only during meetings)
-/MIN.	Minutes
-/NGO.	Statements by nongovernmental organizations
-/R.	Restricted distribution (in theory not generally available to NGOs)
-/PV.	Verbatim records of meetings (procès verbaux).
-/RES.	Texts of resolutions
-/SR.	Summary records of meetings
-/WP.	Working paper

Codes Indicating Modification to Text of Main Document

-/Add.	Addition to text of main document
-/Amend.	Amendment to portion of adopted text
-/Corr.	Corrigendum—corrects errors in the text of the main document
-/Rev.	Revision—replacement version of a document

Electronic Resources

It is impossible to summarize the comprehensive and generally impressive websites maintained by the United Nations; perhaps the best advice is simply to go to the UN home page, http://www.un.org, which is accessible in all six official UN languages, and click on "human rights" to begin your search. In addition, of course, specific addresses may change as a site is revised or updated. Current information on meetings of treaty bodies and other UN organs, including the texts of many of the main documents, can be found through the home page of the UN High Commissioner for Human Rights, http://www.unhchr.ch/.

UN documents also are available on-line through the UN's Official Documents Service (ODS); unfortunately, materials are available only to subscribers to this relatively expensive service. However, a wide range of UN documentation is publicly available through the UN Documentation

Service at http://www.unu.edu/hq/library/UNDC/un_doc_centre.html.

References to other elements of the UN system may be found at http://www.un.org/aboutun/mainbodies.htm; among those sites of particular relevance to human rights are UNICEF, http://www.unicef.org; the International Law Commission, http://www.un.org/law/ilc/index. htm; the UN Division for the Advancement of Women, http://www. un.org/womenwatch/daw/; the UN Development Fund for Women, http://www.unifem.org/; and the UN Crime and Justice Information Network, http://www.uncjin.org/.

Secondary Sources

A great number of books address aspects of the UN's action in the field of human rights. The following are among the more practice-oriented:

Alston, Philip and Frederic Megret, eds. The United Nations and Human Rights: a Critical Appraisal. New York: Oxford University Press, 2004.
> Examines the functions, procedures, and performance of each of the major UN organs dealing with human rights, the relationship between the various bodies, and the potential for major reforms and restructuring.

Bayefsky, Anne F. The UN Human Rights Treaty System: Universality at the Crossroads. Ardsley, NY: Transnational Publishers, 2001.
> A highly critical analysis of the functioning of the UN treaty system.

Bouziri, Néjib. La protection des droits civils et politiques par l'ONU: l'oeuvre du Comité des droits de l'homme. Paris: l'Harmattan, 2003.

Human Rights Internet. For the Record: The UN Human Rights System. Ottawa: Human Rights Internet, 1997– . Annual.
> A comprehensive annual survey of UN human rights documents, in paper and CD-ROM, organized both by country and thematically. English and French. Also available on the World Wide Web at http://www.hir.ca/fortherecord1997. See Serial Publications for address.

Joseph, Sarah, Jenny Schultz and Melissa Castan. International Covenant on Civil and Political Rights. Oxford: Oxford Univ. Press, 2d ed. 2004.

Ksentini, Fatma Zohra. Les Procédures Onusiennes de Protection des Droits de l'Homme: recours et détours. Paris: Publisud, 1994.

McGoldrick, Dominic. The Human Rights Committee: its role in the development of the international covenant on civil and political rights. Oxford: Clarendon Press, 1994 [paper].

O'Flaherty, Michael. Human Rights and the UN: practice before the treaty bodies. Leiden and Boston: Nijhoff, 2d ed. 2002.

Tomuschat, Christian. Human Rights Between Idealism and Realism. Oxford: Oxford Univ. Press, 2003.

International Labor Organization

The most important document for following the ILO's work in supervising ratified conventions is the annual *Report of the Committee of Experts on the Application of Conventions and Recommendations* to the ILO General Conference, though it is generally several years behind. Other important publications include:

International Labor Organization. ILOLEX. Geneva: International Labor Office. See entry under international instruments and documents.

International Labour Office. International Labour Conventions and Recommendations, 1919–1995. Geneva: International Labor Office, 1996. 3 vols. Updated irregularly.

International Labour Office. Official Bulletin. Series A and B. 3/yr.
Series A includes information on the activities of the ILO, texts adopted by the International Labour Conference and other official documents. Series B includes reports of the Committee on Freedom of Association of the Governing Body of the ILO and related material. Subscriptions available in English, French and Spanish at http://www.ilo.org/public/english/support/publ/subs.htm.

International Labour Office. International Labour Standards: A Workers' Education Manual. Geneva: International Labour Office, 4th ed. 1998.
This book provides a brief but thorough introduction to the formulation, adoption, and application of internationally agreed standards of good practice in labor matters; covers developments up to mid-1997.

International Labour Conference. Record of Proceedings. Annual.
All conference documents available in English, French, and Spanish at http://www.ilo.org/public/english/support/publ/books.htm.

International Labour Review. Geneva: ILO. 4/yr.
Offers analysis by economists, lawyers, sociologists, policy-makers, and other experts on the many factors determining the level, quality, and distribution of employment and reviews of recent publications in the field of employment and labor. In English, French and Spanish. On-line or paper subscription information available at http://www.ilo.org/public/english/support/publ/books.htm.

International Tribunals

Although not technically human rights bodies, since they deal with international crimes against humanity, war crimes, and genocide, a number of international criminal tribunals have been created since the mid-1990s. Their activities are obviously relevant to the prevention of gross violations of human rights, and basic information on their activities is set out below.

International Criminal Court (ICC) (Maanweg, 174, 2516 AB The Hague, The Netherlands; Tel: 31 70 515 8515 Fax: 31 70 5158555).
Statute, signatories, official records of the assemblies of states parties, and rules of procedure and evidence available at http://www.icc-cpi.int/php/show.php?id=basicdocuments.

International Criminal Tribunal for the Former Yugoslavia (ICTY) (Churchil-lplein 1 2517JW, The Hague, The Netherlands; Tel: +31 70 416 5233 Fax: +31 70 416 5355).

The ICTY publishes annual reports covering the activities of each organ of the Tribunal; a monthly *Judicial Supplement* with summaries of significant decisions, orders, and judgments; *Basic Documents*, including the statute, rules of procedure and evidence, and other regulatory instruments; and *Yearbooks*, collections of official documents issued in a given calendar year either by the Tribunal itself (regulatory texts, indictments, reports, addresses by senior officials) or in relation to the Tribunal (Security Council or General Assembly Resolutions, implementing legislation passed by States, agreements). It also features biographies and a bibliography. Much of this information is also available on-line, at http://www.un.org/icty/index.html. Judgments, judges' separate opinions, and related press releases are at http://www.un.org/icty/cases/jugemindex-e.htm.

International Criminal Tribunal for Rwanda (ICTR) (Arusha International Conference Centre, P.O. Box 6016, Arusha, Tanzania Tel. 1-212-963-2850/255-27-250-4369/72 Fax 1-212-963-2848-9/255-27-250-4000/4373).

The ICTR has published two volumes of *Basic Documents and Case Law (1995–2000 and 2000–2001),* available in English and French (2nd volume also available in Kinyarwanda) and on CD-ROM. It also publishes on-line versions of a monthly *Bulletin,* a *Newsletter,* and a *Quarterly Bibliography* (all available at http://www.ictr.org/default.htm). A two-volume set of *Reports of Orders, Decisions and Judgments* (through 1998) may be ordered from Brulant Publishing, Rue de la Regence 67, B-1000 Brussels, Belgium Tel. 32-2512-9845 Fax 32-2511-7202 e-mail info@bruylant.be). The ICTR has also compiled an on-line database of all public (non-confidential) judicial records of the Tribunal, such as indictments, motions, responses, decisions, transcripts, and judgments, at http://www.ictr.org/default.htm.

Publications and Electronic Resources

American Non-Governmental Organizations Coalition for the International Criminal Court.

AMICC is a coalition of nongovernmental organizations committed to achieving full United States support for the International Criminal Court (ICC) and the earliest possible U.S. ratification of the Court's Rome Statute. The website is a repository of information about the U.S. and the ICC: http://www.amicc.org/index.html.

Bassiouni, M. Cherif. Introduction to International Criminal Law. Ardsley, NY: Transnational Publishers, 2003.

Bassiouni, M. Cherif. The Statute of the International Criminal Court and Related Instruments: Legislative History, 1994–2000. Ardsley, NY: Transnational Publishers, 2001.

Cassese, Antonio. International Criminal Law. Oxford: Oxford Univ. Press, 2003.

Cassese, Antonio, ed. The Rome Statute for An International Criminal Court. Oxford: Oxford Univ. Press, 2002.

Coalition for the International Criminal Court, http://www.iccnow.org/.
  A comprehensive resource on latest developments related to the ICC.
  Publishes a quarterly newsletter, the *ICC Monitor*, in English, French, and
  Spanish, and a monthly bulletin the *ICC Update*, with versions specific to
  Ibero-America (*Agenda CPI*) and to Europe (*European Newsletter*), all avail-
  able at http://www.iccnow.org/publications.html.
Coalition for International Justice, http://www.cij.org/index.cfm?fuseaction=
  homepage.
  Supports the international war crimes tribunals for Rwanda and the former
  Yugoslavia, and justice initiatives in East Timor, Sierra Leone, and Cambodia.
Delgado, Isabel Lirola and Magdalena Martin Martinez. La Corte penal inter-
  nacional: justicia versus impunidad. Madrid: Dykinson ed. ARIEL, 2001.
Global Policy Forum, http://www.globalpolicy.org/wldcourt/index.htm .
  Tracks developments at the international ad hoc tribunals, the ICC, and special
  international criminal courts. Includes a special section on the Milosevic trial.
Gutman, Roy and David Rieff, eds. Crimes of War: What the Public Should Know.
  New York: Crimes of War Project, nd.
  Full text available in English at http://www.crimesofwar.org/thebook/
  book.html. Also available in Arabic, Chinese, English, French, German,
  Hungarian, Italian, Russian, Serb-Croat and Spanish. The Crimes of War
  Project also publishes a monthly magazine, available at http://www.crime-
  sofwar.org/index-mag.html.
Illuminati, Giulio, Luigi Stortoni and Maria Virgilio, eds. Crimini internazionali
  tra diritto e giustizia: dai Tribunali penali internazionali alle Commissioni
  Verità e riconciliazione. Torino: Giappichelli, 2000.
Stromseth, Jane E., ed. Accountability for Atrocities: National and International
  Responses. Ardsley, NY: Transnational Publishers, 2003.
University of Chicago, International Criminal Court: Resources in Print and
  Electronic Format, http://www.lib.uchicago.edu/~llou/icc.html#books.
  A comprehensive listing of books, journal articles, and Internet links related
  to international criminal law in general and the ICC in particular.
University of Minnesota, Human Rights Library, http://www1.umn.edu/human-
  rts/links/intrib.html.
  A list of links related to international criminal tribunals.
War Crimes Research Office. American University Washington College of Law,
  http://www.wcl.american.edu/warcrimes/.
  Posts regular status reports and tables on proceedings before the ICTY,
  ICTR, the special court for Sierra Leone, and the special panels for serious
  crimes in East Timor, as well as judgment summaries for the ICTY and ICTR.
Zappala, Salvatore. International Criminal Trials and Human Rights. Cary, N.C.:
  Oxford University Press, 2003.

Refugees

There is no substitute for detailed examination of domestic laws relating to applications for asylum and refugee status. However, the following publications and resource centers should be particularly helpful to
the practitioner.

Print Resources

Goodwin-Gill, Guy. The Refugee in International Law. New York: Oxford University Press, 2d ed. 1996.

The standard general work.

Hathaway, James. The Law of Refugee Status. London: Butterworths, 1991.

This comprehensive examination emphasizes Canadian law but also surveys national legislation in other states.

Mbuyi, Benjamin Mulamba. Refugees and International Law. Scarborough, Ontario: Carswell Thompson, 1993.

Contains texts of instruments concerning refugees, bibliographical references, and index. In English and French.

Office of the High Commissioner for Refugees. Handbook on Procedures and Criteria for Determining Refugee Status under the 1951 Convention and the 1967 Protocol Relating to the Status of Refugees. Geneva: UNHCR, rev. ed. 1992.

This is the basic text for those concerned with refugee determination issues, as revised by practice and conclusions and recommendations of the UNHCR's Executive Committee. Full text available at: http://www.asylum-support.info/publications/unhcr/handbook.htm.

Office of the High Commissioner for Refugees. United Nations Resolutions and Decisions Relating to the Office of the UN High Commissioner for Refugees. Geneva: UNHCR, 1989–. 1v. [loose-leaf]. Updated periodically.

United Nations. REFWORLD 2003(4 CD-ROM collection). New York: United Nations. Annual. UN Sales No. E.GV.01.0.5.

This is an expensive but valuable collection on CD-ROM of international and national documents relating to refugees, including over 700 laws and regulations from more than 150 countries. Published annually, with a mid-year update. Reduced rates for NGOs, clinics, and individuals representing asylum seekers.

Periodicals

International Journal of Refugee Law. Oxford: Oxford University Press, v. 1, 1988–. Quarterly.

Subscription information, contents of past volumes, and purchase of individual articles available at: http://www3.oup.co.uk/reflaw/.

International Migration Review. New York: Center for Migration Studies, v. 1, 1966–. Quarterly.

Subscriptions available at: http://cmsny.org/cmspage2.htm.

Journal of Refugee Studies. Oxford: Oxford University Press, v. 1, 1988–. Quarterly.

Subscription information, contents of past volumes, and purchase of individual articles available at: http://www3.oup.co.uk/jnls/list/refuge/.

Refugee Survey Quarterly. Oxford: Oxford University Press, on behalf of UNHCR. Quarterly.

Subscription information, contents of past volumes, and purchase of individual articles available at http://www3.oup.co.uk/refqtl/.

Electronic and Other Resources

Amnesty International. International Secretariat (1 Easton Street, London WC1X 8DJ)

> Amnesty International devotes substantial resources to documenting conditions in countries that produce refugees. Its headquarters in London has an extensive collection of refugee materials and can provide information on the many documentation centers that AI maintains in other cities. The AI home page is at http://www.amnesty.org.

Center for Gender and Refugee Studies, University of California at Hastings.

> The Center for Gender and Refugee Studies provides multiple legal resources focused on female asylum seekers and refugees. Anyone representing women refugees or interested in issues affecting women seeking asylum should consult the website at http://www.uchastiings.edu/cgrs.

Center for International and European Law on Immigration and Asylum (Passerelle) (University of Konstanz, 78457 Konstanz, Germany).

> Extensive directory of refugee and immigration sites; in German and English, at http://www.uni-konstanz.de/FuF/ueberfak/fzaa/index-en.html.

Centre for Refugee Studies, York University (4700 Keele Street, Toronto, Ontario M3J 1P3, Canada).

> Includes research reports and an extensive list of refugee resources at http://www.yorku.ca/crs/.

European Council on Refugees and Exiles (ECRE). Country Reports. London. Annual.

> Covers asylum developments, changes in asylum legislation, and numbers of asylum applicants in twenty-five European countries. Full country reports since 1999 and a wide range of other publications addressing various refugee issues available at http://www.ecre.org/policy/publications.shtml. A full database of ECRE member organizations and their local media and policy experts is available at http://members.ecre.org/cgi-bin/directory.pl?view= all.

European Legal Network on Asylum (ELENA). Index of Useful Addresses. London: ECRE. Annual.

> Provides current information for twenty-five European countries on organizations offering refugee services and counseling, documentation centers, and lawyers and legal experts assisting refugees. Includes names, addresses, and telephone numbers of several hundred individuals who can help refugees and asylum-seekers, as well as inform human rights practitioners about the pertinent national system. Copies also are distributed by Schweizerische Zentralstelle für Flüchtlingshilfe (SFH/OSAR), Postfach 279, 8035 Zürich, Switzerland. More information about ELENA is available at http://www.ecre.org/about/elena.shtml.

Human Rights Watch (350 Fifth Avenue, 34th floor, New York, NY 10118–3299)

> Human Rights Watch issues many reports on refugee-producing situations, and its website has a special section focusing on refugee issues. The Human Rights Watch home page is at http://www.hrw.org.

Informationsverbund Asyl/ZDWF (Zentrale Dokumentationsstelle der Freien Wohlfahrtspflege für Flüchtlinge) (Postfach 11 10, 53701 Siegburg, Germany)

This cooperative effort of several NGOs in Germany that are working to protect the rights of asylum seekers has multiple useful resources available at their website, in German, at http://www.asyl.net/.

Legal Assistance through Refugee Law Clinics, The Refugee Law Reader.

The Refugee Law Reader is a comprehensive on-line resource for the complex and rapidly evolving field of international asylum and refugee law. In includes access to complete texts of the core legal materials, instruments, and academic commentary at http://refugeelawreader.org.

Office of the United Nations High Commissioner for Refugees (UNHCR).

The UNHCR website has what many consider to be the most extensive collection of resources concerning refugees. Its home page is http://www.unhcr.ch.

United States Committee for Refugees (1717 Massachusetts Avenue, NW, Suite 200, Washington, DC 20036–2003)

The U.S. Committee for Refugees defends the rights of refugees, asylum seekers, and displaced persons worldwide. It produces, among many other publications, an annual world refugee survey. Its home page is http://www.refugees.org.

University of Michigan Law School Refugee Caselaw Site.

In order to promote transnational analysis of refugee law, this center provides extensive coverage of judicial opinions in multiple national jurisdictions. Professor James Hathaway of the University of Michigan Law School and Professor Walter Kalin of the Faculty of Law at the University of Bern oversee the postings at http://www.refugeecaselaw.org.

Regional Protection of Human Rights

Africa

The African Commission on Human and Peoples' Rights (P.O. Box 673, Kairaba Avenue, Banjul, The Gambia) publishes communiques of each of its two annual sessions at http://www.achpr.org/english/_info/past_en.html and annual activity reports (from 1996) at http://www.achpr.org/english/_info/index_activity_en.html. Information about the activities of the African Center for Democracy and Human Rights Studies, an independent nongovernmental organization that was established in accordance with Article 25 of the African Charter to "promote and ensure, through teaching, education and publication, respect of the rights and freedoms contained in the Charter and to see to it that these freedoms and rights, as well as corresponding obligations are understood," can be found at http://www.acdhrs.org/. Other useful sources include the following:

Africa Centre. Contemporary Africa Database, http://africadatabase.org/.

An on-line directory of current information concerning prominent Africans, African organizations, and dates in the African calendar. In Arabic, English, French, KiSwahili, and Portuguese.

African Commission on Human and Peoples' Rights et al., eds. Documents of the African Commission on Human and Peoples' Rights. Oxford: Hart Publishing, 2001.

Eteka Yemet, Valère. La Charte Africaine des Droits de l'Homme et des Peuples. Paris: L'Harmattan, 2000.

Evans, Malcom D. and Rachel Murray, eds. The African Charter on Human and Peoples' Rights: The System in Practice, 1986–2000. Cambridge: Cambridge University Press, 2002.

Human Rights Internet. African Directory: Human Rights Organizations in Africa. Ottawa: Human Rights Internet, 1996. Can be ordered at http://www.hri.ca/publications/afdir/.

Institute for Human Rights and Development in Africa. Compilation of Decisions on Communications of the African Commission on Human and Peoples' Rights 1994–2001. Banjul, 2002.
> Collects all Commission jurisprudence, indexed both by the provisions of the African Charter that have been breached by states parties, and according to the countries against which communications have been submitted. May be ordered in English or French at http://www.africaninstitute.org/html/order_the_compilation.html.

Matringe, Jean. Tradition et Modernité dans la Charte Africaine des Droits de l'Homme et des Peuples. Brussels: Bruylant/Nemesis, 1996.

Murray, Rachel. The African Commission on Human and Peoples' Rights and International Law. Oxford: Hart Publishing: 2000.

Osterdahl, Inger. Implementing Human Rights in Africa: the African Commission on Human and Peoples' Rights and Individual Communications. Uppsala: Lustu Forlag, 2002.

Ouguergouz, Fatsah. The African Charter on Human and Peoples' Rights, A Comprehensive Agenda for Human Dignity and Sustainable Democracy in Africa. The Hague: Martinus Nijhoff, 2003.

Umozurike, U. Oji. The African Charter on Human and Peoples' Rights. The Hague: Martinus Nijhoff, 1997.

University of Minnesota Human Rights Library. Africa Human Rights Resource Center, http://www1.umn.edu/humanrts/africa/.
> Includes human rights instruments and institutions, links to African NGOs, and information on the International Criminal Tribunal for Rwanda.

University of Minnesota Human Rights Library. Decisions of the African Commission on Human and Peoples' Rights, http://www1.umn.edu/humanrts/africa/comcases/comcases.html.
> Comprehensive and up-to-date on-line catalogue of all decisions of the Commission, indexed by country and by article.

Welch, Claude E. Protecting Human Rights in Africa: Strategies and Roles of Non-Governmental Organizations. Philadelphia: University of Pennsylvania Press, 1995.

Europe

Council of Europe: Official publications

The essential publication containing the European Convention and its Protocols, the Rules of Procedure of the European Court of Human Rights, and other information is Council of Europe, *European Convention on Human Rights: Collected Texts* (1998), with revised 1998 texts of the Convention and Rules of Court. A two-volume trilingual (English, French, and German) collection of all European treaties from 1949 to 1998 was published in 1998 by the Council of Europe.

Until the merger of the Commission and Court in 1998, decisions (both as to admissibility and on the merits) of the European Commission of Human Rights were first published separately in soft-cover format; most also were collected in *Decisions and Reports* (replacing the previous *Collection of Decisions*), which was published several times a year and is available from the Council of Europe. The Commission also issued an annual *Stocktaking on the European Convention on Human Rights*, which summarized major decisions.

Decisions and judgments of the European Court of Human Rights are published in a similar soft-cover format when they are first issued; Series A comprises judgments and decisions, and Series B contains pleadings, oral arguments, and documents. Court materials are available from the Council of Europe as *Reports of Judgments and Decisions* and also are published commercially by Carl Heymanns Verlag, Luxemburger Straße 449, D-50939 Köln, Tel: (49) 221 94 37 30; Fax: (49) 221 943 73 901, http://www.heymanns.com. A new compilation of *Key case-law extracts* was published by the Council of Europe in 2004.

Selections of both Commission and Court materials, as well as information on other Council of Europe activities and the domestic implementation of European human rights law, may be found in *Yearbook of the European Convention on Human Rights* (Leiden: Nijhoff, edited by the Council of Europe Directorate of Human Rights) and *Human Rights Information Bulletin*; the latter is available free of charge within Europe from the Council of Europe and on-line at http://www.humanrights. coe.int/Bulletin/eng/presenting.htm. Current decisions of the European Commission and Court also are published in the monthly *European Human Rights Reports* (London: Sweet and Maxwell).

For those with access to it, the best source for Council of Europe documents and the jurisprudence of the European Court of Human Rights is through the Council of Europe's website. The Council's home page is http://www.coe.int/DefaultEN.asp; that of the Court is: http:// www. echr.coe.int and includes a searchable case-law database and an index of recent judgments and decisions by subject. For an annual fee, the

Justis Databases (http://www.justis.com/database/human_rights. html) provide access to ECHR case law, European human rights conventions and protocols, the United Kingdom's Human Rights Act (1998), and expert commentary.

Organization for Security and Cooperation in Europe: Official publications

The OSCE has published a wide range of the documents, reports, journals, and decisions issued by its various negotiating and decision-making bodies since 1973. Most OSCE summits and other meetings result in issuance of a "concluding document" that contains the principles or decisions to which the participating states have agreed. The Prague Office of the OSCE Secretariat will mail selected documents upon request, including OSCE's Annual Reports (from 1993); a video documentary on the history of the OSCE; a monthly newsletter; regularly updated factsheets on different aspects of OSCE missions, operations and institutions; and feature publications.

The consolidated texts of all of the OSCE mechanisms and procedures may be found in OSCE Doc. SEC.GAL/92/98 (1998), available from the OSCE Secretariat in Vienna. The OSCE also maintains a reasonably up-to-date website with a good selection of current and past documents, available in English, French, German, Italian, Russian, and Spanish; the home page is http://www.osce.org.

Secondary sources

Alston, Philip A., ed. The EU and Human Rights. Oxford: Oxford University Press, 1999.
Published in French in 2001 as L'Union Européenne et les Droits de l'Homme (Brussels: Editions Bruylant).
Betten, Lammy and Nicholas Grief. The European Union and Human Rights. London: Longman, 1998.
Amato, Giuliano and Judy Batt. Minority Rights and EU Enlargement to the East. Florence: European University Institute, 1998.
One of a series of policy papers on different aspects of European integration. Available in full at http://www.iue.it/RSCAS/WP-Texts/98_05p.htm.
Berger, Vincent. Jurisprudence de la Cour Européenne des Droits de l'Homme. Paris: Sirey, 6th ed. 1998.
Clements, L.J., Nuala Mole and Alan Simmons. European human rights: taking a case under the Convention, London: Sweet & Maxwell, 1999.
Council of Europe. Collected Edition of the "Travaux Préparatoires" of the European Convention on Human Rights. Dordrecht: Martinus Nijhoff, 1985. 8 vols. [in English and French].

A comprehensive survey of the preparatory work in 1949–52 that led to adoption of the European Convention.

Council of Europe. Digest of Strasbourg Case-Law relating to the European Convention on Human Rights. Köln: Carl Heymanns, 1982. 6 vols.

Now dated, but a comprehensive selection of materials, including unreported decisions, organized and indexed by article.

Dijk, Pieter van and G.J.H. van Hoof. Theory and Practice of the European Convention on Human Rights. Deventer: Kluwer, 3d ed. 1998.

European Human Rights Reports. London: Sweet & Maxwell, 1979–.

Covers ECHR case law from 1979 to present day.

Gomien, Donna. Short Guide to the European Convention on Human Rights. Strasbourg: Council of Europe Publishing, 2002.

On-line version available free of charge at http://www.coe.int/T/E/ Human_rights/h-inf(2002)5eng.pdf.

Gomien, D., D.J. Harris and L. Zwaak. Law and Practice of the European Convention on Human Rights and the European Social Charter. Strasbourg: Council of Europe Publishing, 1997.

Harris, D.J., M. O'Boyle and C. Warbrick. Law of the European Convention on Human Rights. London: Butterworth, 2001.

Excellent survey of European jurisprudence, arranged both on an article-by-article basis and according to various procedural issues.

Janis, Mark W., Richard Kay and Anthony Bradley. European Human Rights Law: Text and Materials. New York: Oxford University Press, 2d ed. 2001.

JUSTICE. Putting Rights into Practice: the JUSTICE Series. Oxford: Hart Publishing. 2000–.

Series of books examining the impact of the UK Human Rights Act 1998, and the interaction between it and different areas of the law. Available from: http://www.justice.org.uk/reports/puttingrightsintopractice.html.

Kempes, Peter. A Systematic Guide to the Case Law of the European Court of Human Rights: 1960–2000. The Hague: Martinus Nijhoff, 2000, 3 vols.

Lambert-Abdelgawad, Elisabeth. The Execution of Judgments of the European Court of Human Rights. Strasbourg: Council of Europe Publ., 2002.

Lawson, R.A. & H.G. Schermers. Leading Cases of the European Court of Human Rights. Nijmegen: Ars Aequi Libri, 1999.

Leach, Philip. Taking a Case to the European Court of Human Rights. London: Blackstone Press, 2002.

Marguénaud, Jean-Pierre. La Cour Européenne des Droits de l'Homme. Paris: Dalloz, 2d ed. 2002.

Merrills, J.G. The Development of International Law by the European Court of Human Rights. Manchester: Manchester University Press, 2d ed. 1993.

Neuwahl, N. and Allan Rosas, eds. The European Union and Human Rights. The Hague, Kluwer Law International, 1995.

Ovey, Clare, Francis G. Jacobs and Robin C.A. White. The European Convention on Human Rights. Oxford: Oxford University Press, 3d ed. 2001.

Pettiti, Louis-Edmond, Emmanuel Decaux and Pierre-Henri Imbert. La Convention Européenne des Droits de L'Homme: commentaire article par article. Paris: Economica, 2d ed.1999.

Samuel, Lenia. Fundamental Social Rights: Case law of the European Social Charter. Strasbourg: Council of Europe Publishing, 2d ed. 2002.

> The Council of Europe also began in 1995 to publish a series of separate monographs on Social Charter issues, such as conditions of employment, migrant workers, women, and children. For a full list of social charter monographs, see http://book.coe.int/EN/ficheouvrage.php?PAGEID=39&lang=EN&theme_catalogue=100071.

Sudre, Frederic, Louis-Edmond Pettiti and Stefan Trechsel. L'interprétation de la Convention Européenne des Droits de L'Homme: actes du colloque des 13 et 14 mars 1998. Brussels: Bruylant, 1999.

The Hague, Oslo, and Lund Recommendations. The Hague: Foundation on Inter-Ethnic Relations, 1996–1999.

> Expert recommendations, adopted under the auspices of the High Commissioner on National Minorities, regarding the rights of national minorities with respect to education (The Hague); language (Oslo), and political participation (Lund). Also available in many OSCE languages at the High Commissioner's website, http://www.osce.org/hcnm/documents/recommendations.

Wallace, Rebecca M.M. Companion to the European Convention on Human Rights. London: Trenton Publishing, 2 vol, available through www.justis.com.

> Volume I contains commentaries on the Convention, and Volume II contains commentaries on cases.

The Americas

Official publications

Organization of American States (OAS) serial and occasional publications on human rights in the inter-American system carry the document designation OEA.Ser.L/V/II.—[number assigned in chronological order of publication in the series]. These and other OAS publications are available in English and Spanish (some also in French and Portuguese). The essential collection for the practitioner is *Basic Documents Pertaining to Human Rights in the Inter-American System*; the most recent edition is OEA/Ser. L.V./I.4 rev. 9 (2001), and subsequent amendments are available on the OAS website, http://www.oas.org.

The Inter-American Commission on Human Rights submits an annual report to the OAS General Assembly which includes the decisions it takes in individual cases, as well as summaries of the Commission's other work. Detailed reports on the human rights situations in various countries are issued by the Commission irregularly. Both the annual report and country reports are available directly from the Inter-American Commission on Human Rights at http://www.cidh.oas.org/publications.htm.

The Inter-American Court of Human Rights is based in San Jose, Costa Rica. It also submits an annual report to the OAS General Assembly, and its judgments and decisions are published in soft-cover as they are rendered: Series A includes advisory opinions and judgments; Series B includes written pleadings, oral arguments, and documents relative to Series A; Series C includes decisions and judgments in contentious cases; Series D includes written pleadings, oral arguments and documents related to Series C; and Series E includes provisional measures. (The Court's official site is www.corteidh.or.cr, and annual reports starting with 2002 and other Court documents may be found at http://www1.umn.edu/humanrts/iachr/iachr.html.)

Three Inter-American Yearbooks on Human Rights were published by the OAS covering, respectively, the years 1960–1967, 1968, and 1969–1970; the Inter-American Commission on Human Rights subsequently published *Ten Years of Activities 1971–1981*. Since 1985, annual *Yearbooks* have been published commercially by Martinus Nijhoff/Kluwer (Dordrecht, The Netherlands); see http://www.wkap.nl/prod/s/IAHR. The *Yearbooks* include general information, material on the work of the Court and of the Commission (much of which duplicates the material in the annual reports), and resolutions of the OAS General Assembly concerning human rights.

Secondary sources

Buergenthal, Thomas, and Robert Norris. Editors and Compilers. Human Rights in the Inter-American System. Dobbs Ferry: Oceana, 1982. 2 vols. Looseleaf.
    Obviously dated, but includes the travaux préparatoires of the American Convention on Human Rights and other documents.
Buergenthal, Thomas, and Dinah Shelton. Protecting Human Rights in the Americas. Kehl, Germany, and Arlington, VA: N.P. Engel, 4th ed. 1995.
Comisión Andina de Juristas. Informe Regional. Serial. Annual.
    Report on the situation of human rights in the Andean region. In Spanish with English executive summary.
Comisión Andina de Juristas. Protección de los Derechos Humanos, Definiciones Operativas. Lima: Comisión Andina de Juristas, 1997.
Davidson, Scott. The Inter-American Human Rights System. Aldershot: Dartmouth Publishing, 1997.
    A legal, textual analysis, organized by institution and subject-matter rather than following articles of the American Convention.
Harris, David and Stephen Livingston, eds. The Inter-American System of Human Rights. Oxford: Clarendon Press, 1998.
    An edited volume whose chapters address major issues within the inter-American system, such as reparations, amnesties, states of emergency, indigenous peoples, and the rights protected; political as well as legal in analysis.
Instituto Interamericano de Derechos Humanos. Bibliografía anotada sobre el Sistema Interamericano de protección de Derechos Humanos. San Jose, Costa Rica: Instituto Interamericano de Derechos Humanos, http://www.iidh.ed.cr/comunidades/herrped/Docs/PedagogicasEspecializado/10.htm.

Instituto Interamericano de Derechos Humanos. Revista IIDH. San Jose, Costa Rica: Instituto Interamericano de Derechos Humanos. Serial.

Inter-American Court of Human Rights. Systematization of the Contentious Jurisprudence of the Inter-American Court of Human Rights 1981–1991. San Jose, Costa Rica: IACHR, 1996.

Medina-Quiroga, Cecilia. The Battle of Human Rights: Gross, Systematic Violations and the Inter-American System. Dordrecht: Nijhoff, 1988.

Mendez, Juan E. and Francisco Cox, eds. El Futuro del Sistema Interamericano de Protección de los Derechos Humanos. San Jose: Instituto Interamericano de Derechos Humanos, 1998.

Mendez, Juan E. La Comisión Interamericana de Derechos Humanos. San José, Costa Rica: Instituto Interamericano de Derechos Humanos, 2002. Available on-line at http://www.iidh.ed.cr/comunidades/herrped/Docs/Pedagogicas Especializado/16.htm.

Pasqualucci, Jo. The Practice and Procedure of the Inter-American Court of Human Rights. Cambridge: Cambridge Univ. Press, 2004.

Robles, Manuel Ventura. Sistema Interamericano de Derechos Humanos: La Corte Interamericana de Derechos Humanos. San José, Costa Rica: Instituto Interamericano de Derechos Humanos, 2001. Available on-line at http://www.iidh.ed.cr/comunidades/herrped/Docs/PedagogicasEspecializado/21.pdf.

Wlasic, Juan Carlos, et al., eds. Convención Americana sobre Derechos Humanos: Anotada y Concordada con la Jurisprudencia de la Corte Interamericana de Derechos Humanos. Rosario: Editorial Juris, 1998.

Appendix B: Checklist to Help Select the Most Appropriate Forum

The following series of questions is designed to elicit the basic information needed in order to decide what courses of action would be most appropriate to redress a particular human rights violation, as outlined in chapter 2. Used in conjunction with the Model Communication in Appendix C, an individual or NGO should be able to make a preliminary assessment of what forums might be available to address the human rights concern; reference should then be made to the detailed substantive chapters in Parts II–IV.

I. In *which country* did the violations occur?
   A. Is it a *party to* any human rights or other relevant *treaties?*
      1. Global—International Covenants or other conventions concerning racial discrimination, discrimination against women, discrimination in education, apartheid, refugees, slavery, torture, children, migrant workers? International Labor Organization conventions?
         a. Has the country accepted the right of individual petition under CCPR, CERD, CAT, or CEDAW?
      2. Regional—Europe, the Americas, or Africa?
   B. Is it a country of *special interest to international bodies?*
      1. Israeli-occupied territories?
      2. A country being investigated by a special rapporteur of the UN Commission of Human Rights?
      3. Subject of a confidential investigation under ECOSOC Res. 1503?
      4. Subject of an on-going study by the Inter-American Commission on Human Rights?
   C. To which *international organizations* does the country belong?
      1. United Nations?
      2. UNESCO?
      3. International Labor Organization?
      4. regional organizations?

D. Even if a state has not ratified any relevant treaty, it may still be investigated under procedures such as ECOSOC Resolutions 1235 or 1503 for violations of rights set forth in the Universal Declaration of Human Rights or other widely accepted norms, such as prohibitions against torture, genocide, slavery, or discrimination. It also remains subject to mechanisms created by the ILO and UNESCO. All members of the Organization of American States fall within the jurisdiction of the Inter-American Commission on Human Rights.

II. *What rights* have been violated? Are they the subject of specialized conventions, agencies, or procedures?

A. Trade union rights or freedom of association? (ILO)

B. Cultural, educational, or social rights or scientific freedom? (UNESCO)

C. Racial discrimination? (Convention on Racial Discrimination)

D. Discrimination or violence against women? (Convention on Elimination of Discrimination against Women, Commission on Human Rights rapporteur)

E. Children's rights? (Convention on the Rights of the Child, Commission on Human Rights rapporteur)

F. Disappearance of the victim? (Commission on Human Rights working group)

G. Summary or arbitrary execution? (Commission on Human Rights rapporteur)

H. Arbitrary detention? (Commission on Human Rights working group)

I. Freedom of expression? (Commission on Human Rights rapporteur)

J. Torture? (Convention against Torture, European and inter-American conventions against torture, Commission on Human Rights rapporteur)

K. Religious discrimination? (Commission on Human Rights rapporteur)

L. Contemporary forms of slavery? (Sub-Commission working group)

M. Indigenous rights? (ILO, Sub-Commission working group, Permanent Forum on Indigenous Issues)

N. Minority rights? (Sub-Commission working group, European Framework Convention on Minorities)

O. Rights to asylum or refugee status? (UN High Commissioner for Refugees)

III. Is the complainant a victim of an *individual violation* or of a widespread *pattern of violations*?

A. If an *individual* violation, who is complaining?
  1. Victim himself or herself?
  2. Relative or legal representative?
  3. Non-governmental organization or person unconnected to the victim?
     a. If not connected to the victim, what is the basis for the complaint on his or her behalf?
     b. Does the NGO have direct and/or reliable knowledge of the alleged violations?
  4. Does the chosen procedure permit individual as opposed to general complaints?
B. If there are *widespread* violations, there may be no requirement to exhaust domestic remedies (see below), but communications also are less likely to lead to an adversarial procedure in which the complainant can participate equally with the government concerned. Among the available procedures are:
  1. ECOSOC Resolution 1503 ("consistent pattern of gross violations")
  2. UN procedures, such as the country rapporteurs of the Commission on Human Rights; the working groups on slavery, indigenous peoples, and minorities of the Sub-Commission on the Promotion and Protection of Human Rights
  3. Relevant ILO conventions (available only to recognized employers' or employees' groups)
  4. Treaty-body supervision of periodic country reports which are required to be submitted under various conventions
  5. Communications raising the general issue of human rights in a particular country under the procedures of the Inter-American Commission on Human Rights or regarding a "series of serious or massive violations" under the African Charter on Human and Peoples' Rights
  6. Confidential investigations by the Committee against Torture or Committee on the Elimination of All Forms of Discrimination against Women under their respective treaties
IV. What steps have been taken to obtain *redress at the domestic* (national) *level?*
A. Are there effective administrative or judicial procedures available?
  1. If so, have they been fully exhausted? If not, explain why they are either ineffective or inadequate.
  2. Individual complaint procedures *do* generally require exhaustion.
B. Those procedures which address country situations involving large-scale violations, as well as noncomplaint procedures such

as UN rapporteurs or working groups, do *not* generally require prior exhaustion of domestic remedies.

V. What *remedy* is sought?
   A. Publicity only?
      1. Is there any reason to assume that the media will be particularly interested in the case, such as the visit of a head of state, a pending decision on economic assistance, or examination by an oversight body of a state's periodic report on the situation of human rights in the country?
   B. Fact-finding and investigation to obtain further information?
   C. Changes in national legislation?
   D. Individual remedies?
      1. Urgent action—e.g., stay of execution or deportation, protection from torture, release from detention?
      2. Specific redress—e.g., compensation, restitution of property, granting of exit permit or visa, change in civil status?
   E. Even confidential procedures may create diplomatic pressure on a responsive government, and they may have a greater chance of resolving individual cases than more public procedures. In the case of widespread violations, however, maximum publicity may be more important than the quiet or partial resolution of only a few individual cases.
VI. Can *more than one procedure* be utilized at the same time? Can the same situation be treated both as an individual complaint and cited as an example of a pattern or practice of violations?
VII. What *resources* are available to the complainant?
   A. Are the procedures so complex or the violations so massive that the assistance of a lawyer, NGO, or even a government is essential?
   B. What actual costs (research, photocopying, travel, translation fees, etc.) are involved?
   C. What political (in a broad sense) resources are available—e.g., help from a friendly government, sympathetic trade union, church group, domestic political groups, journalists, parallel interest groups?

Appendix C: Model Communication

Each procedure discussed in the present book should be examined carefully to ensure that a communication or complaint meets the technical and substantive requirements imposed by that particular system. Two bodies—UNESCO and the European Court of Human Rights—require that applicants use a form that each provides upon request. For communications to the Human Rights Committee, Committee against Torture, Committee on the Elimination of All Forms of Racial Discrimination, or Committee on the Elimination of All Forms of Discrimination against Women, a sample form for complaints is available, but its use is not required. No special forms have been developed for other procedures.

The following composite or sample form can be utilized as a model for any of the procedures discussed in this book, with the caveat that careful attention must be paid to the specific scope of each. For example, some procedures permit any person or NGO to raise questions of human rights violations; others permit only the alleged victim or a direct representative to file a complaint. The requirement to exhaust domestic remedies is common to nearly every procedure, but its interpretation varies considerably.

This form should be used in conjunction with the Checklist in Appendix B, which will help identify the proper forum for complaints or communications.

I. *Name of the country* considered responsible for the alleged violation

_____

II. *Information concerning the alleged victim(s) of the violations*
    Name (in full) _____
    Nationality _____
    Date and place of birth _____
    Occupation _____
    Present address _____

_____

Address to be used in correspondence (if different from the above)

_____

_____

[If known, other means of identification such as passport or other identification number should also be included.]

III. If the author of the communication is *not* the same person as the victim described in II, *the same information should also be provided for the author*
Name (in full) _____
Nationality _____
Date and place of birth _____
Occupation _____
Present address _____

Address to be used in correspondence (if different from the above)

_____

_____

Relationship (in any) to the alleged victim _____
[Any supporting documents which establish a relationship between the victim and the author should be included, e.g., birth certificate, power of attorney, personal letter authorizing the representative to work on the victim's behalf, etc.

If the author is a nongovernmental organization, a *brief* description of the organization should be included along with an explanation of why the NGO is submitting the communication.]

IV. *Human rights allegedly violated*
[Particularly if the communication/complaint is based on a specific international instrument, a summary listing of the specific articles relevant to the violations is often helpful. If there is no relevant convention or treaty to which the state is a party, reference can be made to the Universal Declaration of Human Rights, the two International Covenants, or (in the Americas) the American Declaration of the Rights and Duties of Man.

If the procedure is specialized, e.g., UNESCO or ILO, this section should point out the connection between the alleged violation and the specific areas of interest and competence of the body to which the communication is addressed.]

V. *Statement of the facts*
[If the complaint concerns an *individual* or group of individuals who is a victim of a specific violation, a detailed chronological narrative of the incidents that violated the victim's rights should be set forth. As much specific information as possible should be included,

such as the date, time, and place of the incident(s); name, rank, or description of the government official(s) responsible; authority under which the acts took place (laws, regulations, emergency decrees, etc.); place of detention; and the names and addresses of witnesses or others with special knowledge of the events.

[If the communication concerns a *widespread practice* of human rights, a brief historical summary of the situation in the country might be included as an introduction, although overtly political or ideological observations should be avoided. If many rights have been violated (as opposed to a single right or rights, such as the right to form trade unions or freedom of expression), it may be a good idea to include a separate narrative for each right (which will already have been mentioned in part IV). Again, the information should be as specific as possible and should refer to the laws or regulations involved; the dates, times, and places of specific incidents; the names of both victims and witnesses; and the reasons for holding the government responsible, if it is not obvious that government officials were involved.

[In either case, the source(s) of the information should be given, and documentation should be included as annexes to the communication itself. Such documentation might include affidavits from victims and witnesses, texts of laws and regulations, medical reports, press reports, findings or reports of NGOs, and any other information that supports the allegations. It is best *not* to include general political analyses or large quantities of material, unless this is directly relevant to the alleged violations (e.g., the texts of seized documents might be included to demonstrate that they were within the limits of normal political activity and not subversive or a threat to state security).]

VI. *Means of redress attempted*

Domestic: [Any steps taken to obtain redress from domestic authorities should be described in detail, including formal or informal complaints or reports made to the police or other government officials; administrative appeals; requests for information about a detainee and any response from the authorities; and judicial remedies, including details as to any actions commenced, type of writ filed (e.g., *habeas corpus, amparo*), dates and texts of any decisions reached, and the results of any appeal.

[If no domestic remedies have been attempted or remedies have been only partially exhausted, explain why there are no adequate or effective remedies. This may be due to many factors, e.g., nonexistence of remedies to challenge the law or regulation which authorized the acts complained of, existence of a pattern of acts which indicates that any attempt at remedies would be useless, long delays in any remedies theoretically available, lack of independence of the judiciary, failure of similar attempts in the past, fear of reprisals, etc.]

International: [Has this complaint or communication been submitted to any other international body for investigation? If so, what is the status of that communication?]

VII. *Purpose of the communication*

[If appropriate, a specific request or prayer for relief may be included, e.g., permission for access to a detainee by a relative, lawyer, or doctor; release from detention; return of seized materials; investigation by an international body; a declaration that international human rights norms have been violated and a request that a practice be halted or a law or regulation repealed; or a request for appropriate compensation for the victim.]

VIII. *Confidentiality of the communication*

[The author should state whether he or she wishes any part of the communication to remain confidential, such as the identify of the author, victim, or witnesses. Some procedures, e.g., UNESCO Decision 104 EX/3.3, require that the author's name be divulged to the government concerned.]

IV. *Signature and date*

[If someone other than the victim is submitting the complaint, the representative identified in part III should sign the communication.]

Appendix D: Addresses of Intergovernmental Organizations

Telephone and fax numbers change frequently, as do the exact addresses of Websites. The following information was accurate as of March 2004.

United Nations Office of the High Commissioner for Human Rights

Office of the High Commissioner for Human Rights
c/o OHCHR-UNOG
CH-1211 Geneva 10
SWITZERLAND
tel.: + 41 (22) 917-9000; fax: (41) (22) 733-9879
Home page: http://www.unhchr.ch/hchr_un.htm

Urgent action cases should identified as such and be emailed or faxed to one of the numbers below.

All communications under any UN procedure should be sent to the above address. It also may be used to send information to members of the Commission on Human Rights and Sub-Commission on the Promotion and Protection of Human Rights. However, *the envelope and the communications themselves should clearly identify the mechanism to which they are addressed.* A communication to one of the treaty bodies should specify whether it is an individual complaint or whether the author is providing information to committee members regarding their examination of a report from a state party.

In addition, separate contact points have been created for the following mechanisms:

Individual petitions to treaty bodies (Human Rights Committee, CAT, CERD, CEDAW)
email: tb-petitions@ohchr.org
fax: + 41 (22) 917-9022

1503 communications to the Commission on Human Rights:
email: 1503@ohchr.org
fax: + 41 (22) 917-9011

Thematic rapporteurs or working groups on extrajudicial, summary, or arbitrary executions; violence against women; arbitrary detention; disappearances; sale of children, child prostitution, and child pornography; and human rights defenders
fax: + 41 (22) 917-9006

Thematic rapporteur on freedom of opinion and expression
fax: + 41 (22) 917-9003

Urgent action messages to any mechanism not mentioned above
email: urgent-action@ohchr.org
fax: + 41 (22) 917-9006

New York Office of the High Commissioner for Human Rights

United Nations
Room S-2914
New York, NY 10017
USA
tel.: (1) (917) 367-8005; fax: (1) (212) 963-4097
UN human rights home page: http://un.org/rights

This is a much smaller office than the one in Geneva and may be contacted for informal information or in urgent cases; individual petitions or other formal communications to the United Nations concerning human rights should be directed to Geneva.

United Nations Division for the Advancement of Women

Department of Economic and Social Affairs
2 UN Plaza, DC-2, 12th Floor
New York, NY 10017
USA
fax: + 1 (212) 963-3463
e-mail address: daw@un.org
Home page: http://www.un.org/womenwatch/daw

This address should be used for all correspondence concerning the Convention on the Elimination of All Forms of Discrimination against Women and the UN Commission on the Status of Women. Faxes also may be sent to Geneva (+ 41 (22) 917-9022), but the New York address is preferable.

United Nations High Commissioner for Refugees

Case Postale 2500
CH-1211 Geneva 2 Dépôt
SWITZERLAND
tel.: + 41 (22) 739-8111
Home page: http://www.unhcr.ch

E-mail contact with UNHCR and its national offices may be made
through links provided on the Website. A list of UNHCR national offices
can be obtained from the Public Information Office at the above address
or, for those in North America, from:
Washington Office of the UNHCR
1775 K Street, N.W., Suite 300
Washington, DC 20006
USA
tel.: + 1 (202) 296-5191; fax: + 1 (202) 296-5660
e-mail: usawa@unhcr.ch

International Labor Organization

Director-General
International Labour Office
c/o International Labour Standards and Human Rights Department
4, route des Morillons
CH-1211 Geneva 22
SWITZERLAND
tel.: + 41 (22) 799-6111; fax: + 41 (22) 798-8685
e-mail: ilo@ilo.org
Human rights home page: http://www.ilo.org/public/english/stan-
dards/index.htm
For complaints, representations, and all other communications. Contact
information for specific ILO offices may be found at http://www.ilo.org/
public/english/depts/dir_gva.htm

United Nations Educational, Scientific and Cultural Organization (UNESCO)

UN Educational, Scientific and Cultural Organization
Director of the Office of International Standards and Legal Affairs
7, place de Fontenoy
F-75352 Paris 07 SP
FRANCE
tel.: + 33 (1) 45-68-10-00; fax: + 33 (1) 45-68-55-75

Human rights home page: http://portal.unesco.org/shs/en/ev.php@ URL_ID=1827&URL_DO=DO_TOPIC&URL_SECTION=201.html Information regarding communications under UNESCO procedure 104 EX/3.3 is found under Legal Instruments, http://portal.unesco.org/en/ ev.php@URL_ID=15243&URL_DO=DO_TOPIC&URL_SEC-TION=201.html; for additional information via email, contact sec.cr@ unesco.org.

United Nations Centre for International Crime Prevention

United Nations Office for Drug Control and Crime Prevention
P.O. Box 500
A-1400 Vienna
AUSTRIA
tel: + 43 (1) 26060-4269; fax + 43 (1) 26060-5898
Home page: http://www.uncjin.org/CICP/cicp.html
The UN Crime and Justice Information Network website is http://www. unodc.org/unodc/uncjin.html.
For information and texts on international criminal justice norms, including materials of the Commission on Crime Prevention and Criminal Justice.

Council of Europe

Avenue de l'Europe
F-67075 Strasbourg Cedex
FRANCE
tel.: + 33 (0388) 412000 or 412033; fax: + 33 (388) 412745
e-mail: infopoint@coe.fr
Human rights home page: http://www.coe.int/T/E/Human_rights

The European Court of Human Rights may be contacted at the same address. Its home page, which includes an application form in approximately thirty languages, is http://www.echr.coe.int; email is webmaster@ echr.coe.int.

A list of e-mail contacts for, e.g., the European Commissioner for Human Rights, Framework Convention on National Minorities institutions, and European Committee for the Prevention of Torture and Inhuman or Degrading Treatment or Punishment, may be found at http://www.coe. int/t/e/general/contact.asp.

Organization for Security and Cooperation in Europe

The political organs of the OSCE have no formal mechanism under which they can be approached by NGOs or individuals. However, the High Commissioner on National Minorities and the Representative on Freedom of the Media may be sent information directly.

OSCE Secretariat
Kärntner Ring 5-7
A-1010 Vienna
AUSTRIA
tel.: (43) (1) 514-36-180; fax: (43) (1) 514-36-105
e-mail: info @osce.org

OSCE home page: http://www.osce.org
e-mail for specific document requests: docs@osce.org
Office of Democratic Institutions and Human Rights (ODIHR)
Aleje Ujazdowskie 19
PL-00 557 Warsaw
POLAND
tel.: (48) (22) 520-0600; fax: (48) (22) 520-0605
e-mail: office@odihr.pl

Office of the High Commissioner on National Minorities
P.O. Box 20062
NL 2500-FB The Hague
THE NETHERLANDS
tel.: (31) (70) 312-5500; fax: (31) (70) 363-5910
e-mail: hcnm@osce.org
Home page: http://www.osce.org/hcnm

OSCE Representative on Freedom of the Media
Kärtner Ring 5-7, Top 14, 2.DG
1010 Vienna
AUSTRIA
tel.: (43) (1) 512-21450; fax: (43) (1) 512-21459
e-mail: pm-fom@osce.org
Home page: http://www.osce.org/fom

Inter-American Commission on Human Rights

Inter-American Commission on Human Rights
1889 F Street, NW
Washington, DC 20006
USA
tel.: + 1 (202) 458-6000; fax: + 1 (202) 458-3992
e-mail: cidhoea@oas.org
Home page: http://www.cidh.oas.org/DefaultE.htm

For all communications under the American Declaration on the Rights and Duties of Man or the American Convention on Human Rights, as well as country-specific information related to Commission reports. Instructions for filing communications may be found at http://www.cidh.oas.org/denuncia.eng.htm.

Inter-American Court of Human Rights

Apartado Postal 6906-1000
San José
COSTA RICA
tel.: + 506 234 0581 Fax: + 506 234 0584
COSTA RICA
e-mail: corteidh@corteidh.or.cr
Home page: http://www.corteidh.or.cr/index-ingles.html (English)
For information and documentation only.

African Commission on Human Rights

P.O. Box 673
Kairaba Avenue
Banjul
THE GAMBIA
tel.: + 220 392 962; fax: + 220 390 764
e-mail: achpr@achpr.org
Home page: http://www.achpr.org/

Appendix E: Ratifications of Selected Human Rights Instruments

(as of November 2003, unless Otherwise Indicated)

International Covenant on Civil and Political Rights:

Afghanistan, Albania, Algeria (a), Andorra (ab), Angola (a), Argentina (a), Armenia (a), Australia (ab), Austria (ab), Azerbaijan (ab), Bangladesh, Barbados (a), Belarus (a), Belgium (ab), Belize, Benin (a), Bolivia (a), Bosnia and Herzegovina (ab), Botswana, Brazil, Bulgaria (ab), Burkina Faso (a), Burundi, Cambodia, Cameroon (a), Canada (a), Cape Verde (ab), Central African Republic (a), Chad (a), Chile (a), Colombia (ab), Congo (a), Costa Rica (ab), Côte d'Ivoire (a), Croatia (ab), Cyprus (ab), Czech Republic (a), Democratic Republic of the Congo (a), Denmark (ab), Djibouti (ab), Dominica, Dominican Republic (a), Ecuador (ab), Egypt, El Salvador (a), Equatorial Guinea (a), Eritrea, Estonia (a), Ethiopia, Finland (ab), France (a), Gabon, Gambia (a), Georgia (ab), Germany (ab), Ghana (a), Greece (ab), Grenada, Guatemala (a), Guinea (a), Guyana (a), Haiti, Honduras, Hungary (ab), Iceland (ab), India, Iran, Iraq, Ireland (ab), Israel, Italy (ab), Jamaica, Japan, Jordan, Kenya, Kuwait, Kyrgyzstan (a), Latvia (a), Lebanon, Lesotho (a), Libya (a), Liechtenstein (ab), Lithuania (ab), Luxembourg (ab), Madagascar (a), Malawi (a), Mali (a), Malta (ab), Mauritius (a), Mexico (a), Moldova, Monaco (b), Mongolia (a), Morocco, Mozambique (b), Namibia (ab), Nepal (ab), Netherlands (ab), New Zealand (ab), Nicaragua (a), Niger (a), Nigeria, Norway (ab), Panama (ab), Paraguay (a), Peru (a), Philippines (a), Poland (a), Portugal (ab), Republic of Korea (a), Romania (ab), Russia (a), Rwanda, Saint Vincent and the Grenadines (a), San Marino (a), Senegal (a), Serbia and Montenegro (ab), Seychelles (ab), Sierra Leone (a), Slovakia (ab), Slovenia (ab), Somalia (a), South Africa (ab), Spain (ab), Sri Lanka (a), Sudan, Suriname (a), Sweden (ab), Switzerland (b), Syria, Tajikistan (a), Tanzania, Thailand, The Former Yugoslav Republic of Macedonia (ab), Timor-Leste, Togo, Trinidad and Tobago (a), Tunisia, Turkey, Turkmenistan (ab), Uganda (a), Ukraine (a), United Kingdom, United

341

States, Uruguay (ab), Uzbekistan (a), Venezuela (ab), Viet Nam, Yemen, Zambia (a), Zimbabwe

(a) Has ratified the Optional Protocol permitting individual complaints

(b) Has ratified the Second Optional Protocol (abolishing the death penalty)

International Covenant on Economic, Social and Cultural Rights:

Afghanistan, Albania, Algeria, Angola, Argentina, Armenia, Australia, Austria, Azerbaijan, Bangladesh, Barbados, Belarus, Belgium, Belize, Benin, Bolivia, Bosnia and Herzegovina, Brazil, Bulgaria, Burkina Faso, Burundi, Cambodia, Cameroon, Canada, Cape Verde, Central African Republic, Chad, Chile, China, Colombia, Congo, Costa Rica, Côte d'Ivoire, Croatia, Cyprus, Czech Republic, Democratic People's Republic of Korea, Democratic Republic of the Congo, Denmark, Djibouti, Dominica, Dominican Republic, Ecuador, Egypt, El Salvador, Equatorial Guinea, Eritrea, Estonia, Ethiopia, Finland, France, Gabon, Gambia, Georgia, Germany, Ghana, Greece, Grenada, Guatemala, Guinea, Guinea-Bissau, Guyana, Honduras, Hungary, Iceland, India, Iran, Iraq, Ireland, Israel, Italy, Jamaica, Japan, Jordan, Kenya, Kuwait, Kyrgyzstan, Laos, Latvia, Lebanon, Lesotho, Liechtenstein, Libya, Lithuania, Luxembourg, Madagascar, Malawi, Mali, Malta, Mauritius, Mexico, Moldova, Monaco, Mongolia, Morocco, Namibia, Nepal, Netherlands, New Zealand, Nicaragua, Niger, Nigeria, Norway, Panama, Paraguay, Peru, Philippines, Poland, Portugal, Republic of Korea, Romania, Russia, Rwanda, Saint Vincent and the Grenadines, San Marino, Senegal, Serbia and Montenegro, Seychelles, Sierra Leone, Slovakia, Slovenia, Solomon Islands, Somalia, Spain, Sri Lanka, Sudan, Suriname, Sweden, Switzerland, Syria, Tajikistan, Tanzania, Thailand, The Former Yugoslav Republic of Macedonia, Timor-Leste, Togo, Trinidad and Tobago, Tunisia, Turkmenistan, Turkey, Uganda, Ukraine, United Kingdom, Uruguay, Uzbekistan, Venezuela, Viet Nam, Yemen, Zambia, Zimbabwe

International Convention on the Elimination of All Forms of Racial Discrimination:

Afghanistan, Albania, Algeria (a), Antigua and Barbuda, Argentina, Armenia, Australia (a), Austria (a), Azerbaijan, Bahamas, Bahrain, Bangladesh, Barbados, Belarus (a), Belgium, Belize, Benin, Bolivia, Bosnia and Herzegovina, Botswana, Brazil (a), Bulgaria (a), Burkina Faso, Burundi, Cambodia, Cameroon, Canada, Cape Verde, Central African Republic, Chad, Chile (a), China, Colombia, Congo, Costa Rica (a), Côte d'Ivoire, Croatia, Cuba, Cyprus (a), Czech Republic, Democratic Republic of the Congo, Denmark (a), Dominican Republic, Ecuador (a), Egypt, El Salvador, Equatorial Guinea, Estonia, Eritrea, Ethiopia, Fiji, Finland (a), France, Gabon, Gambia, Georgia, Germany (a), Ghana, Greece, Guatemala, Guinea, Guyana, Haiti, Honduras, Holy See, Hungary (a), Iceland (a), India, Indonesia, Iran, Iraq, Ireland (a), Israel, Italy (a), Jamaica, Japan, Jordan, Kazakhstan, Kenya, Kuwait, Kyrgyzstan, Laos, Latvia, Lebanon, Lesotho, Liberia, Libya, Liechtenstein, Lithuania, Luxembourg (a), Madagascar, Malawi, Maldives, Mali, Malta (a), Mauritania, Mauritius, Mexico, Moldova, Monaco, Mongolia, Morocco, Mozambique, Namibia, Nepal, Netherlands (a), New Zealand, Nicaragua, Niger, Nigeria, Norway (a), Oman, Pakistan, Panama, Papua New Guinea, Peru (a), Philippines, Poland (a), Portugal, Qatar, Republic of Korea (a), Romania, Russia (a), Rwanda, Saint Lucia, Saint Vincent and the Grenadines, San Marino, Saudi Arabia, Senegal (a), Serbia and Montenegro, Seychelles, Sierra Leone, Slovakia (a), Slovenia, Solomon Islands, Somalia, South Africa (a), Spain (a), Sri Lanka, Sudan, Suriname, Swaziland, Sweden (a), Switzerland, Syria, Tajikistan, Tanzania, Thailand, The Former Yugoslav Republic of Macedonia, Timor-Leste, Togo, Tonga, Trinidad and Tobago, Tunisia, Turkmenistan, Turkey, Uganda, Ukraine (a), United Arab Emirates, United Kingdom, United States, Uruguay (a), Uzbekistan, Venezuela, Viet Nam, Yemen, Zambia, Zimbabwe

(a) Has recognized the right of the Committee to receive individual complaints under Article 14.

Convention on the Elimination of All Forms of Discrimination against Women:

Afghanistan, Albania (a), Algeria, Andorra (a), Angola, Antigua and Barbuda, Argentina (a), Armenia, Australia, Austria (a), Azerbaijan (a), Bahamas, Bahrain, Bangladesh (a), Barbados, Belarus, Belgium (a), Belize (a), Benin (a), Bhutan, Bolivia (a), Bosnia and Herzegovina (a), Botswana, Brazil (a), Bulgaria (a), Burkina Faso (a), Burundi (a), Cambodia (a), Cameroon, Canada (a), Cape Verde, Central African Republic, Chad, Chile (a), China, Colombia (a), Comoros, Congo, Costa Rica (a), Côte d'Ivoire, Croatia (a), Cuba, Cyprus (a), Czech Republic (a), Democratic Republic of the Congo, Democratic Republic of Korea, Denmark (a), Djibouti, Dominica, Dominican Republic (a), Ecuador (a), Egypt, El Salvador, Equatorial Guinea, Eritrea, Estonia, Ethiopia, Fiji, Finland (a), France (a), Gabon, Gambia, Georgia (a), Germany (a), Ghana, Greece (a), Grenada, Guatemala (a), Guinea, Guinea-Bissau, Guyana, Haiti, Honduras, Hungary (a), Iceland (a), India, Indonesia, Iraq, Ireland (a), Israel, Italy (a), Jamaica, Japan, Jordan, Kazakhstan (a), Kenya, Kuwait, Kyrgyzstan (a), Laos, Latvia, Lebanon, Lesotho, Liberia, Libya, Liechtenstein (a), Lithuania, Luxembourg (a), Madagascar, Malawi, Malaysia, Maldives, Mali (a), Malta, Mauritania, Mauritius, Mexico (a), Moldova, Mongolia (a), Morocco, Mozambique, Myanmar, Namibia (a), Nepal, Netherlands (a), New Zealand (a), Nicaragua, Niger, Nigeria, Norway (a), Pakistan, Panama (a), Papua New Guinea, Paraguay (a), Peru (a), Philippines, Poland, Portugal (a), Republic of Korea, Romania, Russia, Rwanda, Saint Kitts and Nevis, Saint Lucia, Saint Vincent and the Grenadines, Samoa, Sao Tome and Principe, Saudi Arabia, Senegal (a), Serbia and Montenegro, Seychelles, Sierra Leone, Singapore, Slovakia (a), Slovenia, Solomon Islands (a), South Africa, Spain (a), Sri Lanka (a), Suriname, Sweden (a), Switzerland, Syria, Tajikistan, Tanzania, Thailand (a), The Former Yugoslav Republic of Macedonia, Timor-Leste (a), Togo, Trinidad and Tobago, Tunisia, Turkey (a), Turkmenistan, Tuvalu, Uganda, Ukraine, United Kingdom, Uruguay (a), Uzbekistan, Vanuatu, Venezuela (a), Viet Nam, Yemen, Zambia, Zimbabwe

(a) Has ratified the Optional Protocol permitting individual complaints.

Convention against Torture and Other Cruel, Inhuman or Degrading Treatment or Punishment:

Afghanistan, Albania, Algeria (a), Antigua and Barbuda, Argentina (a), Armenia, Australia (a), Austria (a), Azerbaijan, Bahrain, Belarus, Belgium (a), Belize, Benin, Bolivia, Bosnia and Herzegovina, Botswana, Brazil, Bulgaria (a), Burkina Faso, Burundi, Cambodia, Cameroon, Canada (a), Cape Verde, Chad, Chile, China, Colombia, Costa Rica (a), Côte d'Ivoire, Croatia, Cuba, Cyprus (a), Czech Republic, Democratic Republic of the Congo, Denmark (a), Djibouti, Ecuador (a), Egypt, El Salvador, Equatorial Guinea, Estonia, Ethiopia, Finland (a), France (a), Gabon, Georgia, Germany (a), Ghana, Greece (a), Guatemala, Guinea, Guyana, Holy See, Honduras, Hungary (a), Iceland (a), Indonesia, Ireland (a), Israel, Italy (a), Japan, Jordan, Kazakhstan, Kenya, Kuwait, Kyrgyzstan, Latvia, Lebanon, Lesotho, Libya, Liechtenstein (a), Lithuania, Luxembourg (a), Malawi, Mali, Malta (a), Mauritius, Mexico (a), Moldova, Monaco (a), Mongolia, Morocco, Mozambique, Namibia, Nepal, Netherlands (a), New Zealand (a), Nigeria, Norway (a), Panama, Paraguay (a), Peru (a), Philippines, Poland (a), Portugal (a), Qatar, Republic of Korea, Romania, Russia (a), Saint Vincent and the Grenadines, Saudi Arabia, Senegal (a), Serbia and Montenegro, Seychelles, Slovakia (a), Slovenia (a), Sierra Leone, Somalia, South Africa (a), Spain (a), Sri Lanka, Sweden (a), Switzerland (a), Tajikistan, The

Former Yugoslav Republic of Macedonia, Timor-Leste, Togo (a), Tunisia (a), Turkey (a), Turkmenistan, Uganda, Ukraine, United Kingdom (a), United States (a), Uruguay (a), Uzbekistan, Venezuela (a), Yemen

(a) Has accepted the competence of the Committee to consider individual communications under Article 22.

Convention on the Rights of the Child:

Afghanistan, Albania, Algeria, Andorra, Angola, Antigua and Barbuda, Argentina, Armenia, Australia, Austria, Azerbaijan, Bahamas, Bahrain, Bangladesh, Barbados, Belarus, Belgium, Belize, Benin, Bhutan, Bolivia, Bosnia and Herzegovina, Botswana, Brazil, Brunei, Bulgaria, Burkina Faso, Burundi, Cambodia, Cameroon, Canada, Cape Verde, Central African Republic, Chad, Chile, China, Colombia, Comoros, Congo, Cook Islands, Costa Rica, Côte d'Ivoire, Croatia, Cuba, Cyprus, Czech Republic, Democratic People's Republic of Korea, Democratic Republic of the Congo, Denmark, Djibouti, Dominica, Dominican Republic, Ecuador, Egypt, El Salvador, Equatorial Guinea, Eritrea, Estonia, Ethiopia, Fiji, Finland, France, Gabon, Gambia, Georgia, Germany, Ghana, Greece, Grenada, Guatemala, Guinea, Guinea-Bissau, Guyana, Haiti, Holy See, Honduras, Hungary, Iceland, India, Indonesia, Iran, Iraq, Ireland, Israel, Italy, Jamaica, Japan, Jordan, Kazakhstan, Kenya, Kiribati, Kuwait, Kyrgyzstan, Laos, Latvia, Lebanon, Lesotho, Liberia, Libya, Liechtenstein, Lithuania, Luxembourg, Madagascar, Malawi, Malaysia, Maldives, Mali, Malta, Marshall Islands, Mauritania, Mauritius, Mexico, Micronesia, Moldova, Monaco, Mongolia, Morocco, Mozambique, Myanmar, Namibia, Nauru, Nepal, Netherlands, New Zealand, Nicaragua, Niger, Nigeria, Niue, Norway, Oman, Pakistan, Palau, Panama, Papua New Guinea, Paraguay, Peru, Philippines, Poland, Portugal, Qatar, Republic of Korea, Romania, Russia, Rwanda, Saint Kitts and Nevis, Saint Lucia, Saint Vincent and the Grenadines, Samoa, San Marino, Sao Tome and Principe, Saudi Arabia, Senegal, Serbia and Montenegro, Seychelles, Sierra Leone, Singapore, Slovakia, Slovenia, Solomon Islands, South Africa, Spain, Sri Lanka, Sudan, Suriname, Swaziland, Sweden, Switzerland, Syria, Tajikistan, Tanzania, Thailand, The Former Yugoslav Republic of Macedonia, Timor-Leste, Togo, Tonga, Trinidad and Tobago, Tunisia, Turkey, Turkmenistan, Tuvalu, Uganda, Ukraine, United Arab Emirates, United Kingdom, Uruguay, Uzbekistan, Vanuatu, Venezuela, Viet Nam, Yemen, Zambia, Zimbabwe

International Convention on the Protection of the Rights of All Migrant Workers and Members of Their Families:

Azerbaijan, Belize, Bolivia, Bosnia and Herzegovina, Cape Verde, Colombia, Ecuador, Egypt, El Salvador, Ghana, Guatemala, Guinea, Kyrgyzstan, Mali, Mexico, Morocco, Senegal, Seychelles, Sri Lanka, Tajikistan, Uganda, Uruguay

Convention and Protocol Relating to the Status of Refugees:

Albania, Algeria, Angola, Antigua and Barbuda, Argentina, Armenia, Australia, Austria, Azerbaijan, Bahamas, Belarus, Belgium, Belize, Benin, Bolivia, Bosnia and Herzegovina, Botswana, Brazil, Bulgaria, Burkina Faso, Burundi, Cambodia, Cameroon, Canada, Cape Verde (b), Central African Republic, Chad, Chile, China, Colombia, Costa Rica, Côte d'Ivoire, Croatia, Cyprus, Czech Republic, Democratic Republic of the Congo, Denmark, Djibouti, Dominica, Dominican Republic, Ecuador, Egypt, El Salvador, Equatorial Guinea, Estonia, Ethiopia, Fiji, Finland, France, Gabon, Gambia, Georgia, Germany, Ghana, Greece, Guatemala, Guinea, Guinea-Bissau, Haiti, Holy See, Honduras, Hungary, Iceland, Iran, Ireland, Israel, Italy, Jamaica, Japan, Kazakhstan, Kenya, Kyrgyzstan, Latvia, Lesotho, Liberia, Liechtenstein, Lithuania, Luxembourg, Madagascar (a), Malawi, Mali, Malta, Mauritania, Mexico, Moldova, Monaco (a), Morocco, Mozambique, Namibia (a), Netherlands, New Zealand, Nicaragua, Niger, Nigeria, Norway, Panama, Papua New Guinea, Paraguay, Peru, Philippines, Poland, Portugal, Republic of Korea, Romania, Russia, Rwanda, Saint Kitts and Nevis (a), Saint Vincent and the Grenadines, Samoa, Sao Tome and Principe, Senegal, Serbia and Montenegro, Seychelles, Sierra Leone, Slovakia, Slovenia, Solomon Islands, Somalia, South Africa, Spain, Sudan, Suriname, South Africa, Sweden, Switzerland, Tajikistan, The Former Yugoslav Republic of Macedonia, Timor-Leste, Tanzania, Togo, Trinidad and Tobago, Tunisia, Turkey, Turkmenistan, Tuvalu, Uganda, Ukraine, United Kingdom, United States (b), Uruguay, Venezuela (b), Yemen (a), Zambia, Zimbabwe
    (a) Convention only.
    (b) Protocol only.

Convention for the Suppression of the Traffic in Persons and of the Exploitation of the Prostitution of Others (as of February 2002):

Afghanistan, Albania, Algeria, Argentina, Azerbaijan, Bangladesh, Belarus, Belgium, Bolivia, Bosnia and Herzegovina, Brazil, Bulgaria, Burkina Faso, Cameroon, Central African Republic, Congo, Côte d'Ivoire, Croatia,

Cuba, Cyprus, Czech Republic, Djibouti, Ecuador, Egypt, Ethiopia, Finland, France, Guinea, Haiti, Honduras, Hungary, India, Iraq, Israel, Italy, Japan, Jordan, Kuwait, Kyrgyzstan, Laos, Latvia, Libya, Luxembourg, Malawi, Mali, Mauritania, Mexico, Morocco, Niger, Norway, Pakistan, Philippines, Poland, Portugal, Republic of Korea, Romania, Russia, Senegal, Serbia and Montenegro, Seychelles, Singapore, South Africa, Spain, Sri Lanka, Syria, Tajikistan, The Former Yugoslav Republic of Macedonia, Togo, Ukraine, Venezuela, Yemen, Zimbabwe

Convention on the Prevention and Punishment of the Crime of Genocide:

Afghanistan, Albania, Algeria, Antigua and Barbuda, Argentina, Armenia, Australia, Austria, Azerbaijan, Bahamas, Bahrain, Bangladesh, Barbados, Belarus, Belgium, Belize, Bolivia, Bosnia and Herzegovina, Brazil, Bulgaria, Burkina Faso, Burundi, Cambodia, Canada, Chile, China, Colombia, Costa Rica, Côte d'Ivoire, Croatia, Cuba, Cyprus, Czech Republic, Democratic People's Republic of Korea, Democratic Republic of Congo, Denmark, Dominican Republic, Ecuador, Egypt, El Salvador, Estonia, Ethiopia, Fiji, Finland, France, Gabon, Gambia, Georgia, Germany, Ghana, Greece, Guatemala, Guinea, Haiti, Honduras, Hungary, Iceland, India, Iran, Iraq, Ireland, Israel, Italy, Jamaica, Jordan, Kazakhstan, Kuwait, Kyrgyzstan, Laos, Latvia, Lebanon, Lesotho, Liberia, Libya, Liechtenstein, Lithuania, Luxembourg, Malaysia, Maldives, Mali, Mexico, Moldova, Monaco, Mongolia, Morocco, Mozambique, Myanmar, Namibia, Nepal, Netherlands, New Zealand, Nicaragua, Norway, Pakistan, Panama, Papua New Guinea, Paraguay, Peru, Philippines, Poland, Portugal, Republic of Korea, Romania, Russia, Rwanda, Saint Vincent and the Grenadines, Saudi Arabia, Senegal, Serbia and Montenegro, Seychelles, Singapore, Slovakia, Slovenia, South Africa, Spain, Sri Lanka, Sweden, Switzerland, Syria, Tanzania, The Former Yugoslav Republic of Macedonia, Togo, Tonga, Trinidad and Tobago, Tunisia, Turkey, Uganda, Ukraine, United Kingdom, United States, Uruguay, Uzbekistan, Venezuela, Viet Nam, Yemen, Zimbabwe

Regional Instruments:
Members of the Organization of American States:

Antigua and Barbuda, Argentina, Bahamas, Barbados, Belize, Bolivia, Brazil, Canada, Chile, Colombia, Costa Rica, Cuba, Dominica, Dominican Republic, Ecuador, El Salvador, Grenada, Guatemala, Guyana, Haiti, Honduras, Jamaica, Mexico, Nicaragua, Panama, Paraguay, Peru, Saint Kitts and Nevis, Saint Lucia, Saint Vincent and the Grenadines, Suriname, Trinidad and Tobago, United States, Uruguay, Venezuela

American Convention on Human Rights:

Argentina (a), Barbados (a), Bolivia (a), Brazil (a), Chile (a), Colombia (a), Costa Rica (a), Dominica, Dominican Republic (a), Ecuador (a), El Salvador (a), Grenada, Guatemala (a), Haiti, Honduras (a), Jamaica, Mexico (a), Nicaragua (a), Panama (a), Paraguay (a), Peru (a), Suriname (a), Trinidad and Tobago (a), Uruguay (a), Venezuela (a)
    (a) Filed declaration under article 62, accepting jurisdiction of the Inter-American Court

Additional Protocol to the American Convention on Human Rights in the Area of Economic, Social and Cultural Rights:

Argentina, Brazil, Colombia, Costa Rica, Ecuador, El Salvador, Guatemala, Mexico, Panama, Paraguay, Peru, Suriname, Uruguay

Protocol to the American Convention on Human Rights to Abolish the Death Penalty (not yet in force):

Brazil, Costa Rica, Ecuador, Nicaragua, Panama, Paraguay, Uruguay, Venezuela

Inter-American Convention to Prevent and Punish Torture:

Argentina, Brazil, Chile, Colombia, Costa Rica, Dominican Republic, Ecuador, El Salvador, Guatemala, Mexico, Panama, Paraguay, Peru, Suriname, Uruguay, Venezuela

Inter-American Convention on the Prevention, Punishment and Eradication of Violence against Women:

Antigua and Barbuda, Argentina, Bahamas, Barbados, Belize, Bolivia, Brazil, Chile, Colombia, Costa Rica, Dominica, Dominican Republic, Ecuador, El Salvador, Grenada, Guatemala, Guyana, Haiti, Honduras, Mexico, Nicaragua, Panama, Paraguay, Peru, Saint Kitts and Nevis, Saint Vincent and the Grenadines, Saint Lucia, Trinidad and Tobago, Uruguay, Venezuela

Inter-American Convention on Forced Disappearance of Persons:

Argentina, Bolivia, Costa Rica, Guatemala, Mexico, Panama, Paraguay, Peru, Uruguay, Venezuela

Inter-American Convention on the Elimination of All Forms of Discrimination against Persons with Disabilities:

Argentina, Bolivia, Brazil, Chile, Costa Rica, El Salvador, Guatemala, Mexico, Nicaragua, Panama, Paraguay, Peru, Venezuela

Members of the Organization for Security and Cooperation in Europe:

Albania, Andorra, Armenia, Austria, Azerbaijan, Belarus, Belgium, Bosnia and Herzegovina, Bulgaria, Canada, Croatia, Cyprus, Czech Republic, Denmark, Estonia, Finland, France, Georgia, Germany, Greece, Holy See, Hungary, Iceland, Ireland, Italy, Kazakhstan, Kyrgyzstan, Latvia, Liechtenstein, Lithuania, Luxembourg, Malta, Moldova, Monaco, Netherlands, Norway, Poland, Portugal, Romania, Russia, San Marino, Serbia and Montenegro, Slovakia, Slovenia, Spain, Sweden, Switzerland, Tajikistan, The Former Yugoslav Republic of Macedonia, Turkey, Turkmenistan, Ukraine, United Kingdom, United States, Uzbekistan

European Convention on Human Rights (as of March 2004):

Albania, Andorra, Armenia, Austria, Azerbaijan, Belgium, Bosnia and Herzegovina, Bulgaria, Croatia, Cyprus, Czech Republic, Denmark, Estonia, Finland, France, Georgia, Germany, Greece, Hungary, Iceland, Ireland, Italy, Latvia, Liechtenstein, Lithuania, Luxembourg, Malta, Moldova, Netherlands, Norway, Poland, Portugal, Romania, Russia, San Marino, Serbia and Montenegro, Slovakia, Slovenia, Spain, Sweden, Switzerland, The Former Yugoslav Republic of Macedonia, Turkey, Ukraine, United Kingdom

Protocol No. 1:

Albania, Armenia, Austria, Azerbaijan, Belgium, Bulgaria, Croatia, Cyprus, Czech Republic, Denmark, Estonia, Finland, France, Georgia, Germany, Greece, Hungary, Iceland, Ireland, Italy, Latvia, Liechtenstein, Lithuania, Luxembourg, Malta, Moldova, Netherlands, Norway, Poland, Portugal, Romania, Russia, San Marino, Serbia and Montenegro, Slovakia, Slovenia, Spain, Sweden, The Former Yugoslav Republic of Macedonia, Turkey, Ukraine, United Kingdom

Protocol No. 4:

Albania, Armenia, Austria, Azerbaijan, Belgium, Bosnia and Herzegovina, Bulgaria, Croatia, Cyprus, Czech Republic, Denmark, Estonia, Finland,

France, Georgia, Germany, Hungary, Iceland, Ireland, Italy, Latvia, Lithuania, Luxembourg, Malta, Moldova, Netherlands, Norway, Poland, Portugal, Romania, Russia, San Marino, Serbia and Montenegro, Slovakia, Slovenia, Sweden, The Former Yugoslav Republic of Macedonia, Ukraine

Protocol No. 6:

Albania, Andorra, Armenia, Austria, Azerbaijan, Belgium, Bosnia and Herzegovina, Bulgaria, Croatia, Cyprus, Czech Republic, Denmark, Estonia, Finland, France, Georgia, Germany, Greece, Hungary, Iceland, Ireland, Italy, Latvia, Liechtenstein, Lithuania, Luxembourg, Malta, Moldova, Netherlands, Norway, Poland, Portugal, Romania, San Marino, Serbia and Montenegro, Slovakia, Slovenia, Spain, Sweden, Switzerland, The Former Yugoslav Republic of Macedonia, Turkey, Ukraine, United Kingdom

Protocol No. 7:

Albania, Armenia, Austria, Azerbaijan, Bosnia and Herzegovina, Bulgaria, Croatia, Cyprus, Czech Republic, Denmark, Estonia, Finland, France, Georgia, Greece, Hungary, Iceland, Ireland, Italy, Latvia, Lithuania, Luxembourg, Malta, Moldova, Norway, Poland, Romania, Russia, San Marino, Serbia and Montenegro, Slovakia, Slovenia, Sweden, Switzerland, The Former Yugoslav Republic of Macedonia, Ukraine

Protocol No. 13:

Andorra, Austria, Belgium, Bosnia and Herzegovina, Bulgaria, Croatia, Cyprus, Denmark, Estonia, Georgia, Hungary, Ireland, Liechtenstein, Malta, Portugal, Romania, San Marino, Serbia and Montenegro, Slovenia, Sweden, Switzerland, Ukraine, United Kingdom

European Convention for the Prevention of Torture and Inhuman or Degrading Treatment or Punishment:

All members of the Council of Europe are party to this convention.

European Social Charter (as of March 2004):

Austria, Belgium (a), Croatia (a), Cyprus (a), Czech Republic, Denmark, Finland (a), France (a), Germany, Greece (a), Hungary, Iceland, Ireland (a), Italy (a), Latvia, Luxembourg, Malta, Netherlands, Norway (a), Poland, Portugal (a), Slovakia, Spain, Sweden (a), Turkey, United Kingdom
   (a) Accepted system of collective complaints

Additional Protocol to the European Social Charter
(as of March 2004):

Belgium, Croatia, Czech Republic, Denmark, Finland, Greece, Italy,
Netherlands, Norway, Slovakia, Spain, Sweden

Protocol Amending the European Social Charter (as of March
2004) (not yet in force):

Austria, Belgium, Croatia, Cyprus, Czech Republic, Finland, France,
Greece, Hungary, Iceland, Ireland, Italy, Latvia, Malta, Netherlands,
Norway, Poland, Portugal, Slovakia, Spain, Sweden

European Social Charter (Revised) (as of March 2004):

Albania, Armenia, Belgium, Bulgaria, Cyprus, Estonia, Finland, France,
Ireland, Italy, Lithuania, Moldova, Norway, Portugal, Romania, Slovenia,
Sweden

Framework Convention for the Protection of National Minorities
(as of March 2004):

Albania, Armenia, Austria, Azerbaijan, Bosnia and Herzegovina, Bulgaria,
Croatia, Cyprus, Czech Republic, Denmark, Estonia, Finland, Germany,
Hungary, Ireland, Italy, Liechtenstein, Lithuania, Malta, Moldova,
Norway, Poland, Portugal, Romania, Russia, San Marino, Serbia and
Montenegro, Slovakia, Slovenia, Spain, Sweden, Switzerland, The Former
Yugoslav Republic of Macedonia, Ukraine, United Kingdom

European Charter for the Protection of Regional or Minority
Languages (as of March 2004):

Armenia, Austria, Croatia, Cyprus, Denmark, Finland, Germany,
Hungary, Liechtenstein, Netherlands, Norway, Slovakia, Slovenia, Spain,
Sweden, Switzerland, United Kingdom

African Charter on Human and Peoples' Rights:

Algeria (a), Angola, Benin, Botswana, Burkina Faso (a), Burundi (a),
Cameroon, Cape Verde, Central African Republic, Chad, Comoros (a),
Congo, Côte d'Ivoire (a), Democratic Republic of Congo, Djibouti,
Egypt, Equatorial Guinea, Eritrea, Ethiopia, Gabon, Gambia (a), Ghana,
Guinea, Guinea-Bissau, Kenya, Lesotho (a), Liberia, Libya (a), Madagascar,

Malawi, Mali (a), Mauritania, Mauritius (a), Mozambique, Namibia, Niger, Nigeria, Rwanda (a), Sahrawi Arab Democratic Republic, Sao Tome and Principe, Senegal (a), Seychelles, Sierra Leone, Somalia, South Africa (a), Sudan, Swaziland, Tanzania, Togo (a), Tunisia, Uganda (a), Zambia, Zimbabwe

(a) Party to the African Court on Human and Peoples' Rights

African Charter on the Rights and Welfare of the Child:

Algeria, Angola, Benin, Botswana, Burkina Faso, Cameroon, Cape Verde, Chad, Egypt, Equatorial Guinea, Eritrea, Ethiopia, Gambia, Guinea, Kenya, Lesotho, Libya, Malawi, Mali, Mauritius, Mozambique, Niger, Nigeria, Rwanda, Senegal, Seychelles, Sierra Leone, South Africa, Togo, Uganda, Zimbabwe

OAU Convention Covering Certain Aspects of the Refugee Problem in Africa:

Algeria, Angola, Benin, Botswana, Burkina Faso, Burundi, Cameroon, Cape Verde, Central African Republic, Chad, Congo, Côte d'Ivoire, Democratic Republic of Congo, Egypt, Equatorial Guinea, Ethiopia, Gabon, Gambia, Ghana, Guinea, Guinea-Bissau, Kenya, Lesotho, Liberia, Libya, Malawi, Mali, Mauritania, Mozambique, Niger, Nigeria, Rwanda, Senegal, Seychelles, Sierra Leone, South Africa, Sudan, Swaziland, Tanzania, Togo, Tunisia, Uganda, Zambia, Zimbabwe

Appendix F: Citations for Major International Human Rights Instruments

(Listed in Order of Adoption)

Global Instruments

Convention Concerning Forced or Compulsory Labour (I.L.O. No. 29), adopted 28 June 1930, entered into force 1 May 1932, 39 U.N.T.S. 55

American Declaration of Rights and Duties of Man, signed 2 May 1948, O.A.S. Off. Rec. OEA/Ser.L/V/II.23, doc. 21, rev. 6

Convention on the Prevention and Punishment of the Crime of Genocide, opened for signature 9 Dec. 1948, entered into force 12 Jan. 1951, 78 U.N.T.S. 277

Universal Declaration of Human Rights, adopted 10 Dec. 1948, G.A. Res. 217A (III)

Geneva Conventions of 1949: Geneva Convention for the Amelioration of the Condition of the Wounded and Sick in Armed Forces in the Field, opened for signature 12 Aug. 1949, entered into force 21 Oct. 1950, 75 U.N.T.S. 31; Geneva Convention for the Amelioration of the Condition of Wounded, Sick and Shipwrecked Members of Armed Forces at Sea, opened for signature 12 Aug. 1949, entered into force 21 Oct. 1950, 75 U.N.T.S. 85; Geneva Convention Relative to the Treatment of Prisoners of War, opened for signature 12 Aug. 1949, entered into force 21 Oct. 1950, 75 U.N.T.S. 135; Geneva Convention Relative to the Protection of Civilian Persons in Time of War, opened for signature 12 Aug. 1948, entered into force 21 Oct. 1950, 75 U.N.T.S. 287

Convention Relating to the Status of Refugees, signed 28 July 1951, entered into force 22 Apr. 1954, 189 U.N.T.S. 137

Convention on the Political Rights of Women, adopted 20 Dec. 1952, entered into force 7 July 1954, 193 U.N.T.S. 135

Supplementary Convention on the Abolition of Slavery, the Slave Trade, and Institutions and Practices Similar to Slavery, adopted 7 Sept. 1956, entered into force 30 Apr. 1957, 266 U.N.T.S. 3

Standard Minimum Rules for the Treatment of Prisoners, adopted 31 July 1957, E.S.C. Res. 663C, extended 13 May 1977, E.S.C. Res. 2076 (LXIII)

Convention Concerning the Abolition of Forced Labour (I.L.O. No. 105), adopted 25 June 1957, entered into force 17 Jan. 1959, 320 U.N.T.S. 291

Convention Concerning the Protection and Integration of Indigenous and Other Tribal and Semi-Tribal Populations in Independent Countries (I.L.O. No. 107), adopted 26 June 1957, 328 U.N.T.S. 247

Declaration on the Rights of the Child, adopted 20 Nov. 1959, G.A. Res. 1386 (XIV)

UNESCO Convention against Discrimination in Education, adopted 14 Dec. 1960, entered into force 22 May 1962, 429 U.N.T.S. 93

Declaration on the Elimination of All Forms of Racial Discrimination, adopted 20 Nov. 1963, G.A. Res. 1904 (XVIII)

International Convention on the Elimination of All Forms of Racial Discrimination, adopted 21 Dec. 1965, entered into force 4 Jan. 1969, 660 U.N.T.S. 195

Protocol Relating to the Status of Refugees, opened for signature 31 Jan. 1967, entered into force 4 Oct. 1967, 606 U.N.T.S. 267

International Covenant on Economic, Social and Cultural Rights, adopted 16 Dec. 1966, entered into force 3 Jan. 1976, 993 U.N.T.S. 3

International Covenant on Civil and Political Rights, adopted 16 Dec. 1966, entered into force 23 Mar. 1976, 999 U.N.T.S. 171

Declaration on the Rights of Disabled Persons, adopted 9 Dec. 1975, GA Res. 3447 (XXX)

Declaration on the Protection of All Persons from Being Subjected to Torture and Other Cruel, Inhuman or Degrading Treatment or Punishment, adopted 9 Dec. 1975, G.A. Res. 3452

Protocol II Additional to the Geneva Conventions of August 12, 1949, and relating to the Protection of Victims of Non-International Armed Conflicts, opened for signature 12 Dec. 1977, entered into force 7 Dec. 1978, 1125 U.N.T.S. 609

Convention on the Elimination of All Forms of Discrimination against Women, adopted 18 Dec. 1979, entered into force 3 Sept. 1981, 1249 U.N.T.S. 13

Declaration on the Elimination of All Forms of Intolerance and of Discrimination Based on Religion or Belief, adopted 25 Nov. 1981, G.A. Res. 36/55

Convention against Torture and Other Cruel, Inhuman or Degrading Treatment or Punishment, adopted 10 Dec. 1984, entered into force 28 June 1987, 1465 U.N.T.S. 85

Convention Concerning Indigenous and Tribal Peoples in Independent Countries (I.L.O. No. 169), adopted 27 June 1989, entered into force 5 Sept. 1991

Convention on the Rights of the Child, adopted 20 Nov. 1989, entered into force 2 Sept. 1990, G.A. Res. 44/25

International Convention on the Protection of the Rights of All Migrant Workers and Members of Their Families, adopted 18 Dec. 1990, entered into force 1 July 2003, G.A. Res. 45/158

Declaration on the Rights of Persons belonging to National or Ethnic, Religious or Linguistic Minorities, G.A. Res. 47/135, 18 Dec. 1992

Regional Instruments

European Convention for the Protection of Human Rights and Fundamental Freedoms, signed 4 Nov. 1940, entered into force 3 Sept. 1953, 312 U.N.T.S. 222

European Social Charter, signed 18 Oct. 1961, entered into force 26 Feb. 1965, 529 U.N.T.S. 89

Convention Governing the Specific Aspects of the Refugee Problems in Africa, adopted 10 Sept. 1969, entered into force 20 June 1974, 1001 U.N.T.S. 45

American Convention of Human Rights, signed 22 Nov. 1969, entered into force 18 July 1978, O.A.S.T.S. No. 36

Final Act of the Conference on Security and Cooperation in Europe, adopted 1 Aug. 1975, reprinted in 14 Int'l Legal Materials 1292 (1975)

African Charter on Human and People's Rights, adopted 27 June 1981, entered into force 21 Oct. 1986, O.A.U. Doc. CAB/LEG/67/3 Rev. 5

Inter-American Convention to Prevent and Punish Torture, signed 9 Dec. 1985, entered into force 28 Feb. 1987, O.A.S.T.S. No. 67, O.A.S. Off. Rec. OEA/Ser.A/42 (SEPF)

Protocol to the American Convention on Human Rights to Abolish the Death Penalty, adopted 8 June 1990, O.A.S.T.S. No. 73

Additional Protocol to the European Social Charter, signed 5 May 1988, entered into force 4 Sept. 1992, Europ. T.S. 128

European Convention for the Prevention of Torture and Inhuman or Degrading Treatment or Punishment, signed 26 Nov. 1987, entered into force 1 Feb. 1989, Europ. T.S. 126; Protocol No. 1, signed 4 Nov. 1993, entered into force 1 March 2003, Europ. T.S. 151; Protocol No. 2, signed 4 Nov. 1993, entered into force 1 March 2003, Europ. T.S. 152

Additional Protocol to the American Convention on Human Rights in the Area of Economic, Social and Cultural Rights, signed 17 Nov. 1988, entered into force 16 Nov. 1999, O.A.S.T.S. No. 69

Document of the Copenhagen Meeting of the Conference on the Human Dimension of the Conference on Security and Cooperation in Europe, adopted 29 June 1990, reprinted in 29 Int'l Legal Materials 1305 (1990)

Protocol amending the European Social Charter, signed 21 Oct. 1991, Europ. T.S. 142

Inter-American Convention on Forced Disappearance of Persons, adopted 9 June 1994, entered into force 28 Mar. 1996

Inter-American Convention on the Prevention, Punishment, and Eradication of Violence against Women ("Convention of Belém do Pará"), adopted 9 June 1994, entered into force 5 Mar. 1995

European Charter for Regional or Minority Languages, signed 5 Nov. 1992, entered into force 1 Mar. 1998, Europ. T.S. No. 148

Framework Convention for the Protection of National Minorities, signed 1 Feb. 1995, entered into force 1 Feb. 1998, Europ. T.S. No. 157

Additional Protocol to the European Social Charter providing for a System of Collective Complaints, signed 9 Nov. 1995, entered into force 1 July 1998, Europ. T.S. 158

European Social Charter (Revised), signed 3 May 1996, entered into force 1 Nov. 1998, Europ. T.S. 163

Protocol to the African Charter on Human and Peoples' Rights on the establishment of an African Court on Human and People's Rights, signed 9 July 1998, entered into force 25 Jan. 2004

Inter-American Convention on the Elimination of All Forms of Discrimination against Persons with Disabilities, adopted 7 June 1999, entered into force 14 Sept. 2001

Optional Protocol to the Convention on the Elimination of All Forms of Discrimination Against Women, opened for signature 10 Dec. 1999, entered into force 22 Dec. 2000, GA Res. A/54/4

Contributors

Evelyn Ankumah is Director of Africa Legal Aid, a human rights organization with offices in Maastricht, The Netherlands, and Accra, Ghana. She is the author of a monograph on *The African Commission on Human and Peoples' Rights, Practice and Procedure* (1996).

Richard B. Bilder is Foley & Lardner Emeritus Professor at the University of Wisconsin Law School. Before entering teaching, he served for some years as an attorney in the Office of the Legal Adviser of the U.S. Department of State. Among other positions, he has served as Vice-President, Honorary Vice-President, and Counselor of the American Society of International Law; member of the Board of Editors of the American Journal of International Law; Chair of the Committee on Diplomatic Protection of the International Law Association; member of the Advisory Board of the International Human Rights Law Group; a member of U.S. delegations to international conferences; and an arbitrator in international and domestic disputes. He is the author of *Managing the Risks of International Agreement* (1981) and a number of other articles and scholarly publications in the field of international and foreign relations law.

Kevin Boyle is the former Director of the Human Rights Centre of the University of Essex, Colchester, UK, and professor of law. He previously held academic posts at Queen's University, Belfast, and the National University of Ireland, Galway. He is a barrister in Ireland and Britain and has extensive experience pleading cases before the European Commission and Court of Human Rights. In 2001–2002, Professor Boyle served as special assistant to the UN High Commissioner of Human Rights; he served as the first Director (1986–89) of the London-based NGO, Article 19, and now sits on its International Board. He has written extensively on the conflict in Northern Ireland and international human rights and co-edited *Freedom of Religion or Belief: a World Report* (with J. Sheen) (1997).

Stephanie Farrior is Professor of Law at the Pennsylvania State University, Dickinson School of Law, where she teaches courses on international law, international organizations, and gender and human rights. She has also taught at the New York University School of Law and the University of Oxford, and she is former Visiting Scholar at Georgetown University Law Center and Visiting Researcher at Harvard Law School. Professor Farrior is the immediate past Legal Director of Amnesty International at its International Secretariat in London. She has represented Amnesty International at the United Nations and other intergovernmental organizations, and has worked closely with numerous UN human rights bodies and with many NGOs. Professor Farrior's publications focus on international legal issues relating to discrimination, state accountability for human rights abuses by non-state actors, and the rights of women. Professor Farrior holds a J.D. degree from The American University, Washington College of Law, an M.A. from the University of Pennsylvania, and an LL.M. from Harvard Law School.

Cees Flinterman became professor of human rights, Director of the Netherlands Institute of Human Rights, and Director of the Netherlands School of Human Rights Research at the University of Utrecht, The Netherlands, in 1998; he was formerly professor of international law at Maastricht University. He has served as an alternate member to the UN Sub-Commission on Prevention of Discrimination and Protection of Minorities (1987–1991) and chaired the Netherlands delegation to the UN Commission on Human Rights (1993, 1994) and the Second World Conference on Human Rights (1993). Since 1992, he has chaired the Advisory Committee on Human Rights and Foreign Policy, and he has been a member of the United Nations Committee on the Elimination of Discrimination against Women (CEDAW) since 2003.

Maryellen Fullerton is Professor of Law at Brooklyn Law School, where she teaches courses in international law, refugee law, and procedural law. She has written widely in these fields. Her current research and scholarship focus on refugee law. As a Fulbright Scholar to Belgium and the Federal Republic of Germany in 1986–1987, she conducted research on developments in refugee law in Western Europe. As a German Marshall Research Fellow in 1994–1995, she lived in Hungary and studied refugee policy in Central and Eastern Europe. She has been sent by Human Rights Watch to lead two fact-finding missions to Germany and has written human rights reports concerning violence against foreigners in Germany and concerning the increasing restrictions imposed on asylum seekers in Germany. As a Visiting Scholar at the Center for the Advanced Study of the Social Sciences in Madrid in 2002, she expanded her research to refugee law developments in Spain and Portugal.

Hurst Hannum is Professor of International Law and Co-Director of the Center for Human Rights & Conflict Resolution at The Fletcher School of Law and Diplomacy of Tufts University, where he teaches courses in international human rights law, minority rights, self-determination, and nationalism. He has served as counsel in cases before the European and Inter-American Commissions on Human Rights and the United Nations; he also has been a member of the boards of several international human rights organizations. Among other publications, he is author of *Autonomy, Sovereignty, and Self-Determination: The Accommodation of Conflicting Rights* (rev. ed. 1996); and *International Human Rights: Problems of Law, Policy, and Process* (with Richard Lillich) (4th ed. forthcoming 2005).

Siân Lewis-Anthony is a freelance researcher specializing in international human rights law and is currently researching justice in the Middle East and North Africa, for the Euro-Mediterranean Human Rights Network. She was a Senior Lecturer in Law at Oxford Brookes University from 1991 to 1997, where she introduced a course on international human rights law; she also taught international human rights law at the Notre Dame Summer Law Program in London in 1995–1997. She has published on the right to freedom of assembly and association, political autonomy, and economic and social rights. She has written a series of human rights training materials for judges and lawyers in Central and Eastern Europe and has trained judges for the Council of Europe in Kosovo and Albania. She has worked as Legal Officer at Interights, a London-based nongovernmental organization, where she represented and advised clients before international bodies such as the European Commission on Human Rights, the UN Human Rights Committee, and the Inter-American Commission on Human Rights. Ms. Lewis-Anthony received her B.A. degree from the University of Durham and an LL.M. from the London School of Economics. She is a member of Grays Inn and was called to the Bar of England and Wales in 1985.

Stephen P. Marks is the François-Xavier Bagnoud Professor of Health and Human Rights at the Harvard School of Public Health and Director of the François-Xavier Bagnoud Center for Health and Human Rights (FXB Center). He directs the Program on Human Rights in Development at the FXB Center and teaches courses on Development and Human Rights, Health and Human Rights, and the International System, among others. Until July 1999, he was Director of the United Nations Studies Program and Co-Director of the Human Rights and Humanitarian Affairs Concentration at the School of International and Public Affairs (SIPA) of Columbia University. In addition to several teaching positions, he has served as head of human rights education, training, and information for the United Nations

Transitional Authority in Cambodia (UNTAC); Deputy Independent Jurist for the United Nations Mission for the Referendum in the Western Sahara (MINURSO); Director of the Program in International Law and Human Rights at Cardozo School of Law; program officer for international human rights at the Ford Foundation; senior program specialist in the Division of Human Rights and Peace of UNESCO; Secretary to the Committee on Conventions and Recommendations of the Executive Board of UNESCO; and senior staff member at the International Institute of Human Rights in Strasbourg.

Sir Nigel Rodley KBE is Professor of Law at the University of Essex and former UN Special Rapporteur on Torture. He was knighted in the 1998/1999 New Year's Honours List. From 1973 to 1990, he founded and led Amnesty International's Legal Office, contributing to the development and functioning of several UN mechanisms for the protection of human rights. He has written widely in the fields of international law and human rights and is the author of *The Treatment of Prisoners under International Law* (2d ed. 1999).

Dinah L. Shelton is research professor of international law at the George Washington University Law School. She previously taught at the universities of Santa Clara, Stanford, California (Berkeley), Notre Dame, and Robert Schumann (Strasbourg, France). She received her B.A. and J.D. degrees from the University of California, Berkeley, and has been an associate at the International Institute of Human Rights in Strasbourg, France; a lawyer in private practice; and director of staff attorneys for the United States Court of Appeals for the Ninth Circuit (1987–89). She is a Counselor of the American Society of International Law and member of the Board of Editors of the American Journal of International Law. Professor Shelton is the author or editor of numerous articles and studies, including *Protecting Human Rights in the Americas* (with Thomas Buergenthal) (1995), awarded the book prize of the Inter-American Bar Association; *Remedies in International Human Rights Law* (1999), awarded the American Society of international Law Certificate of Merit; and *International Human Rights in a Nutshell* (with Thomas Buergenthal and David Stewart) (3d ed. 2002).

Ralph G. Steinhardt is the Arthur Selwyn Miller Research Professor of Law at the George Washington University Law School. He is also the co-founder and co-director of the Programme in International Human Rights Law at New College, Oxford University, where he has taught courses on Human Rights Lawyering and the International Law of Criminal Procedure. Professor Steinhardt is an active litigator of international human rights norms, having represented *pro bono* various human rights organizations, as well as individual human rights victims, before all levels of the federal judiciary, including the U.S.

Supreme Court. The most recent case in which he appeared as counsel is United States v. Alvarez-Machain, which challenged the legality of the abduction of a Mexican national in Mexico by agents of U.S. government. He is the author of numerous books and articles, including *International Civil Litigation: Cases and Materials on the Rise of Intermestic Law* (2002), *The Alien Tort Claims Act: An Analytical Anthology* (with Tony D'Amato) (1999), and *International Law and Self-Determination* (1994). Professor Steinhardt received his B.A. *summa cum laude* from Bowdoin College, where he was elected to Phi Beta Kappa, and his J.D. from Harvard Law School. He practiced law for five years in Washington, D.C., before joining the faculty at the George Washington University Law School.

Lee Swepston is chief of the Equality and Employment Branch, and is Human Rights Coordinator, of the International Labor Office in Geneva. A graduate of the University of North Carolina and Columbia University Law School, he worked with the International Commission of Jurists before joining the ILO. He has published various works on human rights, including the ILO's supervisory system, child labor, and indigenous and tribal peoples.

Jiri Toman is professor of law at Santa Clara University School of Law. Born in Prague in 1938, he studied in Prague (JUDr.) and Geneva (Ph.D. in Political Science), and began his teaching career at the School of Economics and School of Law of Charles University in Prague. From 1969 to 1990, he was Director of the Henry Dunant Institute in Geneva, during which time he taught at the University of Geneva and was a visiting professor at several universities in Europe and United States. He has served as a consultant to several international and regional organizations (including UNESCO, UNDRO, UNCTAD, the UN Center for Human Rights, and the Council of Europe), is a member of the editorial boards of several journals, and is a foreign member (academician) of the Russian Academy of Natural Sciences. Among his numerous publications in the areas of international law, human rights, humanitarian law, and criminal law are *The Laws of Armed Conflicts* (4th ed. 2004 in English, 1996 in French), *The Protection of Cultural Property* (1994 in French, 1996 in English, 2004 in Spanish), *The Spirit of Uppsala* (1984), and *International Dimensions of Humanitarian Law* (1988).

David S. Weissbrodt is the Fredrikson & Byron Professor of Law at the University of Minnesota, where he teaches international human rights law, administrative law, immigration law, and torts. During 1996–2003 he served as a member of the United Nations Sub-Commission on the Promotion and Protection of Human Rights and was elected Chairperson of the Sub-Commission for the year 2001–02. He also was designated the UN Special Rapporteur on the rights of noncitizens in 2000–03. Among many other publications, he is author of *The Right to a Fair Trial Under the Universal Declaration of Human Rights and the International Covenant on Civil and Political Rights: Background, Development, and Interpretations* (2001) and *International Human Rights: Problems of Law, Policy, Process* (with Joan M. Fitzpatrick and Frank C. Newman) (3d ed. 2001).

Index